RUSSIAN UNEMPLOYMENT AND ENTERPRISE RESTRUCTURING

Russian Unemployment and Enterprise Restructuring

Reviving Dead Souls

Guy Standing
International Labour Office
Geneva

First published in Great Britain 1996 by
MACMILLAN PRESS LTD
Houndmills, Basingstoke, Hampshire RG21 6XS
and London
Companies and representatives
throughout the world

A catalogue record for this book is available
from the British Library.

ISBN 0–333–66872–3

First published in the United States of America 1996 by
ST. MARTIN'S PRESS, INC.,
Scholarly and Reference Division,
175 Fifth Avenue,
New York, N.Y. 10010

ISBN 0–312–16134–4

Library of Congress Cataloging-in-Publication Data
Standing, Guy.
Russian unemployment and enterprise restructuring : reviving dead
souls / Guy Standing.
p.   cm.
Includes bibliographical references and index.
ISBN 0–312–16134–4
1. Labor market—Russia (Federation)   2. Unemployment—Russia
(Federation)   3. Structural adjustment (Economic policy)—Russia
(Federation)   4. Russia (Federation)—Economic policy—1991–
I. Title.
HD5797.2.A6S73   1996
331.13'7947—dc20   96–18545
                                                              CIP

10   9   8   7   6   5   4   3   2   1
05   04   03   02   01   00   99   98   97   96

Printed in Great Britain by
The Ipswich Book Company Ltd
Ipswich, Suffolk

For **T.C.**
who dared to be free

Contents

List of Figures

List of Tables

Preface: Dead Souls –
a Cautionary Tale

This book sets out to paint a picture and tell a story, as best a labour economist can. Almost the whole of the book is devoted to a presentation of statistics in the hope that it will provide a start for empirical labour-market analyses. A start is the best that one can hope to achieve, for little is what it seems to be in the Russian labour market. That is one reason for the subtitle of this book, derived from the title of Nikolai Gogol's famous novel.

In the 1970s and 1980s the huge enterprises that operated like giant fiefdoms across the former Soviet Union were locked into cosy relationships of power and patronage. The number of workers attached to these enterprises was immense, and a visitor to a complex in which many, many thousands of people worked could scarcely be unimpressed, even if the drudgery of the work was clear and the equipment and buildings visibly dated from the nineteenth century, and in some cases much earlier. Yet part of the administrative game of the managements was to maximise the number of 'posts', for the more posts there were, the greater the status of enterprise and management, enhancing the senior employees' power and income and enlarging the wage fund and social consumption funds allocated by the line ministry in Moscow.

Many of those posts were occupied by silent colleagues, who existed on paper only; and if the spirits that filled some of them were alive, they were not in the factory to prove it. Some posts went unfilled because of the contrived 'labour shortage'. Others were occupied by aged pensioners attending from time to time to keep in touch with their former colleagues, obtain something from the enterprise shop or visit the health clinic. Much better than the well-known quip, 'They pretend to pay us, we pretend to work', they could have muttered as they came and went, 'You pretend to need us, we pretend to be workers'.

Estimates of the dead souls who swelled the employment figures can only be guesses. Yet in the 1980s counting began, for with *glasnost* and *perestroika* there was a sporadic drive to improve efficiency and restore a sense of reality, and many of the posts began to disappear, particularly in government organisations. Octogenarians were kindly retired, and many younger pensioners followed. By 1990–1 a flurry of legislative initiatives had successfully disturbed labour relations and had ushered in an era of experimentation. By 1991 the era of dead-soul posts was gone, or rapidly disappearing. There was almost a sense of euphoria about the prospects for labour-market realism in the immediate aftermath of the establishment of the Russian Federation and the much-postponed introduction of a new framework law legitimising unemployment for the first time for nearly fifty years, known succinctly as The Fundamentals of Employment Legislation of the USSR and the Union Republics, 1991.

Then came a painful lesson for those thinking that the Russian labour market would evolve in the same way as anywhere else. Output plunged, employment plunged, incomes plunged, and yet unemployment appeared to stay stubbornly and absurdly low – or at least it appeared to do so according to the only available statistics. Commentators, international agencies and a bevy of foreign 'economic advisers to the government' dismissed every other statistic as unreliable or meaningless – but not those on unemployment. The economists advocating the attempted 'shock therapy' economic reform strategy comforted themselves and disarmed their critics by stating that there was 'no unemployment' and that, until there was much higher unemployment, reforms would be ineffective. Many dry-eyed economists argued for tougher monetary and fiscal policy, citing the low unemployment rate as proof that a tougher macroeconomic policy was needed.

The reality was that those drifting out of the factories, off the farms and off the government's payrolls were the new dead souls of the Russian labour market. Most of the unemployed were not becoming unemployed. They were not registering in the way the system intended them to register, for reasons that will be shown in Chapter 2. They were neither employed nor unemployed: they were conveniently out of the way. But there was a much more sinister development. It seems that many of the unemployed were, rather more literally, 'dead souls'. This was made particularly vivid in a conversation with a cabinet minister in late 1992, who, in response to a question wondering why there was a lack of protest among the growing number of unemployed and impoverished, said ruefully, 'They are going into their homes and dying'. Many of the unemployed, it seems, were not turning up in the registration totals for the awkward reason that they were no longer around to do so.

Flash forward. In one city covered by this study, one of a series of visits to the sole employment exchange yielded a monthly report that was being filed, almost certainly to be forgotten and never read by anybody in Moscow or even in the city administration. It gave a series of percentages – X per cent of those registered were women, Y per cent were under the age of 25, Z per cent had been unemployed for more than six months – and then stated, 'This year 61 unemployed have died'. It promptly went back to the percentages and the statistics, among which was one that showed that the average unemployment benefit was just below the income needed for 'physiological survival'.

The impact of such a report, written by a junior official in a crowded office, lingers far longer than the empty platitudes of the economic advisers explaining that there was no unemployment because enterprises were not changing their behaviour. The awful fact is that, in the period of economic reform, the life expectancy of the Russian population has fallen enormously – by seven years in seven years. This is not short-term pain for long-term gain. This is the aphorism of Keynes turned around to mock those economists who believe there is a simple macroeconomic strategy that can be applied with equal success in Bolivia, Mexico, Poland and Russia. By 1994 the average male life expectancy at birth was just over 58 years, well below the level of many so-called developing countries. And mortality rates had risen fastest for young and middle-aged men. As noted later, impoverishment, personal stress of adjustment and unemployment were behind that awful development. It is hard to stay dispassionate in the face of such realities.

Yet there was another new form of dead souls growing alongside the non-recognition of the unemployed and the disappearance of many of those who would have swelled the ranks of the unemployed. In the 1990s the number of employed was artificially inflated, because many of those turning up for work were not being paid and many more were being put on long-term administrative leave. The irony of the reality should not be lost, for whereas in the 1980s there were posts without workers, now there were many, many thousands of employed workers without posts. Realistically, these were unemployed, but it suited too many people to treat them as employed. In labour-market terms, they were dead souls, neither employed nor unemployed, nor even economically inactive. Some went, no doubt, into the growing informal or black economy, others retired while keeping their work-history book in the enterprise, just in case something happened and in order to make use of the enterprise's facilities. Yet surely for most it was an unrewarding experience. For policy makers the distortionary images of a labour market with minimal unemployment were potentially disastrous. Why devote time and money to tackling unemployment if it scarcely exists?

Little is what it seems to be. Images of dead souls have flickered across the imagination throughout the period in which this book was conceived and written. Nothing in the following should be interpreted as belittling the enormous efforts made by some officials to come to terms with the new realities. They deserve respect and support. Yet whether going round a sprawling factory built in 1874 that should have been shut many decades ago or talking to officials coming to terms with notions that were not part of their vocabulary five years earlier, one could not escape the feeling that the reforms were generating an unnecessarily large number of dead souls.

Should the observer be pessimistic? This question is often posed. One could answer with the famous aphorism of Antonio Gramsci – pessimism of the intellect, optimism of the spirit. Yet there are grounds for longer-term optimism, in the labour-market and social-policy sphere as in some others. As long as an era of social and economic experimentation is encouraged, and as long as that is done in a democratic and equitable manner, what is happening in some of the *oblasts* (regions), in some of the enterprises and in some of the local authorities could emerge as viable 'models' for the country as a whole, and perhaps set examples for other countries to follow. A fear is that such indigenous experimentation will be checked by uninformed policies imposed through poor advice. In 1994 there were signs that both the Russian authorities and those trying to provide assistance were coming to terms with that imperative.

This book has been an adventure amidst the long period of hard work, much of it spent trekking the streets between factories, collecting information from managers, trade unionists, local employment exchanges and a host of federal authorities. An incalculable debt is owed to so many people, from government ministers to managers and workers in factories, many of whom have expressed their views so forcefully. Above all, deep gratitude is due to the Centre for Labour Market Study in the Institute of Economics in Moscow, to whom this book is dedicated.

Among many others, some inadvertently and inexcusably omitted, thanks are also due, in alphabetical order, to Galina Bukhova, Ivan Dubov, Tatyana Gorbachova (Head of Labour Statistics of *Goskomstat* RF – the State Committee of Statistics of the Russian Federation), Vladimir Kosmarski (former First Deputy Minister of Labour), Vladimir Kostakov, Nicolai Ormonsky (Director of the St Petersburg Region Employment Service), Ella Pamfilova (former Minister of Social Protection), Mario Nuti, Peter Peek, Fyodor Prokopov (Director of the Federal Employment Service), Marina Moscovina (Deputy Director of the Federal Employment Service), Ziniada Ridgikova, Alexander Samorodov, Pavel Smirnov, Marina Sukhova, Jim Windell, Slava Zavilov and László Zsoldos. The last-mentioned provided superb assistance in data processing and programming for the final two rounds of the main survey on which the book is based.

Some of the results of the work were presented in conferences organised in Moscow and St Petersburg, attended by officials, academics, managers of industrial enterprises, trade union leaders and groups of officials from the World Bank, who drew on the results in their subsequent work. Papers were also presented in seminars at the Institute of Economics of the Russian Academy of Sciences in Moscow, in Ivanovo (kindly chaired by the mayor), in Nizhny Novgorod, in the ILO in Geneva, and at Columbia University in New York at a conference devoted to an assessment of the economic development of Nizhny Novgorod, attended by the political leadership of that city.

A preface is a place to say *mea culpa*, not as a lame excuse for sloppy analysis or dogmatic conclusions held against the balance of the steady dripping of evidence, but as a way of stimulating fresh thought. In the course of the following the writer takes issue with some of the conclusions and views of others digging in the same territory. He does so with respect for those authorities, not to belittle their efforts. It is simply too early in the development of empirical labour-market research in the Russian Federation validly to hold strong opinions on many issues. As with all surveys and attempts to interpret reality empirically, the only point on which to be certain is that one always makes mistakes. This is not an excuse; it is almost a boast, since unless we make mistakes the next round of diggers will make the same mistakes and not just their own.

In the following chapters, some of the numerous statistics are presented rather baldly, with little discussion. To try to analyse all the data in detail would and should take many more months of work, and it was felt that presenting the material in its current form, while the data are still topical, is preferable to further delay. In any case a change of job, bringing with it a new round of distractions and demands, makes the completion of a more comprehensive analysis difficult to envisage. Technical papers on some of the topics should follow. As regards the sketchiness of the treatment of some of the issues, we feel that the bare bones may well be useful for future students of labour markets.

It is hoped that the story told in the twelve chapters of this book is narrated with the sense of fascination that I experienced in visits to the Russian Federation during its preparation, and trust that the unfolding developments come across to the reader. Those in the Russian labour market deserve more concern than was shown in the first four years of economic transition, whatever the future may bring.

1 The Russian Labour Market and 'Shock Therapy'

1.1 INTRODUCTION

One of the founding fathers of modern economics, Alfred Marshall, exhorted his successors to leave their studies and 'go into the factory' if they wished to learn economic realities. If one wished to analyse the emergence of the Russian labour market in the 1990s, Marshall's dictum would surely be sound advice, for although a large and growing number of Russians work – or do not work – outside factories, industrial enterprises have had a pervasive influence on Russian life.

The old Soviet system was based on gigantic industrial enterprises creating 'enterprise cities' across the vast area of the USSR, cities in which one or two massive conglomerates employing many thousands of workers dominated the economic and social landscape, coexisting in a stable, untroubled balance, mostly polluting the atmosphere, underinvesting and slowly stagnating. Some were very old, with buildings dating from the nineteenth century or earlier, and with working practices as well as equipment preserved for many decades. The technical division of labour was essentially 'Tayloristic' – rigid and detailed, following the work methods espoused by the American Frederick Taylor, based on the separation of mental and manual labour – due in part to its advocacy by Lenin and the early Bolsheviks.[1] The uncritical adoption of so-called 'scientific management' led to the erosion of workers' control and factory committees and to rigid management control, ironically coinciding with a rhetoric devoted to the power of the 'work collective' and the proletariat.

Those directing the great industrial enterprises gauged their status largely by reference to the number of workers under their control. There was a relentless pressure to expand employment, as a result of which there were more 'posts' than workers to fill them. To a certain extent the fiction took over the reality, with employment being measured in part by the number of existing posts, whether filled or not. There was a pervasive and contrived 'labour shortage'.

However it would be a mistake to state that there was no labour *market*. The apparently chaotic developments in the labour market of the

1

Russian Federation since its inception in 1991 can be traced in part to the distortions and peculiar characteristics of the labour market that it inherited.

This book is an attempt to present a picture of the emerging industrial labour market as traced through analysis of data from the first four rounds of an enterprise survey, which we have called the *Russian Labour Flexibility Survey* (RLFS), carried out between 1991 and 1994. It gives most attention to the fourth round of the RLFS, carried out in mid 1994 in five major industrial regions of the Russian Federation and covering over 303000 workers. It also draws on a report prepared for the Russian Federal Employment Service and on data from a two-round jobseekers' survey of 2295 unemployed jobseekers carried out in the Leningrad *oblast* (region) in 1993–4 and, to a small extent, on a women workers' survey carried out in two cities in 1994, although analyses of those are presented elsewhere. Those wishing to find a full account of institutional and legislative developments in the labour market will be disappointed, since an effort has been made to concentrate on the basic data from the hundreds of factories visited and revisited between 1991 and 1994.

The analysis sets out to present a rudimentary picture of the Russian industrial labour market, focusing on the dynamics of adaptation in a truly traumatic period, in terms of employment restructuring, wages and benefits, training, the impact on women, older workers and other groups, changing labour relations and the restructuring of 'corporate governance', insofar as it reflects and affects the labour market. It concludes by presenting, in Chapter 11, a perspective that will certainly not be to everybody's taste – proposing that for economic and social restructuring to succeed in the Russian Federation, the authorities should promote democratic 'human development enterprises'.

Before reaching that stage, it tries to explain how enterprise employment restructuring has occurred. As such, no more is claimed for the following analysis than that it is intended as a contribution to the creation of an empirical base on which future labour economists can build. Many of the hypotheses tentatively put forward in the following pages will be refuted or refined by others, and one should be aware that much of the picture is painted with a broad brush, precisely because of the desire to present an impressionistic picture of the 'industrial labour market'. Time will tell, once the hundreds of emerging labour economists in Russia have been able to turn impressions into more sophisticated images, whether the picture is reasonably accurate. All one can be sure about is that in the period in which this work was undertaken, no one could claim to be an expert on the emerging labour market, and a part of the explanation was that the concepts and data were largely undeveloped.

1.2 THE INITIAL LABOUR-MARKET REFORMS

Under the Soviet system there was a very high level of employment. It was a labouring system in which unemployment was banned as a 'parasitic activity' and in which workers remained in jobs well past the official retirement age, largely because the pension was so low that it made continued employment almost a necessity. For many years until the 1990s there was a contrived labour shortage, in which there were artificially created posts, 'dead souls in dead places', because what might be described as the enterprise art was to expand the wage fund allocated by the central ministry. Labour mobility was actually quite high, for although geographical mobility was limited by the *propiska* (residence permit) system, and occupational mobility was restricted by rigid job structures and the lack of incentives, there was considerable interenterprise 'job hopping', typically in pursuit of higher fringe benefits, most notably housing.

Wages were very low, due in part to the Leninist ideology of 'labour decommodification', by which the long-term objective was to achieve a 'withering away of the wage'. There was a heavy ideological emphasis on the virtues of the 'proletariat' (manual wage labour), so that wages were distorted in favour of manual, semiskilled labour. Based on a complex, rigid, tariff wage structure and on enterprise wage funds, the system resulted in the average wage being close to the minimum wage, and led to narrow and distorted wage differentials between sectors and occupational groups. In terms of earnings, the extent of so-called 'levelling' was less than some analysts believed, but as money incomes were so low the main source of inequality was selective and privileged access to social benefits was provided by enterprises, including subsidised food, consumer goods, housing, holiday facilities and health services. Ironically, one of the main factors that led enterprises to become the main channel for social benefits was that labour turnover was regarded as excessive in the 1950s. After 1956, when the social insurance system was recodified to strengthen the links between duration of uninterrupted service in an enterprise to entitlement to benefits, the industrial enterprise became increasingly the fulcrum of society and the distribution system. As with any social insurance system, it had implications for income distribution. In the Soviet system the enterprise-based system of social benefits was encouraged, and was based on the presumption of, a norm of a two-earner nuclear family, in which women were expected to be as integrated into the labour force as men.

Thus the huge enterprises on which the Soviet economy was based were 'total institutions', in many cases creating what were essentially 'company towns'. These enterprises often produced a vast range of goods and services, and employed many thousands of workers, in some cases hundreds of thousands. Managements and union leaders within enterprises were little more than state functionaries acting as 'transmission belts' for Communist Party commands that typically emanated through industrial ministries based in Moscow.

In the 1980s this command structure started to crumble, with *perestroika* and *glasnost* increasingly allowing economic pluralism and what the then chairman of the State Committee for Labour and Social Welfare described as efforts to establish 'a level playing field' in which more diversified relations of production could coexist. This era produced a spate of what at the time was radical legislation, which led to a rapid growth of so-called cooperatives and leaseholdings, as well as self-employment.[2] And there was an equally impressive legislative drive to create a more open labour market. It was a popular refrain in the mid 1990s to contrast the radicalism of the reforms in the early 1990s with the hesitancy of the late 1980s. In labour-market terms that was unfair, for the real breakthrough came at the end of the decade.

This phase culminated in what we may call for short the *1991 Employment Act*, a piece of framework legislation that recognised open unemployment as legitimate for the first time since the 1920s, and which established a system of unemployment benefits, and declared an official commitment to labour-market policies to assist jobseekers and promote employment restructuring. Also, with the emergence of the Russian Federation, legislative changes accelerated the recognition and promotion of ostensibly independent employer organisations and pluralistic trade unions. How substantive the changes were is debatable, but there is no doubt that the rhetoric was transformed in this period.

Drafting and redrafting the Employment Act was a protracted process, with much misunderstanding. Much was wrong with it, yet it was a radical break with the Soviet era that in future years will be judged more favourably for what it removed than for what it established. Even before the Act came into effect in early 1992 it aroused criticism, in part because there were ample reasons to expect that it would result in a widespread disguising of unemployment.[3] But in any case, the Act legitimised unemployment and set in train the development of a very different labour market. That it also disguised the level of unemployment could not conceal subsequent trends. What happened to the Russian economy in the early 1990s would have created mass unemployment in almost any circumstances.

1.3 THE ECONOMIC IMPACT OF SHOCK THERAPY

The failed putsch of 1991 ushered in an era in which the rhetoric of reform was intensified and the pace of reform was accelerated. In 1992–3 there was an attempt to reform by 'shock therapy', which was an attempt to follow the lines of the strategy pursued in Poland and in countries where structural adjustment was pursued in the 1980s. The most important aspect for our analysis is that it envisaged a particular *sequencing* of reforms. Essentially the sequencing involved price liberalisation first, coupled with the removal of many price subsidies, followed by an attempt to impose a tighter monetary and fiscal policy to squeeze the inflationary pressure out of the economy, including a tax-based incomes policy by which wage inflation was meant to be controlled by a punitive tax on wage increases above a certain amount. As a result of the monetary and fiscal measures, it was foreseen that the real economy would be deflated, threatening to lead to extensive poverty and disemployment, so that in the next stage of the sequencing a social safety net was foreseen, to provide income protection for the losers.

The next stage was to be mass privatisation, which in turn would lead to enterprise restructuring, and thus labour absorption in the new dynamic private economy. It was believed by economic advisers to the government and by some officials in international agencies that only with privatisation would enterprise restructuring occur, and that only then would managements move away from what has been called a 'soft budget constraint'.

A major difficulty with this sequencing is that the huge industrial enterprises that had dominated the Soviet industrial landscape were left intact and neglected as economic entities.[4] Many of these had unchecked monopolistic characteristics, either within their regions or nationally or within the Comecon area. Indeed the Soviet system was based on the wholesale monopolisation of economic and social institutions, so that the attempt to institutionalise reform, financial measures and macroeconomic policy without implementing a strong microeconomic restructuring strategy was doomed to generate persistent stagflation.[5] Most crucially, most industrial enterprises, being monopolistic and having segmented market power, were able to adjust output prices upwards by much more than would have been the case, so that price liberalisation had a much greater inflationary impact, which in turn necessitated a much greater deflation of aggregate demand to squeeze the inflationary pressure to acceptable proportions. The failure to dismantle the huge monopolistic enterprises in the early days of reform – when there was widespread public support for change and when the directors of those enterprises and their agents within them, in the local authorities and in the political sphere, were demoralised and on the defensive – was a failure of monumental proportions. Restructuring should have started before price liberalisation.

This was not merely a matter of destroying monopolistic or simply massive enterprises *per se*, but of removing the monopolistic institutional reflexes. The successful industrialised market economies have all relied on monopolistic corporations in key sectors, but their monopolistic tendencies, such as price fixing, have been regulated. There was no such regulation in this case.

An irony of the shock therapy was that it lacked a *strategy* for economic restructuring. It assumed that market-oriented institutions would evolve speedily as normal agents of economic individualism, neglecting basic institutional dynamics and economic history.[6] Structures condition behaviour, and a strategy worthy of the name surely must integrate the restructuring of institutions, particularly the centres of production and distribution. The economy is not a self-contained system; it is embedded in the socio-historical fabric of society.

In one sense at least the initial set of reforms was not radical enough, for it was surely an error to maintain price control over energy, which simply encouraged industrial enterprises to persist with their profligate use of such resources. There was also an erratic process of partial price liberalisation in practice, such that regional authorities commonly changed policies. In 1992 and 1993 about a quarter of all the regions reintroduced some price controls over basic consumption goods, compounding the sense of uncertainty and reflecting the lack of central authority or capacity to pursue consistent macroeconomic policy.[7]

Another difficulty was that the attempted shock-therapy reform started in most unpropitious circumstances. The economy was extremely fragile after a prolonged period of stagnation. In late 1991, when the economic reformers came into office, the budget deficit was running at about 31 per cent of GDP, trade with the Soviet republics was collapsing, foreign exchange reserves were minimal and production had been stagnating or declining for some years. Unfortunately, although imports fell by nearly 50 per cent in 1991, the International Monetary Fund and the G7 group of leading economies did not provide any balance-of-payments support, and this undoubtedly eroded the basis of an economic stabilisation programme.[8] The price liberalisation of early 1992 sparked off a stagflationary spiral, which was followed by an austere monetary policy to squeeze out inflationary pressures that in turn led enterprises to lurch into a chain of indebtedness and to the development of a united 'industrialists' lobby', seen by many as able to resist whatever pressures there were for rapid restructuring.[9]

Under mounting political pressures in 1993, monetary policy was relaxed, the young reformist government effectively lost control of policy implementation and the ensuing power struggle led to a referendum in early 1993, which in the end gave the president a new lease of legitimacy. Again a tighter monetary policy was pursued, the most important elements for the following analysis being the reduction of credit to enterprises and government organisations and the abolition of import subsidies. In the name of reducing debt, and because of the official belief that there was little unemployment, the government even blocked World Bank loans designed to assist in the financing of social policy. The G7 and the IMF held back. It seemed that only the shock of the general election results in December 1993 gave renewed impetus to foreign assistance. The new government relaxed the attempted shock-therapy approach and postponed the implementation of the new bankruptcy law, which in principle came into force in March 1993. In the ensuing year there was talk of an industrial policy, but little was achieved in 1994 beyond completion of a remarkable process of privatisation, a process that will almost certainly be known under another more appropriate name when the ideological dust has settled.

What was the economic and social outcome of the attempted shock therapy and its aftermath? After declining slightly in 1989 and 1990, between 1991 and the end of 1994 national output dropped by at least a third, and has continued to fall, with the government expecting it to drop by a further 8 per cent or more in 1995.[10] The IMF estimated that production fell by 12 per cent in 1994, roughly the same as in 1993, after falling by about 19 per cent in 1992. The European Bank for Reconstruction and Development (EBRD) estimated that real GDP fell by 19 per cent in 1992, 12 per cent in 1993 and 15 per cent in 1994, and projected that it would fall by 7 per cent in 1995.[11] Although some informal production went unmeasured (which would have been partially offset by a decline in other forms of unrecorded output), this is an awesome decline, which no architect of the economic policies, or adviser or institution pressing for them, had forecast.[12] Most awkwardly, there was a disastrous decline in agricultural production, which prompted a growth of food imports, so that by 1994 about 70 per cent of all food consumption in the major cities of Moscow and St Petersburg consisted of imports.

Table 1.1   Indebtedness of industrial enterprises, Russian Federation, January–July 1994 (number and percentage of enterprises with debts, including manufacturing, construction, transport and agriculture)

	January		July	
	(Number)	*(Per cent)*	*(Number)*	*(Per cent)*
Total in debt	32600	45.3	39000	54.8
to suppliers	29500	40.9	35600	50.0
to state budget	14000	19.5	22000	30.9
to banks	9200	12.8	10900	15.3

Note: The figures are rounded to the nearest hundred. Many firms were in debt to more than one creditor.
Source: *Goskomstat* of the Russian Federation, Moscow.

Interenterprise indebtedness became severe in 1992.[13] One IMF analysis suggested that its growth reflected an indifference to prices and a general belief that the government would pay off the debt in due course.[14] This view was certainly found during 1992 and 1993 in some of the factories visited during the course of the work for this book. Some foreign economists dismissed its significance. However it continued to grow, and as it did so the fear that a mass collapse of industry would take place if the chain were broken seemed to become a barrier to a radical programme of enterprise restructuring. In August 1994 the government estimated that interenterprise debt amounted to 90000 billion roubles, or about US$40 billion.[15] By then, over half of all industrial enterprises were known to be in serious debt (Table 1.1), most being in debt to other enterprises.

Consumer price inflation was over 2300 per cent in 1992, and although the rate of price increases declined, it remained very high by international standards throughout 1993 and 1994. In the latter year it was estimated to be 294 per cent. The EBRD estimated that consumer price inflation was 231 per cent in 1992, 841 per cent in 1993 and 205 per cent in 1994, with a projected rate of 100 per cent in 1995.[16]

In the initial period, producers had enough market power to compensate for cost increases by mark-up pricing.[17] Producer prices rose faster and further than consumer prices throughout the initial phase of the radical macroeconomic policy. In January 1992 alone, producer prices rose by 382 per cent while consumer prices rose by 245 per cent, and in most months throughout 1992 and 1993 producer prices continued to rise more than consumer prices. Mark-up pricing, plus unbudgeted import subsidies, extended the inflationary pressures, which were insufficiently taken into account. Subsequently the monetary squeeze was deep and prolonged in response to the structural inflation.

As for enterprise reactions, in 1992–3 a particular combination of factors – price liberalisation, deflationary monetary policy that was insufficient to squeeze out inflationary pressure in the context of the monopolistic structure of production, and the resultant negative real interest rates – led to a tremendous buildup of stocks and a disruption of commercial ties between enterprises, as well as the growth of interenterprise indebtedness.[18] All this merely postponed the restructuring of investment and employment. Even with the restructuring of property forms of enterprise in 1993–4, limits were placed on the autonomy of firms to cut employment in the initial period, and thus in one way or another the combination of economic policies in the 1992–4 period perversely slowed down the restructuring of enterprises.

The extent and depth of *poverty* soared after 1991, and in mid 1994 the president stated that over half the population was living below the modest official poverty line.[19] The statutory minimum wage, supposed to be the anchor of the social protection system and the wage system, was allowed to fall to an extraordinarily low level. By mid 1994 the minimum wage had fallen to just over 9 per cent of the average wage, and that represented less than a quarter of the official estimate of the income required for subsistence. Because the minimum wage was made the determinant of many social benefits, an absurd situation arose in which it was held down well below any meaningful level of survival subsistence on the ground that raising it would have worsened the budget deficit. The answer should have been to *delink the minimum wage from the determination of social benefits*. But this is not what happened.[20] Similarly the minimum and average pension fell relative to the average wage – the minimum falling from 31 per cent of the average wage in 1991 to 19 per cent in 1993, and the average pension falling from 52 per cent in 1991 to 35 per cent in 1993. In that year about 60 per cent of pensioners were receiving the minimum pension, which was insufficient for survival (Table 1.2).[21] Old-age poverty became an endemic feature of Russian society and influenced the demographic development of the industrial labour force, as shown in Chapter 10.

Real wages were already very low at the outset of price liberalisation at the beginning of 1992; they were a factor in the low and stagnant labour productivity, and explained why one in every five workers was combining a slack 'full-time' job with a secondary job of some kind or another.[22] Even so, real wages plunged in 1992 and in 1993–4 continued to be well below the 1991 levels. All available evidence also supports the widely

Table 1.2   Minimum wage, pensions and subsistence, Russia, 1993–4

	1993		1994	
	January	*June*	*January*	*June*
Min. wage as % of subsistence	16.2	25.9	31.0	18.8
Min. wage as % of average wage	5.7	9.0	10.9	7.0
Min. pension as % of subsistence	40.6	49.1	31.0	24.4
Average pension as % of subsistence	144.0	n.a	88.6	44.0*

* August, 1994; June figure for average pension not available.
Source: *Goskomstat* of the Russian Federation, Moscow.

held view that income inequality grew dramatically.[23] One of the most drastic developments was the widening of wage differentials between the budgetary sphere (public sector services, such as education, health and culture) and other sectors. This reflected the government's direct control in the former. Thus those working in education, public health, culture and art were earning considerably less than workers in industry and less than the national average. Their average incomes were not only less than double the minimal subsistence income, but they were rarely paid in full and were usually paid in arrears. Public sector impoverishment became a widespread reality.

One relatively neglected aspect of the early economic policy was the systematic neglect of the *public sector*, most notably public administration. This is a crucial background consideration when assessing labour market developments. Attempts to cut the public budget included successful efforts to hold down wages and salaries in the public sector. They fell to such low levels in real terms that they were almost guaranteed to induce petty and more serious corruption, woeful inefficiency, sabotage and opportunism of the most rank kind. This undermined the capacity of the state to introduce and operate essential regulations of a 'market economy'. Public corruption was thus in part due to the macroeconomic policies, and this ironically made the reform process more 'gradualist' than intended.

Another development was a substantial increase in *regional disparities* in output, inflation, incomes and employment.[24] Some observers felt that the combination of price liberalisation and attempted budgetary balancing at the federal level merely intensified the regionalisation of the Russian economy, in part because local authorities in the *oblasts* were inclined to retain a higher share of tax revenues, which were shrinking in real terms. But the fall in revenue going to the federal level restricted the national government's capacity to implement interregional redistribution. The growing regional inequalities were accentuated by the decentralisation of social policy, whereby the *oblast* authorities took increasing responsibility for social protection, taxation and direct intervention. As will be shown with respect to unemployment benefits, this decentralisation may cause major labour market dislocation if unemployment levels continue to rise.

As for the most basic aspect of all, simple survival, opinion polls regularly conducted by the All-Russian Central Institute of Public Opinion in Moscow indicated that the vast majority of the population found life scarcely tolerable. In 1992 the size of the country's population began to shrink.[25] Suicides rose, the overall death rate mounted alarmingly, the birth rate fell and the abortion rate rose.[26] And of course, with all those economic and social difficulties, political developments did not make reform any easier. What emerged was a politically weak nation 'state', in which laws and regulations at the local and enterprise levels could be ignored with impunity.

One could paint this picture in great detail. Much of it is depressing and disappointing, yet it must be balanced by the recognition that there were major reforms in the 1991–4 period, which included the development of some semblance of monetary policy to limit inflation and very extensive voucher-led property-form restructuring that has gone under the name of 'privatisation'. It is generally recognised that the Ministry of Privatisation kept to its task of achieving a gigantic and complex process of property restructuring between 1992 and 1994. By mid 1993 about one third of all small firms had been privatised in some way, and over half of all large units had been transformed from old-style state property.[27] By mid 1994 the first phase of privatisation had been completed, in which 15000 medium-sized and large enterprises had been auctioned off, accounting for about 86 per cent of Russia's industrial labour force. The Federal Bankruptcy Agency had also become firmly established, taking action against 2000 companies by early 1995.[28] In some other respects there was restructuring, which we will try to identify at the microeconomic level in Chapter 3.

It is in the context of stagflation, property reform and other forms of restructuring that one has to consider what is likely to have happened in the labour market, in particular to the level and pattern of employment and unemployment, as well as to wages and benefits. Before we turn to developments in the enterprise labour markets, it seems appropriate to assess the peculiar characteristics of Russian unemployment, which is the subject of the next chapter. By 1991 the fear and expectation of mass unemployment had become pervasive.[29] Like so many developments in the Russian labour market, what happened was neither what was expected nor what it seemed to be.

1.4 CONCLUSIONS

> In the old days, engineers who constructed a railway bridge in Russia had to stand under it when the first train crossed.[30]

Critics and apologists for the early economic reform policies have typically posed the issue in terms of 'speed', postulating a dichotomy of 'big bang' and 'gradualism'.[31] This way of putting it has always seemed simplistic. The real failure was in the *sequencing,* in the relative speed of different aspects of reform, and in the neglect of institutional restructuring, including public administration. Enterprise restructuring was given far too little attention.

One can quibble with the official statistics – and few observers have resisted the temptation to do so, if doing so supported their particular interpretation of developments – yet no objective observer could doubt the enormous transformation stagflation that the country experienced after 1991, or that it was much greater than any official body had forecast. Although the private economy – and the 'black economy' most of all – expanded, that could not have made more than a dent in the huge decline in the officially recorded economy, especially bearing in mind that official statistics tried to take account of private-sector growth.

Although the initial economic reform was guided by understandable euphoria, the neglect of institutional restructuring reflected a naive dichotomy of state socialism and the free market, coupled with a belief that if macroeconomic policies were implemented properly, and if the state withdrew from the economic domain rapidly in a spirit of 'deregulation', then society would gravitate towards an economic 'natural state' – the so-called 'end of history' – characterised by individualism in the economy and political democracy in civil society. This neglected the uniquely monopolistic and segmented nature of Russian production. It also neglected the nexus of transactions – or implicit mechanisms of 'contract' – that made up the Soviet economic system, or what some economists would describe as the sphere of 'bounded rationality'.[32] Altering relative prices induces behavioural reactions that are contingent on the institutional structures and the complex set of social relations of production and distribution. As Karl Polanyi, Joseph Schumpeter, Herbert Simon, Oliver Williamson and many others have taught, a market economy does not emerge through the simple levers of macroeconomic policy. It emerges through a complex rearrangement of institutions and regulations, so that we may say that *ownership matters* and *institutions of contract matter*. Altering relative prices and monetary flows in one institutional context can be valid, doing so in another could be disastrous.

The radical macroeconomic policies in the economic environment of institutional decay that was clear in 1991–2 produced a non-viable situation characterised by low institutionalisation, high flexibility and high uncertainty, so characteristic of the informal or second economy. This is not to argue in favour of gradualism. It is to argue that economic reform can be sustainable only if there is a substitution of rules for personalised discretion.[33] Institutions and legitimised regulations may reduce some forms of flexibility, yet they also produce credibility gains, encouraging agents to adapt and take a longer-term perspective, rather than indulge in short-term opportunism and behavioural inertia.

Most fundamentally, reform of public administration was desperately needed in the early 1990s, but the ideology of shock therapy, with its 'state desertion', hindered the emergence of an efficient administrative apparatus, which had extensive ramifications for labour-market and enterprise restructuring. The distinction between formal rules and laws and actual behaviour was magnified. In Weberian terms, neither the old state apparatus nor the emerging one was a rule-observing bureaucracy.

As far as regulatory mechanisms in the labour market was concerned, the impact of macroeconomic stabilisation policies removed the two main pillars that had legitimised the former labour market – employment security and income security, even though both had been at a low level in the 1980s. There had been the assurance of guaranteed employment, while subsidised prices and direct benefits had provided social protection. In 1992, the authorities and their advisers anticipated that there would be slow labour shedding from state enterprises as budgetary constraints tightened in the period of stabilisation, and then more rapid shedding as privatisation accelerated, when the emerging private sector would absorb the freed labour and there would be only modest unemployment. There was little reason to expect such a smooth transfer. In other countries that practised some variant of shock-therapy reform, most notably Poland, the reality was what Janos Kornai has called, somewhat charitably, a deep 'transformation recession', typically associated with mass unemployment in excess of 15 per cent.[34] Should the Russian Federation in the 1990s have been any different?

2 The Mystery of Unemployment: Triumph of Wishful Thinking?

2.1 INTRODUCTION

> What kind of shock therapy is it . . . when unemployment is only 1 per cent? (Boris Fyodorov, Finance Minister, on resigning, January 1994).

> Contrary to initial expectations, unemployment remains not only low, but declining.[1]

This chapter deals with one of the most fundamental and most misunderstood aspects of the Russian labour market – the emergence of large-scale *open unemployment*. This can be defined as the number of adults with no income-earning activities but wanting, seeking and being readily available for employment. The conventional view is that employment in the Russian Federation scarcely declined in the period covered by this study.[2] As a result, it has been claimed, unemployment remained minimal.[3] This view, repeated by numerous casual observers and the international media, is a triumph of wishful thinking, an unusual case of acceptance of official Russian data by those who have questioned almost all other data on the Russian economy.

In the early 1990s those economists advocating a shock-therapy strategy proclaimed that unemployment was one issue on which there was no need for concern, and thus there was no need to expand public expenditure to deal with it. Indeed a World Bank loan of US$70 million, designed to assist in the development of policies to combat unemployment, was held up for over two years, effectively because of the belief that the problem did not merit it. However this sanguine view of unemployment ignored available official and unofficial statistics and defied basic economic theory. If national income fell by, say, 10 per cent in any industrialised market economy, would any economist doubt that there would be mass unemployment? Would they accept official statistics suggesting otherwise? Why should the Russian Federation in the mid 1990s have been any different?

In later chapters, devoted to data from the RLFS, we shall consider the

14

microeconomic reasoning that has led some economists to the view that there is no unemployment. Here we very briefly refer to the statistics and the reasons and evidence for their being misinterpreted.

2.2 TRENDS IN REGISTERED UNEMPLOYMENT

The conventional view that after 1992 unemployment hovered around 1 per cent of the labour force stems from a literal and uncritical reading of the registered unemployment figures.[4] Briefly, the Russian Federal Employment Service (FES), which was split off from the Ministry of Labour and became a separate legal entity in June 1992, is responsible for the monthly reporting of the number of jobseekers registering at district employment exchanges around the country, and divides these into those with 'unemployment status' and others who are presumed to have a job or who do not qualify as unemployed for some identifiable reason. Unemployment status is accorded to registrants who can demonstrate that they have no work, are capable of work, are seeking it, are immediately available for work and satisfy other criteria that will be considered later.

From its base of zero in 1991 the number of workers registered as unemployed grew rapidly in 1992, from 62000 in January to 517900 in December, then stabilised in 1993 (even declining a little). On 1 January 1994 the total stood at 835504. After that it started growing again, moderately, officially reaching about 1.5 per cent in mid 1994. The basic statistics for 1993–4 are presented in Table 2.1.

Every one of those statistics should be subject to a critique, as discussed in an advisory report prepared for the FES.[5] Although they may have valuable uses for officials involved in developing the employment service, one should be extremely wary about utilising the data for monitoring or analysing the labour market.

There are essentially three hypotheses to explain the low registered unemployment.

First, the conventional view in defence of those statistics is, broadly speaking, as follows. There has been little restructuring of old enterprises, so that there has been extensive 'labour hoarding', rigid employment and little change in employment, while the emerging private economy has been absorbing labour-force entrants and those leaving old enterprises.

This interpretation does not stand up to close scrutiny, as we shall see in Chapter 4. There are three points to bear in mind for the later analysis. In the first place, for many years labour turnover has been high in the country, and on reasonable assumptions about jobseeking and time between

Table 2.1 Registered unemployment, Russian Federation, 1993–4

	30 Sept. 1993	1 July 1994	30 Sept. 1994
Non-employed jobseekers	968645	1516102	687895
of whom:			
% Unemployed	72.9	83.1	84.5
of whom:			
% receiving unemployment benefit	63.6	68.6	84.1
% in training schemes	3.0	3.1	3.2
% in public works	2.2	2.3	1.5
Vacancies per registered unemployed	0.7	0.3	0.3
% of vacancies for workers	89.3	84.9	89.3
Number notified for mass release	n.a.	56633	46989

Source: Russian Federal Employment Service, October, 1994.

jobs, one could expect a rate of 'frictional unemployment' (equivalent to what was regarded as unplanned labour turnover, or *tekuchest*) of between 2 per cent and 3 per cent, in itself much more than what was supposed to be total unemployment, as derived from the registration figures. As labour turnover has long averaged over 15 per cent per year, then assuming about two months between jobs on average, that means up to 3 per cent of those classified as employed would have been between jobs, which would have been about two million workers. In the 1980s it was estimated in various studies that the average number of days between jobs varied regionally between about 15 and 53, depending on the availability and activity of a local employment service.[6] Is there any reason to suppose that frictional unemployment was lower in the 1990s, let alone much lower, or that finding new jobs was easier in a shrinking economy than in one that was not?

The second point is that, in their reports to *Goskomstat*, enterprises report the number of 'posts' they have, and there has been a double incentive to report having more employed than is the case, since traditionally the wage fund allocated to them has been determined by the employment level and because firms have had to pay a wage tax determined by the average wage. As of 1994, if the enterprise's wage bill divided by the number of employed was more than four times the statutory minimum wage, the wage was subject to a 35 per cent 'excess wage' tax. This was modified from the tax formula prevailing in 1992–3. Given a double-digit inflation rate in most months, enterprises were raising money wages every month, whereas the minimum wage was raised only very irregularly and not to anything like the same extent. So to avoid too much 'excess wage' tax, there was an incentive to inflate employment figures.

The third point is that, according to all available data, notably from *Goskomstat,* the level of employment has dropped very substantially since the late 1980s – by five million between 1990 and 1994. In 1993 and the first half of 1994 employment fell by about 700000. Yet registered unemployment fell during much of that period, and only rose modestly in early 1994. At the same time the working-age population should have grown slightly, for demographic reasons and because the enrolment rate in post-secondary education and vocational training has declined in recent years. Thus enrolment of 16–24 year olds in secondary and tertiary schooling declined in the period, because of the very low stipends and their need for current income. At the same time there was no evidence that pension-age workers were withdrawing from the labour force, which was not surprising given the low and declining level of pensions. So employment fell and the labour force should have grown – yet we are supposed to accept that unemployment remained insignificant by any standard, and was much lower than in any industrialised market economy or in any other country undergoing similar economic transitions in central Europe.

The second, related hypothesis is that the official statistics on employment do not include the private economy. Undoubtedly there is a rampant black economy and an underrecorded streetside economy. However one should not leap to conclusions. One could make a reasonable case for expecting that many of those involved in the black economy would have recorded jobs as well, while most of those involved in such activities are doing them as 'survival activities' and are essentially unemployed. To see middle-aged women standing on a curb by the road holding out Coca-Cola bottles or bunches of drooping flowers should be a sufficient antidote to the claim that such people are employed in any meaningful sense of the term.

Moreover the official employment statistics *do* include private sector employment. Indeed in mid 1994, for the first time ever, according to official statistics, only a minority of total employment in the country was in state enterprises and organisations – an almost unnoted yet momentous fact (Table 2.2).

The third hypothesis is that the registered unemployment statistics have chronically understated actual unemployment. There is rather devastating evidence in support of this hypothesis. There are also ample explanations of why the statistics do not measure what some observers persist in claiming.

Table 2.2   Distribution of employment, by property form, Russia, 1990–4

	1990	1991	1992	1993	1994*
Total (in millions)	75.3	73.3	72.0	71.0	70.3
Total (in per cent):					
Public sector	82.6	75.5	68.9	52.1	49.2
Mixed property forms	4.0	10.1	11.7	20.6	26.3
Individual (private)	12.5	13.3	18.3	26.2	23.4
Funds, social institutions	0.8	0.9	0.8	0.7	0.7
Joint ventures	0.1	0.2	0.3	0.4	0.4

* First half.
Source: *Goskomstat* of the Russian Federation. The 'private sector' includes those in 'mixed property form', such as joint stock companies and cooperatives.

Table 2.3   Economically active population, aged 15–72, by gender, Russia, December 1993

	Total	Men	Women	% Men
Economically active	75.1	38.7	36.4	51.6
Of whom:				
Have job for wage or income	71.0	36.6	34.4	51.6
Not employed, looking for a job (unemployed)	4.1	2.1	2.0	51.8
Percentage of economically active	69.7	75.6	63.9	—
Percentage unemployment	5.5	5.4	5.5	—
Of which registered	1.1	0.7	1.6	—
Average duration of unemployment (months)	5.8	5.2	6.5	—
Average duration of registered unemployment (months)	5.4	5.2	5.5	—

Source: Labour force survey of the Russian Federation, December 1993.

The basic evidence is that in two very large national labour force surveys the extent of open unemployment has been shown to be much higher than the registered totals.[7] These surveys defined the unemployed as those without employment but seeking and being available for employment in a given reference week. The second of these surveys was carried out in late 1993, and the basic findings are reproduced in Table 2.3. The key point to note is straightforward: *actual unemployment was five times the registered total.* There are also some rather important secondary points. As can be seen, at the end of 1993 the size of the economically active population was over 75 million, whereas employment was just over 71 million and still declining. The official *Goskomstat* employment data shown in Table 2.2 indicate that employment fell further in 1994.

If one took the ratio of actual to registered unemployed from the survey and extrapolated it to the figures on registered unemployed for mid 1994, then open unemployment would have been something like 7.5 per cent. Even this would probably be an underestimate, for three reasons.

First, in all the statistics the employment level is inflated. For example, since an amendment to the Employment Act in mid 1992, an unemployed person sent on a training course is counted as employed and a woman on two-year maternity leave is often counted as employed.[8]

Second, the *Goskomstat* labour force survey made the age range 15–72, but in effect included pensioners only if they were employed, so that in calculating the unemployment rate the denominator was inflated, thus artificially lowering the unemployment rate. The normal procedure is to include only the working-age population, which in the Russian Federation would be 15–54 for women and 15–59 for men. In the Russian context, this must have considerably lowered the recorded unemployment rate.

Third, the labour force survey used a one-week reference period for job-seeking to classify someone as unemployed, and in many areas, particularly isolated rural communities, that is likely to have resulted in some of those available and wanting employment not being counted as unemployed, simply because jobseeking would be more sporadic in communities where direct knowledge of employment opportunities would be strong. The shorter the reference period, all other things being equal, the lower the measured unemployment rate.

There are other structural reasons for believing that actual unemployment is considerably higher than 7.5 per cent, which will be considered in detail later. However it might be useful to list the main factors that should make all analysts, policymakers and commentators realise that they should give no credence to registered unemployment figures showing that 'unemployment in Russia is low'.

2.3 WHY MEASURED UNEMPLOYMENT IS SO LOW

In 1992–3 a series of visits were made to employment exchanges in the *oblasts* covered by the RLFS, the survey that is the main focus of this book. These were made as part of background work for a technical report prepared for the FES on the limitations of the existing statistics and to make recommendations on the design of a labour market information system. In the course of that work a two-round 'tracer' survey of 2295 jobseekers in 18 districts was carried out.[9] Drawing on the survey and numerous discussions with federal officials, *oblast* and district employment service officials, jobseekers, factory managers and trade unionists, the following 12 factors seem to explain the chronic underrecording of unemployment. In considering the influence of those factors, one must bear in mind that the main reasons for going to an employment exchange in Russia, as elsewhere, are to obtain employment or unemployment benefits. In that context, the following would have made registration less likely.

Stigma

Perhaps the most fundamental reason for the unemployed not to register was reluctance to visit an employment exchange. For nearly 70 years unemployment was designated a 'parasitic' activity, if not a criminal one, and for many decades employment exchanges were almost exclusively for social misfits, alcoholics, ex-prisoners and 'unemployables'. Employment exchanges had a negative connotation that would have had to be overcome by the attractiveness of potential benefits and prospective job offers.

Number of exchanges

By 1994 there were only about 2500 state employment exchanges in this huge country of over 148 million people, meaning that many of those becoming unemployed either did not know where their district employment exchange was located or had very far to go, in some cases more than 60 kilometres. In some districts there were reports suggesting that some had to go over 80 kilometres. In addition the number of employment service staff was correspondingly small by international standards. In 1993 there were 0.28 staff per 1000 persons of official working age, compared with nearly four times as many in the United Kingdom and twice as many in Germany. There were scarcely any private employment agencies, and of the estimated number of 142, only a tiny fraction were licensed.

Cost and time of registration

A key barrier to registration was the financial and time costs involved. Given the distance that many had to travel, reaching the exchange could take a great deal of time. If the unemployed were able to afford that, and could find the employment exchange, there were further costs to take into account. Only a very limited number of staff in employment offices were available to register jobseekers, and thus the time spent in queues was considerable. In one employment office visited, each staff member was expected to deal with up to 50 jobseekers a day, and the unfortunate people waiting their turn were having to wait for hours. The fact that those registered had to report twice a month further raised the cost of registration. That cost will become much higher as unemployment rises, and thus the increasing cost will act as a hindrance to the recording of that growth in unemployment.

Failure to send the unemployed to the employment service

Employers are statutorily required to send workers leaving their firm to the employment service to register, but in the jobseekers' survey 61 per cent of the women and 80 per cent of the men had not been informed by their previous employer of the need to register as unemployed. According to the fourth round of the Russian Labour Flexibility Survey (RLFS4), as shown in Chapter 8, in 1994 over one fifth of managements admitted that they did not send workers to register. There is actually an incentive for employers not to send workers to the employment service, as they have to pay the third month of severance pay only if the worker has registered at the local employment exchange.

Severance pay condition

This seems to be one of the main factors limiting registration, and is quite unlike the situation in other countries. Under the 1991 Employment Act a person released from a job is entitled to two or three months' severance pay from the enterprise making him or her redundant. The amount payable is determined by his or her previous average wage, and three months' pay is awarded if, and only if, that person registers at the employment exchange. During those months, such workers are not entitled to unemployment benefit, and this acts as a major deterrent to registration, especially as most workers suddenly confronted by unemployment for the first time – or for the first time in a radically transformed labour market – tend to believe they will find a job within two or three months. This almost certainly explains the low percentage of registered unemployed who have been 'released' from employment. It also helps explain why some employers do not send redundant workers to register, for if they do not register they will lose their entitlement to the third month of severance pay.

This has produced a state of affairs – what one was inclined to call a 'Catch 22' situation when finding examples during the course of fieldwork – that partly explains why only a minority of the registered unemployed have been classified as having been made redundant from previous jobs, and why some observers have been misled into thinking that most of the unemployed have quit their previous jobs voluntarily. If a worker was released from a job he or she could not receive unemployment benefit while receiving severance pay. There was therefore little incentive to travel a long distance to wait in a queue in an uncomfortable employment exchange in order to register. Yet, probably unknown to the newly unemployed, unless they registered within a few days of becoming unemployed they would automatically lose their entitlement to unemployment benefit when their severance-pay period ended after two months. Imagine being a newly unemployed labourer in an industrial town in which unemployment had been condemned as parasitic for nearly fifty years. The probability of acting in the correct manner must be fairly low.

Low probability of employment

All other things being equal, the probability of registering and being counted as unemployed is inversely related to the probability of obtaining a job as a result. The fact is that, although it might be hoped that this will change, most Russian employers have not recruited workers through employment exchanges. In 1994, according to RLFS4, as shown in Chapter 6, 61.5 per cent of firms reported that they had recruited none of their workers from the employment service and a further 32.2 per cent had recruited less than 10 per cent; only 4.4 per cent had recruited more than one quarter through the district employment exchange.

Moreover, less than two thirds of the firms had reported vacancies to the FES, despite the law requiring them to do so. Outside Moscow, over 40 per cent had not reported vacancies. Even those that had reported vacancies had done so rarely; less than one quarter had reported vacancies monthly. As smaller firms have tended not to report, and as restructuring should result in more employment being found in such firms, the tendency to register vacancies may decline further.

Discouragement deregistration

Because of the low probability of obtaining a job and for other reasons, a majority of the registered unemployed who leave the register do not obtain a job, according to FES statistics. In the first quarter of 1994 only 37.5 per cent of those leaving registered unemployment obtained a job, 7.9 per cent went into 'early retirement' and 54.5 per cent simply dropped off the register.[10]

Low probability of receiving unemployment benefit

This is a key factor, for although a growing proportion of the registered unemployed in 1992–4 were receiving unemployment benefit, this was likely to have reflected tighter screening procedures in employment offices. If one combines the registered and unregistered unemployed, then in 1993–4 only about 13 per cent of unemployed were receiving unemployment benefit, and until 1994 only about two thirds of the registered unemployed (half the registered jobseekers) had received any benefits. The main reasons for non-entitlement to benefit are as follows:

1. Incomplete work-history book.
2. Receipt of severance pay.
3. Registration for less than ten days.
4. Dismissal from previous job.
5. Failure to report twice a month as required.
6. Refusal of two job offers deemed acceptable by the employment office.
7. Absence of a *propiska* (residence permit).
8. Absence of a health certificate or educational certificate.

In the 1993–4 jobseeker survey, all the above were found to have affected entitlement to unemployment benefit. Thus, for example, in February 1994 17.3 per cent of the jobseekers who had gone to the employment exchange were not entitled to benefit because they were deemed to have left their previous job voluntarily.

In some districts, local practices have actually been more restrictive than the official reasons have suggested. In one major city the employment exchange found that its staff was overstretched, so a side office was set aside for two 'lawyers' to interview potential applicants. The jobseekers were told what they should bring with them if they wished to register and were then told to return two weeks later to register. According to the two lawyers, quite a few of those interviewed were concerned that their work-history book was incomplete or incorrect, and did not return. Such a precondition for entitlement to unemployment benefit does not exist in most countries. In Russia it has meant that for at least the first two weeks of unemployment the unemployed person has automatically been excluded from the official unemployment figures.

Low level of unemployment benefits

Perhaps the greatest deterrent to registration is that unemployment benefit is dismally low. Under the Employment Act, people gaining unemployed status through satisfying all the various, and in some cases ambiguous, conditions are entitled to receive benefits for up to 12 months. For the first four months they should receive 75 per cent of their previous wage, for the next four months 60 per cent and for the final four months a mere 45 per cent, subject to a minimum equivalent to the statutory minimum wage.

This formula means that, because an applicant has to wait for a period of two weeks before being entitled to receive the benefit, or three months if made redundant, and because of rapid wage inflation, most of the unemployed actually receive very little indeed. If workers were put on unpaid or partially paid administrative leave prior to being made redundant, their average wage in the period just prior to their becoming unemployed would be so low that the 75 per cent rule would never come into effect.[11] Even ignoring that phenomenon, consider an example of what the formula has meant. A worker receiving what was the average wage of 7379 roubles when he or she became unemployed in September 1992 would, at best, have received 5534 roubles per month in December 1992. By then, the actual average wage in the country was 16071 roubles, so that the unemployed worker would have been receiving only 34 per cent of the wage he or she would have been earning had he or she stayed in employment. By the fourth month, collecting the benefit would scarcely have justified the two journeys to the employment exchange.

Another difficulty of the benefit formula is that many of the unemployed come from jobs paying low wages, so from the outset they only qualify for the minimum wage amount. In the jobseekers' survey of 2295 unemployed, it turned out that more than half the women registering at the exchanges had been earning the equivalent of, or less than, the *current* minimum wage and nearly a third of the men had been earning less than it. So, although nominally earnings-related, from 1992–4 the average benefit received was about equal to the minimum wage, in a period when the minimum wage dropped to about a quarter of the 'physiological survival' subsistence income. In some months, FES data, according to the average unemployment benefit was much less than the minimum wage – for instance, only 80 per cent of it in July 1993.

Expressed in another way, the average monthly unemployment benefit was the equivalent of about US$7 per month, and this had to be collected in two instalments, involving a visit to the employment exchange every two weeks. This was scarcely an incentive to register as unemployed.[12] First-time jobseekers and those returning to the labour market after a prolonged absence were entitled to only 75 per cent of the minimum wage, which in early 1995 was still a little over 15000 roubles, or about 7500 rouldes (US$2) for each two-week claim. There was no possibility of surviving on that.

'Early retirement'

Some of the older unemployed have been shifted off the register by being given an early retirement pension rather than unemployment benefit. As this involves women aged 53–4 and men aged 58–9, many thousands who would have been counted as unemployed in most countries have merely had their statistical status changed. As the minimum pension rose above the minimum wage, or the expected unemployment benefit, many workers in their 50s would have been encouraged to rely on their pension rather than be counted as unemployed.

Propiska

To move one's area of residence or work in Russia, a residence permit is required and formerly this was required for entitlement to benefits as well. Obtaining a *propiska* is difficult and time-consuming, especially without a sponsor. A decree in 1994 declared that a *propiska* was no longer a condition for unemployment benefit. Thus it should no longer be a factor constraining the unemployed from registering. However in mid and late 1994 some employment exchanges (including all those visited by us) were continuing to impose that condition, indicating that the regulatory reach of Moscow is neither long nor strong.

Disability status

Those with a classified disability have tended to move out of employment without going into registered unemployment, simply because they receive a disability allowance and not unemployment benefit. From 1991–4 employment of workers with disabilities shrank extraordinarily (by about 600000), yet hardly any turned up in the registered unemployment figures.[13]

2.4   THE REGIONAL FEAR

One factor threatening to reduce further the monthly recording of unemployment is the formula for operating the Employment Fund. Under FES regulations, unemployment benefits are paid out of the Employment Fund, which since January 1993 has been financed by contributions of 2 per cent (previously 1 per cent) of the wage bill from all enterprises. These funds are collected at the district level. Part is sent to the *oblast* employment service and just 20 per cent is transferred to the FES for staff costs and so on, and for redistribution to where the funds are most urgently required. Before July 1994 only 10 per cent was transferred to Moscow from the *oblasts*. In principle, the district employment service retains 40 per cent of the contributions and transfers the other 40 per cent to the *oblast* employment service headquarters, or to the local authorities. During the course of discussions some city and district office directors complained that they had been unable to retain anything like 40 per cent. But the essential structural problem arises from the fact that most of the money is retained at the local level.

The implication of this institutional arrangement is that a district with rising unemployment and falling employment will experience both declining contributions, because firms cannot or will not pay the 2 per cent of their wage bill, and rising demands for transfers, whereas more prosperous, low-unemployment districts will have more contributions and fewer demands. This must accentuate regional inequalities, and as national unemployment rises those areas with above-average rates of unemployment will face a threat of bankruptcy, leading to an inability to pay unemployment benefits and an inability to use funds for employment-saving policies or to provide labour-market training.

In 1994 it was estimated that if the national level of registered unemployment rose to about 3 per cent, a large number of *oblasts* with above-average unemployment would be unable to pay their costs and unemployment benefits from the Employment Fund.[14] Already in 1994 some *oblasts*, including one covered by the RLFS, were in acute financial difficulty. The announcement that the Employment Fund was to become part of the consolidated federal budget in 1995 made the situation even more fraught with uncertainty, since it opened up the prospect that the fund would cease to be primarily an employment fund to deal with unemployment and labour-market restructuring, but would instead be used to reduce the government's budget deficit. Whether or not that fear was justified, the fact remained that the decentralised nature of the Employment Fund undermined the potential for regional unemployment policy.

2.5 THE INCIDENCE OF REGISTERED UNEMPLOYMENT

Much attention was paid from 1991–4 to the pattern or incidence of unemployment, again interpreting the registration figures as representative. If there are good grounds for doubting the validity of registration figures as a means of measuring the overall rate of unemployment, is there any reason to suppose they will adequately capture the incidence of unemployment? A full analysis of this should be made through use of successive rounds of the national labour force survey. Here we will merely mention a few points of relevance for our analysis of enterprise restructuring in later chapters.

First, with regard to *gender*, in the early 1990s the number of women registered as unemployed was more than twice the number of men. Many commentators have used the registration data to state that 'unemployment has mainly involved women'. In fact this is wrong. As Table 2.3 has shown, when account is taken of the non-registered unemployed there have been more unemployed men, although the male unemployment rate has been very slightly lower than that of women. One reason for more women being registered as unemployed, according to the jobseeker survey, seems to be that priority has often been given to the reemployment of men within the first ten days of registration, during which time a person is not counted as unemployed. We will consider possible explanations for the gender distribution of unemployment in Chapter 9.

Second, it is believed that the *duration of unemployment* is relatively short, on average. For example in April 1994 only 8.8 per cent of the registered unemployed were classified as unemployed for more than a year and only 12 per cent were unemployed for between eight and twelve months. This apparent incidence of relatively long-term unemployment is much less than in Western or Central Europe. But again the registration statistics should not be taken as a reliable guide. One reason for this is that a majority of those who drop off the register do so for reasons other than job placement (Table 2.4). The distribution is very similar for men and women. However the labour force survey data for November 1993 suggests that use of the registration statistics leads to an underestimation of the average duration of unemployment for women in comparison with men. Another reason is that, as noted earlier, those registering are not counted as unemployed for at least the first ten days.

A third aspect of the incidence of unemployment is *age distribution*. In 1991–2 it was widely assumed that older workers would bear the brunt of unemployment, followed by youths unable to obtain entry-level posts. As far as industry is concerned, the actual developments will be considered

Table 2.4 Reasons for leaving the unemployment register in selected regions of the Russian Federation, first quarter, 1994 (percentage distribution of those deregistering)

	Received job	*Early retirement*	*Other reasons*
Russian Federation	37.6	7.9	54.5
Moscow	12.0	36.4	51.6
St Petersburg	40.0	5.7	54.3
Nizhny Novgorod	39.8	18.9	41.3
Ivanovo	39.1	3.2	57.7

Source: Federal Employment Service.

in Chapter 10. The registration data are hard to interpret, as most older workers becoming unemployed do not qualify for unemployment benefit since they are in receipt of some form of pension. There has also been a tendency for employment exchanges to put unemployed workers in their 50s – 53–4 for women, 58–9 for men – into early retirement, as suggested by Table 2.4.

The youth age group has also accounted for a smaller proportion of the registered unemployed than many expected, or a smaller proportion than would have been expected according to the pattern in most other countries. In the FES statistics 'youth' has been defined as people aged 16–29, and at the end of the first quarter of 1994 that group comprised 35 per cent of the total, and only 16 per cent in Moscow. Of those who had left the register during the preceding three months, only 36.3 per cent had been placed in jobs.

One feature of the jobseeker survey carried out in 18 districts in 1993–4 was the low percentage of young unemployed persons attending employment exchanges, and the consequent fact that the average age of those registering was around 35, which is not the norm in other countries. Unemployed youths simply have a lower propensity to register, and thus one should be wary about reading too much from the registered unemployment totals when calculating the age distribution of unemployment.

Nevertheless, if we include both the registered and the unregistered unemployed that were identified in the 1992 and 1993 labour force surveys, it is clear that youths made up a greater proportion of the unemployed than the registered figures alone suggested, as shown in Table 2.5. The mean average age of those employed was about five years higher than that of the unemployed. But it would be misleading to describe the unemployment problem in the Russian labour market as primarily one of youth unemployment.

Table 2.5 Age distribution of employed and unemployed, Russian Federation, October 1992 and 1993 (percentage distribution of total employment or unemployment)

	October 1992		October 1993	
Age	Employed	Unemployed	Employed	Unemployed
15–19	3.0	15.5	3.0	13.6
20–24	7.6	15.8	8.4	16.8
25–29	10.3	11.6	9.9	11.9
30–49	55.9	39.6	56.3	43.4
50–54	11.4	6.5	10.0	5.6
55–59	6.8	5.3	7.8	5.1
60+	5.0	5.7	4.6	3.6

Source: Labour force survey, 1992 and 1993, *Goskomstat* of the Russian Federation. The unemployed were defined as those seeking and available for paid employment in the reference week.

A final aspect of the incidence of registered unemployment that is worth noting is that the *educational and occupational* pattern is not concentrated on low-level skills. At the end of the first quarter of 1994, 65 per cent of those registered were classified as 'workers', 23.7 per cent were 'employees' and only 11.3 per cent were 'without occupation'. The first two national labour force surveys indicated that the more highly educated had a lower rate of unemployment than the less educated, but the differences were not substantial. At the end of 1993, 17.7 per cent of employed people had not completed secondary schooling, compared with 21.1 per cent of the unemployed. A year earlier the figures were 18.5 per cent and 21.8 per cent respectively.

In sum, these statistics suggest that it would be inappropriate to describe unemployment as 'structural' in terms of the characteristics of the unemployed. While some groups do appear to have a higher probability of being unemployed than others, there is little evidence to suggest that unemployment is concentrated among particular groups that could be described as 'hard to employ'.

2.6 CONCLUSIONS

There can be little doubt that actual unemployment in the Russian labour market in the early 1990s was much greater than suggested by the registration statistics, which should not be cited as a realistic guide to the extent of unemployment. Nor should regional unemployment distribution be regarded as a good proxy for statistical analysis. In some regions, such as the high-unemployment region of Ivanovo, the labour force survey estimated that unemployment was less than twice the registered rate, whereas in Moscow City it was 19 times the registered rate. According to the registration data, Nizhny Novgorod and St Petersburg had the same rate of unemployment, but according to the labour force survey St Petersburg's rate was nearly 60 per cent higher.

This chapter has drawn attention to a formidable set of barriers and disincentives that deter people from registering as unemployed. It is therefore not surprising that the registration count has led to incorrect analysis. What is incredible is that some economists have believed the figures and suggested that unemployment in the early 1990s was lower than in the 1970s and 1980s, before the tremendous slump in production and removal of the guarantee of full employment.[15]

In February 1995 the director of the Russian Federal Employment Service forecast that the number of registered unemployed would rise to ten million by the end of 1995. This was by no means the first time he had made such a dire prediction. The FES had consistently and understandably forecast a much greater number than actually transpired, but the danger of 'crying wolf' was that the warnings would not be heeded when the real upsurge took place.

Perhaps it is time to pose a rather basic question. Was there something systemic that made it hard for registered unemployment to rise above a certain level, that slowed down the growth of measured unemployment and increased the difference between registered and total unemployment? The image is of a bath in which the taps are turned on at the same time as the plug is out of its hole. In reality, at the district and *oblast* levels there has been considerable discretion in the registration and treatment of the unemployed. Anecdotes and case studies may not provide strong evidence, yet surely do provide material for hypotheses. In one major *oblast* the director of the employment service said he knew they could not afford to pay benefits to everybody affected by rising local unemployment. He was sure that no men in their thirties or forties could be unemployed, so was trying to exclude them from the register. Elsewhere the queuing restriction on registration was operating. No doubt those with no prospect of receiving unemployment benefit were likely to drift away from crowded or depressing employment exchanges, especially if the weather was bitterly cold and they believed there was little chance of obtaining a job through waiting.

What is important to stress in this respect is that there is no reason to suggest that employment service officials in Moscow or elsewhere were trying to conceal the degree of unemployment. They were merely responding in rational ways to an increasingly onerous situation.

Sadly, another factor has surely played a part in concealing the extent of rising unemployment. If the employment dislocation were limited, how is it that the average life expectancy in the country has declined so precipitously? It is worth reiterating that by 1994 the average life expectancy of males had dropped to a little over 58, compared with 65 in 1987. Most striking of all, according to official data the death rates of young and middle-aged men have risen sharply, and this is associated with stress and insecurity linked to labour-market and economic upheavals. This is the sombre context in which one has to consider economic and labour-market restructuring.

3 Restructuring in Russian Industry: The RLFS

3.1 INTRODUCTION

For many decades Russian industry was the backbone of the Soviet economy, and although the service industry is now expected to play a more significant role, it is a common mistake to divide the soviet economic system into primary, secondary and tertiary sectors, where primary refers to agriculture, forestry and mining; secondary to industry, mainly manufacturing; and tertiary to services. In reality, for better or worse, industrial enterprises in the Soviet system were far more than just industrial.

The huge enterprises that came to dominate the economic and social system were 'total institutions', in which hundreds of workers carried out functions, that in other economies would have been conducted by other sectors. This is important to bear in mind, since the restructuring of enterprises, which remains the critical issue for the economic restructuring and regeneration of the Russian economy, will also entail an occupational redivision of labour between types of enterprise.

This book is concerned with the restructuring of the industrial labour market, and most specifically with the restructuring of the 'internal labour market' of industrial enterprises. It is based on findings from four rounds of the Russian Labour Flexibility Survey (henceforth the RLFS, followed by the number corresponding to the round). Since its inception in 1991, the RLFS has been charting the industrial restructuring process and attempting to document the changing labour and employment practices of factories. An underlying theme, which was reinforced by numerous visits and discussions with enterprise managements from 1991 onwards, is that the economic reform strategy launched in 1991 committed a grave error when it relegated enterprise restructuring to late in the reform sequencing. This 'state desertion' resulted in neglect of the productive potential of the older structures, helped to make the economic slump much worse than it should have been, and distorted the restructuring, which occurred, of necessity, in defensive mode.

That point was critically relevant in 1995, since both in the Russian Federation and in other countries of the former Soviet Union – which were mostly well behind Russia on the road to economic reform – reform of what are called 'corporate governance' and 'internal labour markets' was still urgently required.

3.2 THE RUSSIAN LABOUR FLEXIBILITY SURVEY

The idea of the survey arose during preparatory work for an international conference convened in Moscow in October 1990, jointly organised by the ILO's Employment Department and the USSR State Committee for Labour and Social Affairs. It was quite clear that analysis of the labour market was being severely impeded by a dearth of reliable information and that existing data were sufficient to indicate that profound changes were taking place.

Consequently, during the year following that conference informal case studies of firms were carried out as a means of developing an instrument for collecting information on aspects of the restructuring and on the various labour and employment developments taking place in industrial enterprises. This exercise became a 'pre-pilot' for a statistical survey – given that it is always risky to generalise from a few cases.[1] These factory visits involved detailed discussions with top managers, personnel managers or their equivalents, union representatives, chief engineers and others. The main objectives were to clarify the issues, refine the questionnaires, clarifying the concepts and obtain the respondents' views on a wide range of labour-related issues.

The resultant first round of the RLFS, launched in late 1991, was effectively an attempt to monitor the changes in labour and employment practices in Soviet industrial enterprises within the context of the government's attempts to promote economic 'pluralism' (including a diversity of property forms – notably what were euphemistically called 'cooperatives' at the time), decentralisation of decision making under the rubric of 'cost accounting', more flexible payment systems, a general tightening of budgetary constraints in the enterprises and what the chairman of the State Committee on Labour and Social Affairs described as 'a level playing field in industrial relations'. It was still an era of perceived labour shortage, or at least the legacy of that era was still evident.

The survey had a quirky uniqueness in several respects. It was not intended to be representative of the country as a whole, nor of all sectors. It was intended to be representative of the manufacturing industry in three major *oblasts*. The uniqueness was that it began in one country and concluded in another, since the fieldwork coincided with the dissolution of the Soviet Union and the emergence of the Russian Federation as a separate entity, and it began in one city but ostensibly concluded in another, in that one of the three *oblasts* was Leningrad at the outset but St Petersburg before the end. The fieldwork was difficult. The weather was harsh, transport between factories was not particularly easy and administrative support was complicated by upheavals in the various authorities. Nevertheless the response rate among top managers of the factories visited was remarkably good, and the political vacuum existing at the individual enterprise level was conducive to a frankness that might not have been possible even a year earlier. It was a frankness that highlighted what was palpably a unique moment for reform, when uncertainty and even bewilderment at the enormity of the changes taking place around them meant that managements would surely have accepted radical change, and many expected it.

The first round of the RLFS covered 503 industrial firms, or what are called 'establishments' in statistical terms.[2] The basic results were presented at two large conferences held in Moscow and St Petersburg over a week at the end of October 1992. Among the participants were employers, trade union leaders, cabinet ministers, statisticians, academics and representatives of international agencies. By then the fieldwork for a follow-up survey, the second round, had been completed in the three *oblasts*, covering 191 firms, 109 of which had been in the first round.

The methodology of the RLFS was as follows. A representative sample of manufacturing establishments was drawn up by the statistical authorities in the *oblasts* covered by the survey, stratified by industry and drawn from all registered firms in manufacturing, regardless of property form. The intention was to have representativeness in terms of property form and industry. Each of the four rounds of the RLFS was intended primarily as an independent survey, in that each was complete in itself. However in successive rounds there was an attempt to include a sufficiently large and representative number of firms that had been included in previous rounds.

The technique of data gathering was labour-intensive and could be described as a combination of case study and statistical survey. The basic survey instrument consisted of two long questionnaires, both directed at top management. The first was delivered to the factory and covered basic statistical material on production, sales, capacity utilisation, property form, employment, vacancies, labour turnover and wages and benefits. At that first visit arrangements were made for a prolonged visit or visits to interview senior managers on labour-market practices, employment, training and labour relations, through the second questionnaire.

For each round of the RLFS there was a 'pre-pilot' stage along the lines described earlier. This was followed by the training of those selected as supervisors for the fieldwork and of the enumerators, using a lengthy training manual and lectures on basic concepts, questions, interview techniques and various practical matters.[3] Then there was a pilot survey of a few firms to test the finalised questionnaires as well as enumerator skills and respondent reactions.[4] Once the lessons of the pilot survey had been digested, the fieldwork began. In most cases, teams of two enumerators visited each factory, and often two or more visits were necessary or desirable. Random field checks were made, and it is believed that the two-round approach ensured a high standard of reliability of the data. In the course of the four rounds, some factories were visited a dozen times or more.

The survey questionnaires were refined and modified over the four rounds of the RLFS, in part because certain questions needed to be modified, in part because certain issues became less relevant or were shown to be less relevant than had been believed at the outset, and in part to take account of the rapidly changing problems and challenges facing managements and workers. In some cases, subjects included in one round were dropped or considerably reduced in a subsequent round simply because new issues demanded priority, and it was judged prudent to include new topics only if there were cuts elsewhere in the questionnaires.

The basic numerical details of the RLFS are shown in Table 3.1. This shows that RLFS1 was the largest of the four rounds in terms of the number of firms and workers covered, although the geographical coverage of the survey was extended in 1993 to include the supposedly dynamic 'growth pole' city of Nizhny Novgorod – described by many as the economically most dynamic industrial region of Russia and the recipient of more foreign aid than any other – and then further in 1994 to balance the previous extension by including the supposedly economically depressed city of Ivanovo – seen by many as the most depressed in Russia. The five regions covered by the fourth round may not be representative of the country as a whole, but they do represent the major industrial regions of the country. It is hoped that the type of survey used for our analysis will be replicated in other regions, and at the time of writing this was being planned.

The dates of the four rounds mentioned in Table 3.1 refer to the period of fieldwork, when the factories were visited. The 'reference period' is the period covered by retrospective information collected during the fieldwork, often by means of inspecting a copious number of statistics collected in the administrative offices in factories.[5] Some questions related to the recent past, but it was considered inappropriate to go back very far with most data. For example data on employment were regarded as relatively reliable for the past month and for the corresponding month one year earlier,

Table 3.1 Characteristics of the Russian Labour Flexibility Survey, 1991–4

Round	Date	Reference period	Number of establishments*	Panel	Workforce covered	Region
RLFS1	Nov. 1991–Jan. 1992	1990–1	503(503)	—	529250	Moscow City Moscow Region St Petersburg
RLFS2	June 1992	1990–2	200(191)	109	166895	Moscow City Moscow Region St Petersburg
RLFS3	July 1993	1991–3	350(340)	240	308969	Moscow City Moscow Region St Petersburg, Nizhny Novg.
RLFS4	July 1994	1992–4	400(384)	340	303333	Moscow City Moscow Region St Petersburg Nizhny Novg. Ivanovo

* Figures in parentheses indicate number of establishments completed; the first figure is the initial sample for the round. The unit of observation is the establishment, not the enterprise, which may consist of more than one establishment.

whereas on some behavioural issues only current data were collected. To complement the retrospective information, on some issues respondents were asked about plans or expectations over the next year or two.

'Number of establishments' (fourth column of Table 3.1) refers to the number sampled, and the number completed is shown in parentheses. In RLFS1 the response rate was less impressive than it seems, for replacements were drawn from the registered industrial establishments by *Goskomstat*. In some cases one or two visits were insufficient to obtain responses, and there were a few where five or six were required. In general, however, the response rate was very good for this type of survey.

The fifth column ('Panel') refers to the number of firms in the designated round that were in one or more of the preceding rounds. The number does not mean they were in all previous rounds. Thus in the fourth round (1994) 340 factories had been included in one or more previous rounds, yet only 229 of those had been included in the 1993 survey. This feature of the RLFS is not ideal from a statistical point of view, yet on many issues the possession of two or more years of data from the same subsample of firms should be valuable for assessing the dynamics of firm behaviour.[6]

In the following chapters, most attention is paid to the results of the fourth round of the RLFS, for several reasons. (One is tempted to put the main reason in a footnote in the hope that the reader will overlook it.) The most pragmatic reason is that to present the full results of all four rounds would be a monumental task that would span several volumes, take much longer to write and result in a more dated analysis, albeit probably a better one. At the time of writing the data for 1994 were the most topical and in some respects the most complete, because of the modifications made as a result of the analysis of preceding rounds.[7] Nevertheless information is presented from all four rounds, with least attention being given to the second round, which was the smallest and least innovative in terms of issues covered.

In the remainder of this chapter the characteristics of the firms covered by the RLFS are presented, the main objective being to identify the process of restructuring that occurred in the traumatic period of 1991–4. In most respects this was a reactive restructuring, rather than a strategic restructuring led by a coherent strategy.

3.3 RESTRUCTURING IN CRISIS CONDITIONS

Successive rounds of the RLFS have chronicled the changing character of Russian industrial enterprises, and it is a central hypothesis that these

Figure 3.1   Industrial distribution of establishments, all regions, 1994 (percentage distribution of factories in RLFS4)

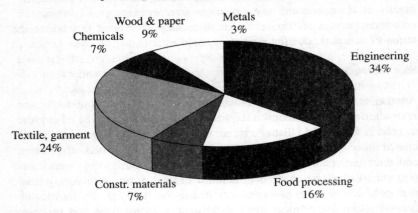

Source: RLFS4, n = 384.

aspects of restructuring shaped the dynamics of labour market developments in the period of stagflation. Six potential aspects of restructuring are discussed below.

Industrial restructuring

In terms of the changing composition of the manufacturing industry, there were few major changes in the early 1990s. The Soviet system gave high priority to 'material production', and this was further boosted by the military–industrial orientation of production. So it was no surprise that engineering represented the largest group in 1991 and this continued to be the case, although its share did decline – from 39.1 per cent of the total in late 1992 to 33.6 per cent in mid 1994 (Figure 3.1).[8] This decline cannot be interpreted as a decline in engineering, although it will be shown that important employment and production shifts could be interpreted as a decline.

In 1991, 1992 and 1994 the second largest group consisted of textiles and garments, followed by food processing. Compared with 1993 and RLFS3, the increased share of textiles and garments in RLFS4 reflected the inclusion of Ivanovo and the composition of industry in Ivanovo, long known as a garment-producing area and 'the women's city' because of the high ratio of women to men in the population.

Analysis of factories included in several rounds of the RLFS revealed no instances of a firm changing industry in terms of its main products. It is also known that no firms went bankrupt during the period. Thus, superficially at least, one can say that there was no evidence of substantial conversion across sectors, although there may have been conversion in terms of actual products, to which we will return.

Size restructuring

Another form of restructuring is what can be described as *workforce size restructuring*. For efficiency and other reasons, one may regard this aspect as crucial. One should distinguish between 'downsizing' due to redundancies or other employment cuts and restructuring due to a break-up of firms and the creation of medium-sized and small firms. Although workforce size changes will be covered in the next chapter, it is worth noting here that there was some *restructuring by divestment*. In 1993, 12 per cent of firms divested one or more units (8 per cent in Ivanovo), as had 15.1 per cent of state establishments. However the percentage of workers involved in such detachments was very small (about 1.5 per cent of the workforce on average), and in none of the four rounds of the RLFS was there much evidence of size restructuring of firms (except a generalised shrinkage due to demand factors).

In 1991, 24 per cent of the factories had more than 1000 workers and 29 per cent had fewer than 250; by 1993 the relative shares were 20 per cent and 34 per cent. This suggests there had been some shift, although it tells us little about restructuring. The existence of slightly more small firms in 1994 at least partly reflects the inclusion of firms from Ivanovo (Figure 3.2). Proportionately more of the factories in Ivanovo were small (54.5 per cent had fewer than 250 workers), whereas St Petersburg and Nizhny Novgorod had the largest share of large factories, St Petersburg having 49 per cent with more than 500 workers.

Property-form restructuring

The most topical aspect of enterprise restructuring is *property-form restructuring*. During the period of the RLFS this was nothing less than revolutionary. In late 1991, as indicated in RLFS1, 57.5 per cent of establishments were state-run and a further 32.3 per cent were leaseholdings (*arenda*), which were essentially still state enterprises. The latter were little more than profit-sharing enterprises that lacked the possibility to engage in independent restructuring efforts.

In mid 1992 still well over half (55.1 per cent) were state-run and 26.6

Figure 3.2 Distribution of establishments by workforce size, all regions, mid 1994 (percentage distribution of factories in RLFS4)

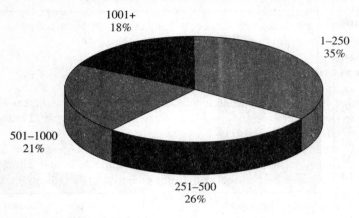

Source: RLFS4, n = 384.

Figure 3.3 Property-form distribution of establishments, all regions, mid 1994 (percentage distribution of current property forms in RLFS4)

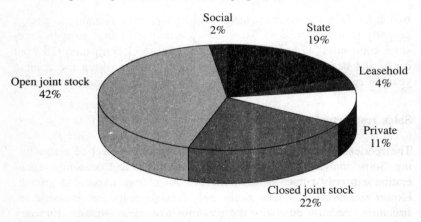

Source: RLFS4, n = 384.

per cent were leaseholdings. By mid 1993 the state enterprise share had shrunk to 36 per cent, and by mid 1994 state establishments accounted for fewer than one in five (19 per cent) of all factories. By then, as shown in Figure 3.3, the main property form had become open joint stock (42.7 per cent), followed by closed joint stock (21.9 per cent).[9] Moreover, more than

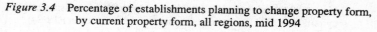

Figure 3.4   Percentage of establishments planning to change property form, by current property form, all regions, mid 1994

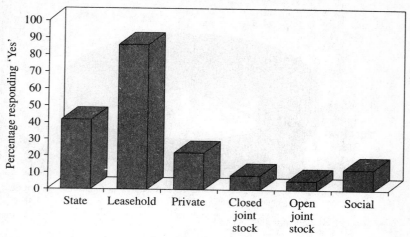

Source: RLFS4, n = 383.

two in five of the remaining state establishments were planning to change property form (Figure 3.4). Most were planning to change to open joint-stock companies (47 per cent) or to closed joint-stock companies (28.8 per cent), and nearly three quarters expected to change within the coming year. In sum, there had been massive restructuring of property form.

Sales restructuring

The reorientation of sales is a relatively neglected aspect of restructuring. Some analysts argue that structural adjustment and economic regeneration can only come, as in South-East Asia, from export-led growth. Export reorientation is seen as the only feasible route for economic restructuring because otherwise the pressures to secure dynamic efficiency will be insufficient to prevent firms from returning to bureaucratic modes of regulation and price setting.

Unfortunately for the prospect of regeneration of Russian industry, most firms have been remarkably oriented towards domestic sales. This was an endemic feature of the unravelling of the Soviet Union, for it seems that the local authorities in the regions, including directors of the dominant enterprises, indulged in semi-autarkic behaviour that in the late 1980s

Figure 3.5   Percentage of sales exported, by industry, all regions, 1992–4

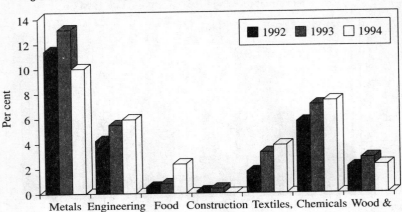

Source: RLFS4, n = 384.

included informal controls over trade so as to retain inside the *oblast* the goods most in demand or need.[10]

For whatever reason, export orientation was very low at the beginning of the 1990s. Thereafter it began to pick up, albeit moderately and very patchily. Although the level was extremely low in 1990, there was a steady upward trend in exports as a share of total output. The trend is important, since exposure to international markets should lead to greater pressure to improve productivity.

Bearing in mind that direct comparisons between rounds of the survey could be slightly misleading, a swing towards exports was nevertheless evident. According to RLFS1, on average the firms exported a tiny 1.32 per cent of their output in 1989 and 1.31 per cent in 1990. In mid 1992 exports seemed to remain static, at about 1.5 per cent of total sales in 1991. According to RLFS3, exports accounted for a mean average of 1.9 per cent of total output for 1992, rising to over 3.9 per cent for factories with over 1000 workers. According to RLFS4, on average the firms exported 4.3 per cent of their sales in the first half of 1994, compared with 3.9 per cent in 1993 and 2.9 per cent in 1992, although not all industries had become more export-oriented (Figure 3.5). It should be noted that the observed growth in exports, compared with previous rounds, occurred despite the inclusion of firms from Ivanovo, which was the area least oriented towards exports.

Figure 3.6 Percentage of sales exported, by property form, all regions, 1992–4

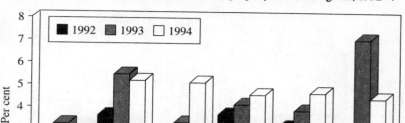

Source: RLFS4, n = 384.

In 1994, private firms exported more than twice as much of their output (5.2 per cent) as state firms (2.2 per cent) (Figure 3.6). State firms had also been less export-oriented than others in 1991, 1992 and in 1993. In all years, the larger the firm, the greater its export orientation. But overall, manufacturing was predominantly producing for the domestic market.

Besides this modest shift towards exports, the economic crisis seems to have induced a striking shift of sales towards barter trade (Figure 3.7). It is generally recognised that this reflected a lack of liquidity in the tightening monetary situation, the increasing uncreditworthiness of many firms and a shortage of goods.[11] But it also reflected the personal bilateral relationships between directors of the various enterprises in particular regions. Thus in many firms visited during the course of the fieldwork we were told of how a firm producing trucks would give a truck to a food-processing plant, in return for which food items were provided to be sold to the workers, usually at non-market prices, in the growing number of shops constructed on the factory grounds.

According to the RLFS1 data, in 1990 barter accounted for a mere 0.74 per cent of total output. In 1991–2 the RLFS2 data suggested that the barter share had risen sharply, particularly in large factories and most of all in state enterprises.[12] At the time there was debate among economists about the fact that, in the wake of the first wave of price liberalisation,

Figure 3.7 Percentage of output bartered, by industry, all regions, 1992–4

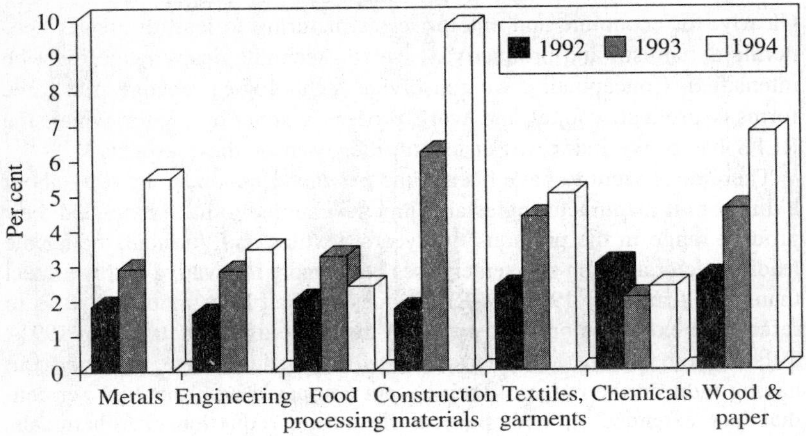

Source: RLFS4, n = 348.

retail sales had fallen more than wholesale sales. Some observers interpreted this as reflecting deliberate stockpiling by firms, attributing it to a desire by enterprise managements to speculate on a rising rate of inflation. Stockpiling may have been part of the story, although it seems a little too sophisticated to be convincing. It is more likely that the relatively rapid decline in sales compared with output in 1992 reflected a shift into barter and intra-enterprise transfers, which the RLFS2 also recorded. Two pieces of evidence support that interpretation – barter rose as a percentage of output (non-sold output) and the growth of barter was greatest in establishments that recorded a fall in sales.

In the third round it seemed as if barter had peaked in 1992 and was significant only in medium-sized and large firms. However, according to RLFS4, it continued to rise, accounting for 2.1 per cent of total sales in 1992, 3.6 per cent in 1993 and 4.4 per cent in 1994.[13] It was particularly common in the economically depressed region of Ivanovo, whereas it was insignificant in Moscow City. Across industries, it was greatest in building materials (9.8 per cent). It was positively correlated with size of establishment, and was greater in firms that had cut total employment than in those that had increased it or kept it constant, with barter accounting for 8 per cent of sales in those firms that had cut jobs by over 20 per cent. Why had barter increased? The most likely explanation was the liquidity constraint associated with enterprise indebtedness.

Technological restructuring

Clearly, for economic and enterprise restructuring to lead to greater economic dynamism and productivity growth, technological change must be intensified. Conceptually, we can divide technological change into three forms – product, capital and work process innovations – for which the RLFS has proxy indexes. Let us consider each of these aspects.

There does seem to have been some *product innovation*. In 1991 about a third of all manufacturing establishments claimed to have extended their product range in the previous two years, textiles and garments being the leading sector and non-state enterprises being more innovative in this respect than state firms. By 1993 the RLFS question had been modified so as to refer to an extension or a narrowing of the range of products. From 1991–3 there seemed to be a net narrowing of the product range, 30.6 per cent having reduced the range of their output compared with the 24.4 per cent that had extended it, with particularly strong reductions in chemicals, engineering, and textiles and garments plants. Given the huge conglomerate nature of Russian industrial enterprises, this seemed to be the harbinger of a rationalisation process. However in 1993–4 29.7 per cent of firms had increased their product range the previous year while 24.5 per cent had cut their range, the food-processing sector being relatively more likely to have increased the range (42.6 per cent) and the chemicals sector most likely to have reduced it (39.3 per cent). State establishments were most likely to have decreased their product range (38.4 per cent), whereas private firms (35.7 per cent) and closed joint-stock firms (34.5 per cent) were apparently most likely to have increased it. This latter finding may be indicative of some restructuring of output associated with property-form restructuring, but more detailed analysis than is possible here would be required to identify any other major trend, if there were one.

It is indicative of some tentative capital innovation that in 1993–4 43.6 per cent of firms had introduced some *new technology in production*, again with food processing (51.6 per cent) generally being the most innovative, along with chemicals (57.1 per cent) and wood and paper products (52.8 per cent). State firms were least likely to have made this form of technological innovation (41.1 per cent, compared with 46.3 per cent for private). In the first round of the RLFS 54 per cent of firms stated that they had made capital innovations during the previous two years, although most of those had been minor. In RLFS3 48.2 per cent of firms stated they had introduced a change of some sort, with nearly 59 per cent in food processing. In all rounds of the survey the major changes were listed as new equipment, but the overall impression was that the changes were mostly

Table 3.2   Product, capital and work process innovation, by property form, all regions, 1993–4 (percentage of establishments having made a change)

Property form	Changed product range		New technology	Changed work process
	Increase	Decrease		
State	21.9	38.4	41.1	47.2
Leasehold	35.7	21.4	42.9	35.7
Private	19.5	22.0	46.3	53.7
Closed joint stock	34.5	20.2	42.9	39.3
Open joint stock	32.3	20.7	43.9	42.7
Social	37.5	37.5	57.1	62.5

Source: RLFS4, n = 345.

small. Except in the first round, the fact that stood out was that a majority had made no changes over a two-year period. In an economy undergoing a major economic upheaval, this was bad enough; it would be inconceivable in any of the industrially dynamic countries of the world.

As regards *work process innovation*, in RLFS1 about 44 per cent of the factories had introduced some form of work reorganisation during the previous two years. This remained about the same in subsequent years (1992–3 and 1993–4) (Table 3.2).

In 1994 private firms were relatively more likely to have introduced some form of work reorganisation. Although this was not the case in earlier years, in 1993–4 the main change had been to cut out administrative tiers of employees in response to the changing structure of decision making, or as some managements put it, 'to tighten work organisation'. The second most common change had been to increase the range of work tasks for manual jobs, which probably also reflected the reduction in administrative workers.

In sum, the evidence suggests that it would be incorrect to describe the firms as technologically stagnant, yet the innovation was limited and slow. The perceived effects on employment will be considered in later chapters.

Corporate governance restructuring

As critical as property-form restructuring is *management restructuring*, or what might be called *corporate governance restructuring*. Governance involves issues of ownership of property rights and possession of control rights, and establishments should be analysed in terms of governance structures rather than simply in terms of production functions.[14] Essentially governance concerns *accountability*, which means the range of responsibilities and controls exercised by management and workers, and by their intermediary institutions, as well as the internal pressures influencing decision making within the firm.

For the longer-term revival of Russian industry, perhaps the most important change in industrial relations in the mid-1990s was the change in the position of senior managers. Some have described this as the 'privatisation of management',[15] although a better description would be the 'destatisation of management'. Whatever the term used, the transformation of management and the management labour market have been distinctive aspects of enterprise restructuring, and may have been as least as important as the transformation of the property rights of ownership. For dynamic efficiency, management governance requires *incentives* for risk-taking and profit orientation combined with substantial *monitoring* of their behaviour. Providing adequate incentives for managerial agents without monitoring could lead to recklessness, short-termism and opportunism, to the detriment of the interests of their principals, whether the latter be the workers, in their capacity as shareholders, or others. Rigid monitoring without adequate incentives is likely to promote shirking or sloth, illicit appropriation of assets and an unwillingness to take risks. Epitomised by the giant agencies and enterprises of the Soviet system, bureaucratic organisations are chronically prone to 'hard' (rigid) monitoring coupled with 'soft' budget constraints that combine to produce both opportunism and shirking.

Issues of corporate governance relate to many aspects of labour-market restructuring, so it may be useful to make some conceptual distinctions. One can distinguish between *external governance* and *internal governance*. The former refers to the structure of managerial, employee and external stakeholder rights of ownership or property, and to rights of control over the distribution of assets and investment. The latter refers to relations of production and distribution within the work process, most notably the incentive and monitoring structures. Much of the literature on privatisation and the economic transition in Central and Eastern Europe has dealt with aspects of external governance. The analysis in the following chapters mostly deals with aspects of internal governance, particularly when considering the changing wage system and the evolving structure of industrial relations. However the impact of alternative external governance relations are given some attention.

In the Soviet era, external enterprise governance involved a primary role for the Communist Party, whereby managers of industrial enterprises were induced to behave opportunistically in an hierarchical series of transactions – with line ministries, party functionaries, local authorities, worker brigades, union leaders and consumers. Industrial managers were typically motivated by the desire for revenue maximisation subject to a broadly predetermined profit constraint. While total revenue or total sales determined their bonuses, it was the level of the establishment's output and the size of the firm's workforce that determined not just their earnings but their local power and status. This ideal-type manager was answerable to a line ministry and was linked into a regional network of reciprocal relationships with other functionaries.

Decentralisation and the move towards self-management in the late 1980s increased the scope for opportunistic behaviour on the part of managers, since relaxation of central control reduced the directive strength of regulations and external bureaucracies. It strengthened the scope for local coalitions between managers, local authority representatives, party functionaries and union leaders. The nature of the changes must have influenced the balance of control between those agents, particularly weakening the position of union leaders, since they were fatally compromised in serving a managerial function, as discussed in Chapter 7. In that regard, the reforms of the late 1980s probably strengthened the position of managers. But there was little to suggest that the resultant decentralisation fundamentally altered the structure of incentives so as to encourage a greater orientation towards profit generation and dynamic efficiency.

In 1992, with price liberalisation and the pressure for commercialisation, it was widely expected that there would be changes in management behaviour, but that only after privatisation would the primary motivation be profit maximisation. That at least was the basic expectation, on the ground that the management would cease to be concerned primarily with matters other than profit only when they were answerable to external shareholders.

The evolving process of property-form restructuring had implications for both external and internal corporate governance. One can make an heuristic if crude distinction between what have been called *outsider* models of privatisation and *insider* models.[16] Outsider models have figured strongly in the reforms in Central Europe in the 1990s, reflecting the dominance of advice from national and international financial agencies based in the United States and Western Europe. This follows the American and British practice, for example, whereby share ownership is expected to be highly dispersed and incumbent managements are pressurised to maximise profits by the existence of a large number of external stakeholders. Acceptance of the outsider model has often meant a search for a large, single stockholder in the form of a mutual fund or other financial institution. The insider model is closer to the system that has developed in Germany and Japan, in which commercial banks hold equity and are closely involved in management of the firms.

The outsider model's relevance to corporate governance restructuring is that it relies on the emergence of financially strong intermediary institutions and puts a high premium on *uncertainty*. If a management is uncertain about the identity or stability of intermediary groups of stakeholders, it will be inclined to act opportunistically and focus on short-term benefits for itself. This was surely a feature of the difficult transition in corporate governance in the early 1990s. In Russian industry there was effectively a hybrid form of privatisation in that the dominant model adopted after 1991 involved a process by which insiders in firms were allowed and encouraged to acquire up to 51 per cent of the firm at 1.7 times the book value, unadjusted for inflation, while investment funds were limited to 10 per cent of the shares. This brought insider acquiescence and provided insiders with an incentive to restructure, while the authorities promoted it because they anticipated the rapid emergence of a substantial secondary market for shares. However there were very few cases of enterprises having substantial 'blockholders', that is, single shareholders holding a large percentage of the total stock. One study of a small number of enterprises suggested that in early 1994 the average blockholder owned 11 per cent of an enterprise's stock.[17]

The danger of any hybrid model is that it could create greater uncertainty than a clearly defined alternative, and thus induce greater short-term opportunism by both managers and workers. Thus in Russian industry the slow process of corporate governance restructuring and the lack of enterprise restructuring, in terms of breaking up the huge entitities that had dominated the Soviet system, meant that the 'debt overhang' that emerged in the early 1990s gave unclear signals to creditors about management, which undermined the effectiveness of the hybrid form of property-form restructuring.[18] If the objective was to guide foreign and domestic investment to potentially profitable firms through financial stakeholders, this guidance was impeded by the unclear character of enterprise indebtedness. Was it due to inefficient management, to efficient management having to respond to distorted incentives and information, or to a fundamental lack of viability that exonerated management from direct responsibility? Although many observers assume it was the first, one cannot be sure.[19] Some observers believe that blockholders are the most effective means by which management can be monitored. However their emergence was hesitant. By 1994 there were reported to be 640 investment funds holding the shares of millions of voucher holders, but that was not new capital for investment. It was estimated that 2.4 per cent of general directors of Russian firms had been appointed by investment fund holders, while 9.5 per cent of firms had investment-fund representatives on their boards of directors. Clearly there is a long way to go before the emergence of a predominant model of governance becomes evident.

That issue aside, management behaviour can be expected to depend on whether property-form restructuring gives a high or low degree of ownership to workers, managers and outside stakeholders. The most crucial element may be the degree of uncertainty. Thus if managers are faced by indebtedness and imminent accountability for inadequate profits, they might respond by accelerating the firm's decapitalisation if they perceive the debt as a threat to their personal survival as managers. In this way they could increase their short-term income and provide surplus for distribution to stakeholders to bolster their chances of reappointment.

Similarly if managers do not know what the property rights are going to be, they are unlikely to be able to decide rationally between short-term and long-term investment and behavioural strategies. This is probably more important than the distinction that is usually the focus of attention, that is, between employee-owned and outsider-owned firms. If outsider stakeholders are in assured control, the firm's management is likely to be oriented towards particular objectives, and typically be more concerned with short-term profits to be paid out as dividends. If insider stakeholders, notably workers, are the main owners of shares, there will be a tendency towards trade-offs between wage levels and employment stability.[20] There is no reason to suppose that outsider control will necessarily reduce opportunism by managers, since worker shareholders are more likely to have information that allows identification of opportunism and thus will be able to threaten miscreants with retribution. Both workers and managers require reciprocal monitoring and a balanced capacity to impose sanctions.[21]

Thus the type of short-term and long-term objectives should vary according to the mode of managerial governance, rather than be oriented towards or away from short-termism. In contrast, *uncertainty* of ownership rights or management rights could be expected unambiguously to orient managers' behaviour towards short-termism and opportunism.

Various aspects of corporate governance restructuring are highlighted in the RLFS, some of which are examined in the course of the following chapters. Among the most important changes are the mechanisms by which senior management have been appointed and reappointed. Although change in management roles was a feature of *perestroika* in the late 1980s, when work collectives were given the right to elect heads of enterprise

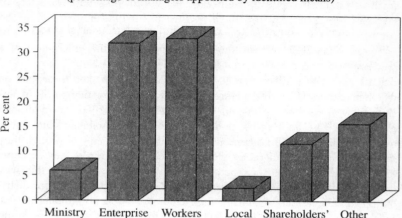

Figure 3.8 Means of appointment of top management, all regions, mid 1994 (percentage of managers appointed by identified means)

Source: RLFS4, n = 384.

administration, at that time production decisions and financing decisions were still concentrated in ministries and other state agencies. So-called 'self-management' was largely restricted to questions of distribution and social functions.[22] This began to change after 1991. By the mid 1990s decentralisation of managerial decision making had gone much further, often as a precursor of property-form restructuring and often as a part of that process.

Information on management appointment was not sought in the first two rounds of the RLFS. In 1993, at the time of the third round, most managers had been appointed by line ministries; by mid 1994 a mere 5.7 per cent of senior managers had been appointed by ministries and 2.4 per cent by local authorities, compared with the 32.6 per cent who had been formally appointed by the work collective (corresponding to the predominance of closed and open joint-stock enterprises as the main property forms), the 31.8 per cent who had been appointed by enterprise boards (these would have consisted mainly of appointees from outside the establishment) and the 11.5 per cent appointed through shareholders' meetings, who would have consisted largely of workers (Figure 3.8).

These diverse forms of appointment mean it would be too simple to state that by the mid 1990s managements were firmly in control of enterprises,[23] and we visited several factories where the management had been voted out by worker shareholders. A further reason for doubting the existence of absolute control is that the duration of appointment was variable, and had become generally much shorter than in the Soviet era, and this was surely having an effect on the climate of decision making. Over a third of the general managers (36.3 per cent) had been appointed for a period of two years or less, 14.3 per cent for three or four years, 27.1 per cent for five years and 22.4 per cent for no fixed term, without a formal contract. Managers in open joint-stock firms were far more likely to have been appointed for two years or less (57.3 per cent), whereas state enterprise managers typically had longer-term contracts. Managers appointed by enterprise boards or by shareholder meetings were more likely to have been appointed for two years or less than those appointed by a ministry or local authorities.

In the restructuring of corporate governance, by mid 1994 *worker share ownership* had become widespread and extensive. On average, including those state firms and social organisations where there were no shares, workers and employees of the firms owned 46.4 per cent of all shares by possessing 93 per cent of the shares in closed joint-stock companies and 56 per cent of those in open joint-stock companies. This substantial worker 'stakeholding' was creating the basis for a possibly unique evolution of corporate governance, a reversal of the old socialist vision – privatisation of ownership coupled with socialisation of management.

Much has been said and written in Russia about managements taking advantage of property restructuring to acquire financial control through the acquisition of shares. In that context, it was reported by the accounts departments of the factories visited in mid 1994 that about 11.6 per cent of the shares of those firms that had issued them were possessed by managers. But in closed joint-stock firms the managers held nearly 26 per cent, which meant that their capacity to control decision making was considerable, since apart from the state agency they were the largest shareholders.

One potentially interesting aspect of the restructuring of corporate governance is the additional *rights* associated with worker shareholdings. In 1994, in most firms (82 per cent) there were apparently none, according to the managers. A few said that worker shareholders could obtain low-interest loans, and a few said that such workers would receive privileged employment protection in the event of mass redundancy. Worker shareholders were apparently more likely to have additional privileges in closed joint-stock firms than in open joint-stock companies (31.2 per cent as against 14.3 per cent).

With all these changes taking place, we could divide corporate governance structures into three main types – *state* (in which managers are appointed by ministries or local authorities, which accounted for 8.1 per cent of the total in 1994), *internal* (in which they are appointed by the 'work collective' or at shareholder meetings in those firms in which workers and employees own more than 50 per cent of the shares, representing up to 44.1 per cent of the total) and *external* (in which appointment is by an enterprise board or a mixed process, usually involving the state and external bodies that have an influence, accounting for up to 47.8 per cent of the total, possibly plus some of those appointed by shareholder meetings). As can be appreciated, this approach causes some haziness in classification.

An alternative way of classifying corporate governance structures is by taking account of the property form of the establishment, the character of share owning and the form of appointment of management. We can classify governance into four main types:

1. *State governance,* where the establishment is still state-owned and the senior manager is appointed by a line ministry or local authority; or where it is state-owned and nominally the work collective and the ministry or local authority are responsible for managerial appointments.
2. *Private governance,* the other end of the spectrum, where there is private ownership or a joint-stock arrangement in which the employees do not own more than 50 per cent of the shares and the manager is appointed by an enterprise board or at a shareholders' meeting, as long as the employees do not possess more than 50 per cent of the shares.[24]
3. *Employee governance*, where the property form is joint stock, the workers and management together own more than 50 per cent of the shares, *without the workers owning 50 per cent or more*, and the top manager is appointed by an enterprise board, by a shareholders' meeting or by some other non-state mechanism.[25]
4. *Worker governance,* where the property form is joint stock, the workers own 50 per cent or more of the shares and management is appointed by the workers or by a shareholders' meeting.

As of mid 1994 the distribution of governance types in the industrial establishments covered by RLFS4 showed that 20.5 per cent were state governance structures, 17.1 per cent were private governance, 23.5 per cent were employee governance and 38.9 per cent were worker governance structures.

Without wishing to conclude at this stage that any particular governance structure is superior to another (given the recency of the changes), a

Table 3.3 Structural characteristics, by type of governance, all regions, mid 1994

Characteristic	Type of Governance			
	State	*Employee*	*Worker*	*Private*
Product range extended	22.1	33.1	35.6	20.3
Product range narrowed	36.4	15.9	19.9	31.3
New production technology	40.3	50.0	41.1	42.2
Work reorganisation	47.4	43.2	40.4	48.4
Debt status: net debtors	22.1	19.3	36.7	26.6
Fearing bankrupcy	15.6	17.1	18.4	21.9
Capacity utilisation, May 1994	60.1	59.5	53.3	61.2

Source: RLFS4, n = 374.

few pointers are worth further consideration as the restructuring process continues in the latter part of the 1990s. In terms of the measures of technological restructuring, in mid 1994 employee and worker governance were substantially more likely to have reported that they had extended their product range (Table 3.3), and correspondingly those with state or private governances were more likely to have reduced their product range. In terms of new technology in production, there was less difference, although more of the employee-governed seemed to have made innovations. In terms of debt, 60.7 per cent of worker-controlled firms owed more than was owed to them, compared with 49.4 per cent of state-governed firms.

One should not expect too much from the first phase of these novel forms of governance or the new forms of managerial appointment, since no doubt many former managers succeeded in having themselves reappointed. Yet the ethos of accountability was likely to develop, and this was found in a few large firms that we visited on several occasions to make illustrative case studies.[26] Thus if managerial control had increased during the 1990s, it was nevertheless circumscribed by the actual and potential – real and imagined – monitoring controls available to worker shareholders.

This was vividly brought home in one factory visited three times over two years, where the confident general director of the first visit was a nervous *parvenu* at the time of the second and no longer there at the time of the third. By then he had been replaced by his deputy, who had been elected by the work collective and had set up a special department to monitor the share dealings of the workers for fear of blocks of shares being built up that would threaten his position in the medium term. More

Figure 3.9 Sales change in previous year, by industry, all regions, mid 1994 (percentage of establishments in sector reporting sales change in real terms)

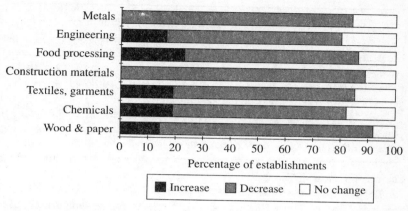

Percentage of establishments

■ Increase ■ Decrease □ No change

Source: RLFS4, n = 379.

generally, it was reported that in early 1994 about 10 per cent of general managers had been voted out of office during shareholders' meetings, and it was likely that many others had jumped before they were pushed.[27]

3.4   THE CRISIS INDICATORS

So from 1991–4 there were six types of restructuring, which were tentative in most cases, more substantial in others. Yet the limited restructuring took place in a context of sharply shrinking output and sales. The prolonged economic crisis was reflected in the RLFS in various ways. Most fundamentally, the value of *sales* fell in real terms. In 1993 about 62 per cent reported that sales in real terms had declined over the past year, compared with the 25 per cent that reported an increase. The sector in which increased sales were most likely was food processing, which reflected the sharp shift towards an increase in proportional expenditure on food due to falling real incomes.[28] In 1994 two thirds of all firms had experienced declining sales over the past year, compared with only 15.9 per cent with rising sales (Figure 3.9). In all sectors the majority of firms had experienced falling sales.

In mid 1994 Russian factories were in a parlous state. When asked what was their main economic problem, 40.6 per cent of the managements cited inability to sell their products and 24.2 per cent cited high taxes. The problems had become severe. Numerous reports in the national and international media have testified to an enormous growth of *interenterprise debt* and of enterprise debt to banks and the state. According to official *Goskomstat* data, 39000 enterprises were in serious debt in mid 1994. This was 6400 more than in January 1994, which meant that whereas 45.3 per cent of all enterprises in the country were deeply in debt at the beginning of the year, by the middle of the year 54.8 per cent were in that position. The vast majority owed money to other enterprises, although many were also in debt to banks and/or the federal authorities.

One feature of the reaction of enterprises to the economic upheavals of the early 1990s was non-payment for inputs and the resultant spiralling of interenterprise debt. For a while this received considerable attention, amid fears that a disruption of the chain would lead to a domino effect of enormous proportions.[29]

The pervasiveness of indebtedness was brought out in RLFS4, in which only 11.7 per cent of all firms had no debts to banks or other enterprises. A majority of firms owed a large amount and were in turn owed a lot, but 56.3 per cent of firms stated that they owed more than was owed to them. About 26.8 per cent claimed they were owed more than they owed, and 4.9 per cent claimed that their debts were in balance with what was owed to them. A much higher percentage of firms in Ivanovo claimed to be owed more than they themselves owed (38.6 per cent compared with 17 per cent in Moscow City).

There is the related issue of *subsidies*. According to anecdotal reports, many enterprises have been bolstered by direct subsidies from local or national government agencies. One can only speculate on how extensive that practice has been, but it seems to have declined, perhaps reflecting the state's inability or unwillingness to support industrial enterprises. In mid 1994 only 6.3 per cent of all establishments reported that they were receiving a subsidy to assist in production (Figure 3.10). Large firms with more than 1000 workers were twice as likely to have a subsidy, and firms in Nizhny Novgorod were twice as likely to be receiving a subsidy as firms elsewhere, probably reflecting the large number of military–industrial enterprises in that region. Subsidies were most likely to come from federal authorities.

There is also the much discussed issue of *bankruptcy*, which was made official by legislation in 1993 but was effectively suspended throughout 1993 and 1994. In 1993 managements were asked whether they feared or expected bankruptcy within the next 12 months. At that time 16 per cent considered there was a high probability of going bankrupt and a further 17 per cent were uncertain. No less than 44 per cent of firms in the chemicals

Figure 3.10 Share of establishments receiving subsidies, by industry, all regions, mid 1994 (percentage of establishments in sector receiving federal or local authority subsidy)

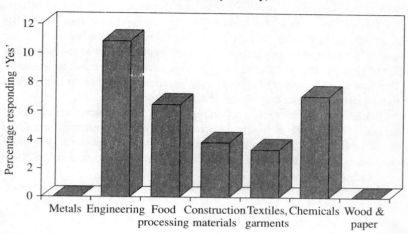

Source: RLFS4, n = 384.

sector foresaw bankruptcy, and other sectors in which pessimism was rife were engineering and textiles and garments. In contrast food-processing plants were relatively sanguine. Overall the main reason for expecting bankruptcy was indebtedness to other firms, which was cited by 45.5 per cent of all those anticipating bankruptcy, followed by 16.4 per cent who thought their firms would go bankrupt because of the cuts in subsidies.

In mid 1994, according to RLFS4, the fear of bankruptcy was reported to be 'strong' in 5.7 per cent of all factories, 'fairly strong' in a further 12.2 per cent and 'moderately worrying' in a further 33.3 per cent. With 3.4 per cent reporting that they did not know, this left a minority (45.3 per cent) that did not expect to go bankrupt within a year. The fear of bankruptcy was strongest in building materials, textiles and garments, and again least in food processing (Figure 3.11). In 1994, among those expecting or fearing bankruptcy, the cause most often mentioned was difficulty in selling their output; the second most common reason was the high or rising price of raw materials.

The two notable changes in sentiment about prospective bankruptcy between 1993 and 1994 were, first, that the engineering sector showed a relative recovery, which may have reflected the change of government and the views expressed about preserving production, and second, that there was a decline in concern about interenterprise indebtedness.

Figure 3.11   Percentage of establishments believing bankruptcy likely within a
year, by region, 1994

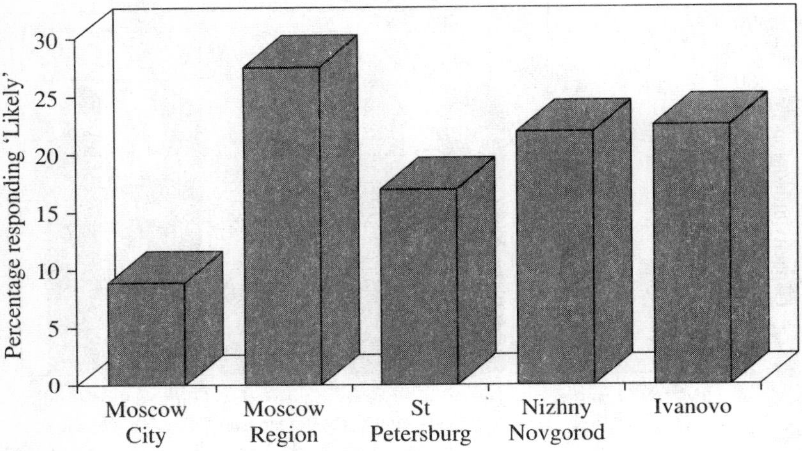

Source: RLFS4, n = 384.

3.5 THE SLUMP IN CAPACITY UTILISATION, 1989–94

With sales shrinking sharply and against a background of deepening stagflation in the Russian economy in 1992, one of the most striking trends
observed in the second round of the RLFS was a sharp fall in what managements estimated was the level of capacity utilisation of their plants. No
questions had been included on this issue in RLFS1.

Overall, capacity utilisation dropped from 88.3 per cent at the end of
1989 to 82.9 per cent at the end of 1991 and 75.8 per cent in June 1982.
So during the period of price liberalisation there was an accelerated
decline. All sectors experienced a decline over the two-and-a-half years,
although chemicals showed the greatest slump, followed by basic metals
and engineering.[30] On average, state enterprises had the lowest capacity
utilisation rates in all periods, but even for non-state firms the decline was
substantial. Declines were remarkably similar for all size categories of
factory, suggesting that it was predominantly a recession-induced decline
rather than a reflection of restructuring.

It is worth noting that, according to *Goskomstat* data, overall industrial
capacity utilisation peaked in the mid 1970s, and that except for a brief
revival in 1988 it declined steadily from about 1975. As the declines in the
1980s must reflect sharp cuts in production and not growth in potential

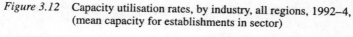

Figure 3.12 Capacity utilisation rates, by industry, all regions, 1992–4, (mean capacity for establishments in sector)

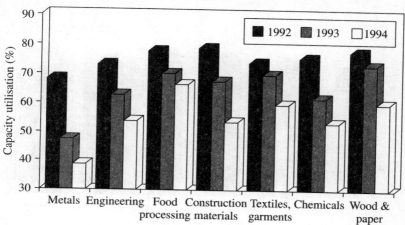

Source: RLFS4, n = 384.

capacity, it seems right to conclude that much of the unused capacity in 1992 was rapidly becoming part of Russian industrial history, neither to be revived nor much lamented. If so, the low utilisation rate was giving an illusion of the extent of untapped reserves. But surely it would have been wrong to write off all 25 per cent of the unused capacity as unusable. The main reason for this contention is that, even though many firms would have had negative value added, the disruption to previous markets meant that time was required to allow for restructuring and the penetration of alternative markets.

According to RLFS3, capacity utilisation levels continued to decline in 1993. Overall, for the firms in the four regions covered in 1993, capacity had fallen from 83.2 per cent in mid 1991 to 74.5 per cent in mid 1992 and 70 per cent in mid 1993. Again, worst affected was the chemicals sector, where in mid 1993 firms were operating at only 55.4 per cent of their capacity. State enterprises were operating at the lowest level, on average.

There was no evidence of any reversal of the trend in 1994. Overall, according to RLFS4, in early 1992 the average level at which factories were operating was 74.7 per cent. By early 1993 it was 66.3 per cent, and by early 1994 it was a mere 57.3 per cent. This was certainly the lowest level ever recorded in the country. Food processing had held up best, while metals had fallen most (Figure 3.12). Worst affected of all were

Figure 3.13   Capacity utilisation rates, by property form, all regions, 1992–4, (mean capacity for establishments in prevailing property form)

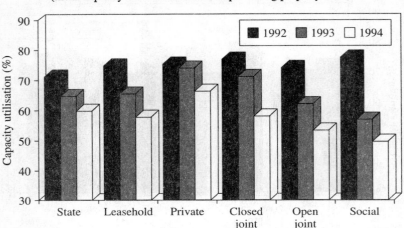

Source: RLFS4, n = 384.

'social organisations' (sheltered factories), in which capacity utilisation had slumped by over 25 per cent (Figure 3.13).[31] For those establishments that were in both RLFS3 and RLFS4, capacity utilisation dropped from 82.9 per cent in December 1991 to 74.1 per cent in December 1992, 69.4 per cent in June 1993, 65.4 per cent in December 1993 and 56.2 per cent in June 1994. For those factories the fall between 1991 and 1994 was greatest in basic metals and least in chemicals.

The drop in utilisation was much greater in large factories, implying that the overall drop was even greater than the mean average suggested (Figure 3.14). Most surprising was that Ivanovo suffered the lowest drop, even though the level there had been lowest in 1992 (Figure 3.15).

3.6   CONCLUSIONS

Between 1991 and 1994 there was some enterprise restructuring in a situation of falling output, declining sales and some reorientation in output (notably a resurgence of barter and a modest shift towards exports). Property-form restructuring was extensive and there were signs of change taking place in corporate governance. Although it is questionable whether the evolving enterprise arrangements were conducive to dynamic efficiency,

Figure 3.14 Capacity utilisation rates, by employment size, all regions, 1992–4

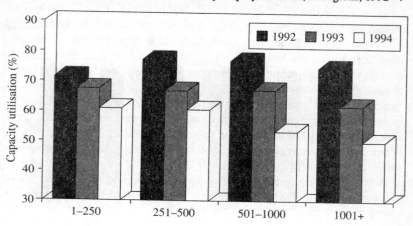

Source: RLFS4, n = 384.

Figure 3.15 Capacity utilisation rates, by region, 1992–4

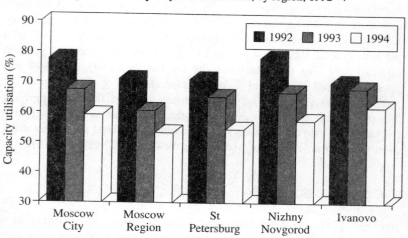

Source: RLFS4, n = 384.

new forms of organisation were coming into existence that may make the labels of capitalism and socialism seem inappropriate. That is a subject for study in the longer term and should provide rich material for institutional economic analysis. Essentially the task should be to formulate policies that steer the institutional developments in directions favouring dynamic efficiency while recognising that firms are not simple production functions but governance structures.[32]

Both the deep economic crisis and the disjointed restructuring could be expected to have a broad range of labour-market and employment effects. It is on those implications that the remainder of our analysis concentrates, beginning with the impact on the level of labour utilisation and the various forms of unemployment.

In the following chapters there is one hypothesis that deserves to be highlighted: in the Russian Federation, employment restructuring has been impeded by excessive labour-market flexibility in several key respects.

4 Disappearing Jobs: Crisis of 'Concealed Unemployment'

4.1 INTRODUCTION

Employment fluctuations are part of a dynamic economy and a dynamic labour market, part of the process of what the Austrian economist Joseph Schumpeter called 'creative destruction'. Both the image and the reality of the Soviet system at the end of the 1980s were that enterprises were motivated by the objective of maximising employment, concentrated in enormous enterprises in which labour hoarding was endemic.

With the slump in production after 1990 the common image was that employment was maintained and that labour surplus grew correspondingly. In this chapter we shall examine the evidence on employment dynamics between 1990 and 1994, exploring the impact of the limited restructuring of firms on employment and the extent of 'concealed unemployment'. In the main, the primary objective is to lay out the essential facts, leaving interpretation of the pattern of employment dynamics to the end and to subsequent chapters.

Throughout this analysis we refer to notions of 'labour surplus', 'labour hoarding', 'underemployment' and 'concealed unemployment'. None of these terms is unambiguous. However one thing is obvious: Russian industry had long suffered from surplus labour, and undoubtedly the scope for raising labour productivity was enormous. The ensuing slump in production would have intensified the extent of surplus labour unless a really massive shedding of jobs occurred. Yet there was scope for both, or one to the relative exclusion of the other.

In considering what actually happened, we should make a conceptual distinction between *short-term* (or *'visible'*) *surplus labour* and *long-term* (or *'dynamic'*) *surplus labour*. The first refers to the perception by management of the amount of underutilised labour or to the measured number of workers in full-time equivalents who could be displaced without reducing output, with given technology, capital and work organisation. Dynamic labour surplus means the amount of employment that could be cut if work were reorganised and the available technological options were

63

utilised. The analysis concentrates on the former. We may surmise with confidence that, whatever the level of visible surplus labour with current levels of output, technology and work organisation, the dynamic surplus would be some multiple of a visible surplus greater than one.

4.2 EMPLOYMENT IN 1990–1: LEGACY OF A SHORTAGE ECONOMY

The firms included in the first round of the RLFS exhibited the classic features of Soviet industry. Questions were asked about employment in late 1991 and one year earlier. The mean average number of workers and employees was 1154 in September 1990, and 24 per cent of all firms had more than 1000 workers.[1] Although 28.8 per cent had fewer than 250, the size distribution was much more skewed than was typical internationally.[2] Factories in the engineering sector were by far the largest, with a mean of over 1500 and nearly a third of its establishments with over 1000 workers. In basic metals the mean was over 1300 and in textiles and garments it was over 1000.

In the real sense of the term, this was a transition phase for Russian factories. There was a mixture of a growing realisation of labour surplus with a continued perception of labour shortage. There were various signs of the latter. Despite declining output and economic stagnation, in September 1991 the average job vacancy rate was 6 per cent, expressed as a percentage of total employment. It ranged from 2.7 per cent in food processing to 9.4 per cent in construction materials. Vacancies were more numerous in state enterprises and, strangely, in firms that had relatively high wages, prompting the speculative hypothesis that average wages were higher precisely *because* supposedly funded 'posts' were left vacant.[3] As discussed later, this managerial practice was to evolve into a clever cost-reducing tactic and a primary source of concealed unemployment.

The second legacy was that, despite declining sales and output, only a little over 10 per cent of the managements reported that during the previous year they had too little work for the workforce for periods of a month or more. This ranged from under 7 per cent in the textiles and garments sector to over 21 per cent in chemicals. Most notably, some of those firms believing they had too little work for their workers had expanded employment over the previous year.

A third pattern suggesting that factories were still experiencing the legacy of contrived labour shortage was that most managements claimed they had had difficulty recruiting or retaining workers. Over 42 per cent of those reported that the main cause was labour shortage, 25.9 per cent said it was due to low wages and 24.3 per cent cited poor working conditions; contrary to a common belief, less than 1 per cent cited lack of housing. The real meaning of the perceived labour shortage came out in response to the question about what management thought had been the main effect of the supposed difficulty. Although a third of managers thought it had limited production, over a third said it had had no effect and only a little over 10 per cent said it had resulted in greater work intensity.

Yet at the same time – and contrary to orthodox opinion – sizeable employment cuts were already taking place. Overall, among the factories in RLFS1, from September 1990 to September 1991 employment was cut by 48934, or an average of nearly 98 employees per establishment. The mean employment size of industrial establishments fell to 1056, and the overall employment decline during the year was 7 per cent, the largest being in Moscow City (8.4 per cent), followed by St Petersburg (8.3 per cent) and Moscow Region (3.7 per cent). Over 80 per cent of all factories in Moscow City cut employment.

With the exception of food processing, all sectors experienced a net decline, with the chemicals sector suffering most of all. This was significant, for already there was the beginning of a trend in which declining incomes were leading people to spend a greater proportion of their income on food, which at that time was mostly produced domestically, although imports were beginning to replace internal produce.

The other notable feature of the pattern of employment decline in 1990–1 was that it appeared to be primarily demand-induced, in that there was a general 'downsizing' rather than any conspicuous restructuring effect that might have come with demonopolisation, or with a systematic reduction in market power through a break-up of large firms into smaller units as a means of creating a more competitive market economy. The latter was most unlikely; indeed those with the largest fixed assets seemed to have cut employment by less than the average.

Finally, at the end of 1991 there was widespread pessimism among managements about employment prospects for 1992. About a third expected or planned to cut employment in the coming year and only about 12 per cent thought it would increase. One might have expected even more to be thinking of employment cuts, but there was widespread ambiguity in this regard. This was graphically illustrated in the case of a garments factory that was visited a few times. In late 1991 the respondents had said they were unsure what would happen to employment even though they were having great difficulty selling their clothes. In the three months between visits they had reduced employment from 788 workers to 703, a cut of nearly 11 per cent. There was also widespread reluctance to recognise the need for employment cuts, which other observers also noted.[4] However the prevailing sense of employment stability did not stop managements from making cuts through non-replacement of those who left for one reason or another. Even this was beginning to change, because nearly a third of all firms reported that they actually expected or planned to make redundancies during 1992, a high percentage bearing in mind the long tradition of employment maximisation, contrived labour shortage and employment security.

4.3   EMPLOYMENT DYNAMICS IN 1992–3

By mid 1992, at the time of RLFS2, with capacity utilisation and sales crashing there was an even more widespread perception by managements that they had surplus labour and the employment crunch had arrived. One cannot make direct comparisons with the full results from RLFS1, but the changing picture was clear enough. By now few firms were reporting problems of labour shortage and 55 per cent of all establishments reported that they could produce the same level of output with fewer workers than they currently employed. In the basic metals sector the figure was 89 per cent, and in engineering over 63 per cent. Large factories were more inclined to report this form of underemployment. Not surprisingly, those firms that had cut capacity utilisation over the previous year were more likely to report that they could cut employment without further cutting output, highlighting the evidently lagged reaction of changes in employment in response to changes in output. Although there were few private firms at the time, there was no appreciable difference in their perception of labour surplus and property form.

Those firms that reported that they could cut employment without reducing output were asked to estimate what percentage cut they could make, other things remaining equal. Overall they estimated they could cut their workforces by 18 per cent. In construction materials the figure was 29 per cent. The average for private firms was 15 per cent, for leaseholdings (*arenda*) 17.5 per cent and for state firms 19 per cent. The most important point was that managements were recognising that they had a labour surplus, and their response was an indicator of the forthcoming employment crisis, since they were deliberately holding on to many more workers than needed.

Over 62 per cent of firms in mid 1992 reported that they had had too little work for their workforces for periods of a month or more in the

Table 4.1 Main and second main measures taken in response to surplus labour, besides retrenchment and transfer, all regions, 1991–2 (percentage distribution of measures taken if too little work for workforce)

Measure	Main	Second
None	20.0	5.3
Cut normal hours	25.8	13.2
Cut overtime	5.0	3.9
Extended vacations	0.5	2.6
Partially paid leave	8.3	9.2
Long unpaid leave	10.0	26.3
Encouraged resignations	20.0	23.7
Cut wages	0.8	5.3
Cut production	5.8	5.3
Other	3.3	1.3

Note: The percentage distribution refers only to firms that gave main reasons.
Source: RLFS2.

past year, with no less than 75 per cent of chemicals plants experiencing that situation.[5] However it was not the number that was of primary interest but the managements' responses. In June 1992, 51 per cent of those reporting a labour surplus in the past year had cut employment by various means, and on average had cut it by more than 10 per cent in the preceding nine months. However they had also taken a variety of other actions to limit or avoid actual cuts. Besides retrenchment – which, as indicated in Chapter 8, was already more widespread than some economists were claiming – many managements responded by cutting working time, 'encouraging' resignations and putting workers on extended paid or unpaid leave (Table 4.1). Furthermore nearly 72 per cent of all establishments reported that they had transferred workers within their enterprises in order to limit redundancies.

Yet the main employment development of 1991–2 was what can now be seen as the beginning of a major jobs haemorrhage. For the whole sample of 191 establishments, in the nine months from September 1991 to June 1992 *total employment fell by 8.2 per cent*, from 166895 workers to 154213. For those firms that were in both the first and second rounds of the RLFS, between September 1990 and June 1992 *total employment declined by over 15 per cent*, a substantial decline by any standards. Most significantly the percentage decline accelerated during the period, being equal in the nine months between the first and second rounds to the rate of decline for the whole of the preceding 12 months. In September 1990 the 109 factories that were in both rounds employed 82949 workers, by September 1991 the number had reduced to 74774 and by June 1992 it was down to 67907.

As this was a period of unprecedented stagflation, employment fell across the board, although in percentage terms it fell most in state establishments. The claim that state enterprises were simply holding on to all or almost all their workers – through inertia, 'soft budget constraints' or whatever – is simply not supported by these data. They may not have cut employment by as much as their output, yet they were shedding a very large number of jobs.

In 1992 property-form restructuring was already taking place, even if the nature of the changes was mainly the creation of hybrid forms of enterprise. Those changes were intended and expected to make firms more cost conscious and thus less likely to hold on to surplus labour. The responses to RLFS2 suggested that something like this was happening. Over 55 per cent of all those that had changed property form in the past year reported that the change itself had led to a reduction in employment.

There was also a direct link between sales and employment, suggesting that managements were beginning to respond to market factors. Thus over the period 1990–2 employment fell more in firms that experienced a decline in sales in real terms. But it also fell in those that had managed to expand their sales, which at least suggested that some had brought about an improvement in labour productivity.

Expectations about employment in mid 1992 were no more encouraging than had been the case six months earlier. For all factories in RLFS2, more than two in five expected employment to fall during the coming year and only 11 per cent thought it would rise. Since this was a time of acute depression in the military–industrial sector, it was not surprising that engineering plants were the most pessimistic.

There was also a useful pointer to a change in attitude towards employment levels. Expectations of employment change reported in the first round of the survey had mostly proved too optimistic or not pessimistic enough. Those that reported in the first round that they expected employment to fall experienced a 12 per cent drop between the two rounds. But on average, those that had said they expected employment to rise actually experienced a fall of 5 per cent, while those that had expected no change did in fact cut employment by 6 per cent. Once more, one sensed that the former determination to preserve as large a labour force as possible was evaporating under the impact of the economic depression.

By mid 1993 the depth and nature of the labour surplus had further intensified. While capacity utilisation had declined to unprecedentedly low

Figure 4.1 Percentage of firms that could produce the same output with fewer workers, by industry, all regions, mid 1993

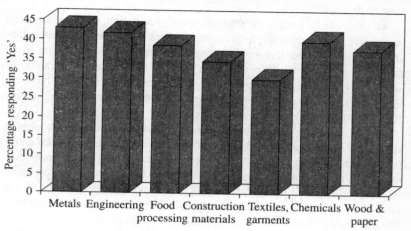

Source: RLFS3, n = 332.

levels, more than one in three managements (37.6 per cent) reported that they could have produced the same output with fewer workers, with more than two in five factories in basic metals and engineering making this observation (Figure 4.1).

This was less than had been reported in 1992, although it was indicative of a severe labour surplus problem. Larger firms were far more likely to have a labour surplus in that sense (nearly half of those with more than 500 workers reported this problem). Those operating at lower levels of capacity utilisation were more likely to estimate that they could maintain their current level of output with fewer workers. Over half of all those that had cut capacity utilisation by 10 per cent or more during the previous year felt they could cut employment without affecting their output (Figure 4.2). So although labour hoarding was continuing, with managements living in hope that the government would arrest the economic decline, there was widespread recognition of a severe labour surplus. On average, those establishments that reported that they could maintain production with fewer workers estimated that they could cut employment by 6.7 per cent.

Given the pressure the government put on privatised firms in 1993–4 not to cut employment in the immediate aftermath of a change in property form, it was perhaps not surprising that managements of leaseholding and open joint-stock enterprises were relatively more likely to estimate that

Figure 4.2   Percentage of establishments that could produce the same output with fewer workers, by change in capacity utilisation, all regions, mid 1993

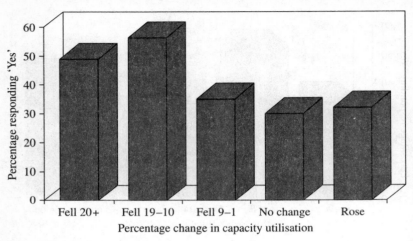

Source: RLFS3, n = 332.

they could cut jobs without affecting output (Figure 4.3). One anticipated that they would shed many more jobs in 1994, when restrictions on their doing so were to be removed.

In 1993 managements were asked whether there had been occasions that year when they had had too little work for the workforce for periods of two weeks or more, rather than for a month as was the measure in the previous rounds.[6] As in those rounds, this second proxy for labour surplus was used mainly to lead to questions about managerial reactions. Overall 41.5 per cent reported that they had had a labour surplus in this sense of the term, with establishments in the metals and chemicals sectors being most affected. Again this perception was much more common in larger firms.

As for managerial reactions, there had been a considerable change since 1992. Whereas cutting working time had been the main response to surplus labour a year earlier, by 1993 the pattern had been set for firms to resort to unpaid and partially paid leave, although many still cut the number of normal working hours (Table 4.2). This important new phenomenon will be considered more systematically later.

In 1993 numerous establishments (49.5 per cent) reported that they had also resorted to *internal transfers* specifically to limit redundancies (Figure 4.4), including firms that had not allowed a situation of prolonged labour slack to emerge.

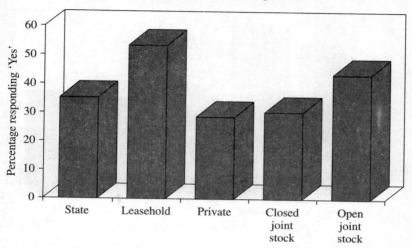

Figure 4.3 Percentage of establishments that could produce the same output with fewer workers, by property form, all regions, mid 1993

Source: RLFS3, n = 340.

Table 4.2 Main and second main measures taken in response to surplus labour, besides retrenchment and transfer, all regions, 1992–3 (percentage distribution of measures if too little work)

	Main measure	*Second main*
None	0.5	0.0
Cut normal hours	20.7	20.3
Cut overtime	0.8	1.6
Paid leave	3.3	3.1
Unpaid leave	41.3	21.9
Partial paid leave	15.7	26.6
Cut wages	1.7	6.3
Cut production	9.9	15.6
Other	1.7	4.7

Note: The percentage distribution refers only to firms that gave main reasons.
Source: RLFS3, n = 121 (col.1) and 64 (col.2).

Figure 4.4 Percentage of establishments making internal transfers to avoid redundancies, by industry, all regions, 1992–3

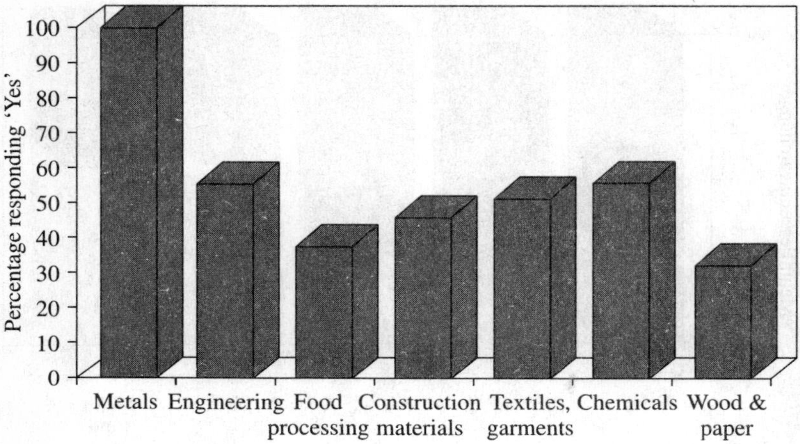

Source: RLFS3, n = 331.

This leads us back to the most crucial trend. *Employment decline* in 1992–3 continued at a similarly rapid rate as that observed in RLFS2 for the period 1991–2 and in RLFS1 for 1990–1. *Between mid 1992 and mid 1993 industrial establishments cut employment by an average of 8.8 per cent*, from 308969 workers to 281749, or a cut of 27220 jobs. This is very close to the rates of decline observed in the first two rounds, so that, taking account of changes in the number of enterprises and the addition of the Nizhny Novgorod region to the third round, employment had declined by 25–30 per cent since 1990.

Although employment fell in all four of these major industrial regions, the rate of decline was significantly lower in Nizhny Novgorod: less than 3 per cent compared with well over 10 per cent in Moscow City and St Petersburg. Given the distinctive restructuring strategy in that region based on an extraordinary concentration of foreign financial aid and technical assistance, this deserves to be highlighted.

Another feature is that, contrary to the belief that there would be employment cuts and restructuring only after privatisation, *employment cuts were greatest in state enterprises*, as had been observed in 1991–2. Thus in 1992–3 employment was cut by nearly 13 per cent in state enterprises and a little over 5 per cent in closed and open joint-stock enterprises (Figure 4.5).

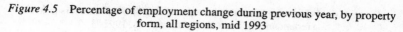

Figure 4.5 Percentage of employment change during previous year, by property form, all regions, mid 1993

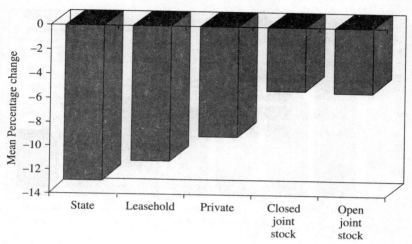

Source: RLFS3, n = 336.

As in both 1991 and 1992 employment fell more in establishments where sales had declined during the previous two years (9.8 per cent). However it also fell substantially in those that had experienced rising sales (7.1 per cent). In the longer term, the latter *may* be encouraging since it may imply that labour productivity was rising. In the short term, it was not promising in terms of employment generation.

Regression analysis suggested that, controlling for whether an establishment had divested part of its productive capacity during the preceding year, employment fell less in wood products, food processing and construction materials than in other sectors, controlling for the influence of employment structure, region, sales change and property form. Those with a high percentage of manual workers cut more jobs. The regression suggested that, taking account of other factors, the region of location made no difference to employment change.

State enterprises made more cuts than closed joint-stock or open joint-stock firms, even controlling for other characteristics, and firms with a large number of employees in 1992 actually cut employment proportionately less than others. It is also worth noting that, controlling for other factors, the extent of the cuts did not seem to depend on whether managements owed their appointment to election by the work collective. This is important in the context of claims that such 'industrial democracy' would

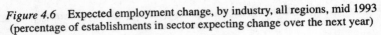

Figure 4.6 Expected employment change, by industry, all regions, mid 1993 (percentage of establishments in sector expecting change over the next year)

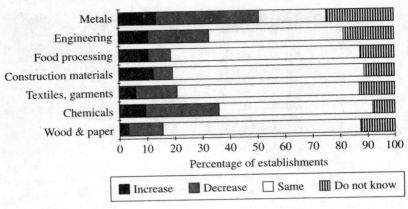

Source: RLFS3, n = 334.

prevent a decline in employment. This finding may be due to the fact that much of the decline resulted from 'natural wastage', that is, no replacements were hired to fill vacancies.

What is clear is that the decline in employment was considerable. Nor were future prospects encouraging. Nearly 18 per cent of all firms expected to cut employment during the following year and only 8 per cent expected it to grow. Most worrying – albeit expected – was that 35 per cent of large establishments with more than 1000 workers foresaw employment cuts in the near future. It should be recalled that in the Russian industrial context large firms still account for a very large share of total employment, and the figures on expected employment change are unweighted for size of establishment. The sectors with the most pessimistic outlook were metals, chemicals and engineering, that is, the traditional core of the Russian economy (Figure 4.6).

As for property form, state enterprises were just as likely as others to expect to make employment cuts (Figure 4.7). However, among those state enterprises anticipating a property-form change in the near future, 23 per cent expected the change to lead to employment cuts whereas only 9.5 per cent expected it to increase employment. All large-scale firms with over 1000 workers planning an ownership change foresaw employment cuts. About a third of those that expected the change to result in a loss of jobs thought the cuts would amount to more than 10 per cent of total employment. It seemed that factories in Nizhny Novgorod were less concerned about the threat to jobs than those elsewhere.

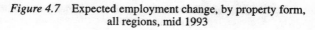

Figure 4.7 Expected employment change, by property form, all regions, mid 1993

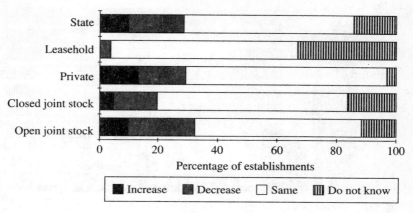

Source: RLFS3, n = 333.

As in 1991 and 1992, those firms that had cut employment the preceding year were also slightly more likely to expect to have to cut jobs in the near future. In the previous two rounds of the RLFS there had been a strong tendency for managements to be overoptimistic about future employment, and many that had not expected to make cuts had subsequently been forced to do so. The figures on expected employment decline should therefore be taken as an underestimate.

4.4 THE SPREAD OF UNPAID LEAVE IN 1993

One means by which managements responded to the economic slump in 1992–3 was by putting workers on administrative leave, usually without pay. In the Russian labour market context it was more rational for an employer to take that particular course of action than to release the worker, who would then be entitled to two or three months' severance pay. For the worker it was more rational to take unpaid leave than to become unemployed because there was hope of returning to the job and the worker would also retain access to the social benefits and facilities offered by many firms that were social enterprises providing a very wide range of social amenities and services.[7]

According to responses in RLFS3, in mid 1993 there was a notable amount of unpaid and partially paid administrative leave, excluding formally designated holidays. Conceptually it is difficult to distinguish

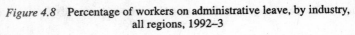

Figure 4.8 Percentage of workers on administrative leave, by industry, all regions, 1992–3

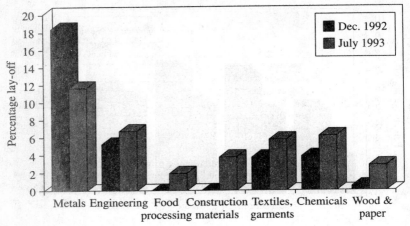

Source: RLFS3, n = 340.

prolonged holidays from unpaid leave. We explicitly exclude fully paid leave because of the statistical haziness of the concept of leave as a measure of labour slack. What is left is a measure that could be defended as a proxy for 'lay-off unemployment' – a measure that is likely to result in a considerable underestimate of the full extent of unemployed workers still nominally attached to their former workplace.

In total, 5.1 per cent of all workers were in lay-off unemployment, which if translated across the Russian labour market would represent *three times the level of official unemployment*. As unpaid leave was greatest in large establishments, the extent was underestimated by simple averages.

The leave or lay-off rate in mid 1993 varied from a very low 1.9 per cent in food processing to 11.6 per cent in the basic metals sector (Figure 4.8). Since 1992 the rate had increased for all sectors, with the exception of the small basic metals sector. Lay-offs were substantial in all property forms (Figure 4.9), but were clearly much higher in St Petersburg than elsewhere, and rare in Nizhny Novgorod.

Besides lay-offs, it turned out that actual working hours were only 35.8 per week for employees and 36.7 for workers. The 'normal' time recognised administratively as short-time working accounted for 1.1 hours per week per employee and per worker, although if one took a 40-hour working week as the norm it should have been 4.2 hours for employees

Figure 4.9 Percentage of workers on administrative leave, by property form, all regions, 1992–3

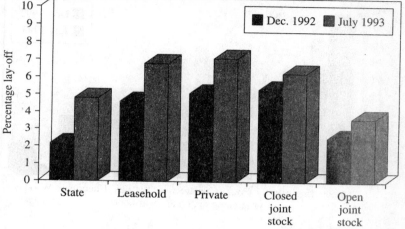

Source: RLFS3, n = 340.

and 3.3 hours for workers, or 10.5 per cent of standard working hours for employees and 8.2 per cent for workers. Administrative short-time working was greatest in St Petersburg and lowest in Nizhny Novgorod.

When account is taken of the employment cuts, the recourse to fewer working hours and the perception of labour surplus represented by the view that employment could be cut without reducing output, one can see the real depth of labour displacement taking place in Russian industry, and dismiss the view that little or no change in employment has taken place.

4.5 THE CRISIS OF CONCEALED UNEMPLOYMENT IN 1993–4

By mid 1993 it was clear that two trends were coexisting – shrinking industrial employment and growing concealed unemployment. The one did not preclude the other. By the time of the fourth round of the RLFS it was essential to probe the nature and extent of concealed unemployment. There is no standard way of doing this, so the following is an experimental means of identifying the main forms of visible surplus labour. The extent of each is estimated and then a composite *index of suppressed unemployment* is presented – a sort of 'labour market overhang' that

Figure 4.10   Percentage of establishments that could produce the same output with fewer workers, by industry, all regions, mid 1994

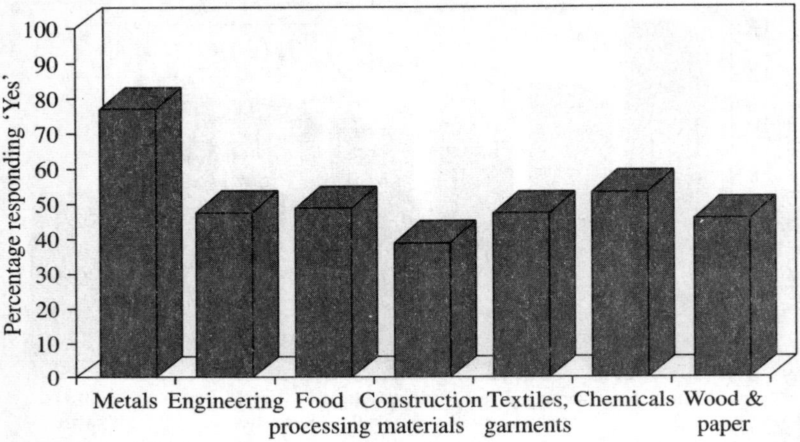

Source: RLFS4, n = 382.

could spill over into mass unemployment at any time and very rapidly. The first- and last-mentioned forms are hard to integrate into an index, the first because of its subjective nature and the last because of the ambiguity inherent in trying to interpret an institutional practice.

Managerially perceived surplus labour

First, as in previous rounds managements were asked if they could maintain the same level of output with fewer workers. As capacity utilisation levels were extraordinarily low, no less than 48.2 per cent said they could do so, with 76.9 per cent in the metals sector and 53.6 per cent in chemicals (Figure 4.10). This was more than 10 per cent more than one year earlier. Non-state establishments had higher levels of perceived labour surplus, and large firms were far more likely to believe they could cut their workforces without affecting output. Thus 63.2 per cent of firms with more than 1000 workers reported that they could produce the same amount with fewer workers.

Those establishments operating at relatively low capacity had a higher probability of being able to cut employment without reducing their output. And although those that had cut employment in the past year were more likely to estimate that they could cut employment in the current year, more

Figure 4.11   Percentage of fewer workers needed to produce the same output, by industry, all regions, mid 1994

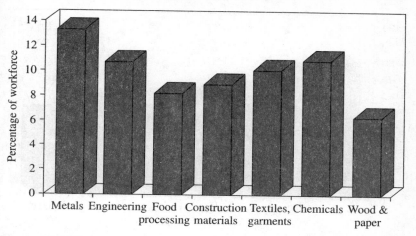

Source: RLFS4, n = 382.

than a third of those that had increased employment also believed they could cut jobs without lowering their current output.

For all firms, including those that did not believe they could cut jobs, on average managements estimated they could reduce employment by 9.8 per cent without affecting output, the highest percentage being in metals, chemicals and engineering (Figure 4.11). In other words nearly 10 per cent of the entire industrial workforce was in concealed unemployment or was surplus labour according to this definition. On average, those reporting they could produce the same amount with fewer workers estimated they could cut one in five jobs.

Intriguingly, this form of labour surplus was higher in private than in state establishments (Figure 4.12). Furthermore large firms had a greater labour surplus than small firms in percentage terms. Those factories that had cut capacity estimated they could cut employment to a greater extent than others, thus indicating a likely lag between changes in capacity utilisation and employment change.

Production stoppages

A second form of surplus labour has arisen from spells of *complete* or *partial stoppage of production*, for economic reasons. There is anecdotal

Figure 4.12   Percentage of fewer workers needed to produce the same output, by property form, all regions, mid 1994

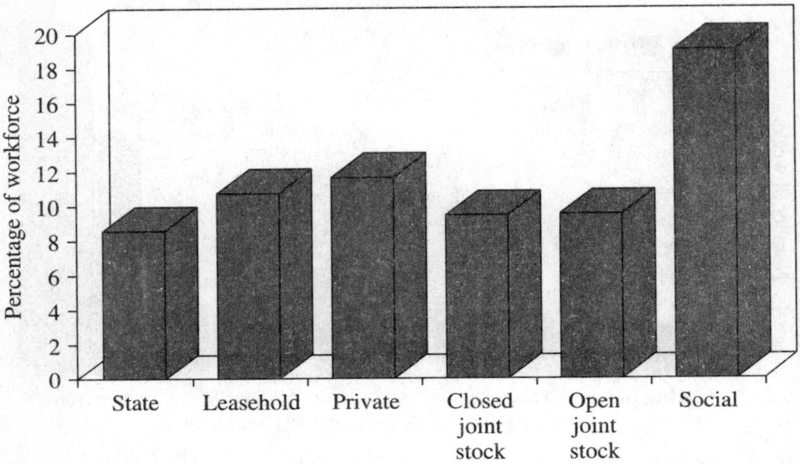

Source: RLFS4, n = 382.

evidence that this phenomenon became pervasive throughout Russia in 1994. For instance, during a meeting of the Federal Employment Service's Technical Assistance Advisory Committee on 12 September the FES director, Fyodor Prokopov, said that in July 1994 5000 major enterprises across Russia were not working at all, compared with 2000 a year earlier.

With regard to *complete stoppages*, in RLFS4 many firms reported that during 1993 and 1994 they had completely stopped production for one or more periods or had stopped part of their plant at some time. For all firms, on average the factories had experienced stoppages for 0.63 weeks in 1993 and 0.97 weeks in the first half of 1994, implying a more than threefold increase. In effect, assuming a working year of 48 weeks, the figure implies that for all firms together this accounted for about 4 per cent of working time.

In 1993 the lowest incidence of complete stoppage was in food processing. Regionally it was highest in Ivanovo (1.73 weeks), and the amount of labour time lost through this practice was inversely related to the firm's actual employment change in the period.

Partial stoppages, defined as closure of part of the plant for lack of work, accounted for an average of 1.25 weeks in 1993, with 5.4 weeks in metals. In the first half of 1994 alone the average for all firms was 2.1

Figure 4.13 Number of weeks when production partially or wholly stopped, by region, 1993–4 (whole year for 1993, first six months for 1994)

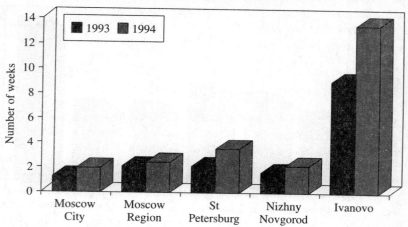

Source: RLFS4, n = 384.

weeks. The highest incidence was in construction materials, the lowest in food processing.

The unweighted average percentage of workers affected by partial stoppages was 15.3 per cent of the workforces of all establishments, or 35.2 per cent of the workforces in those firms in which there had been partial stoppages. The highest level was in Ivanovo, where 47.2 per cent of the workforces in those firms that had partially stopped production had been left idle for some time. The number of workers involved tended to be higher in large firms, implying that the unweighted mean underestimated the total number of workers involved.

We can make a rough calculation of 'labour slack due to partial stoppage' by multiplying the total workforce in the establishment by the percentage of workers affected and by the number of weeks they were off work, divided by the size of the workforce multiplied by 48 for 1993 and 24 for 1994, which assumes that a working year consists of 48 weeks.[8]

If we add complete and partial stoppages, with the latter expressed as time lost, as estimated above, *production stoppages for economic reasons accounted for about 6.8 per cent of total labour input during the first half of 1994.* This is probably an underestimate, but it indicates that the labour surplus was substantial. The distribution shows that certain sectors, areas and types of firm were particularly badly affected. Thus Figure 4.13 shows the number of weeks during which production was wholly or partially stopped in 1993 and 1994, and also how bad the situation was in Ivanovo and how it deteriorated in 1994. Time lost was greater in the first half of 1994 than for the whole of 1993. In effect, production stoppages for economic reasons had become a major form of 'suppressed unemployment'.

Administrative leave

A third form of surplus labour is *administrative leave*, or lay-off. This arises when a management tells workers they do not need to turn up for work, but does not make them redundant. To call this practice 'leave' is a convenient euphemism for what is essentially unemployment, except that the worker retains a slim hope that he or she will return to properly paid employment, while the enterprise retains a potential labour supply, available at short notice, and does not have to pay severance pay under Russian legislation, which obliges enterprises to continue to pay released workers for two or three months.

According to *Goskomstat* data, the extent of such leave throughout Russia by mid 1994 was higher than forecast at the beginning of the year and higher than the authorities had expected for the end of 1994 – 11 million workers were on administrative leave or working short time, or 22 per cent of the labour force.[9] This figure should be regarded as illustrative of official realisation that a major problem was distorting the picture of employment and unemployment.

The RLFS divides administrative leave into unpaid, partially paid and fully paid leave, but in practice only the first two have been used in Russia to any great extent. In fact partially paid leave accounted for most of the total, and it is almost certain that the amount paid was usually a token gesture (confirmed in all the factories we visited personally), at most amounting to the minimum wage, which was equal to less than the equivalent of US$8 a month, or less than 10 per cent of the average wage.

Taken overall, the extent of administrative leave rose substantially from early 1993, and in May 1994 accounted for between a low of 7.7 per cent of the workforce in food processing and a high of 23.9 per cent in the metals sector (Figure 4.14).

In terms of property form, Figure 4.15 shows that all types experienced an upward trend in administrative leave, with the exception of 'social organisations'. This latter finding is likely to reflect the acute pressure that such organisations were experiencing, given their previous reliance on budgetary support, the withdrawal of which would have forced them to

Figure 4.14 Percentage of workers on administrative leave, by industry, all regions, 1993–4

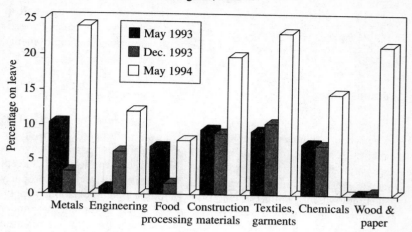

Source: RLFS4, n = 384.

Figure 4.15 Percentage of workers on administrative leave, by property form, all regions, 1993–4

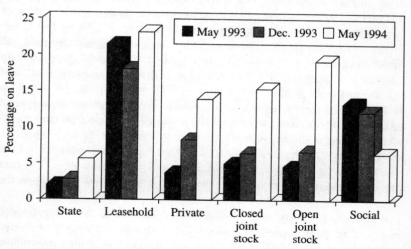

Source: RLFS4, n = 384.

Figure 4.16   Percentage of workers on administrative leave, by employment size,
all regions, 1993–4

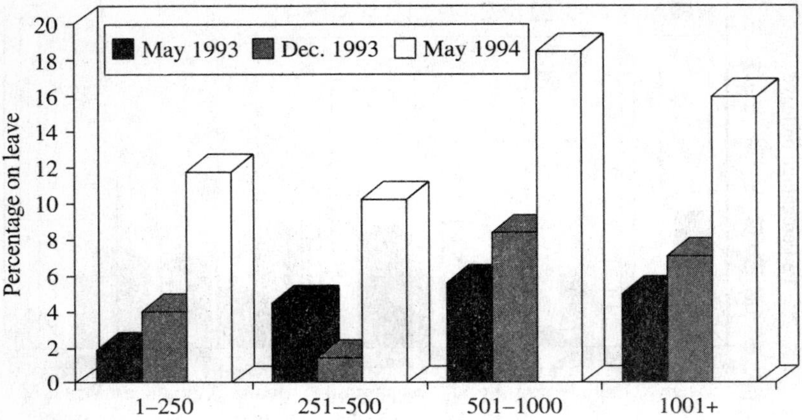

Source: RLFS4, n = 384.

release workers altogether because of the high overhead costs involved
continued responsibility for these workers, many of whom had disabilities.

Administrative leave rose in all size categories of establishment (Figure
4.16) and was highest in medium-sized and large firms, implying that the
unweighted means understated the full extent of lay-offs.

Overall, as in so many other respects, the situation was by far the worst
in the depressed region of Ivanovo, where an extraordinary 40 per cent
of all workers were on lay-off leave (Figure 4.17). Surely that situation
could not be maintained for very long, and there are ample reasons for
not wanting it to persist.

The reasons for this extensive recourse to unpaid administrative leave,
or lay-offs, will be considered later. By 1994 it had become a major form
of suppressed unemployment.

Short-time working

The fourth form of labour surplus consists of workers on *short time*, which
in the RLFS is measured by those working shorter working weeks than
normal for economic rather than personal reasons, subdivided into those
working fewer days than normal and those working fewer hours per day.

It turned out that working fewer days per week was far more common
than working fewer hours per day. Both increased considerably in 1993–

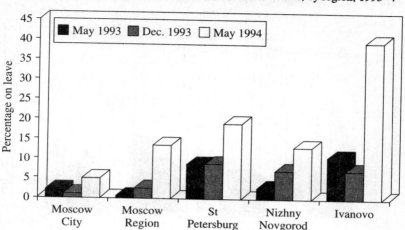

Figure 4.17 Percentage of workers on administrative leave, by region, 1993–4

Source: RLFS4, n = 384.

4. Taking both together, the basic metals, engineering and textiles and garments sectors had the highest levels (Figure 4.18). Most intriguingly, short-time working was much greater in state, social-organisation and leaseholding factories (Figure 4.19), and there is a suggestion that short-time working is a substitute for administrative leave or lay-offs.

Maternity leave

Another feature of Russian industry that could be interpreted as a partial form of surplus labour or hidden unemployment is prolonged maternity leave. One cannot interpret this wholly as hidden unemployment, yet it has been a convenient way of dealing with surplus labour crisies. When there is a shortage of work enterprise managements can simply encourage women to prolong their maternity leave. This is consistent with the fact that, in a country where the birth rate is extremely low, on average no less than 5.9 per cent of the female workforce were on maternity leave in May 1994. Maternity leave was relatively high in textiles and garments (Figure 4.20), in closed joint-stock companies and in large firms. Many of those women might have been replaced at work, yet in official statistics they would have been classified as employed, although more properly they should have been classified either as economically inactive or as being in disguised unemployment. As such, to a great extent the percentage of women on maternity leave could be interpreted as an indicator of surplus labour.

Figure 4.18   Percentage of workers on short time, by industry, all regions, 1993–4

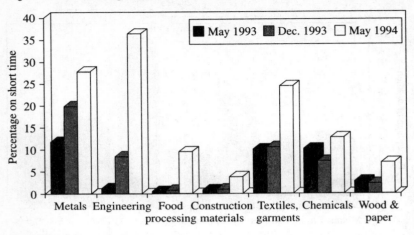

Source: RLFS4, n = 384.

Figure 4.19   Percentage of workers on short time, by property form,
all regions, 1993–4

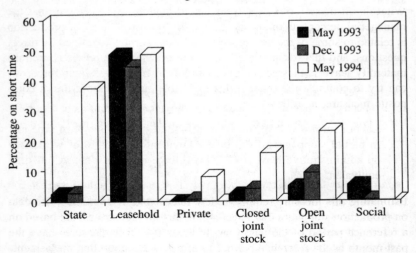

Source: RLFS4, n = 384.

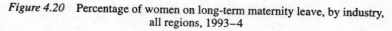

Figure 4.20 Percentage of women on long-term maternity leave, by industry, all regions, 1993–4

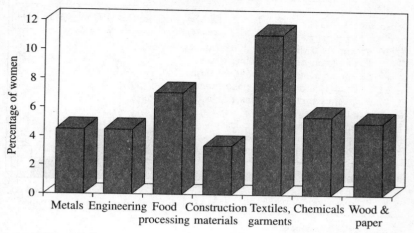

Source: RLFS4, n = 384.

Indexes of total surplus labour

What do all these forms of surplus labour amount to? Assuming that the managerial perception of surplus labour at the current level of production is related to some of the actual forms of labour surplus identified by direct questions, and that (despite the conclusion drawn in the previous section) maternity leave is classed as total withdrawal from the labour force, we can try to combine the other forms of visible surplus labour into a composite measure, as follows:

Labour surplus = % of time lost from total stoppages + % of time lost in partial stoppages in full-time equivalent terms + % of workforce on administrative leave + % of workforce on short-time in full-time equivalent terms.

Estimating this measure requires a few reasonable assumptions. The data on production stoppages due to economic factors (not strikes) are based on a reference period of the past year, whereas the other measures have the past month as the reference period. In effect, we assume that the percentage of time lost over the whole year can be regarded as applying to any particular month. Another assumption is that time lost from partial stoppages is separate from that lost through administrative leave or short-time

Table 4.3   Indicators of surplus labour or concealed unemployment
in Russian industry, all regions, mid 1994

Indicator	%*
1. Could produce the same output with fewer workers	
% employment cut possible, if yes	20.3
% employment cut possible, all firms	9.8
2. Labour unused due to complete production stoppages	4.0
3. Labour unused due to partial production stoppages	2.8
4. Unpaid administrative leave	3.0
5. Partially paid administrative leave	12.2
6. Fully paid administrative leave	0.3
7. Short-time working – fewer days or hours per day	12.3
8. Maternity leave	
% of women	5.9
% of all workforce	4.0
9. Unpaid employment?	

* Percentage of employment in full-time equivalent numbers for all firms, including those with zero. All figures are weighted estimates for size of firm, as of May 1994.

working. It could be that such stoppages are the immediate cause of some administrative leave. Accordingly labour surplus can be estimated as a composite index that excludes partial stoppages, as well as the index that includes them. Another assumption is that those on short time are deemed to have worked half time. Finally, in order to estimate the percentage of time lost from production stoppages we again assume a working year of 48 weeks, which in itself tends to result in an understatement of time lost because the average working year is probably shorter than that.

The averages of the various indicators of surplus labour are summarised in Table 4.3. To give a more complete picture, the table also shows the maternity leave average and refers to the issue of 'unpaid employment', which is covered in a later section.[10] The three groups of indicators are separated to highlight the point that they are somewhat different in character.

If we include labour input that is lost because of partial and complete stoppages of production, the percentage of workers on administrative leave, and the full-time equivalent measure of labour input that is lost because of enforced short-time working, we estimate that *in 1994 suppressed unemployment in Russian industry affected 35.2 per cent of the workforce.*

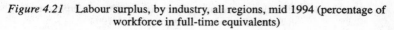

Figure 4.21   Labour surplus, by industry, all regions, mid 1994 (percentage of workforce in full-time equivalents)

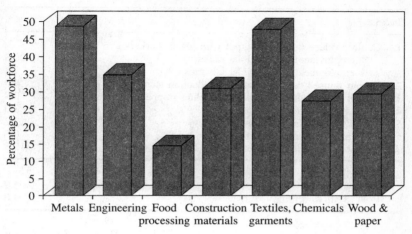

Source: RLFS4, n = 384.

In effect, more than one in three workers might have been released from employment, and in one way or another were released, short of being made openly unemployed. And this excludes extended maternity leave and unpaid leave.

The index of suppressed unemployment varies enormously by sector, area and type of firm. It was particularly high in metalworking plants, and textiles and garments (Figure 4.21). Were it not for food processing, where the labour surplus was less than 10 per cent, the aggregate would be much higher. Even more worrying is the fact that in *large firms with more than 1000 workers, over 37 per cent of workers were effectively redundant.* Also worrying is that surplus labour in mid 1994 was relatively high in open joint-stock firms (Figure 4.22), which so far had been inhibited from releasing large numbers of workers by privatisation agreements. Surplus was lowest in private firms (22.3 per cent) and, significantly for those concerned with corporate governance restructuring, was higher in firms where the management had been formally appointed by work collectives than where they had been appointed by enterprise boards.

The most fundamental question of all is: why has all this surplus labour been retained or unemployment suppressed, rather than conducting a massive process of labour shedding?

There are two hypotheses, the second of which will be considered in

Figure 4.22   Labour surplus, by property form, all regions, mid 1994, (percentage of workforce in full-time equivalents)

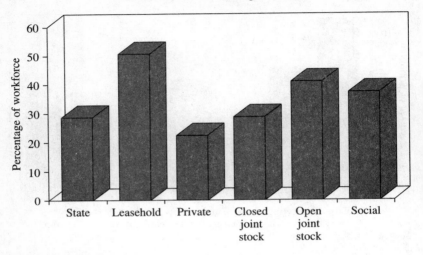

Source: RLFS4, n = 384.

the following chapter. The first is the conventional view that industrial firms have hoarded labour because they have a 'soft budget constraint', are unconcerned by labour costs and accordingly experience 'employment rigidity', intensified by employment protection practices that induce firms to regard labour as a fixed cost. As mentioned in Chapter 1, according to this view it is only with privatisation that internal labour surpluses can be converted into job cuts, as a result of the emergence of a 'hard budget constraint'. The validity of this hypothesis can be considered in terms of what has happened to employment.

4.6   THE JOBS HAEMORRHAGE IN 1993–4

There are two aspects of the first hypothesis. First, it has been argued that employment is 'rigid', making it very hard for managers to cut employment even if they wish to do so. We can deal with this very briefly. Both national data and information from successive rounds of the RLFS show that for many years *labour turnover* has been high, as will be shown in Chapter 8. Thus in 1993–4, as Figure 4.23 shows, labour turnover – defined as all departures from employment – was high in all regions.

Figure 4.23   Labour turnover, by region, 1993–4

Source: RLFS4, n = 384.

Overall it averaged 15.5 per cent, with particularly high rates in the construction materials sector.

Although the share of total turnover attributed to *redundancy* has been very low, this can be explained by three factors. First, 'voluntary' turnover has been sufficiently high to make redundancy less necessary; second, government regulations on mass redundancy make it desirable for firms to disguise redundancy as other forms of departure from employment; third, severance-pay conditions encourage firms to opt for other forms of disemployment, including extended unpaid leave as a means of inducing workers to leave 'voluntarily'. All we wish to stress here is that high labour turnover implies that there has not been employment rigidity. If firms wish to cut employment there are no insurmountable obstacles to doing so. Moreover the *vacancy* rate has been extremely low, ranging from about 1 per cent in Nizhny Novgorod to 2.5 per cent in Moscow Region, giving *prima facie* evidence that there has been a very low demand for labour.

More importantly, actual employment decline has been considerable. Weighted for employment size, *in 1993–4, on average for all establishments, employment was cut by 8.2 per cent, or 26882 jobs*. The decline was greatest in Ivanovo (13.8 per cent), followed by Moscow City (10.8 per cent), Moscow Region (8.4 per cent), St Petersburg (8 per cent) and Nizhny Novgorod (5.9 per cent).

Figure 4.24   Percentage change in employment, by industry, all regions, 1993–4

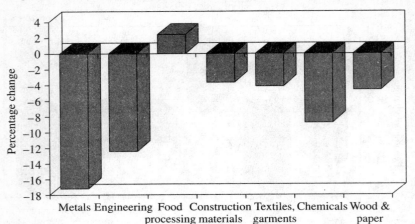

Source: RLFS4, n = 384.

This continued the pace of decline observed in the first three rounds of the RLFS, suggesting there had been a total decline of about 30 per cent since 1990. This is brought out more in analysis of the panel data for establishments that were in more than one round of the RLFS. Of the 126 factories in the first and fourth rounds of the RLFS, on average employment declined by 31.3 per cent between late 1990 and mid 1994. One can see also that the decline was significantly higher in the depressed region of Ivanovo than in the economically more dynamic region of Nizhny Novgorod. Employment declined most in the metals and engineering sectors and rose only in the food processing sector (Figure 4.24).

In terms of property forms, on average only private firms increased their employment level (Figure 4.25), in some cases simply because they had come into existence only recently. The sharp decline in employment in state establishments should be noted, since an average 10 per cent decline in one year for all firms is substantial. The relatively low decline in employment in closed joint-stock firms is also noteworthy, since such firms are closest to being 'employee-owned' and thus could be expected to be concerned with preserving employment for their worker members.

Before we examine the factors that could have determined interfirm differences in employment change, it is worth noting a few patterns perceived by managements.

First, they were asked what effect they thought changes in their sales in

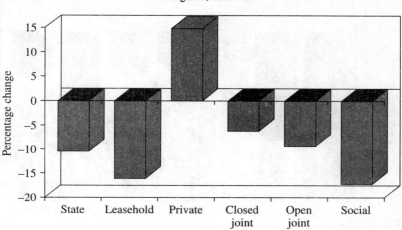

Figure 4.25   Percentage change in employment, by property form, all regions, 1993–4

Source: RLFS4, n = 384.

real terms had made to their firm's employment level. Of those that had experienced declining sales, 59 per cent believed that these had led to cuts in employment, 11.6 per cent to cuts in working time and 11.2 per cent to reduced working intensity. The remainder thought the changes had made no significant difference. In effect, the reactions suggest that many had responded to market pressures, and that they were suffering from a demand shock. The positive employment effect of sales growth was much weaker. Of those that had expanded sales, only 26.7 per cent felt that this had tended to increase employment, a third said it had had no effect and the remainder said they had increased work intensity or made some work-process change to facilitate the increased demand.

Second, on average those firms that had exported a relatively high percentage of their output in 1993 had cut employment by a relatively large amount (Figure 4.26). Why should export-oriented firms have cut employment more than others? Was it because they were uncompetitive or had they tried to respond to the need to be more competitive in the export market by raising labour productivity?

Third, those managements that reported they were planning to change the property form of their firm were asked what impact they thought this change would have on employment. Overall, 20.6 per cent considered it

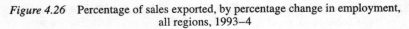

Figure 4.26   Percentage of sales exported, by percentage change in employment, all regions, 1993–4

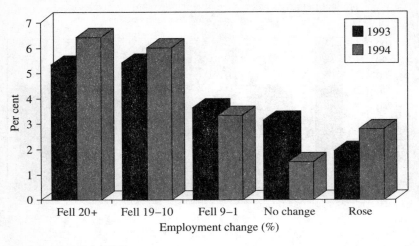

Source: RLFS4, n = 378.

would reduce employment and 17.6 per cent that it would increase it, from which we can infer that privatisation was not perceived to change employment very much.[11] One factor might have been that newly formed joint-stock enterprises were officially prevented from releasing workers for some months, so that any adverse effect would be postponed. However 45.5 per cent of firms with more than 1000 workers expected property restructuring to lead to employment cuts.

Fourth, technological change was often perceived by managements as having been beneficial for employment. Those that had increased their product range tended also to have increased their employment level (Figure 4.27). Those that had introduced new production technology were also relatively likely to believe that this had increased employment (Figure 4.28). As for those that had conducted some work reorganisation, managements tended to be split about the effect (Figure 4.29). Of course one should be wary about deciphering cause and effect in such cases.

Fifth, those establishments that had shed production units during the previous year had cut their employment level by slightly more than others, on average. This is hard to interpret, in that shedding such units could merely have been a form of cutting employment. Although this might become significant, it was not important in 1993–4 since the number of workers detached in this way was very small.

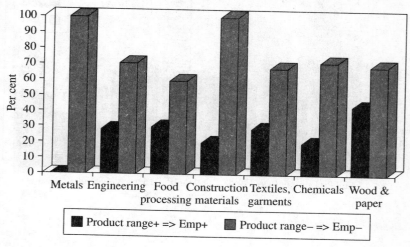

Figure 4.27 Perceived effect of product-range change on employment, by industry, all regions, 1994 (percentage of establishments believing product-range extension increased employment or product-range reduction decreased employment)

Source: RLFS4, n = 384.

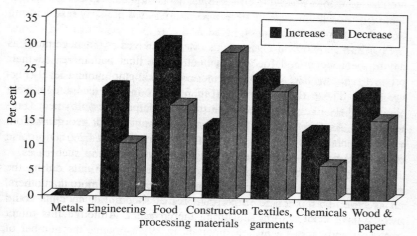

Figure 4.28 Perceived effect of technological change on employment, by industry, all regions, 1994 (percentage of establishments reporting that new technology had increased or decreased labour requirements)

Source: RLFS4, n = 166.

Figure 4.29 Perceived effect of change in work organisation on employment, by industry, all regions, 1994 (percentage of firms reporting increase or decrease)

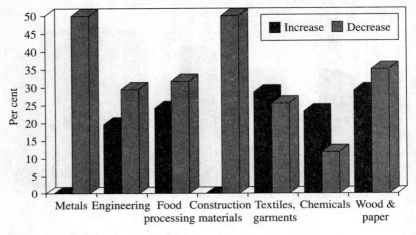

Source: RLFS4, n = 161.

Sixth, those that had cut their employment level the most were operating at a relatively low capacity utilisation level (Figure 4.30). No matter how this is interpreted, it suggests that a 'hard budget constraint' was operating.

Over one third of industrial establishments expected to make employment cuts during the coming year, whereas only 9.4 per cent expected employment to grow. Most pessimistic in this respect were firms in metals, textiles and garments, and chemicals. More than half of the large factories (52.9 per cent) expected to cut jobs, and those that had cut employment most during the past year were the most pessimistic about employment prospects during the coming year (Figure 4.31). In comparison with other property forms, state establishments were relatively unlikely to expect employment either to fall or to increase (Figure 4.32). Of those establishments expecting to change property form in the next year, a majority of those expecting to become fully private were on balance expecting that this change would result in an expansion of employment, although nearly half expected employment to decline as a result. In contrast, more of those expecting to become open joint-stock establishments anticipated that employment would fall as a result of the change, and the mean expected cut was nearly 8 per cent.

Finally, what of the correlations with governance type? Table 4.4 presents

Figure 4.30   Capacity utilisation rates, by employment change during previous year, all regions, 1993–4

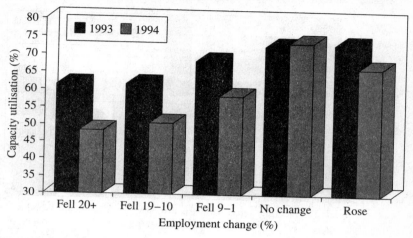

Source: RLFS4, n = 378.

Figure 4.31   Expected employment change, by employment change during previous year, all regions, mid 1994

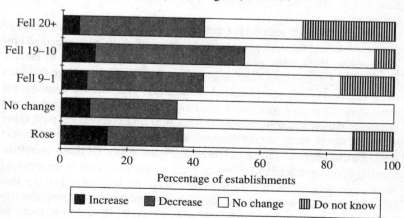

Source: RLFS4, n = 375.

Figure 4.32   Expected employment change, by property form, all regions, mid 1994

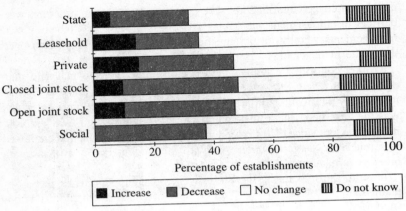

Source: RLFS4, n = 381.

Table 4.4   Employment dynamics, by type of governance, all regions, mid 1994

	Type of governance			
	State	*Private*	*Employee*	*Worker*
Mean % employment change, 1993–4	–11.2	–1.7	–11.4	–6.9
Labour surplus	27.9	29.6	39.1	23.2
% on administrative leave	7.6	22.2	20.7	14.8
% that could produce same output with fewer workers	45.5	54.0	43.2	49.0
% released	0.8	1.6	2.2	1.6
% expecting employment to rise	6.7	9.5	10.2	11.0
% expecting employment to fall	25.3	38.1	35.2	38.4

Note: The employment change figures were weighted for employment size of establishment within governance-type category.
Source: RLFS4, n = 384.

a set of measures of labour surplus and employment change for factories with different corporate governance structures. There were substantial differences in the observed rates of employment cuts, with employee-controlled establishments having the largest reduction in employment, along with state-controlled firms. As with so many correlations, one must be cautious about those results, for the changes in governance were only recent. Nevertheless the picture conveyed is *prima facie* evidence that neither employee-controlled nor state-controlled governance structures were barriers to employment cuts. What was most striking was that non-state managements were more pessimistic about future employment prospects than state managements.

Worker-controlled establishments seemed more able to maintain their employment levels, as would be expected if one accepts that such structures imply that workers influence managerial decision making. But if that was the case here, the management may have internalised their employment behaviour since their perception of labour surplus among the employed was relatively sanguine compared with their counterparts in firms with other governance types.

In sum, the hypothesis that low registered unemployment can be explained simply by labour hoarding because of employment rigidity is not supported. Actual and prospective job cuts have been substantial, and there has been little sign of employment rigidity. The factories surveyed were also evidently prepared for, and planning, further cuts in the near future. This does not mean that a great deal of employment restructuring has taken place. Where we examined employment change across all sectors and areas, multiple regression results (summarised in Appendix 4.1) suggest that the employment decline reflected demand effects, not restructuring. Controlling for other possible influences, the regression shows that sector of production was the main determinant of interfirm differences in employment performance. Large firms were not more likely to have cut employment, property form made no appreciable difference and the higher the share of manual workers the *lower* the reduction in total employment, indicating a lack of occupational restructuring.

None the less employment rigidity cannot explain the persistence and growth of the huge labour surplus in enterprises. Although it does not rule out elements of the first hypothesis, an alternative explanation will be considered in the context of wages. Before doing so, we should note that surplus labour was substantially higher in firms that had cut employment (Figure 4.33). And – most bizarrely – the share of women workers on maternity leave was much higher in firms that had cut employment than in others (Figure 4.34), suggesting either that women were more fertile in such firms or that this sort of leave was being used to disguise unemployment, as hypothesised earlier. That aside, we still have to explain the substantial growth and persistence of suppressed unemployment. We will try to do so in the process of examining what has happened to wages (Chapter 5).

Figure 4.33   Labour surplus, by employment change during previous year, all regions, mid 1994 (percentage of workforce in full-time equivalent terms)

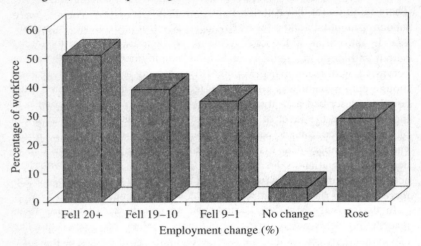

Note: Labour surplus is defined as the percentage of workers on administrative leave, plus those affected by partial and full production stoppages and the percentage on short-time work, in full-time equivalents.
Source: RLFS4, n = 384.

Figure 4.34   Percentage of women on maternity leave, by employment change, all regions, mid 1994

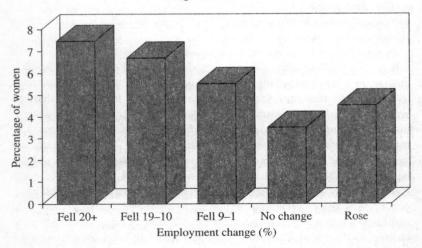

Source: RLFS4, n = 378.

4.7 CONCLUSIONS

There is no doubt that Russian industry entered the 1990s with very low labour productivity and a false self-image as suffering from a labour shortage. In the initial period of stagflation, characterised by sharply falling output and shrinking capacity utilisation, employment schizophrenia was pervasive, with many managements still perceiving a labour shortage even though employment was contracting. Russian industry then entered what could be described as a three-phase process of employment decline.[12] In the first phase the level of employment falls by means of a contraction of vacancies, continued 'voluntary' labour turnover and a delay in filling vacancies. Employment may contract to a lesser degree than the rate of decline of output and sales, yet it does shrink.[13] This first phase was characteristic of Russian industry in 1990–2 and affected the pattern of labour-force changes, as will be discussed in Chapters 9 and 10.

In the second phase, the decline in employment accelerates as firms resort to lay-offs (mostly involving individuals rather than mass redundancies) when they realise that the decline is not likely to be reversed. In this phase induced 'voluntary' departures combine with a growing number of redundancies, which also has implications for the composition of the workforce. Russian industry was still firmly in the second phase during 1993 and 1994, although fewer managers told us that they expected output to expand and thus absorb their surplus labour than was the case in 1991 and 1992.

The third phase involves mass redundancies, plant closures and bankruptcies. It would be truly extraordinary if this phase does not characterise labour-market developments in 1995–6.

From 1990–4 there was a huge loss of industrial jobs in Russia, and this is scarcely consistent with the orthodox view that there had been little change in employment and very low unemployment. One would have to have made the most unrealistic of assumptions to presume that the employment cuts in industry would be smoothly offset by labour absorption in growing sectors, such that substantial 'frictional' and restructuring unemployment would not result. But from early 1995 far worse was surely to come, since the build-up of concealed unemployment could not be sustained. Nor should it have been sustained – it was certainly not a sign of a buoyant and flexible labour market. Yet why did that build-up occur? Was the conventional explanation for the increased retention of surplus workers any better than the orthodox view of minimal employment change and extraordinarily low unemployment? In the following chapter an alternative hypothesis to the view that all could be explained by the existence of a soft budget constraint is proposed through an examination of the changing character of wage determination.

APPENDIX 4.1   REGRESSION ANALYSIS OF EMPLOYMENT CHANGE AND LABOUR SURPLUS, 1993–4

In order to examine the structural determinants of employment change, a straightforward regression function was estimated, in which the dependent variable was the change in the logarithm of total employment between May 1993 and May 1994. It was hypothesised that sectoral, regional and governance factors would explain differential employment change, with demand-side factors being captured by the change in sales in constant prices and the change in capacity utilisation, and structural change factors being proxied by product innovation (extension), work reorganisation and introduction of new technology in production during the preceding year, as well as governance or property form. Because of the correlation between governance and ownership, two functions were estimated, one with the set of corporate governance types, the other with the set of property forms.

Thus the function was the following:

$$EMP = a + b_1\Sigma(IND) + b_2\Sigma(REG) + b_3\Sigma(CORP) + b_4CHPROP + b_5EMP + b_6SALESDN + b_7WORKORG + b_8PRINC + b_9TECH + b_{10}CHCAP + b_{11}\%BC93 + b_{12}\%FEM93 + b_{13}DETACH + e.$$

The independent variables were defined as follows:

$\Sigma(IND)$ = set of binaries for industry of establishment, the omitted sector being textiles and garments.

$\Sigma(REG)$ = set of binaries for region in which establishment located, the omitted region being Moscow City.

$\Sigma(CORP)$ = set of binaries for corporate governance type, the omitted category being state-controlled governance.

CHPROP = 1 if the establishment had changed from a state to a non-state enterprise in the previous 12 months, 0 otherwise.

EMP = employment size of establishment in mid 1993.

SALESDN = 1 if sales decreased in past year in real terms, 0 otherwise.

WORKORG = 1 if the establishment had introduced a work organisation change in the past year, 0 otherwise.

PRINC = 1 if establishment increased product range in past year, 0 otherwise.

TECH = 1 if establishment introduced new production technology in past year, 0 otherwise.

CHCAP = percentage change in capacity utilisation in past year.

%BC = Manual workers as a percentage of total employment in mid 1993.

%FEM93 = Women as a percentage of the total workforce of an establishment in 1993.

DETACH = 1 if establishment shed unit in past year, 0 otherwise.

%MATLV = percentage of total workforce on maternity leave in mid 1994.

The results are presented in Table A4.1. Among the notable points is the lack of significance of corporate governance variables. This raises questions about the impact on employment of the change in management associated with property-form restructuring.[14] However it does not rule out the idea of reactions taking place after a lag. Controlling for sector and other factors, one finds that factories in St Petersburg and Nizhny Novgorod expanded their employment levels relative to Moscow, or rather cut employment less than in Moscow and Ivanovo.

The higher the share of manual workers in total employment in mid 1993, the greater the employment decline in the ensuing year. This suggests that there was some restructuring from manual workers to non-manual. The higher the percentage of women, the larger the cut – although this does not necessarily imply that women were being displaced, since it may mean that the type of factory employing a large number of women was more able to reduce its employment level. As hypothesised in this chapter, putting women on maternity leave seemed to be an alternative to employment cuts, since the more women who were on maternity leave the larger the employment decline.

Sectorally, the regression results suggest that establishments in the 'heavy' industries were particularly likely to have cut employment, that is, engineering, basic metals, chemicals and construction materials. Factories that shed units not surprisingly tended to cut employment by more than others, although as noted earlier this could merely represent a form of employment cut, such that it should not be included as an independent variable. However dropping that variable did not affect the statistical significance of other variables.

Finally, technological-restructuring variables do seem to have had a modest effect, as establishments that introduced technological innovations

Table A4.1 Employment dynamics in Russian industry: per cent and change in log. employment over previous year, 1993–4 (OLS regression results)

Variable	% employment change	Log. emp. change
(Constant)	134.7640	0.3114
Industry		
Metals	−54.1523***	−0.1308***
Engineering	−54.0966***	−0.1355***
Food processing	−21.3836**	−0.0307
Constr. materials	−49.7144***	−0.1105***
Chemicals	−47.7485***	−0.1190***
Wood & paper	−32.4286**	−0.0890***
Corporate Governance		
Purely private	7.6791	0.0132
Employee controlled	−12.8186	−0.0290
Worker controlled	−0.8989	0.0052
Region		
Moscow Region	7.9199	0.0300
St Petersburg	22.9101***	0.0439***
Nizhny Novgorod	9.8361	0.0364**
Ivanovo	−9.2073	−0.0186
Employment size, 1993	−0.0003	0.0000
Change from state to non-state property form	15.2105	0.0291
Sales decrease, 1993	1.8480	−0.0152
New technology	8.4367	0.0219*
Product range increase	10.7272	0.0268*
Product range decrease	−8.9366	−0.0256*
% manual workers, 1993	−1.1085***	−0.0028***
% maternity leave	−1.9207**	−0.0078***
% change in capacity utilisation	−0.2779	−0.0002
Receiving subsidy	−17.8121	−0.0567**
Production unit separated	−13.4705	−0.0455**
% sales exported	−0.0570	−0.0004
Work reorganisation	0.0843	−0.0022
% women, 1993	−0.4366**	−0.0007*
R^2	0.1496	0.2687
F	2.2798	4.7623

* Statistically significant at the 10% level of probability.
** Statistically significant at the 5% level.
*** Statistically significant at the 1% level.
Source: RLFS4, n = 384.

were likely to have cut employment by less than others. Those that reduced their product range were more likely to have cut employment. More sophisticated models of employment change could incorporate the possible endogeneity of these and other variables. What these results suggest is that sectoral and other structural factors can explain interfactory differences in employment dynamics in Russian industry, and that factory managements were responding to market forces.

Similar regression functions as those used to examine employment change were estimated for the percentage of *surplus labour* for mid 1994, using a narrow measure of surplus labour (Index 1) as well as the broadest measure (Index 3). The results are presented in Table A4.2. They suggest that sectoral and regional factors influenced interfactory variation in surplus labour. Food processing plants, construction materials, wood products and engineering plants had relatively low levels of surplus labour. The greater the deline in capacity utilisation, the higher the labour surplus. Perhaps of interest was the finding that firms in Ivanovo, St Petersburg and Nizhny Novgorod had more surplus labour than those in Moscow City. Given the sign and significance of the coefficient in the employment change regression, the results imply that the main difference was in the form of dealing with surplus labour. Were establishments outside Moscow more inclined to believe that the economic depression was temporary?

Not surprisingly, a decline in sales was associated with above-average levels of surplus labour. Those establishments that had cut employment had lower levels of surplus labour, although the relationship was not as strong as one would have expected. Finally, note that the higher the percentage of workers on maternity leave, the lower the level of surplus labour, further testifying to the use of this mechanism as an alternative to lay-offs or other forms of employment cut.

Table A4.2   Employment dynamics in Russian industry: labour surplus indexes, 1994 (OLS regression results)

Variable	Log. labour surplus index 1	Log. labour surplus index 2	Log. labour surplus index 3
(Constant)	1.0933	1.3140	1.1464
Industry			
Metals	0.2673	0.2735	0.2218
Engineering	−0.0390	−0.0994	−0.0532
Food processing	−0.1416	−0.2303	−0.2039
Constr. materials	−0.5518**	−0.2204	−0.3733*
Chemicals	−0.3023	−0.0324	−0.1478
Wood & paper	−0.1266	−0.0407	−0.1927
Corporate governance			
Purely Private	−0.0431	0.0191	0.0159
Employee Controlled	−0.3225*	−0.2344	−0.1645
Worker controlled	0.0441	0.1012	0.0679
Region			
Moscow Region	0.0121	−0.0042	0.0084
St Petersburg	0.2739*	0.2570	0.2761**
Nizhny Novgorod	0.2726	0.0563	0.2159
Ivanovo	0.2707	0.3878*	0.3157*
Employment size, 1994	0.0000	−0.00004*	−0.00004**
Change from state to non-state property form	−0.2146	−0.0942	−0.1073
Sales decrease, 1993	0.0657	0.0575	0.0943
New technology	0.0187	0.0029	0.0290
Product range increase	−0.0638	0.0972	0.0351
Product range decrease	−0.0651	0.0831	−0.0237
% manual workers, 1994	0.0049	0.0017	0.0050
% maternity leave	−0.0096	−0.0069	−0.0091
% change in capacity utilisation	−0.0030	−0.0040	−0.0054
Receiving subsidy	−0.1498	−0.2801**	−0.1351
Production unit separated	0.0018	0.0010	0.0008
% sales exported	−0.0069**	−0.0066**	−0.0064***
Work reorganisation	−0.2466	−0.2649	−0.3161*
% women, 1993	0.0708	0.0706	0.0916
% emp. change, 1993–4	−0.0001	−0.0002	−0.0004
R^2	0.2486	0.2726	0.2826
F	1.4177	1.6060	1.6878

Source: RLFS4, n = 384.

5 The Paradox of Wage Flexibility

5.1 INTRODUCTION

A key to understanding what has happened in the chaotic industrial labour market, and particularly what has happened to employment and unemployment, can be found by unravelling the wage system that characterised the Soviet economic system. Under that system wage levels were always very low, in part because of the ideological commitment to a gradual withering away of the wage mechanism following the Leninist dictate to achieve 'labour decommodification', and in part because of the perceived need to increase the rate of 'social exploitation' in order to pay for arms production and so on. Whatever the relative significance of the factors that kept wages so low, the reality was that money wages were always lower than would have been required for a subsistence standard of living corresponding to national living standards.

The low money wages were compensated for by a wide array of social benefits, provided mainly through the enterprise in which workers were employed, and in which they were expected to spend all their working lives and much of their 'pension age' as well, since the low wages conferred correspondingly low pensions that had to be supplemented by continuing paid employment well past the relatively low pension age. In most industrialised countries enterprises set wages broadly to correspond to actual or perceived labour-market circumstances, whereas in the Soviet system they were set more to correspond to the provision of benefits and price subsidies. Control over labour was exercised by the provision of enterprise benefits, which determined labour turnover and the 'effort bargain' of workers.

Low wages coexisted with modest wage differentials between occupational groups, industrial sectors and regions. Between the 1960s and 1980s most forms of wage differential declined.[1] However it would be a mistake to suggest that there were no differentials. Rather there was a pattern that would not have arisen in labour markets where relative wages were determined by productivity or demand and supply. Although there was a state commitment to a progressive narrowing of wage differentials, there was an ideological bias in favour of manual semiskilled labour in the 'sphere of material production', which meant that manual workers in engineering

107

were a relatively privileged category in industry, which in turn meant that intersectoral wage differentials were actually quite large, in favour of engineering. In effect, from the early decades of the USSR onwards, occupational wage differentials reflected an emphasis on job *status*. Relative wages were shaped by an administrative perception of what was 'socially useful', relying on distinctions between 'productive' and 'unproductive' labour.[2]

It is ironic that the 'proletarianisation' of the workforce meant that manual workers in engineering were paid relatively high wages and that there was a long-term tendency to boost their employment, both in absolute terms and relative to other groups of workers. There may have been a reasonable rationale for setting their wages relatively high in the early phases of industrialisation of the Soviet Union. Yet once established, status-based differentials tend to be rigid under an administrative system, since there is no easy way of altering the relative status of one job or another, let alone revising a whole structure.

For similar reasons, in contrast to the normal pattern in other countries, in the Soviet era there were small wage differentials between 'employees' and 'workers', a conventional distinction that corresponds roughly to the popular distinction between 'white-collar' and 'blue-collar' workers in Western Europe and North America. Some analysts even reported an inverse correlation between workers' schooling and wage rates.[3] Between 1970 and 1990 those working in service jobs, most notably in public education, experienced a sharp decline in relative earnings.

The wage distortions were also influenced by the effect of the centralised direction of the wage 'tariff' scale. The average wage was close to the minimum wage, and the minimum set the pattern of wage differentials, being a unit of account on which the wage tariff was based.[4] Because the minimum wage was low, and because of the complexity of the wage tariff system, which had an in-built bias in favour of manual skills and working conditions, the wage system itself tended to reduce wage differentials and accentuate the distortions in favour of semiskilled manual labour. In effect, most wage differentiation took place via privileged access to work experience and other forms of enterprise-based benefit.

Low wages and distorted wage differentials went with low and declining labour productivity.[5] The links between these three phenomena became increasingly clear in the period of *perestroika* in the late 1980s. Studies showed that workers were increasingly dissatisfied with their wages and they openly admitted that low wages restricted their productivity and discouraged them from working.[6] Other studies showed that the wage structure was an important factor (with the housing shortage and the *propiska* system) impeding geographical labour mobility.[7]

In sum, the wage system was rigid and distortionary, with non-wage benefits comprising a substantial share of total remuneration, and changes in relative wages being sluggish and unrelated to labour market needs or pressures. Since the late 1980s a great deal has changed. This chapter examines the pattern of wages, earnings and benefits in Russian industry since 1991, through analysis of data from RLFS3 and RLFS4. The main hypothesis is that there has been a growth in wage system flexibility, which largely explains the perverse pattern of employment restructuring and concealed unemployment presented earlier.

Another concern is the impact on wages and other forms of remuneration of changes in corporate governance, associated with so-called privatisation and the means by which managers have been appointed.

5.2 LABOUR COSTS

The first point to note is that labour costs have remained fairly low. In industry overall, wage costs have comprised a moderate share of total production costs, although according to RLFS3 they rose between 1991 and 1992 from 20.8 per cent to 22.1 per cent, on average. In both years their share was highest in wood and paper products and the engineering sector, and lowest in basic metals and food processing. While wages as a share of production costs rose in most sectors, they fell slightly in the latter two (Figure 5.1). The average wage-cost share also seemed to be inversely related to size of establishment.

According to RLFS4, which had a slightly larger sample and included firms in Ivanovo (where, as we will see, wages were relatively low), average wage costs were coincidentally 20.8 per cent in 1992 and 23.6 per cent in 1993. The ranking of industries was similar to that shown in 1991 and 1992 in RLFS3, and wage costs remained inversely related to establishment size. They were slightly higher in private and state firms than in joint-stock companies, and were lowest in firms that had increased employment. In 1994 they varied from an average of 17 per cent in food processing and 18.6 per cent in basic metals to 40.6 per cent in wood and paper products and 36.7 per cent in engineering (Figure 5.2). For the firms in both rounds, wage costs rose from 20.2 per cent in 1991 to 21.4 per cent in 1992, according to RLFS3, and from 21.6 per cent in 1992 to 24.1 per cent in 1993, according to RLFS4.

Labour costs – which included 'social consumption' expenditure as well as wages – accounted for 27.5 per cent of total production costs in 1991 and 30.1 per cent in 1992, according to RLFS3, and for 27.6 per cent in 1992 and 31.6 per cent in 1993, according to RLFS4 (Figures 5.3 and 5.4).

Figure 5.1 Wage-cost share of production costs, by industry, all regions, 1991–2

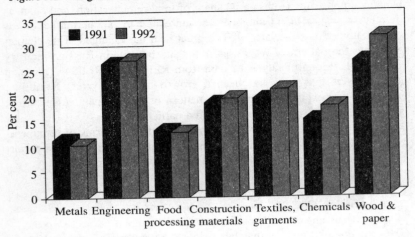

Source: RLFS3, n = 338.

Figure 5.2 Wage-cost share of production costs, by industry, all regions, 1992–3

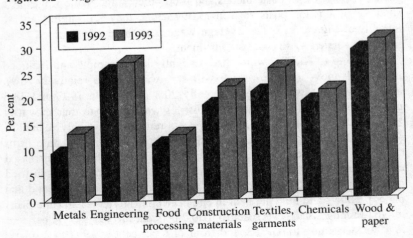

Source: RLFS4, n = 384.

Figure 5.3   Labour-cost share of production costs, by industry, all regions, 1991–2

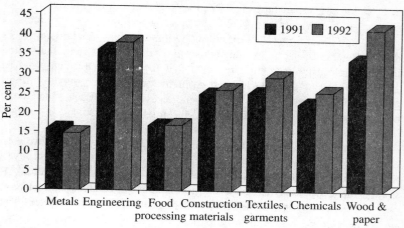

Source: RLFS3, n = 338.

Figure 5.4   Labour-cost share of production costs, by industry, all regions, 1992–3

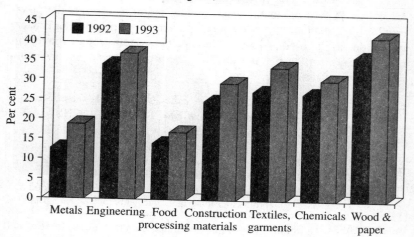

Source: RLFS4, n = 384.

For those firms in both rounds, labour costs rose from 26.7 per cent in 1991 to 29.3 per cent in 1992 and 32.6 per cent in 1993. There were sectoral variations, for instance in 1992 they varied from an average of 14.5 per cent in basic metals to 41.2 per cent in wood and paper products.

Although these figures are quite low by international standards, in 1993 the managements of one in four industrial establishments (and nearly one in three state establishments) reported that they regarded wage costs as likely to be the main labour-related problem facing their firms the following year. This seemed to be due to a general tightening of access to funds, persistent enterprise indebtedness and the high cost of social or 'fringe' benefits, rather than to high wages *per se*.

Between 1991 and 1992, according to RLFS3, social expenditure rose as a share of total labour costs, from 24.4 per cent to 26.6 per cent, even though there was a substantial rise in money wages in that period. Although the share stabilised between 1992 and 1993, as shown by RLFS4, social expenditure still increased its share of total production costs. The rise may have been due in large part to the 'tax-based incomes policy', which, by imposing a punitive tax on high wage rises, encouraged firms to shift to non-monetary forms of remuneration while preventing them from linking wages to productivity growth and converting wages into an effective mechanism for boosting work motivation and efficiency.[8]

In order to examine the variation of labour costs more systematically, an ordinary least-square regression function was estimated in which the wage-cost share of production costs was related to industry, region, property form of establishment or corporate governance form, level of capacity utilisation, size of establishment (with employment size squared to test for non-linearity), and change in sales over the previous year. The following function was estimated:

$$\text{Log.\% wage} = a + b_1\Sigma(\text{IND}) + b_2\Sigma(\text{CORPGOV}) + b_3\Sigma(\text{REG}) + b_4\text{EMPSIZE} + b_5\text{EMPSIZSQ} + b_6\text{CHSALES} + b_7\%\text{CAPUT} + b_8\%\text{BC} + e$$

where

Log.% wage	= logarithm of wage cost as percentage of total production cost.
$\Sigma(\text{IND})$	= a set of binaries (0,1) for the industry of the establishment, the omitted reference category being textiles and garments.
$\Sigma(\text{CORPGOV})$	= a set of binaries for the corporate governance, the omitted category being state enterprises.

Σ(REG)	= a set of binaries for the regional location of the establishment, Moscow City being the omitted category.
EMPSIZE	= size of establishment by number of workers and employees.
EMPSIZSQ	= size by number of workers and employees squared.
CHSALES	= percentage change in sales in real terms during the past year.
%CAPUT	= percentage capacity utilisation rate in mid-year.
%BC	= percentage of manual workers in the workforce of the establishment.
e	= error term.

Separate functions were estimated for the logarithm of 'social consumption' costs as a share of production costs and the logarithm of total labour costs (wages and social benefits) as a share of production costs. The functions were estimated by means of ordinary least-square regressions, the results of which are shown in Tables 5.1 and 5.2 (1992 from RLFS3 and 1993 from RLFS4).

The results were not very strong, although they suggest that wage costs and social costs were relatively high in engineering and relatively low in food processing and basic metals. They declined with increasing size of establishment, suggesting there were economies of scale with social benefits. For 1992 they may have been relatively high in Nizhny Novgorod, and were lower in open joint-stock companies than in state-owned establishments. The latter finding suggests that there would be efficiency gains from property-form restructuring, but the result was not replicated for 1993. Further research is needed to examine labour costs, and these preliminary findings merely point to possible lines of enquiry.

5.3 THE GROWTH OF WAGE-SYSTEM FLEXIBILITY

More germane to our current analysis is the evolution of the wage system. What emerged from the Soviet era was a centralised and administered wage tariff system, and for that reason alone the evolution of the industrial labour market in the wake of the enormous economic shocks and the breakdown of central authority could have been expected to produce a more flexible payment system. Perversely, since the announcement by President Yeltsin in October 1991 that wages were to be 'freed', *the wage system that emerged in the early and mid-1990s could be characterised as one of the most flexible conceivable.*

Table 5.1   Wage, social and labour-cost share of production costs, 1992

Variable	Log. % wage cost	Log. % social cost	Log. % labour cost
(Constant)	1.1833	0.4510	1.2587
Industry			
Metals	−0.1794	−0.1605	−0.1793
Engineering	0.1138**	0.1704***	0.1354***
Food processing	−0.3118***	−0.4063***	−0.3225***
Constr. materials	−0.0444	−0.0274	−0.0471
Chemicals	−0.0400	−0.0316	−0.0224
Wood & paper	0.0996	0.0323	0.0815
Corporate governance			
Private	−0.0068	−0.0425	−0.0253
Employee-controlled	−0.1326*	−0.1008	−0.1399*
Worker-controlled	−0.0427	−0.0675	−0.0556
Region			
Moscow Region	−0.0488	−0.0446	−0.0475
St Petersburg	0.0451	0.0516	0.0415
Nizhny Novgorod	0.0661	0.0551	0.0728
Employment size	−0.00010***	−0.00008**	−0.00009***
Employment size^2	6.4E−09**	4.6E−09	5.7E−09**
% sales change, 1992–3	0.0000	0.0000	0.0000
% capacity utilisation	0.0007	−0.0007	0.0004
% manual workers, 1992	0.0011	0.0058**	0.0022
R^2	0.2827	0.2811	0.3057
F	6.8157	6.7635	7.6136

* Statistically significant at the 10% level of probability.
** Statistically significant at the 5% level.
*** Statistically significant at the 1% level.
Source: RLFS3.

There are various aspects of wage flexibility, the most notable being the responsiveness of wages to market and productive signals. The underlying issues are whether changes in the wage system in Russian industry are creating the basis for increased responsiveness to such signals, and whether this responsiveness is conducive to restructuring, productivity improvement and employment generation. As such, one can have too little or too much wage flexibility, since a spot market could create chronic instability.

In mid 1993 the managers questioned in RLFS3 were asked to name the main factor that had influenced the level of their establishment's wages, besides price rises. Over 62 per cent said no other factor had been influential, while 13.6 per cent said that rising productivity had been the main

Table 5.2   Wage, social and labour-cost share of production costs, 1993

Variable	Log. % wage cost	Log. % social cost	Log. % labour cost
(Constant)	1.2441	0.7838	1.3706
Industry			
Metals	−0.3318***	−0.2343**	−0.3058***
Engineering	0.0600	0.0601	0.0620
Food processing	−0.3070***	−0.3004***	−0.3055***
Constr. materials	−0.0627	−0.0462	−0.0630
Chemicals	−0.1064*	−0.0094	−0.0796
Wood & paper	0.0575	0.0315	0.0508
Corporate governance			
Private	−0.0118	−0.0150	−0.0092
Employee-controlled	0.0391	0.1372**	0.0581
Worker-controlled	−0.0471	0.0129	−0.0352
Region			
Moscow Region	−0.0661	−0.0573	−0.0684
St Petersburg	−0.0032	0.0118	0.0006
Nizhny Novgorod	0.0094	0.0222	0.0152
Ivanovo	−0.0038	0.0228	0.0003
Employment size	−0.00007***	−0.00006**	−0.00007***
Employment size^2	3.7E−09***	2.8E−09*	3.6E−09***
% sales change, 1993–4	0.0000	0.0000	0.0000
% capacity utilisation	0.0005	0.0009	0.0006
% manual workers, 1993	0.0015	−0.0002	0.0012
R^2	0.2504	0.1842	0.2476
F	6.3850	4.3148	6.2895

* Statistically significant at the 10% level of probability.
** Statistically significant at the 5% level.
*** Statistically significant at the 1% level.
Source: RLFS4.

consideration and 10.7 per cent said that an extension in production had been the most important factor. Although other factors were mentioned, none were of widespread relevance. In 1994, 62 per cent stated that price was the only factor influencing their wages, 18 per cent said that productivity was taken into account and 10.2 per cent referred to the expansion of production. What these opinions imply is that a majority of managements had yet to try to change wages in order to influence or reflect economic performance, although a growing number had become conscious of the need to link productivity to pay.

Bearing in mind that any form of flexibility can have positive or negative effects, and should not be regarded as wholly negative or wholly positive, one can assess the extent of wage-system flexibility in Russian factories by considering eight major developments, beginning with the former core of the wage system.

The wage tariff

Traditionally, wages in Russian industry were seen as very rigid because they were determined centrally by means of a complex wage tariff system, which set wages and wage differentials. Thus the first sign of growing wage flexibility was that, although a majority of factories in RLFS4 were still using the state tariff wage system in 1994 (56.3 per cent), over two in five no longer did so, and only 39 per cent of private firms were still using it. The larger the factory, the more likely it was to be still using the wage tariff (over 60 per cent of those with more than 1000 workers), suggesting that if size restructuring were to occur the drift away from it would continue. Use of the wage tariff system was greater in firms that had been shrinking, which also suggested that it was a declining force.

Furthermore, using the wage tariff system did not mean that it was used wholly or that it strongly determined total remuneration. Indeed, because it was based on the statutory minimum wage, which traditionally set the base for wage tariff differentials, by 1994 the tariff system had lost touch with reality, since the statutory minimum wage had been held so far below the subsistence income level that nobody could possibly live on it.

Lest we think that the wage tariff had no effect on actual wages in the 1990s, its role as an anchor to hold down wages should not be forgotten. In those factories still utilising the wage tariff, in 1993–4 average wages rose 50 per cent less than in those not using it.[9] Thus the declining use of the tariff permitted upward as well as downward flexibility.

Wage individualisation

Perhaps as important as the decline in reliance on the wage tariff system, between 1991 and 1994 there was a strong shift away from wage determination based on collective performance towards what might be called 'wage individualisation'.

In mid 1993, according to managerial responses – and one must be cautious about speculating on the strength of any linkage – wages were still set largely according to collective performance rather than individual performance, with 61.3 per cent of managements claiming that the main criterion used to determine remuneration was the performance

Table 5.3 Main performance criterion for wage determination, by industry, all regions, mid 1993 (percentage distribution of management responses by industry)

Industry	Main performance criterion		
	Overall	Unit	Individual
Metals	75.0	25.0	0.0
Engineering	57.3	18.8	23.9
Food processing	69.2	23.1	7.7
Constr. materials	61.5	30.8	7.7
Textiles, garments	54.2	18.6	27.1
Chemicals	70.8	12.5	16.7
Wood & paper	62.5	21.9	15.6

Source: RLFS3, n = 331.

Table 5.4 Main performance criterion for wage determination, by property form, all regions, mid 1993 (percentage distribution within property forms)

Property form	Main performance criterion		
	Overall	Unit	Individual
State	65.8	14.0	20.2
Leasehold	53.8	15.4	30.8
Private	50.0	37.5	12.5
Closed joint stock	59.1	25.8	15.2
Open joint stock	63.8	20.2	16.0

Source: RLFS3, n = 332.

of the establishment as a whole, 20.5 per cent reporting that it was the performance of the work brigade or work unit collective, and 18.1 per cent basing it primarily on individual performance. This pattern varied considerably by sector, with firms in the textiles and garments sector being the most inclined towards an individualised (largely piece-rated) payment system (Table 5.3).

There was little variation by type of property form, implying that by itself commercialisation had not led to individualisation of the payment system (Table 5.4). This latter finding probably reflected the nature of joint-stock forms of management, in which the work collective retained a collective voice, at least in principle.

Table 5.5 Main performance criterion for wage determination, by industry, all regions, mid 1994 (percentage distribution of management responses by industry)

Industry	Main performance criterion			
	Overall	Unit	Individual	Other
Metals	46.2	76.9	30.8	0.0
Engineering	36.7	25.0	58.6	0.0
Food processing	45.2	33.9	30.6	0.0
Constr. materials	34.6	38.5	34.6	0.0
Textile, garments	26.4	18.7	68.1	0.0
Chemicals	46.4	32.1	46.4	3.6
Wood & paper	38.9	25.0	41.7	2.8

Source: RLFS4, n = 348.

In 1993–4 there was a major shift towards individual wage determination. By mid 1994, and bearing in mind that some factories were using a combination of forms of payment, 51.3 per cent of firms reported that they used individual performance to determine pay, 36.7 per cent used establishment performance and 28.1 per cent used the performance of the work unit. Textiles and garments and engineering were leading the way (Table 5.5). For establishments that were surveyed in both 1993 and 1994, the number paying mainly according to individual performance *doubled*. In the textiles and garments sector the share paying according to individual performance (piece-rates mainly) rose from 34 per cent to 64 per cent. In non-state establishments the trend to individualised remuneration was very clear (Table 5.6).

These trends imply what is surely an irreversible movement away from the former system based on the work collective. Not surprisingly, private firms were most inclined to base pay on individual performance, but the trend was similar in all property forms. Given that the property forms had evolved, it is reasonable to conclude that a shift to a very flexible wage-determination system was occurring as part of the restructuring.

The drift towards individualisation of wage determination was associated with higher money wages and the relative decline of the wage tariff system. In those firms that were operating an individual-performance pay system, wages rose in 1993–4 by 42 per cent more than in those that still operated a work-collective pay-determination system. One could conclude that the decentralisation of pay was contributing to money wage inflation. This is a contentious issue among labour economists, and the links between

Table 5.6 Main performance criterion for wage determination, by property form, all regions, mid 1994 (percentage distribution within property forms)

	Main performance criterion			
Property form	Overall	Unit	Individual	Other
State	31.5	26.0	46.6	1.4
Leasehold	57.1	14.3	42.9	0.0
Private	31.7	17.1	63.4	0.0
Closed joint stock	34.5	39.3	53.6	1.2
Open joint stock	40.2	27.4	49.4	0.0
Social	25.0	25.0	62.5	0.0

Source: RLFS4, n = 384.

the level of pay determination and the wage rates will be considered later. The point here is that the payment system itself had become more flexible by virtue of the drift towards individualised remuneration, which allowed greater differentiation and a greater capacity to raise or lower wages.

Bonuses

Other developments also show that the wage system had become quite flexible, in that it was allowing wage adjustments to be made according to enterprise and worker performance. The form of remuneration is indicative of wage flexibility, and in this regard the international trend has been away from fixed wages. This too has begun to be mirrored in Russian industry. For instance most establishments have been paying bonuses of one kind or another, and a substantial share of earnings has consisted of bonus payments.

According to the managements in RLFS3, in 1992 an average of 39.5 per cent of total wage remuneration was paid in the form of bonuses (Figure 5.5). There was little apparent difference between sector, size of establishment or property form. By mid 1993 the bonus share had risen to 43.7 per cent on average, highlighting the fact that the wage tariff system was becoming less binding, and perhaps reflecting the impact of the tax-based incomes policy.

According to RLFS4, on average bonuses comprised about 37.7 per cent of earnings in 1993, with a particularly high share in food processing.[10] In the worsening labour-market conditions of 1994 the bonus payments diminished (Figures 5.6 and 5.7), and accounted for only 32.9 per

Figure 5.5 Percentage of wages paid in bonuses, by industry, all regions, 1992–3 (average percentage of average total earnings in bonuses)

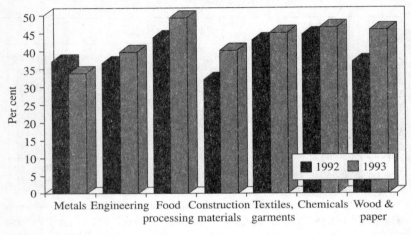

Source: RLFS3, n = 338.

Figure 5.6 Percentage of wages paid in bonuses, by industry, all regions, 1993–4 (average percentage of average total earnings in bonuses)

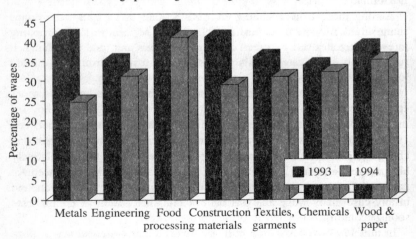

Source: RLFS4, n = 384.

Figure 5.7 Percentage of wages paid in bonuses, by property form, all regions, 1993–4 (average percentage of average total earnings in bonuses)

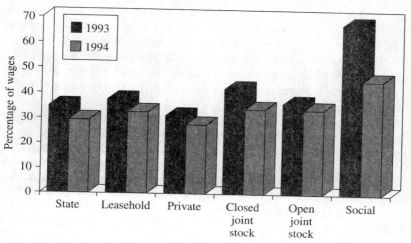

Source: RLFS4, n = 384.

cent of earnings on average, with particularly low bonuses in firms that had made employment cuts, evidence that it was a mechanism for wage flexibility.

Among those firms that were in both RLFS3 and RLFS4, the bonus share shrank from 42.6 per cent in 1993 to 36.7 per cent in 1994, dropping in every sector, albeit by minor amounts in metals and food processing. It rose slightly in private firms and fell in others, most strongly in closed joint-stock enterprises.

In 1993 most establishments in all sectors provided workers with monetary 'incentives'. Although there may have been a slight tendency for incentive payments to decline between 1992 and 1993, and again between 1993 and 1994, this probably reflected incapacity to pay rather than any change in principle.[11] Firms providing incentives tended to pay relatively high wages, although the causal link is unclear. Whether the incentive nature of the payments was strong or weak is a matter for speculation, and in any case many wage analysts believe that such incentive components soon become incorporated into the normal wage.

In mid 1994 over four in five firms reported that they operated a monetary incentive scheme of some kind, and one feels that, however much they were abused as a genuine incentive mechanism, they provided scope for considerable wage flexibility.

Profit sharing

In terms of wage flexibility, one aspect has been singled out for special emphasis in international debates – so-called 'profit-sharing' payments. The economic advantages and disadvantages of tying wages to profit levels and trends have been extensively analysed, both theoretically and empirically.[12] What is fairly clear is that, to the extent that they genuinely operate as profit-sharing mechanisms, they impart a greater degree of wage flexibility into the wage system.

In Russian industry a majority of firms operate some or other system akin to profit sharing. In mid 1993, according to RLFS3, over two thirds of establishments reported that they operated some form of profit sharing, with three quarters of those in the textiles and garments sector and about 85 per cent of closed joint-stock enterprises reporting that system. As would be expected, the practice of profit sharing was linked to managements being elected by the work collective. A majority of establishments (52.2 per cent) reported that the individual worker's profit share payment varied according to the work collective's performance, while 20.8 per cent stated that the payment was a variable share depending on total revenue.

Tabulations suggest that, on average, firms operating some form of profit sharing paid higher wages and earnings. However, as will be shown later, this has not been borne out by the regression results. Profit sharing is the ultimate form of wage flexibility, and although profit sharing is probably a misnomer for what was involved, the depressed state of Russian industry in 1993 allowed firms with a profit-sharing system to lower workers' real earnings relatively easily. Conversely, if production were to pick up, those with profit-share pay should benefit sooner and by more than those on a more fixed wage system. In short, profit sharing is a risk-sharing mechanism, where the danger of economic insecurity for workers is balanced against the advantage of workers having a share of the establishment's profits.

Although various types of arrangement were in operation, some being little more than norm-related bonuses, in mid 1994 67.2 per cent of firms reported that they were operating some form of profit-sharing payment system and 8.1 per cent of firms were paying dividends (13.1 per cent of closed joint-stock firms, 10.4 per cent of open joint-stock firms and 7.3 per cent of other private firms). The proportion of firms operating a profit-sharing mechanism had increased. Of those factories included in both 1993 and 1994, 69.3 per cent operated profit sharing in 1993 and 71.6 per cent in 1994, the greatest increase coming in the food processing sector, where nearly 89 per cent had profit sharing in 1994 compared with 77 per cent a year earlier.

In 1993–4 there was also a historically remarkable growth of worker share-owning. Although by 1994 it had probably not become an established practice to link profits to wages, the existence of the mechanism could have induced a willingness among workers to accept lower wages, as well as a means by which managements could lower wages, especially in the context of rising money wages.

Implicit deregulation

Another indicator of wage flexibility is the limited effect of wage regulations. Three aspects deserve emphasis – the excess wage tax or 'tax-based incomes policy', the statutory minimum wage and the presidential decree of 1993 stipulating a cap on managerial wages.

Most managements were ignoring the *presidential regulation on managerial wages* with impunity, if they were even aware of it. According to that regulation, managers in state establishments were not supposed to receive more than six times the average wage of workers in the enterprise, and managers in other forms of enterprise were strongly recommended not to exceed that limit. According to the managements' responses, in mid 1994 the majority (65 per cent) were unaware of the existence of the regulation, including 80 per cent in the private firms. Most of the remainder were simply ignoring it. This is symptomatic of the realities of the Russian labour market, for if regulations are unknown and ignored, that in itself implies a much greater degree of labour-market flexibility than an examination of the regulation's formal obligations might suggest. In the Russian labour market of 1994 wage controls of any sort were unlikely to have any effect.

One potential impediment to downward wage flexibility is the *statutory minimum wage*.[13] In sharp contrast with the Soviet era, after 1991 its level was allowed to drift downwards relative to the average wage and to well below a level of income required for minimal subsistence.[14] Under a presidential decree of November 1992 a quarterly price indexation adjustment was started in April 1993. Yet not only was there no formula for indexation, but the adjustment was delayed in the final quarter of 1993 and was not raised again until July 1994. In effect, from 1991 onwards the minimum wage ceased to provide any floor of wage protection. Even so, policy makers and analysts continued to regard the minimum wage as the anchor of the wage system and continued to make it the determinant of important social transfers, notably unemployment benefits and child allowances. Its effect on wages would be expected to be primarily through the automatic effect on the wage tariff, of which it was the basis. Outside Russia there have been prolonged debates among labour economists on the effects of minimum wages on average wages and wage differentials, and there has been a tendency among foreign economic advisers to the Russian authorities to advise them to abandon the minimum wage altogether.[15]

In RLFS3 and RLFS4 managers were asked about the influence of changes to the minimum wage on the average wage in the factory and on wage differentials between groups of workers in it. In 1993 nearly two thirds of managements reported that the minimum wage did have some influence on the average wage level. Although there was little sectoral or regional differential in the perceived impact, managers in state and lease-holding establishments were more inclined to perceive an impact than their counterparts in joint-stock companies, and it was also relatively likely to have an effect in very large factories. Over 62 per cent of managers of factories with more than 1000 workers believed that changes to the minimum wage had had an influence on wage differentials, although most believed that they had served to widen such differentials.

These results were surprising given the low level of the minimum wage. The most likely explanation is that the perception was a residual legacy of the time when the minimum wage set the tariff wage structure and when the minimum was close to the average wage. Also, it probably had an effect on the average wage through its being the basis of the excess wage tax, which may also explain the perception among managements that it influenced wage differentials. It may also have influenced the *form* of remuneration, as discussed later. Thus, ironically, the wage tax had probably prevented the minimum wage from becoming a completely marginal factor in wage determination.

By 1994 the effect was ebbing. Over half the firms reported that changes to the minimum wage had had no effect on their wages, a major change from the situation in 1993. In food processing nearly two thirds of all factories reported that it had had no effect. As in 1993, managements in large factories were more likely to report that it had had an effect, which coincided with the fact that the wage tariff was still relatively likely to be used in such firms. Indeed those firms still operating the wage tariff were more inclined to report that the minimum wage had had an impact on average wages than those that did not (52.3 per cent as against 46 per cent). Among those factories visited in both years, the share believing adjustment in the minimum wage had had an effect on average wages declined from 62.3 per cent to 48.7 per cent. The share reporting that they thought it had had no influence on wage differentials rose from 63.4 per cent to 73.2 per cent.[16]

Clearly, in the vast majority of firms the minimum wage had ceased to be influential, and this was corroborated by the fact that, again in contrast with 1993, more than three-quarters of factory managements reported that changes to the minimum wage had had no effect on wage differentials. In short, the minimum wage had become ineffectual, and as such was unable to prevent downward wage flexibility.

The third wage regulation that paradoxically contributed to wage flexibility was the *excess wage tax*, designed to prevent wage inflation in the wake of price liberalisation. This tax was introduced in 1991 to succeed the abortive Abalkin tax, and was modified in 1992, 1993 and 1994. Between 1991 and 1993, when computing profits subject to tax, a firm was allowed to include a wage bill equal to four times the minimum wage multiplied by the number of workers and employees in the firm. If the average wage was between four and eight times the statutory minimum wage, it was subject to a profit, or excess wage, tax of 32 per cent. If the average wage was more than eight times the minimum wage it was subject to a 50 per cent tax rate. In January 1994 the tax was simplified to a straightforward 38 per cent tax on average wages that were more than six times higher than the minimum wage.[17] There have been better taxes.

The tax had a number of labour-market effects. First, although it did not hold down wages to the level where the tax applied, the very existence of the tax discouraged firms from raising wages, as was intended. However, to the extent that it was successful in that respect it was a mixed blessing, given the desirability of raising wages in order to encourage firms to allocate labour resources more efficiently, bearing in mind the extremely low wages inherited from the Soviet era, and in order to encourage a higher 'effort bargain' between workers and enterprises. Low wages breed low effort and low efficiency. And there can be little doubt that a wage that was four times the statutory minimum wage was well below the appropriate optimum 'efficiency wage', since that would have been below the subsistence minimum.

A second effect was to encourage a 'dead souls' employment policy, or the proliferation of concealed unemployment. This is because one simple way of lowering the average wage is to put a worker on unpaid or partially paid administrative leave rather than making him or her redundant. By this means, not only did the firm avoid the cost of three months of severance pay but it also reduced the tax cost. Thus the tax had the perverse effect of slowing the process of employment restructuring.

Moreover, by reducing labour productivity it raised labour costs and could even be inflationary, when the whole rationale of the tax was to reduce inflation.

A third effect was to encourage a shift away from money wages towards other forms of remuneration, particularly enterprise benefits, which again is precisely the opposite of what was required in the 1990s.[18] Because of the tax, it was less costly for an enterprise to use wage funds to pay for benefits such as subsidised rents or holidays than to put the money into wages. This option was particularly attractive in 1992–3, when there was a shortage of food and other basic consumer goods in the open market. We will return to this when reviewing the developments of enterprise benefits.

A fourth effect was more insidious. The minimum wage in 1993 was less than a quarter of the minimal 'physiological survival' income, and thus the 'excess' wage tax was levied on a wage that just about provided enough for bare survival, which would have been well below any realistic notion of an 'efficiency wage'. Thus a fairly punitive tax levied on low wages would have encouraged firms to find ways of evading as well as avoiding the tax, simply because it would not have been perceived as legitimate or just.

In sum, perversely the wage regulations were such as to encourage wage flexibility rather than wage rigidity, and given the extremely low minimum wage and the nature of the excess wage tax, they encouraged downward wage flexibility rather than employment flexibility.

Weak 'voice regulation'

Another indicator of wage flexibility is that managements were under very little effective pressure to pay wages. In effect, workers were unable or unwilling to exercise their 'voice' to obtain the wages to which they were entitled, either directly in protest or through their trade union.

During 1992 and 1993 there was much national and international comment about the rise in average real wages in Russia, as indicated by official *Goskomstat* data. Many commentators suggested that this indicated that the labour and employment situation was not as bad as had been claimed, and that public discontent was limited because those in employment were doing well.

In reality the reported wages from the quarterly forms filled in for *Goskomstat* were the statutory wages to which enterprises were committed, not necessarily those they actually paid. There have been numerous reports that many enterprises did not pay anything like the full amount. Accordingly the firms in the survey were asked if they had had severe

Figure 5.8 Difficulty in paying wages, by property form, all regions, mid 1994

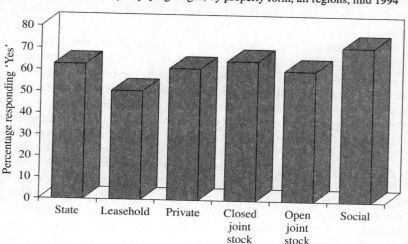

Source: RLFS4, n = 381.

difficulty in paying the wages that they had agreed to pay. In 1993 46.9 per cent of all firms – and 53.8 per cent of state firms – reported that they had had such difficulty, including nearly 60 per cent of engineering firms, many of whom provided products for the military–industrial complex. It seemed that those establishments in which the managers had been elected by the workers were least likely to fail to pay wages – 40.6 per cent of those having acute difficulty in paying compared with 56.5 per cent of those in which the top managers had been appointed by ministries and 60 per cent of those in which they had been appointed by a local authority.

That was bad enough, yet the situation continued to deteriorate. In mid 1994 over 60 per cent of firms reported that they had experienced severe difficulty in paying wages, including over 70 per cent of engineering firms and an even larger share of textiles and garments producers. About three quarters of those employing more than 1000 workers had been experiencing severe difficulty. And it seemed to have affected all property forms of establishment (Figure 5.8). For factories surveyed in both 1993 and 1994, 44.9 per cent had had difficulty in the first year whereas 59.6 per cent were having difficulty in the second, with textiles and garments factories experiencing the greatest deterioration.

In 1993 the main reaction of over half of those that had had difficulty in paying wages (60.5 per cent) had been to pay the wages with a delay

Figure 5.9   Difficulty in paying wages, by percentage employment change during previous year, all regions, mid 1994

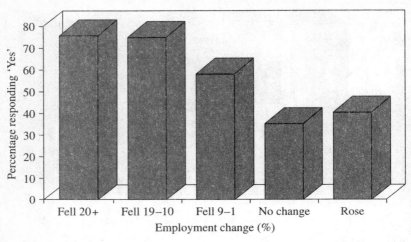

Source: RLFS4, n = 375.

and to pay all workers at that time. Among the other main reactions mentioned, 16.6 per cent took out loans to pay the wages, 12.7 per cent paid some (not all) of their workers with a delay, and 5.7 per cent paid their workers part of their wages.[19] Resorting to loans was far more common among large establishments, being the response of one quarter of factories with more than 1000 workers.

As in 1993, in 1994 those establishments that had made the greatest cuts in their employment levels the previous year were also most likely to have had difficulty in paying wages (Figure 5.9). In 1993, for instance, those factories that had reported such a difficulty had cut employment by 13.4 per cent on average, whereas those that had reported no such difficulty had cut by only 4.7 per cent. Those that had experienced a decline in their rate of capacity utilisation were also relatively likely to have had difficulty in paying wages. There was also a suggestion that state enterprises reporting to government authorities were under greater financial pressure over wages than joint-stock enterprises, irrespective of whether the managers had been appointed by an enterprise board or a work collective.

In 1993 the period in which wages were not paid was relatively long in firms that had made employment cuts (Figure 5.10). This could be interpreted as *prima facie* evidence that not paying wages was a partial alternative to employment cuts, even though non-payment was also associated

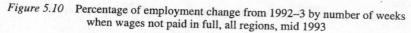

Figure 5.10 Percentage of employment change from 1992–3 by number of weeks when wages not paid in full, all regions, mid 1993

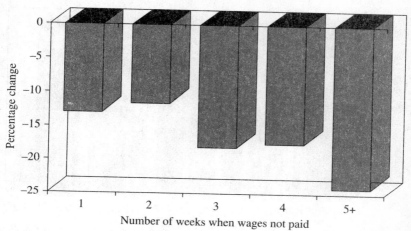

Source: RLFS3, n = 134.

with cutting employment. Between mid 1993 and mid 1994 the average length of time in which wages were unpaid more than doubled.

In sum, there was widespread difficulty in paying wages, a finding that supports the claims made in late 1993 and throughout 1994 by the leadership of the General Federation of Trade Unions (FITUR), among others, that millions of workers had not been receiving the wages due to them.[20] The average wages reported in official statistics should be deflated to take this into account.

In mid 1994 a majority of factories reported that they had experienced difficulty in paying wages – 32.5 per cent had had a chronic problem, 28.9 per cent had experienced some months in which they had had acute difficulty in paying. The most widespread problem was in textiles, garments and engineering. The one industry in which there had not been a problem was food processing, once again highlighting its new-found position of strength. All property forms had experienced difficulty, social organisations by far the most (Figure 5.11). The larger the firm, the more likely the difficulty (Figure 5.12), and those in Ivanovo had had more of a problem than those elsewhere (Figure 5.13).

In a perverse way, the fact that the probability of acute difficulty in paying wages was inversely related to employment change is further evidence that the labour market was functioning (Figure 5.14). Those in most

Figure 5.11   Percentage of establishments with wage arrears, by property form, all regions, mid 1994

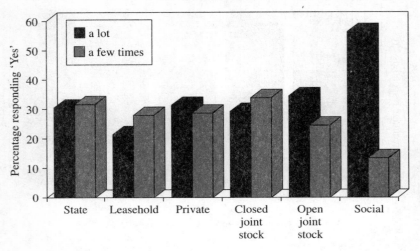

Source: RLFS4, n = 381.

Figure 5.12   Percentage of establishments with wage arrears, by employment size, all regions, mid 1994

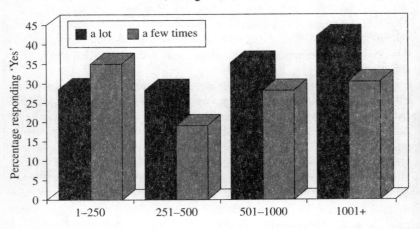

Source: RLFS4, n = 381.

Figure 5.13 Percentage of establishments with wage arrears, by region, mid 1994

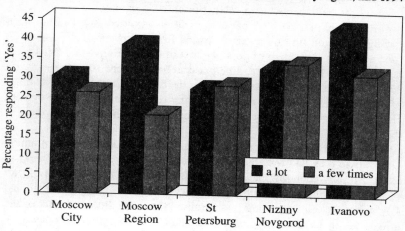

Source: RLFS4, n = 381.

Figure 5.14 Percentage of establishments with wage arrears, by employment change, all regions, mid 1994

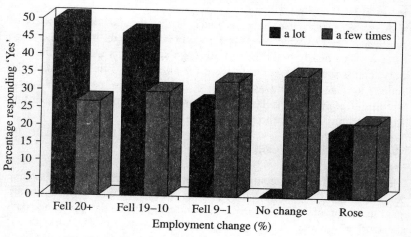

Source: RLFS4, n = 375.

difficulty were making the greatest number of employment cuts, which is what would be expected in a market-oriented economy.

On average, in 1994 47.3 per cent of firms admitted they had not been paying wages on time. The figure varied from a low of 15.4 per cent in food processing to a high of 56.4 per cent in engineering. State firms were more likely to have paid late, 50.3 per cent having done so compared with 37.9 per cent of private firms. The larger the firm, the higher the probability of its paying late. There was also a strong relationship with employment change, and those making cuts were more likely to be in wage arrears to their workers.

When firms were in wage arrears the amount tended to be substantial. On average they had not paid 78 per cent of the wage bill. Particularly in an inflationary economy, late payment is effectively non-payment of part of a worker's earnings. But wage arrears were often really non-payment – in many factories the managers admitted there was little prospect of the arrears being paid.[21] There was also admission of actual non-payment, with no intention or expectation of payment. For all the factories combined, on average 6.4 per cent of wages had not been paid.

In principle voice regulation of wages should be the preserve of the trade union in the enterprise. At the national level, in 1993–4 the main trade unions made a series of protests, including a mass demonstration in October 1994, yet – as will become clear in the next chapter – their role in enterprises was muted.

A related factor, also discussed later, is that the *duration of collective agreements* had become very short, incorporating flexibility into the wage system. Thus nearly two thirds of all wage agreements were for one year only, and a further 21 per cent were for two years. This means that the scope for wage changes was increasing, in part because negotiators would be more likely to build in large wage increases at the outset to compensate for uncertainty and prospective inflation.

Wage flexibility by lay-offs

The rationale for managements to make extensive use of administrative leave in 1994 was clear. First, by putting workers on unpaid or minimally paid leave for a few months the firm avoided having to pay severance pay: the worker's average wage, paid for a period of two or three months. If a worker quit, he or she would lose his or her right to severance pay. If he or she did not quit, and the firm subsequently released him or her, the severance pay would have been much less in real terms, because severance pay was based on the worker's average wage over the previous few months, during which time he or she would have been on leave. In an inflationary context in which average money wages were rising by a considerable amount each month, the average in real terms would have declined even if the firm had calculated it on the basis of the worker's wage when in full-time employment on full pay.

The practice of leave leading to redundancy was quite crude. More subtle was the practice of putting workers on lay-off as a means of lowering the average wage on which the 'excess wage' tax was levied. In mid 1994, according to official *Goskomstat* data, the average (contractual) wage in industry was a little over twice the subsistence minimum. In many firms the actual wage would have been more than six times the minimum wage, and thus liable to the 38 per cent wage tax. Yet by laying off large numbers of their workers they were able to avoid the wage tax. In effect the administrative-leave option allowed managements to increase upward and downward wage flexibility at the same time. As in so many other respects, theoretical policy making was being defeated by institutional realities.

Impoverishment wages

Another, almost unnoticed, aspect of wage flexibility in the Russian labour market of the early 1990s was the growth of a category of workers best described as 'working impoverished'. When firms wished to lower labour costs and the average wage, one way of doing so was to put groups of workers on very low rates of pay. There was little to prevent them from doing this, and it was a convenient way of limiting redundancies.

This phenomenon became apparent during the course of factory visits for RLFS1 and RLFS2 in 1991–2, and the indices of average and occupational wages simply did not show it up. In many factories we were told that some groups of workers were receiving much lower wages than the remainder, even within the same job category. From discussions with managements and workers, it seemed as if the decentralisation and disintegration of the wage tariff system was a primary cause of this development.

Ironically, another contributing factor was the 'excess-wage tax' discussed earlier. One of the justifications given by supporters of this tax was that it would reduce wage differentials by putting a cap on wages, discouraging firms from paying privileged insiders high wages and preventing relatively successful firms from paying much more than others. Hence the irony – the tax actually allowed and encouraged managements to *widen* the differentials in their plant, to give higher wages to highly valued workers and employees and much lower wages to others, simply because the tax was levied on the average wage.

Although there were anecdotal reports of the emergence of very low-paid groups within factories, as of 1993 there were no data. Accordingly in RLFS3 an experimental set of questions was devoted to identifying the lowest-paid groups of workers and employees. These showed that on average the lowest-paid group received 63 per cent of the average wage of manual skilled and unskilled workers, whereas among employees the lowest-paid group received 30.4 per cent of the average monthly salaries of all employees. On average, managerial salaries were over six times the wages received by the lowest-paid groups of workers, a differential accentuated by other forms of payment. Potentially, such wage and earnings differentials might be appropriate as incentives for work performance or labour mobility within and between firms. However wages that were less than one third of the average wage were less than the official subsistence level of income. To the extent that this outcome was due to the excess wage tax, one must lay the charge against it and those who promoted it that it induced impoverishment in employment and hindered employment restructuring by encouraging the alternative managerial option of paying extremely low wages.

A few aspects are worth noting. For all industries combined, in 1993 wage differentiation between the lowest-paid group and the remainder was greater for employees than for workers. But in 1992–3 the lowest-paid workers suffered a deterioration relative to their low-paid counterparts among employees. In mid 1992 the lowest wage averaged 2065 roubles for employees and 1525 for workers, whereas in mid 1993 it averaged 15908 roubles for employees and 10174 for workers. In 1992, among employees the minimum was lower in engineering than in other industries, lower in state enterprises than in other property forms, and relatively low in large firms; whereas among workers the lowest levels were in chemicals and engineering, state enterprises, and factories with more than 500 workers. This pattern changed a little in 1993, when the lowest for both employees and workers were in the metals sector (Figure 5.15), open and closed joint-stock companies and large establishments.

However in 1993 the differential between the lowest-paid group of manual workers and the average wage for such workers was smaller in open and closed joint-stock enterprises than in state enterprises, and the differential was smaller in larger establishments than in large factories. So, for example, in absolute terms the lowest-paid workers in open joint-stock firms were at a disadvantage, but in relative terms, compared with other workers in such firms, they were relatively well off.

In May 1994, according to RLFS4, in all factories the reported minimum for employees averaged 91847 roubles per month, compared with

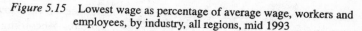

Figure 5.15 Lowest wage as percentage of average wage, workers and employees, by industry, all regions, mid 1993

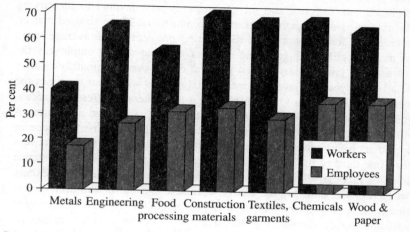

Source: RLFS3, n = 305.

an average for all employees of 171477 roubles.[22] The highest minimum was in food processing, the lowest in textiles and garments. Although there was little variation by property form, the minimum seemed highest in state establishments and lowest in social organisations (Figure 5.16). It was lowest on average in Ivanovo, and much lower in firms that had made employment cuts than in those that had not.

In May 1994 the minimum paid to workers was 44670 roubles monthly (compared with 9514 in May 1993 for the same firms).[23] As in the case of employees, the lowest minimum was in textiles and garments, the highest in food processing. In the firms that were in both rounds of the RLFS, firms in chemicals and engineering had improved their minimum payment compared with other sectors, another indicator of the relative recovery of the engineering sector in 1994, in part due to the new government's more benign approach to that sector. Nevertheless it was in food processing where the minimum was highest. The lowest paid in that sector were receiving over twice as much as the lowest paid in textiles and garments production.

Across property forms, the minimum pay was lowest in social organisations, next lowest in private and highest in closed joint stock. This was as expected, in that firms in which the workers had a high proportion of the shares should have been in a position to prevent the payment of very

Table 5.7 Minimum actual wage as a percentage of the average wage, workers and employees, by industry, mid 1994

| | Employees | | Workers | | | % workers receiving minimum payment | |
	Minimum payment (roubles)	Minimum as % of average	Minimum payment (roubles)	Minimum as % of average		May 1993	May 1994
Metals	91109	72.7	41066	32.8		5.3	18.5
Engineering	84826	60.6	41007	29.3		8.6	12.5
Food processing	147089	82.6	73917	41.5		6.7	8.0
Constr. materials	97273	64.4	50445	33.4		9.1	17.4
Textiles, garments	66850	74.1	31376	34.8		11.3	16.5
Chemicals	89780	64.2	44749	32.0		12.1	16.9
Wood & paper	82817	74.3	38419	34.5		9.2	19.8

Source: RLFS4, n = 384.

Figure 5.16   Lowest wage for workers and employees, by property form, all regions, mid 1994

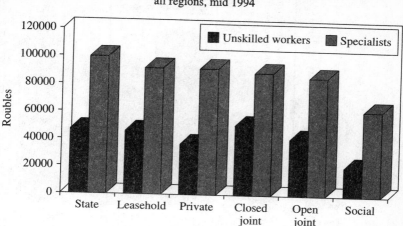

Source: RLFS4, n = 384.

low wages. Regionally, again as expected, the minimum was lowest in factories in Ivanovo.

Perhaps most revealing of the labour-market forces at work, the minimum pay in 1994 was lowest in establishments that had made employment cuts – and the difference between the minimum and average in the firm was greatest in those that had been cutting employment. For instance, for employees (specialists) the lowest paid in firms that had expanded employment were receiving about 50000 roubles more than their counterparts in firms that had cut employment by 10 per cent or more during the previous year. For workers, the corresponding difference was about 22000 roubles.

In mid 1994 no less than 14.3 per cent of all workers were receiving the minimum payment, with only food processing having fewer than 10 per cent (Table 5.7). This meant there had been a sharp increase in the incidence of such wages since May 1993, when 9.2 per cent of workers were receiving the lowest payment. In addition, this substantial minority of workers were only receiving about a quarter of the average wage in the firm, highlighting the radical change in the wage structure from the situation in the 1980s, when the minimum wage was very close to the average wage.

In state establishments only a relatively small proportion of the

Figure 5.17 Percentage of workers receiving minimum payment, by region, mid 1994

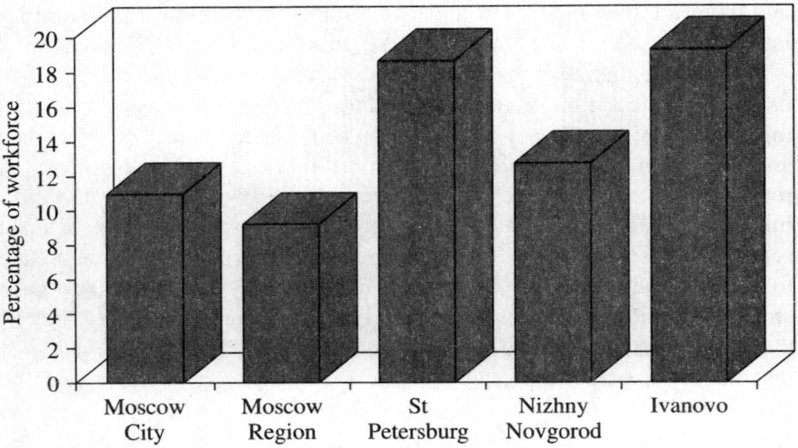

Source: RLFS4, n = 384.

workforces was on the lowest-paid level (perhaps an indication of one means by which property-form restructuring would widen wage differentials). As expected, plants in Ivanovo, besides having the lowest minimum pay, typically had a very high percentage of workers on those minimum payments (Figure 5.17). The rise in the proportion of workers on minimum payments was also greatest in Ivanovo. Also as expected, the proportion of workers on the minimum was much higher in firms that had been cutting employment than in others.

In short, by the mid 1990s the practice of putting groups of workers on very low pay had become a mechanism of wage flexibility, allowing higher wages to be paid to 'insider' groups and in part being a substitute for releasing more workers.

5.4 CONCLUSIONS

The diverse items of information presented in this chapter show that the wage system in Russia during the period studied has become very flexible, even though much of the flexibility is of a perverse and unfortunate kind. And thus we reach the paradoxical explanation for the persistence and intensification of labour surplus – and its associated lack of employment restructuring. There has been *excessive wage flexibility*, excessive in the sense that it has been easy for managements to avoid or reduce wage costs, and therefore they have been under little pressure to remove their surplus labour.

The picture that emerges is of a wage system that is more flexible than its formal structure might imply. The wage tariff remains, yet is of declining relevance; wages are increasingly determined at the decentralised and individual level; bonuses and other flexible non-wage components of remuneration have become a very large proportion of total pay; the minimum wage regulation is of minimal importance, in part because the level set has been so abysmally low; and above all enterprises have been able to put a growing number of workers on extremely low wages, or have simply not paid their workers the wages to which they are entitled. For all these reasons the wage system has become highly flexible, and it is this that largely explains the relatively limited cuts in employment and the huge growth of concealed unemployment documented in the previous chapter. The following chapter briefly examines what has happened to the level and distribution of wages within the industrial labour market.

The conventional approach to explaining the limited cut in employment is incorrect, for it has not been the 'soft budget constraint' (lack of pressure on management) that has put a check on unemployment but the low cost of employment. It is less costly for firms to put workers on unpaid leave or on very low pay than to dismiss them, especially as they can avoid severance pay (three months' average pay) and induce workers to leave 'voluntarily' when they have given up hope of returning to their job. Managements have been quite rational in that respect, and the desirable policy answer is straightforward. Quite simply, *wage contracts should be made more binding*, and both trade unions and the government should take steps to ensure that 'team contracts' are strengthened and enforced. A tightening of contractual regulations, which might be condemned by supply-side economists as a 'rigidity', would actually promote employment flexibility, which is required in the Russian labour market in the second half of the 1990s if enterprise and economic restructuring are to become effective. If employers are obliged to pay the wages they are contractually obliged to pay, then they will not be able to resort to the imposition of unpaid leave and other means of suppressed unemployment, and will either have to try to become more productive or release workers altogether. Only if workers are openly and visibly unemployed can the relevant authorities be expected to respond appropriately with labour-market and unemployment-protection policies.

Another basic message is that distortions in labour markets breed further distortions. The most urgent requirements in the Russian labour market are a stronger set of policies for responding to mass unemployment – which will only emerge if the severity of the situation is recognised – and a reform of the wage determination system, so that it can promote productivity and enterprise restructuring.

In October 1994 the main trade union body, the Federation of Independent Trade Unions of Russia, estimated that enterprises owed workers 5.6 trillion roubles in unpaid wages, which was 38 per cent more than it had been in August that year. Although this referred only to enterprises in which FITUR had representation, it graphically highlights the gravity of the labour-market situation, which was accompanied by real, 'open unemployment' that was much higher than the registered numbers suggested, and by a massive incidence of suppressed unemployment in the form of unpaid leave, short-time working and poverty-level wages.

The non-payment of wages raises questions about International Labour Convention No. 95, which the Russian government has ratified. This is not the place to comment on this convention, other than to note that it requires the regular payment of wages. Yet the really important issue is labour-market and income *security*. What is needed is a rapid move towards effective collective bargaining backed by effective legal redress, not just for the benefit of the workers but to improve the effectiveness of the labour market and facilitate employment restructuring.

This should be accompanied by reform of the 'excess-wage tax', or a tax-based incomes policy. In an effort to limit the rise in wages, as part of the shock-therapy strategy, successive governments have operated a variant of this policy, as advocated by the IMF and the World Bank, *inter alia*. This has encouraged a shift into non-wage forms of remuneration and the use of administrative leave, because putting workers on unpaid leave lowers the average wage for the whole firm, and thus enables it to avoid or limit the wage tax. The tax has encouraged firms to shift into fringe benefits and thus has hindered them from developing the wage mechanism as an incentive and reward for labour productivity. Without productivity growth, economic restructuring will be painfully unrewarding for many years, and without a restructuring of the wage system productivity is unlikely to improve. Can a system of collective bargaining achieve what an administratively operated system has signally failed to achieve?

6 Restructuring and 'De-Levelling' Wages

6.1 INTRODUCTION

The very low money and real wages that characterised the Soviet era contributed to the low productivity, double jobholding and anomic behaviour in the workplace that became symbols of the rottenness of the Soviet system. Between 1991 and 1994 wages rose enormously in nominal terms; they fell drastically in real terms in 1992, though they recovered part of the losses in 1993 and 1994. Yet one should be more wary than some observers have been of reported trends in average wages, as represented by official *Goskomstat* statistics. The main problem with these data is that they relate to contractual or agreed wages, not those actually paid, and as such ignore issues of non-payment and wage arrears, as well as under-the-table payments and payments in kind.

Nominal average wages nearly trebled between late 1993 and late 1994, and the relative ranking by sector changed by much more than one would expect in any market economy, as shown in Table 6.1. To put the figures in better perspective, in November 1994 the national average for all sectors was 2.3 times the officially estimated minimal subsistence income, and in many cases these contractual and estimated wages were well above those that were actually paid.

Turning to manufacturing, as of May 1993, according to RLFS3, the mean average money wage was 34557 roubles per month (about US$35 at the prevailing exchange rate), compared with 3496 roubles in mid 1991, as recorded in the first round of the RLFS.[1] There was a substantial difference between wages and total earnings, the latter including bonuses, incentive payments and other supplements. Thus in May 1993 average earnings were 47250 roubles per month. By May 1994 average wages were 171479 roubles and average earnings were 193767 roubles.[2]

Three general aspects of the changes should be noted. First, because the samples of firms were different, one must be wary of making comparisons, especially as average wages in Moscow City in 1994 were almost twice as high as in Ivanovo, which was not included in earlier rounds of the RLFS. Second, earnings differentials were larger than wage differentials. Taking just those firms that were surveyed in both 1993 and 1994, one finds that

Table 6.1   Average nominal monthly wages, by sector, Russian Federation, 1993–4

	November 1993	November 1994	% of 1994 average	% rise 1993–94
Total economy	101660	281600	—	277
Industry	114200	310600	110.3	272
Construction	147210	390100	138.5	265
Agriculture	53400	133500	47.4	250
Transport	165100	427600	151.8	259
Public health	66130	201700	71.6	305
Education	62064	195500	69.4	315
Culture and art	59940	170800	60.7	300
Banking, insurance	225400	592600	210.4	263
Public administration	110700	326500	115.9	295

Source: *Goskomstat* of the Russian Federation.

whereas average wages rose by 336 per cent, average earnings rose by 400 per cent, implying a relative growth in the more flexible components.

Third, the wages and earnings figures ignore payments in kind. According to RLFS4 data, in the first half of 1994 firms on average 'sold' 0.3 per cent of their output to their workers, ranging from 0.7 per cent in the construction materials sector and 0.5 per cent in food processing to nothing in basic metals and scarcely anything in engineering. Such differences should be borne in mind when making intersectoral comparisons. The share of output sold to workers was highest in closed joint-stock firms, perhaps reflecting the strength of the work collective in such factories.

Presuming the output was sold to workers at subsidised prices, payments in kind represented a form of income, and it is therefore relevant to note that the estimated share of total output disposed of in that way had been cut since 1993. The share of output *given* to workers increased from an insignificant amount in 1993 to 0.3 per cent in the first half of 1994, the beneficiaries being workers in textiles and garments, construction materials and food-processing plants. Output given to workers was greatest in state firms and closed joint-stock firms, and least in private firms. According to responses to identical questions on the extent of total remuneration in non-monetary in-kind payments, the share of output trebled between 1993 and 1994, becoming most widespread in garments and food processing. In the subsample of firms surveyed in both 1993 and 1994, the non-monetary share rose to 3.4 per cent from 0.5 per cent. This reflected the widely reported practice of giving workers output in lieu of

Figure 6.1 Average wages and earnings, by industry, all regions, mid 1993 (average roubles per month for all workers and employees in sector)

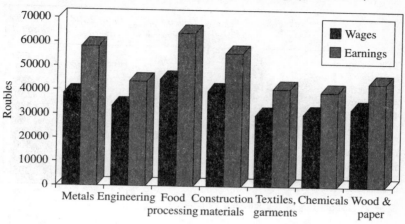

Source: RLFS3, n = 338.

wages. Non-monetary payments rose to about 6 per cent in textiles and garments and to nearly 4 per cent in food processing. Typical of what was happening, a shoe factory in Ivanovo visited several times in 1993 and 1994 was giving workers large boxes of boots to sell on their own account, in lieu of wages, which the firm could not pay.

6.2   INTERINDUSTRY WAGE DIFFERENTIALS

Even so, the most basic change that had occurred by the mid 1990s was in interindustrial wage distribution. This distribution had become more unequal or dispersed since the beginning of the 1990s.[3] The most notable change since the 1980s was that engineering, or heavy industry, was no longer the wage leader. The highest wages and earnings were in food processing, the lowest in textiles and garments (Figure 6.1). This corresponded to the pattern found in the first two rounds of the RLFS.[4] The changes reflect the wage flexibility that emerged in this period.[5] A pattern had emerged in the Russian labour market for wages to be relatively high in sectors associated with raw material processing and relatively low in sectors dependent on modern technology.[6] This probably reflects both productivity factors (due to technological stagnation in Soviet industry in the 1980s, and the excessive labour absorption in engineering-based 'material

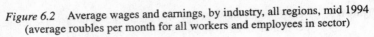

Figure 6.2   Average wages and earnings, by industry, all regions, mid 1994 (average roubles per month for all workers and employees in sector)

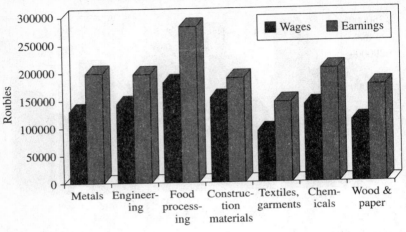

Source: RLFS4, n = 384.

production') and demand factors (low demand for the products of those sectors and a surplus of workers with the skills required by them).

In terms of changes in sectoral wages and earnings between 1993 and 1994 from the sub-sample of 229 firms that were in both rounds of the RLFS, food-processing plants improved their relative position, while engineering and chemicals also recovered a little during that period (Figure 6.2). One reason for those improvements may have been that, as they had the lowest share of earnings coming from bonuses, their wages were relatively sticky in the worsening labour market of 1994.

Substantial regional differences also emerged, and in 1994 there were large gaps between wages in the depressed local labour market of Ivanovo and those in Moscow City (Figure 6.3), which were unlikely to reflect simple differences in costs of living.[7]

Because large, monopolistic enterprises have traditionally been centres of economic and political power in Russia, with an ability to exact privileges from the state, it is not surprising that average wages and earnings were higher in larger establishments (Figure 6.4). However the correlation in 1993 was less pronounced than in 1991 or 1992, and by mid 1994 there was little correlation between size and average wages, although average wages and earnings were lowest in firms with fewer than 250 workers.

If industrial establishments were beginning to respond to market

Figure 6.3 Average wages and earnings, by region, mid 1994 (average roubles per month for all workers and employees in sector)

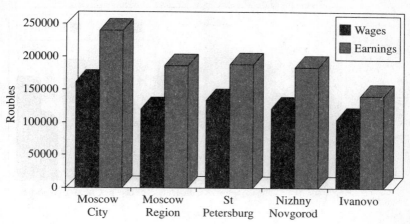

Source: RLFS4, n =384.

Figure 6.4 Average wages and earnings, by employment size, all regions, mid 1993 (average roubles per month for all workers and employees in firm size group)

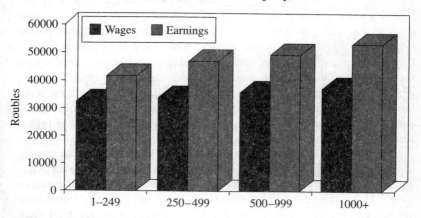

Source: RLFS3, n = 340.

Figure 6.5   Average wages and earnings, by percentage employment change during previous year, all regions, mid 1993 (average roubles per month for all workers and employees in employment change group)

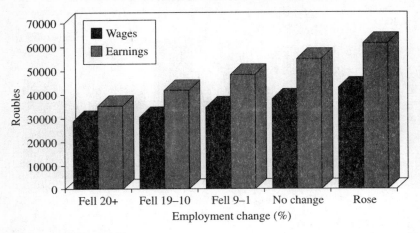

Source: RLFS3, n =337.

pressures, then one would expect that money wages would have risen by less in factories that had cut employment by more than others. In that respect it seemed the labour market was functioning, in that in both 1993 and 1994 average monthly wages were highest in factories that had experienced rising employment and were lowest in those that had cut employment by 20 per cent or more (Figures 6.5 and 6.6). Similarly, in firms where the capacity level of production had risen during the previous year, average wages may have been slightly higher (800 roubles on average) than in those where capacity utilisation had fallen; in terms of average earnings the mean difference was over 1300 roubles.

These relationships were weaker in 1994, when the government seems to have relaxed its financial pressure on enterprises in economic difficulties, or at least signalled that it was doing so. However average earnings rose much more in firms that had experienced rising sales during the previous year (501 per cent) than in those that had experienced a decline, in which average earnings rose by 368 per cent.

As for the impact of enterprise restructuring, there are two aspects of property-form restructuring to consider – ownership and managerial control. Although it has been commonly argued that privatisation will lead to higher wages in Russian industry, one should be wary of assuming this will occur. *A priori*, the relationship is indeterminate. An alternative

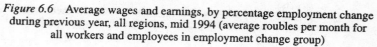

Figure 6.6   Average wages and earnings, by percentage employment change during previous year, all regions, mid 1994 (average roubles per month for all workers and employees in employment change group)

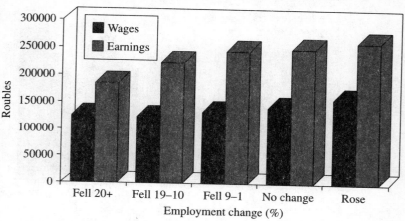

Source: RLFS4, n = 378.

hypothesis is that, with the erosion of the centralised wage tariff system, state-enterprise managements will be the least inclined to hold down wages because of the soft budget constraint, merely borrowing or extending their debt and relying on government agencies to come to their assistance in due course. Conversely the government's attempts to limit wage increases as part of its attempt to curb public expenditure could lead state enterprises to hold down wages more than other enterprises. But offsetting that, private and joint-stock enterprises could be expected to be *more* responsive to market pressures, so although they might exercise greater autonomy in setting wages, the depressed state of the economy could induce them to hold down wages.

In terms of simple correlations, a glance at the data suggests that in 1993 wages and earnings were highest in open joint-stock establishments and relatively low in state and leasehold enterprises (Figure 6.7). In mid 1994, although earnings were still high in open joint-stock firms, they were relatively low in private firms and were highest in the remaining state establishments (Figure 6.8).

Looking at the firms that were in both RLFS3 and RLFS4, one finds that average wages were slightly higher in state-owned firms than in private firms in mid 1994, whereas in mid 1993 wages were lower in state establishments. One difficulty in interpreting these figures is that the number

Figure 6.7   Average wages and earnings, by property form, all regions, mid 1993 (average roubles per month for all workers and employees in property form)

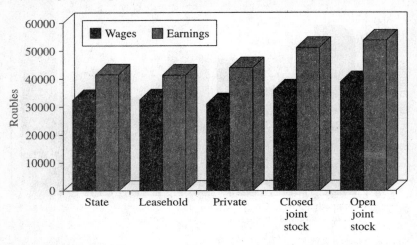

Source: RLFS3, n = 339.

Figure 6.8   Average wages and earnings, by property form, all regions, mid 1994 (average roubles per month for all workers and employees in property form)

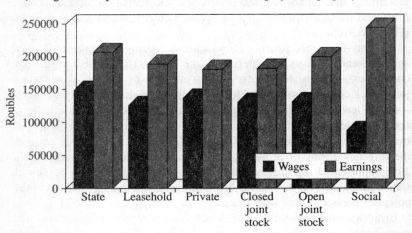

Source: RLFS4, n = 348.

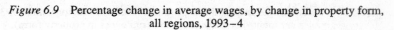

Figure 6.9 Percentage change in average wages, by change in property form, all regions, 1993–4

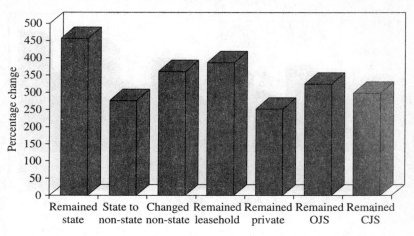

Source: Merged RLFS data, n = 227.

of state-owned firms almost halved during the year, while the number of open joint-stock firms doubled. The average wage increased most in state enterprises that remained state enterprises, and increased least in private firms and those that went from being state enterprises to non-state firms (Figure 6.9).

Property-form restructuring is linked to the changing position of management and workers. Theoretically, the creation of closed joint-stock companies – in which workers hold a majority of 'shares' – and open joint-stock companies – in which they hold a substantial minority of shares – should lead to greater worker control than in cases of what most observers would depict as privatisation, where management and ownership control over the workforce is much greater. However it is debatable whether the different forms of property restructuring of industrial enterprises in 1993 represented real differences for the workforce, given the legacy of state domination and the resultant lack of awareness among workers of the potential pressures they could exert.

Besides ownership, the way in which managements are appointed and reappointed could be expected to make a difference to absolute and relative wages. Moves towards 'economic democracy' within firms, whereby workers periodically vote on management appointments and on a wide range of corporate decisions, have traditionally been criticised as resulting

Figure 6.10   Average wages and earnings, by method of appointing general manager, all regions, mid 1993

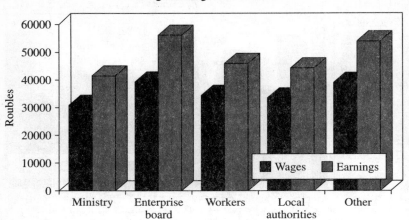

Source: RLFS3, n = 339.

in short-term decision making, whereby the allocation of funds to current wages is given higher priority than investment or enterprise growth, which might raise future wages. This implies that external shareholders would take a longer-term perspective, and that closed joint-stock companies of the type promoted in 1993–4 would pay relatively high wages. However it is equally plausible to argue that workers in a factory in which workers are minority or majority shareholders may have a greater commitment to its survival and growth, and thus be prepared to postpone or forgo wage rises.[8]

Since these were early days in the 'governance restructuring' of Russian industry, it is doubtful whether the destatisation achieved by mid 1994 had led to a substantial growth of economic democracy. Nevertheless average wages and earnings were, if anything, *lower* in factories where top management had been elected by the workers than in those where they had been appointed by an external enterprise board (Figures 6.10 and 6.11).

Thus far the analysis has concentrated on tabulations, which may be affected by the influence of other related factors. Accordingly we estimated wage and earnings functions of the following form:

$$\text{Log.}W, \text{Log. }E = a + b_1\Sigma(\text{IND}) + b_2\Sigma(\text{PROP}) + b_3\Sigma(\text{REG}) + b_4(\%\text{BC})$$
$$+ b_5(\%\text{EMPCH}) + b_6(\text{EMPSIZE}) + b_7(\%\text{FEM}) +$$
$$b_8(\text{PT}) + b_9(\text{SUB}) + b_{10}(\text{PROF}) + b_{11}(\%\text{SALES}) +$$
$$b_{12}(\%\text{UNION}) + e$$

Figure 6.11 Average wages and earnings, by method of appointing general manager, all regions, mid 1994

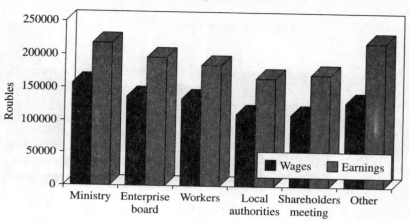

Source: RLFS4, n = 341.

where

log.W	= the average wage in the establishment, in natural logarithm.
log.E	= the average earning in the establishment, in natural logarithm.
Σ(IND)	= a set of binaries (0,1) for the industry of establishment, the omitted reference category being textiles and garments.
Σ(PROP)	= a set of binaries for the property form of establishment, the omitted category being state enterprises.
Σ(CORP)	= a set of binaries for corporate governance forms, as defined earlier, the omitted category being state.
Σ(REG)	= a set of binaries for the regional location of the establishment, Moscow City being the omitted category.
%BC	= percentage of workforce in establishment classified as manual workers.
%EMPCH	= percentage employment change in establishment over past year.
EMPSIZE	= size of establishment in number of workers and employees.
%FEM	= percentage of workforce consisting of women.
PT	= dummy, 1 if firm employed part-timers, 0 otherwise.
SUB	= dummy, 1 if firm was receiving a government subsidy, 0 otherwise.

PROF   = dummy, 1 if firm was operating a profit-sharing pay system,
              0 otherwise.
%SALES   = percentage change in sales in real terms in past year.
%UNION = percentage of workers unionised.
e = error term.

The wage and earnings functions were estimated by means of ordinary least-square regressions. The results for 1993, presented in Table 6.2, show statistically significant inverse relationships between employment change and average wages and earnings, although the quantitative effect is small. The results at least suggest that there was some wage elasticity with respect to changes in employment, and that to some extent the labour market was functioning. The relationship did not emerge from the function estimated with the 1994 data, when, as we saw in Chapter 4, concealed unemployment grew considerably.

Regional factors have influenced wages, regardless of sector, workforce structure and property-form restructuring. In both 1993 and 1994 average wages were significantly lower in Moscow Region and Nizhny Novgorod than in Moscow City, and in 1994 they were also significantly lower in St Petersburg and Ivanovo.

The regressions also show that wages were relatively high in food processing and suggest that other sectoral variations were emerging, with wages in construction materials, metals, engineering and chemicals being relatively high compared with those in wood products and textiles and garments production. The position of food processing is most notable, in that wage costs as a share of production costs were lowest in that sector, despite its having relatively high wages.

The wage regressions also show that, when account is taken of other factors, property-form differences did not appear to exist.[9] This might reflect the nature of the changes, or it might reflect the fact that the restructuring had been too recent to have much effect. However, for reasons mentioned earlier, there may not be a simple direct relationship at all.

More intriguingly, the results for both 1993 and 1994 show that the operation of some profit-sharing payment system was *inversely* related to the average wage, perhaps highlighting that mechanism's role in creating greater wage flexibility in response to the economic performance of the establishment.

It is worth stressing which factors were not significant. Employment size was no longer significant in 1994, which might point to the declining monopolistic power of the large factories. Whether sales in real terms had increased or decreased over the previous year made no difference to

Table 6.2 Log. average wages and average earnings, 1993–4 (OLS regression coefficients)

Variable	Log. average wages/93	Log. average earnings/93	Log. average wages/94	Log. average earnings/94
(Constant)	4.7846	4.8803	2.0974	2.1181
Industry				
Metals	0.0403	0.0654	0.1278**	0.1614**
Engineering	-0.0116	-0.0055	0.1131***	0.0923*
Food processing	0.1491***	0.1517***	0.2878***	0.2935***
Construction materials	0.1087*	0.1113*	0.0967*	0.0769
Chemicals	-0.0552	-0.0574	0.1372***	0.1464***
Wood & paper	0.0239	0.0149	0.0097	0.0341
Property form				
Leasehold	-0.0162	-0.0359	-0.1037*	-0.1004
Private	0.0182	0.0219	-0.0743*	-0.0179
Closed joint stock	0.0257	0.0287	-0.0184	-0.0072
Open joint stock	0.0408	0.0393	-0.0185	0.0028
Social	N/A	N/A	-0.1830***	-0.0506
Region				
Moscow Region	-0.0954***	-0.0692	-0.1138***	-0.1069***
St Petersburg	-0.0313	-0.0267	-0.1081***	-0.0874***
Nizhny Novgorod	-0.0795***	-0.0657*	-0.1380***	-0.1181***
Ivanovo	N/A	N/A	-0.1872***	-0.1997***

Table 6.2 Cont'd

Variable	Log. average wages/93	Log. average earnings/93	Log. average wages/94	Log. average earnings/94
Employment size	0.00002***	0.00003***	0.0000	0.0000
% manual workers	-0.0005	-0.0008	0.0025**	0.0025*
% women	-0.0012	-0.0007	-0.0013*	-0.0011
Part-timers	-0.0154	-0.0108	0.0150	0.0252
Subsidy	0.0080	0.0149	0.0826*	0.0352
Profit sharing	-0.0596**	-0.0816***	-0.0632***	-0.0668**
% sales change	0.0001	0.0001	0.0000	0.0000
% emp. change	0.0012**	0.0022***	0.0003*	0.0002
% unionisation	-0.0665	-0.0520	-0.0447	-0.0034
R^2	0.2477	0.2407	0.3865	0.3058
F	4.2354	4.0781	7.3231	5.1211

* Statistically significant at the 10% level of probability.
** Statistically significant at the 5% level.
*** Statistically significant at the 1% level.

Note: N/A = not applicable, since Ivanovo not included.
Source: RLFS3, n = 348.

average wages or earnings, even controlling for the influence of 'structural' factors. This may change, and perhaps ought to change.[10]

Also, receipt of a government subsidy was not associated with above-average wages. Here there may be a problem of causation. It could be that those enterprises under pressure to cut wages obtained subsidies to enable them to keep them at the level found in otherwise comparable enterprises. So we should perhaps consider the impact of subsidies as *at most* preventing wages from falling.

Finally, the lack of any effect of union presence suggests that trade unions have remained part of management and as intermediaries responsible for the disbursement of social benefits rather than a collective bargainer pushing for higher wages. At least it would seem most unreasonable to blame unions for wage rises in Russian industry.

6.3   OCCUPATIONAL WAGES

In the context of the slow erosion of the centralised wage tariff system and the gradual decentralisation of wage determination, one could hypothesise that relative wages and earnings *within firms* would widen, especially when one recalls the previous 'Leninist' bias in favour of manual labour.

Wage data were collected for seven occupational categories, and although one has to bear in mind that occupational wage variations would have existed within such rather broadly defined categories, the data do provide a picture of the evolution of occupational wages and earnings. We will concentrate on the top category.

According to RLFS3, in May 1993 managerial salaries averaged 59239 roubles a month for the whole sample, ranging from a high of nearly 83000 in food processing to a low of just over 51000 in engineering, a pattern quite unlike that found in most countries, or what prevailed during the Soviet era. The pattern surely reflected the severe depression that had hit the military–industrial complex in 1992–3, as well as the previous heavy overemphasis on engineering, and its military bias. In 1993–4 managers in engineering improved their position, probably reflecting the softening of industrial policy under the new government. Nevertheless managers in food processing continued to earn substantially more than their counterparts in other industrial sectors.

Although to a lesser extent than in 1993, in 1994 managerial salaries were positively related to size of establishment, in terms of number of workers. This too had been a feature of the old regulated system, and is

Figure 6.12   Average earnings for managers, by percentage sales change during previous year, all regions, mid 1993 (average monthly earnings in roubles in size category)

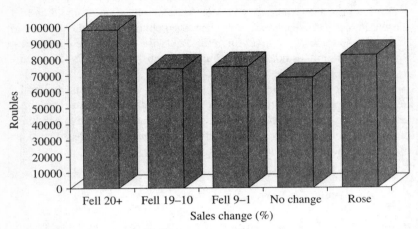

Source: RLFS3, n = 348.

relevant to the widely reported resistance by managerial groups to enterprise restructuring (break-ups), which should be regarded as crucial for the success of economic reform. Under the Soviet system the status-based approach to wage determination meant that size of enterprise was a primary determinant of managerial earnings, and this acted as a barrier to employment planning and cutting. This tendency continued into the mid 1990s. Significantly, for other occupational groups there was no relationship between size of firm and average wages.

To be effective as a mechanism for motivation and reward, managerial salaries should be positively related to profitability and economic performance. On this issue it seems there was little change in the early 1990s. In 1993 and 1994, as Figures 6.12 and 6.13 show, *managerial salaries were not linked to sales performance*, although in 1994 earnings were much lower in establishments in which sales had really slumped (by over 30 per cent). In 1993 they were positively correlated with employment change, being much higher in establishments in which employment had risen over the past year and lowest in those that had cut employment by over 20 per cent (Figure 6.14). This latter pattern did not apply in 1994, even though managerial salaries continued to be highest in firms that had expanded employment (Figure 6.15).

Local labour-market factors have had a differentiating influence on

Figure 6.13 Average earnings for managers, by percentage sales change during previous year, all regions, 1994 (average monthly wage in establishments with given sales change)

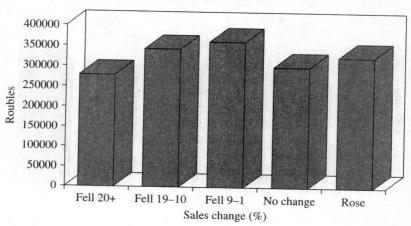

Source: RLFS4, n = 384.

Figure 6.14 Average earnings for managers, by percentage employment change during previous year, all regions, mid 1993 (average monthly earnings in roubles in size category)

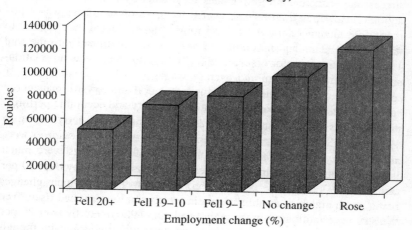

Source: RLFS3, n = 348.

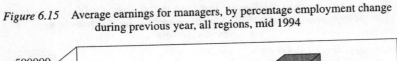

Figure 6.15   Average earnings for managers, by percentage employment change during previous year, all regions, mid 1994

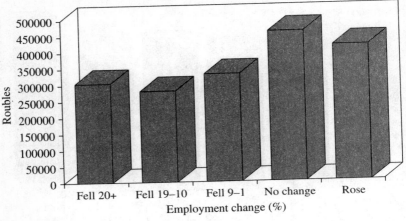

Source: RLFS4, n = 384.

managerial salaries, which tended to be higher in Moscow City than in the other regions in 1993. Intriguingly, in 1994 they were highest of all in Nizhny Novgorod, nearly twice as high as those in Ivanovo. One anticipates that such regional differences will grow in the next few years, as regional disparities in economic prosperity and growth widen.[11]

In 1993 managers seemed to be earning higher salaries in open joint-stock enterprises – and to a lesser extent in closed joint-stock companies – than in state enterprises (Figure 6.16). But in 1994 the managers of the remaining state enterprises were earning relatively high salaries, almost certainly reflecting the changing composition of the remaining state enterprises, selected for their strategic significance. Managers in closed joint-stock companies were on average receiving significantly less than their counterparts in open joint-stock companies, and both groups were receiving substantially less than those in private firms (Figure 6.17).

In 1993 there was also a tendency for managers to be relatively better paid in those factories where they had been appointed by an enterprise board, compared with those in which they had been appointed by a sectoral ministry, local authority or the work collective (Figure 6.18). In 1994 the relationship was clouded by the changing composition of state enterprises (Figure 6.19), yet managers appointed by enterprise boards were still receiving more than those appointed by workers – on average about 24000 roubles per month in wages and 36000 in terms of earnings. But in mid

Figure 6.16 Average earnings for managers, by property form, all regions, mid 1993 (average monthly earnings in roubles in property-form group)

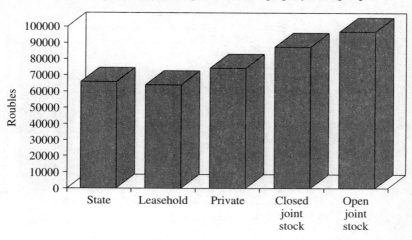

Source: RLFS3, n = 348.

Figure 6.17 Average earnings for managers, by propenty form, all regions, mid 1994 (average monthly earnings in roubles in property-form group)

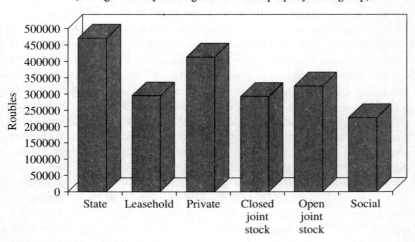

Source: RLFS4, n = 384.

Figure 6.18 Average earnings for managers, by method of appointing general manager, all regions, mid 1993 (average monthly earnings in roubles in appointing group)

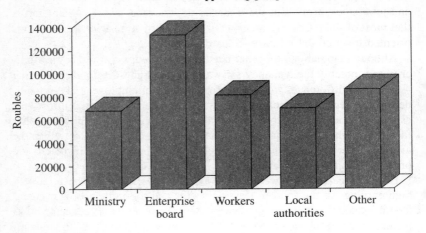

Source: RLFS3, n = 348.

Figure 6.19 Average earnings for managers, by method of appointing general manager, all regions, mid 1994 (average monthly earnings in roubles in appointing group)

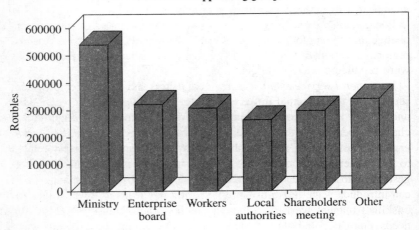

Source: RLFS4, n = 384.

1994 the highest average salaries for managers were paid to those who had been appointed by ministries. There are several possible explanations for this. It might have been due to a tendency to underreport more in private and joint-stock firms. But that issue aside, the most likely explanation is that most of the remaining managers appointed by ministries were in firms oriented towards the military–industrial complex.

Although tabulations for other occupational groups showed some similarity to – notably the tendency for wages to be highest in food processing – and some differences from those for managerial employees, the remainder of this section focuses on the results of occupational wage functions, estimated in an attempt to tease out the relationships controlling for other factors, in which the dependent variable was the logarithm of either the average wage or the earnings for the occupational category. The results are presented in Tables 6.3 and 6.4.

For *managerial employees*, multivariate analysis reveals the relatively high earnings in the food processing sector and the influence of regional labour markets, and shows that when controlling for the influence of other factors, average wages were positively related to size of establishment, supporting the view that because size is related to management incomes, managers in Russian industry have fought to preserve their establishments as large-scale units. Their salaries were also positively related to changes in employment. Note that sales performance does not seem to have had any effect on managerial salaries. As emphasised earlier, this will have to change if a dynamic competitive economy is to evolve.

For *specialist employees*, salaries were positively linked to employment change and to employment size of establishment, as well as to sector and regional location, further suggesting that local labour market conditions were producing wage differentiation.

For *general service employees*, regional factors and sector of employment seem to be the principal influences, whereas for *supervisory, technicians* and *skilled workers* employment size of establishment and employment change appear to be the main differentiating factors. For *unskilled workers*, the most striking result is that wages were strongly inversely related to the existence of some sort of profit-sharing pay mechanism. This suggests that, to the extent that it represents a means by which management can introduce wage flexibility, profit-sharing pay leads to lower wages for unskilled manual workers, although not for other categories. This issue needs more detailed study.[12] The implication is that the growing wage flexibility could widen inequality.

Two general findings should give rise to concern. First, unlike the comparable findings in 1991 and 1992, in 1993 the wages of all occupational

Table 6.3 Occupational wages, mid 1993

Variable	Managers	Specialists	Gen. service	Supervisors	Technicians	Skilled workers	Unskilled workers
(Constant)	5.1178	4.8198	4.5680	4.9896	4.8919	4.9002	4.5751
Industry							
Metals	−0.0439	−0.0372	−0.1179	0.0156	−0.0384	−0.0516	0.0143
Engineering	−0.1694**	−0.1190*	−0.1304*	−0.0845	−0.1526**	−0.0641	−0.1038
Food processing	0.1133**	0.1146**	0.1367**	0.1292***	0.1004**	0.0996**	0.1961***
Constr. materials	−0.0815	−0.0170	−0.0490	−0.0130	−0.0595	0.0341	0.0001
Chemicals	−0.0816	−0.0187	−0.0110	−0.0622	−0.0488	−0.0855	−0.0616
Wood & paper	−0.0972	−0.0131	−0.0633	−0.0644	−0.0814	−0.0926	−0.1271
Property form							
Leasehold	0.0514	−0.0135	−0.0166	0.0003	−0.0428	−0.0592	−0.1037
Private	−0.0463	−0.0435	−0.0541	−0.0525	−0.0558	−0.0551	−0.0668
Closed joint stock	0.0008	0.0055	−0.0165	0.0001	−0.0297	−0.0054	−0.0172
Open joint stock	0.0523	0.0547*	0.0303	0.0609*	0.0434	0.0210	0.0065
Region							
Moscow Region	−0.0964**	−0.1106**	−0.1013**	−0.1076**	−0.1091**	−0.1319***	−0.0875
St Petersburg	−0.0559	−0.0748**	−0.0846**	−0.0623*	−0.0764**	−0.0184	−0.0072
Nizhny Novgorod	−0.1090***	−0.0912***	−0.1278***	−0.0863**	−0.0846**	−0.0887***	−0.0754*

Employment size	0.00003***	0.00002**	0.00002*	0.00002**	0.00002**	0.00002**	0.00003**
% manual workers	0.0063***	0.0061***	0.0068***	0.0055***	0.0066***	0.0043**	0.0045*
% women, 1993	−0.0036***	−0.0029**	−0.0025*	−0.0027**	−0.0032***	−0.0034***	−0.0024*
Part-timers	−0.0228	−0.0014	−0.0282	0.0014	0.0065	−0.0022	−0.0122
Subsidy	−0.0258	0.0148	−0.0287	0.0177	0.00003	0.0049	−0.0166
Profit sharing	−0.0154	−0.0337	−0.0387	−0.0295	−0.0232	−0.0393	−0.0938**
% sales change, 1992–3	0.0001	0.0001	0.0001	0.0001	0.0001	0.0001*	0.00002
% emp. change, 1992–3	0.0016**	0.0018**	0.0015*	0.0019***	0.0016**	0.0015**	0.0018**
% unionisation	−0.2604**	−0.2666**	−0.1809	−0.2930**	−0.3006**	−0.2321**	−0.1887
R^2	0.3682	0.3960	0.3481	0.3679	0.3698	0.3461	0.3739
F	4.5038	5.0664	4.1256	4.4791	4.5340	4.0890	4.6137

* Statistically significant at the 10% level of probability.
** Statistically significant at the 5% level.
*** Statistically significant at the 1% level.
Source: RLFS3, n = 348.

Table 6.4 Occupational earnings, mid 1993

Variable	Managers	Specialists	Gen. service	Supervisors	Technicians	Skilled workers	Unskilled workers
(Constant)	5.1401	4.7580	4.4832	4.9965	4.8349	4.9010	4.5155
Industry							
Metals	-0.0206	0.0061	-0.0373	0.0430	0.0083	-0.0310	0.0649
Engineering	-0.1670**	-0.1061	-0.1078	-0.0763	-0.1340*	-0.0633	-0.0626
Food processing	0.1591**	0.1537***	0.1777***	0.1772***	0.1449**	0.1328**	0.2302***
Constr. materials	-0.0722	0.0030	-0.0171	-0.0020	-0.0424	0.0441	0.0276
Chemicals	-0.0679	0.0119	0.0293	-0.0358	-0.0148	-0.0587	-0.0036
Wood & paper	-0.1023	-0.0145	-0.0600	-0.0635	-0.0888	-0.0705	-0.1311
Property form							
Leasehold	0.0903	0.0365	0.0324	0.0536	0.0130	-0.0292	-0.0830
Private	0.0088	-0.0114	-0.0171	0.0018	-0.0225	-0.0303	-0.0354
Closed joint stock	0.0495	0.0454	0.0236	0.0509	0.0105	0.0241	0.0215
Open joint stock	0.0748*	0.0752*	0.0514	0.0892**	0.0732*	0.0441	0.0354
Region							
Moscow Region	-0.1004*	-0.1184**	-0.1053*	-0.1102**	-0.1091**	-0.1136**	-0.0586
St Petersburg	-0.0572	-0.0749*	-0.0843***	-0.0607	-0.0716*	-0.0038	0.0067
Nizhny Novgorod	-0.1112**	-0.0957**	-0.1264***	-0.0909**	-0.0843**	-0.0697*	-0.0680

Employment size	0.00003***	0.00002**	0.00002*	0.00003**	0.00002**	0.00002**	0.00003**
% manual workers	0.0073***	0.0069***	0.0074***	0.0063**	0.0075***	0.0048**	0.0047*
% women, 1993	-0.0045***	-0.0034**	-0.0027*	-0.0034**	-0.0037***	-0.0038***	-0.0024
Part timers	-0.0115	0.0065	-0.0197	0.0080	0.0174	-0.0116	-0.0223
Subsidy	-0.0190	0.0208	-0.0177	0.0077	0.0005	0.0001	0.0015
Profit sharing	-0.0285	-0.0359	-0.0389	-0.0359	-0.0291	-0.0490	-0.1063***
% sales change, 1992–3	0.0001	0.0001	0.0001	0.0001	0.0001	0.0002*	0.0001
% emp. change, 1992–3	0.0022**	0.0025***	0.0023***	0.0026***	0.0025***	0.0023***	0.0027***
% unionisation	-0.2449	-0.2166	-0.1252	-0.2564*	-0.2509*	-0.1840	-0.1351
R^2	0.3539	0.3916	0.3533	0.3599	0.3855	0.3478	0.3861
F	4.2325	4.9735	4.2217	4.3440	4.8468	4.1207	4.8602

* Statistically significant at the 10% level of probability.

** Statistically significant at the 5% level.

*** Statistically significant at the 1% level.

Source: RLFS3, n = 348.

groups except unskilled workers were lower the higher the percentage of women in the factory workforce. This raises the issue of the changing position of women in Russian industry, which will be analysed in Chapter 9. Second, whether or not the workers were represented by a trade union made no difference to the level of wages of any group, and in the analysis this applied irrespective of whether the independent variable used was presence of a trade union or the percentage of workers unionised. Indeed the sign of the regression coefficient is negative for all groups and weakly statistically significant for higher-level manual workers. Had there been a situation of strong independent trade unions bargaining for workers, one would have expected the regression coefficients to be positive and highly significant.[13] The results lend substance to the view that trade unions have continued to be part of management or are concerned with social issues rather than wage bargaining, an issue considered in the next chapter.

Property form of establishment seemed to make little difference to some occupational wage levels, although there was a weak positive impact associated with open joint-stock enterprises for high-grade, higher-status groups. This weak relationship may be due to the fact that most non-state enterprises had only recently changed property form, or it may be due to the limited nature of the changes.[14] However the overall results point to a widening of wage differentials linked to property-form restructuring.

The comparable results for 1994 indicate the following relationships:

1. *Managerial employees*: as for 1993, managerial wages were highest in food processing. Regional labour markets remained influential, with much lower wages in Ivanovo and Nizhny Novgorod than in Moscow or St Petersburg. It seems that the higher the percentage of women in the workforce, the less administrative employees earned. No other variable is statistically significant, suggesting that size of firm was no longer a major determinant of managerial salaries. If that were the case, it was weakening one factor causing the industrialist lobby to resist enterprise restructuring.

2. *Specialist employees*: sectoral and regional factors are significant, with food processing paying high wages, and Ivanovo and Nizhny Novgorod paying lower wages. Those in open joint-stock firms earned more than those in state factories; the more women in the firm, the lower the wage; and the higher the percentage of manual workers, the higher the earnings of specialist employees.

3. *General service*: the most notable result for this group is that the coefficients for open joint-stock and closed joint-stock firms are negative and significant, while receipt of a subsidy is positively related

to the wage paid. Regional differences are as for other groups, and the coefficient for food processing is also positive and significant.

4. *Supervisors*: wages are positively related to working in food processing and chemicals, and the regional variations are as for other groups. No other factor is significant, again highlighting the declining relevance of factory size. In the earnings function, the higher the percentage of manual workers, the higher the earnings of supervisors.

5. *Technicians*: the results are similar to those for supervisors, although working in wood products in 1994 was also associated with higher wages and the coefficients for open and closed joint-stock companies are negative and significant, suggesting that wage differentials within the manual workforce were more limited in those property forms. The existence of profit sharing was associated with lower earnings.

6. *Skilled production workers*: the results for this group are the most indicative of the evolving labour market in 1994. Sectorally, the coefficients are positive and significant for food processing and engineering. Regionally, the coefficients for Ivanovo, Nizhny Novgorod and Moscow Region are all negative. And most pertinently, the coefficient is negative and significant for open joint-stock companies, again suggesting that the intermediate form of property restructuring was reducing wages.

7. *Unqualified workers*: the most notable result for unqualified workers is that this is the only group for which sales changes seem to have made a difference. If sales had declined, then wages were relatively low. Otherwise the positive coefficients for food processing and chemicals are significant, and the regional variables are as for other groups. Property form *per se* is not significant.

We can conclude that interfirm variations in occupational wages were linked to structural factors such as location of enterprise, employment change and industrial sector. To that extent, a labour market was operating, although one may expect that property form, union strength and economic performance will have more significant influences in the near future.

6.4 OCCUPATIONAL WAGE DIFFERENTIALS

For many years, occupational wage differentials in Soviet industry were apparently narrow and subject to the rhetoric of 'levelling'.[15] Although the differentials were distorted more than levelled, a narrowing of wage differentials was part of the ideology of the Soviet labour system. There is

Table 6.5 Wage ratio of occupational groups compared with unskilled workers, by industry, all regions, mid 1993

Industry	Managerial	Specialist	Gen. service	Supervisory	Technician	Skilled
Metals	3.54	2.01	1.21	2.84	2.07	1.78
Food processing	3.73	2.24	1.33	2.94	1.67	2.40
Constr. materials	2.94	1.80	1.32	1.82	1.30	1.57
Textiles, garments	3.34	2.22	1.42	2.69	1.86	2.23
Chemicals	3.84	2.35	1.72	2.98	1.69	1.95
Wood & paper	3.91	2.63	1.51	3.13	2.00	2.13
Engineering	3.79	2.75	1.53	2.82	1.65	2.33

Source: RLFS3. These refer to wage ratios; earnings ratios were generally wider.

Table 6.6 Wage ratio of occupational groups compared with unskilled workers, by industry, all regions, mid 1994

Industry	Managerial	Specialist	Gen. service	Supervisory	Technician	Skilled
Metals	3.65	2.44	1.58	2.78	1.99	2.63
Engineering	4.20	1.98	1.32	2.99	1.83	2.23
Food processing	3.25	2.23	1.52	2.26	1.81	1.79
Constr. materials	3.04	1.96	0.79	2.42	1.55	1.90
Textiles, garments	4.14	2.62	3.13	3.41	2.47	2.08
Chemicals	4.01	2.10	1.73	3.28	2.24	1.79
Wood & paper	4.17	2.47	1.65	3.24	2.02	2.12

Source: RLFS4, n = 348.

also some evidence that wage differentials *within* sectors were modest in the early 1980s.[16] Developments since the 1980s have become increasingly controversial.

The basic hypothesis is that as a result of the decline of the wage tariff system, property restructuring and the drift to more individualised, 'flexible' wage determination, *occupational wage differentials have widened rapidly and considerably.*

Within industrial firms, according to RLFS3, wage differentials between occupational categories had widened since the first two rounds of the RLFS in 1991 and 1992.[17] For instance, whereas managers on average earned salaries that were 2.4 times the wages of unskilled workers in 1991, the results for 1993 suggest that they were earning 3.6 times as much. According to RLFS4, this continued to be the differential in 1994, which almost certainly understated the actual figure, since the higher the status of the group, the more likely was an underestimate of earnings. For other occupational categories, the differential between them and unskilled workers also increased between 1991 and 1993–4.[18] However this stabilisation reflected the change in the sample. For those firms included in both 1993 and 1994, wage differentials widened during the two years.

There was intersectoral variation, with occupational differentials in 1993 being greatest in wood and paper production and least in construction materials (Table 6.5). The big change against the upward trend was in food processing, and if that sector were excluded, it can be seen that in all other sectors the managerial-to-unskilled worker differential continued to widen in 1993–4 (Table 6.6). Differentials widened most in sectors that had been hit hardest in 1993–4, most notably textiles and garments.

Differentials tended to be much wider in labour-intensive firms where the labour-cost share of production costs was relatively high. In 1993 there was no apparent difference by size of establishment, but in 1994 workers in unskilled jobs had evidently suffered particularly acutely in larger firms, for in all cases the wage ratio was highest in large firms (Tables 6.7 and 6.8).

One might interpret the finding that wage differentials were wider in factories in which employment had fallen as evidence that wage elasticities were greater for workers than for managerial and administrative employees (Figures 6.20 and 6.21). In other words, the labour market was working more for workers than for employees.

Occupational wage differentials were wider in firms outside Moscow, and in 1994 were widest in the depressed labour market of Ivanovo, where managerial wages, for example, were six times the average wages of unskilled production workers, and where skilled production workers

Table 6.7 Wage ratio of occupational groups compared with unskilled workers, by employment size, all regions, mid 1993

Employment size	Managerial	Specialist	Gen. service	Supervisory	Technician	Skilled
1–250	3.44	2.25	1.17	2.49	1.09	2.19
251–500	3.81	2.40	1.66	2.96	1.80	2.17
501–1000	3.37	2.11	1.50	2.59	1.92	1.91
1001+	3.55	2.08	1.44	2.72	2.06	2.01

Source: RLFS3, n = 348.

Table 6.8 Wage ratio of occupational groups compared with unskilled workers, by employment size, all regions, mid 1994

Employment size	Managerial	Specialist	Gen. service	Supervisory	Technician	Skilled
1–250	2.96	1.70	1.27	2.21	1.63	1.68
251–500	2.91	1.83	1.34	2.28	1.35	1.66
501–1000	3.06	1.94	1.13	2.64	1.94	1.80
1001+	4.37	2.25	2.16	3.23	2.07	2.18

Source: RLFS4, n = 348.

Figure 6.20   Ratio of managerial to unskilled wages, by percentage employment change during previous year, all regions, mid 1993

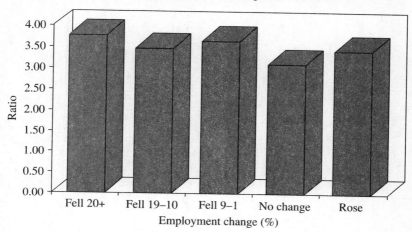

Source: RLFS3, n = 305.

Figure 6.21   Ratio of managerial to unskilled wages, by percentage employment change during past year, all regions, mid 1994

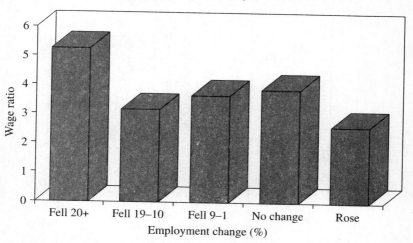

Source: RLFS4, n = 348.

Table 6.9 Wage ratio of occupational groups compared with unskilled workers, by property form, all regions, mid 1993

Property form	Managerial	Specialist	Gen. service	Supervisory	Technician	Skilled
State	3.66	2.36	1.42	2.68	1.55	2.18
Leasehold	3.89	2.08	1.53	2.87	1.87	2.32
Private	3.69	2.40	1.51	2.98	1.41	2.02
Closed joint stock	3.29	2.10	1.32	2.65	1.47	2.08
Open joint stock	3.51	2.16	1.46	2.61	1.90	1.99

Source: RLFS3, n = 242.

Table 6.10 Wage ratio of occupational groups compared with unskilled workers, by property form, all regions, mid 1994

Property form	Managerial	Specialist	Gen. service	Supervisory	Technician	Skilled
State	5.09	1.66	1.15	2.61	1.22	1.83
Leasehold	3.62	1.93	1.29	2.36	1.99	1.52
Private	3.57	3.12	0.85	3.25	2.98	2.16
Closed joint stock	2.77	1.78	1.98	2.40	1.61	1.55
Open join stock	3.72	2.12	1.34	2.95	2.09	2.07
Social	3.94	2.67	1.98	3.13	2.26	1.82

Source: RLFS4, n = 348.

were receiving three times the wages of the unskilled. In effect, regional disparities in labour-market conditions influenced average wages and widened differentials within occupational groups. This is further indication of the existence of labour-market flexibility.

As for the effect of property form, in both 1993 and 1994 differentials were relatively small in closed joint-stock enterprises. Although one must be sceptical about its extent, implicit economic democracy may have played a role in limiting the growth of wage differentials between workers and management in such firms. They were smaller there than in any other type of firm (Tables 6.9 and 6.10). There was also evidence that the differentials were much narrower where the corporate governance form was worker-controlled.

This result may be stronger than it seems. There have been anecdotal reports that managerial salaries have been severely understated following the growth of the unregulated private economy and the decentralisation and weakening of the old wage-tariff, wage-fund system.[19] This understatement would probably be much less in firms in which workers were major shareholders, although the limiting effect of their 'voices' has probably been small, so far. However it may be because the wages and salaries of higher-level employees were held down by a perception of *relatively* strong worker control (or constraint), and that average wages were actually lower in factories where workers were able to vote on management appointments. This is worth emphasising, since it raises questions about the widespread view that 'worker control' leads to higher wages. By limiting wage differentials, the reverse could be the reality.

In most cases wage differentials continued to widen in 1993–4, with technicians gaining most relative to unqualified workers. The wages of managerial and specialist employees improved relative to those of unskilled workers, in large but not in small firms. The ratio of managerial to unskilled workers' wages seems to have been greater in firms that cut employment, suggesting that wage elasticity with respect to employment was much greater for unskilled workers than for managerial employees. A similar relationship emerged for the wage differential between supervisors and unskilled workers. These results would not surprise students of industrial labour markets in recession in other countries.

6.5   ENTERPRISE-BASED SOCIAL BENEFITS

Finally, we turn to one of the most complex aspects of the remuneration system in Russian industry. Since social benefits were largely enterprise-based in the Soviet system, industrial establishments came to provide a wide array of benefits. These were distributed or operated mainly by the trade unions, and comprised a large share of total remuneration.[20] Most were 'universal benefits' in the sense that they were, in principle, an entitlement for all employees and workers, although their distribution was commonly based on discretionary decisions by managements and union officials.

In moving away from a command economy, the system of social protection must shift away from enterprises on to the state, in the interest of social equity and efficiency. It was one of the great mistakes of the early period of reform in 1991–2 that no direct action was taken to restructure social policy by transferring social functions from enterprises to local authorities and/or special agencies. Indeed a paradox was that the tax-based incomes policy had the effect of encouraging firms to shift away from money wages to non-wage forms of remuneration and benefits, because they were not subject to the punitive tax that ordinary wages almost inevitably involved.

Consequently it was not surprising that (according to the various rounds of the RLFS) there was a shift from the wage funds to social development funds in the 1990–2 period and that in both 1991–2 and 1992–3 the social-cost share of production costs rose in Russian factories. This applied to almost all sectors, size categories of establishment and property forms, as illustrated for 1992–3 in Figures 6.22–6.24. Besides benefits, many large

Figure 6.22   Social-cost share of production costs, by industry,
all regions, 1992–3

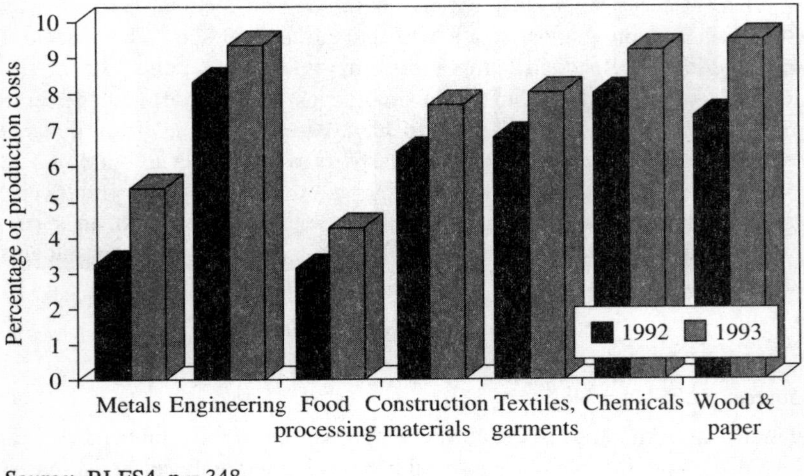

Source: RLFS4, n = 348.

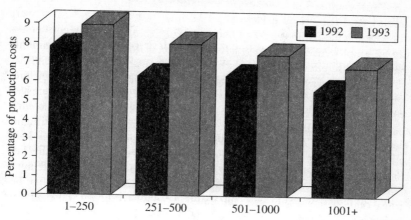

Figure 6.23   Social-cost share of production costs, by employment size, all regions, 1992–3

Source: RLFS4, n = 348.

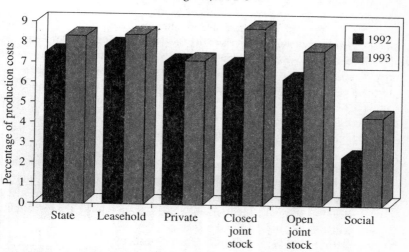

Figure 6.24   Social-cost share of production costs, by property form, all regions, 1992–3

Source: RLFS4, n = 348.

industrial enterprises operated their own agricultural holding. In 1991 over 10 per cent of the factories included in RLFS1 had farms, including more than two in five large firms.

Despite these short-term trends, there were strong signs that, under pressure to cut costs and commercialise their activities, firms were beginning to curtail the range of benefits provided for workers and employees, although entitlements remained extraordinarily broad. At least in terms of the range of benefits, they were provided almost as much to regular workers as to employees, and the only group formally disentitled to many benefits were casual and contract workers.

Since it can be expected that non-regular workers will comprise a growing share of employment, as in other countries, the shift to such 'flexible' categories will in itself be associated with an erosion of entitlement to enterprise benefits, and may accentuate one of the worst phenomena of the Russian labour market: the polarisation or fragmentation of the workforce into those receiving secure incomes and a wide range of social benefits and entitlements and those with very low wages and limited access to social benefits. In 1994 it was simply too easy for labour economists to assert that workers were prepared to take wage cuts because they had access to enterprise benefits. That may have been true to some extent, but it is just as likely that many of those pushed into low-wage casual employment were denied access to those benefits as well.

Between 1993 and 1994 there was the beginning of what may become known as the great withering away of the Russian 'social enterprise'. In 1993, according to RLFS3, industrial establishments were continuing to provide a broad range of benefit entitlements, and in the main these were provided to regular workers to the same extent as to managerial employees (Table 6.11 and Appendix 6.1).[21] Only for casual or contract workers were benefit entitlements restricted.

Among the patterns of benefit entitlement suggested by the statistics were:

1. Workers and employees in engineering and textiles and garments had a lower probability of entitlement to most benefits than those in other sectors. This implies that benefit distribution was broadening interindustrial earnings inequality, since the sectors having fewer benefits were also relatively low-wage sectors.
2. Non-regular workers had a much lower probability of receiving benefits, although they were relatively less disadvantaged in the case of sickness benefit, bonuses, subsidised food and subsidised consumer goods.
3. Benefits were generally less likely to be provided in small establishments with up to 250 workers, although beyond that size there were only minor differences, with only a few of the benefits being much

Table 6.11 Benefit entitlement, by worker category, all regions, mid 1993
(percentage of establishments providing specified benefit)

Benefit	Admin. workers	Regular workers	Non-regular workers
Paid vacation	100.0	100.0	39.8
Additional vacation	48.7	69.6	10.3
Rest house	67.3	67.3	10.3
Sickness benefit	99.1	99.1	65.5
Paid health services	49.6	50.1	18.9
Subsidised rent	13.3	15.0	2.9
Subsidies for kindergarten	48.1	49.0	12.1
Bonuses	85.0	84.7	44.2
Profit sharing	65.7	65.4	19.2
Loans	92.0	92.0	24.8
Retirement assistance	76.1	76.4	12.4
Supplementary pension	9.4	9.7	1.2
Possibility for training	75.2	77.9	20.1
Subsidised food	34.5	34.8	23.3
Subsidy for canteen or benefit for meal	61.7	62.8	41.0
Subsidised consumer goods	21.2	21.2	14.5
Transport subsidies	34.2	34.5	16.6

Source: RLFS3, n = 338.

    more likely to be found in large units, notably health services, subsidised kindergartens and access to training.

4. There was little evidence that property-form restructuring had led to any widespread erosion of the provision of benefits, but for some benefits workers in joint-stock enterprises were more likely to be entitled to them, notably health services and subsidised food.

5. Privatised firms were less likely than state enterprises to be providing subsidised housing for workers.

6. Establishments in sectors paying relatively high wages tended to be providing benefits to a greater extent than those in sectors where wages were relatively low, implying that benefits were a means by which income inequality was being intensified.

Between 1993 and mid 1994 a substantial number of firms ceased to provide certain benefits. In particular, whereas in 1993 over two thirds of firms provided employees and workers with access to rest houses or holiday homes, in mid 1994 less than half did so, and only one in five private firms. There was even some erosion of the provision of sickness benefit. Above all, far fewer firms were providing subsidised food or canteen

Table 6.12   Benefit entitlement, by worker category, all regions, mid 1994
(percentage of firms providing specified benefit)

Benefits	Admin. workers	Regular workers	Non-regular workers
Paid vacation	99.7	99.5	48.6
Additional vacation	47.9	65.9	18.6
Rest house	44.8	44.5	20.7
Sickness benefit	93.0	93.5	55.9
Paid health services	51.0	51.3	28.1
Subsidised rent	15.6	16.4	5.8
Subsidies for kindergarten	44.8	45.3	19.2
Bonuses	72.1	72.7	41.5
Profit sharing	66.1	65.6	27.8
Loans	81.8	82.3	37.6
Retirement assistance	73.2	73.4	24.4
Supplementary pension	7.0	7.0	2.4
Possibility for training	50.3	51.8	18.9
Subsidised food	18.5	18.8	11.1
Subsidy for canteen or benefit for meal	51.3	53.1	31.5
Subsidised consumer goods	9.9	9.9	7.6
Transport subsidies	30.2	31.8	14.4
Unpaid shares	25.3	25.3	7.1

Source: RLFS4, n = 348.

meals, and even the ubiquitous 'company store' was less likely to provide consumer goods at subsidised prices (Tables 6.12 and 6.13). There was also a polarisation between large and smaller factories. For instance in mid 1992 workers were more than twice as likely to have access to holiday homes if they worked, for a firm with more than 500 workers than those working for a smaller one, and were also much more likely to have subsidised meals, kindergartens and paid health services.

It was a little surprising that in mid 1994 non-regular workers were more likely to be entitled to a few benefits than in 1993 (Table 6.14). One can only speculate about the reason for this, which may not stand up to later scrutiny. It may reflect a growing tendency for firms to put more workers in an intermediary category of insecure employment with partial benefits; or it could reflect a composition change, due to some firms ceasing to employ casual workers while others had started to employ such workers.

There was flexibility even here. Some factories had added new benefits over the previous year, the main items being subsidised food, shares and transport. However, in comparison with early rounds of the RLFS, in 1993–4 more firms had cut some benefits (28 per cent) than had added some. In terms of the main benefits cut, over 9 per cent had dropped the provision

Table 6.13 Benefit entitlement, by worker category, all regions, mid 1993
(merged sample of factories; percentage providing benefit)

Benefit	Admin. workers	Regular workers	Non-regular workers
Paid vacation	100.0	100.0	38.4
Additional vacation	46.7	71.2	8.3
Rest house	65.1	65.1	10.0
Sickness benefit	100.0	100.0	67.2
Paid health services	48.9	49.8	19.7
Subsidised rent	11.8	14.0	2.2
Subsidies for kindergarten	50.2	51.5	12.7
Bonuses	82.1	81.7	40.2
Profit sharing	67.7	67.2	20.5
Loans	91.7	91.7	23.1
Retirement assistance	76.9	77.3	12.7
Supplementary pension	9.6	10.0	1.7
Possibility for training	75.5	77.3	21.8
Subsidised food	33.2	33.2	21.8
Subsidy for canteen or benefit for meal	62.0	63.8	40.6
Subsidised consumer goods	21.0	21.0	13.5
Transport subsidies	34.5	34.5	17.1

Source: RLFS3, n = 229.

Table 6.14 Benefit entitlement, by worker category, all regions, mid 1994
(merged sample of factories; percentage providing benefit)

Benefit	Admin. workers	Regular workers	Non-regular workers
Paid vacation	99.6	99.6	53.3
Additional vacation	46.3	69.4	22.0
Rest house	45.0	45.0	22.5
Sickness benefit	93.0	93.9	61.7
Paid health services	54.6	54.6	31.3
Subsidised rent	15.3	16.6	6.2
Subsidies for kindergarten	41.5	42.4	21.6
Bonuses	75.9	77.3	50.2
Profit sharing	69.9	69.9	32.2
Loans	84.3	84.3	41.9
Retirement assistance	78.2	78.6	29.5
Supplementary pension	7.9	7.9	2.2
Possibility for training	51.5	54.6	21.1
Subsidised food	19.7	19.7	13.3
Subsidy for canteen or benefit for meal	55.0	56.8	35.7
Subsidised consumer goods	9.6	9.6	9.3
Transport subsidies	31.4	33.2	18.5

Source: RLFS4, n = 229.

of subsidised food, 3.1 per cent had dropped subsidised vacations and 2.9 per cent had dropped the provision of subsidised consumer goods.[22]

What will be the consequences for social protection of an effective enterprise restructuring strategy? If large enterprises were broken into smaller units, the pattern of benefits suggests that this would lead to a general narrowing of the range of enterprise benefits, since most forms of benefit are less likely to be provided in factories with fewer than 250 workers, and the cost burden is probably larger in small units. Among those surveyed, although the differences in probability of entitlement between factories of different sizes were small for most benefits, in some cases, as in the provision of training opportunities and access to subsidised rent for accommodation, the differences were substantial. So size restructuring could be expected to accelerate the decline in enterprise benefits.

What about the longer-term effect of property-form restructuring? There must be a high probability that this will be associated with increasing differentiation, as well as a decline in the range of benefits and enterprise expenditure on them.[23] One would expect that state firms will continue to provide a wide range of benefits, although fiscal pressures may force them to cut back. One would expect smaller private firms to reduce their benefit provision and shift towards greater reliance on those that involve workers paying partly or wholly for them. And one would expect that closed joint-stock enterprises, and to a lesser extent open joint-stock enterprises, would provide the widest range, in view of the potentially powerful voice of worker–shareholders in such firms. Although it was too early for it to be conclusive evidence, in 1994 it seemed as if in most cases closed joint-stock firms did have the highest probability of providing benefits, as Tables 6.15–6.17 indicate. There was also a suggestion that the corporate governance structure will make a difference, since in most cases the probability of entitlement to a benefit seemed highest in worker-controlled structures (Tables 6.18–6.20).

Benefits were most likely to be cut in value terms if enterprise restructuring involved both size restructuring and property-form restructuring, since the share of production costs devoted to social expenditure was highest in state enterprises and had risen most in state factories compared with those that had restructured in property terms. Although to some extent this may reflect the type of enterprise that had restructured or some behavioural change associated with restructuring, the data suggest that enterprise restructuring will accelerate the withering of enterprise benefits. It will be essential for local authorities to take over the provision of many of these, and it was apparent in factory revisits in late 1994 in Ivanovo and Nizhny Novgorod that to some extent this was beginning to happen. Factories had to turn from being social institutions to being commercial

Table 6.15   Benefit entitlements for management, by property form,
all regions, mid 1994

Property form	State	Lease	Private	CJS	OJS	Social
Paid vacation	100.0	100.0	100.0	100.0	99.4	100.0
Additional vacation	43.8	35.7	46.3	45.8	50.3	87.5
Rest house	37.0	42.9	26.8	47.6	49.4	87.5
Sickness benefit	89.0	92.9	95.1	91.7	94.5	100.0
Paid health services	41.1	42.9	43.9	58.3	54.3	50.0
Subsidised rent	11.0	7.1	17.1	21.4	15.9	0.0
Subsidies for kindergarten	41.1	35.7	43.9	52.4	45.1	12.5
Bonuses	69.9	64.3	56.1	78.6	73.6	87.5
Profit sharing	45.2	21.4	61.0	81.0	73.2	62.5
Loans	74.0	64.3	82.9	86.9	83.5	87.5
Retirement assistance	69.9	71.4	43.9	77.4	81.1	50.0
Supplementary pension	6.8	14.3	4.9	9.5	5.5	12.5
Possibility for training	42.5	57.1	31.7	63.1	51.2	50.0
Subsidised food	15.1	14.3	12.2	20.2	20.2	37.5
Subsidy for canteen or benefit for meal	38.4	50.0	39.0	53.6	59.1	50.0
Subsidised consumer goods	5.5	7.1	12.2	11.9	10.4	12.5
Transport subsidies	32.9	42.9	22.0	34.5	27.4	37.5
Unpaid shares	1.4	21.4	9.8	42.9	32.5	0.0

Source: RLFS4, n = 229.

Table 6.16   Benefit entitlements for regular workers, by property form,
all regions, mid 1994

Property form	State	Lease	Private	CJS	OJS	Social
Paid vacation	100.0	100.0	100.0	100.0	98.8	100.0
Additional vacation	58.9	57.1	51.2	66.7	72.0	87.5
Rest house	35.6	42.9	26.8	47.6	49.4	87.5
Sickness benefit	89.0	92.9	95.1	92.9	95.1	100.0
Paid health services	41.1	42.9	46.3	58.3	54.3	50.0
Subsidised rent	11.0	7.1	17.1	21.4	17.7	0.0
Subsidies for kindergarten	42.5	35.7	46.3	53.6	44.5	12.5
Bonuses	69.9	64.3	58.5	78.6	74.4	87.5
Profit sharing	43.8	21.4	61.0	81.0	72.6	62.5
Loans	74.0	64.3	82.9	88.1	84.1	87.5
Retirement assistance	69.9	71.4	43.9	77.4	81.7	50.0
Supplementary pension	6.8	14.3	4.9	9.5	5.5	12.5
Possibility for training	45.2	57.1	36.6	61.9	52.4	62.5
Subsidised food	15.1	14.3	14.6	20.2	20.2	37.5
Subsidy for canteen or benefit for meal	38.4	50.0	41.5	56.0	61.6	50.0
Subsidised consumer goods	5.5	7.1	12.2	11.9	10.4	12.5
Transport subsidies	32.9	42.9	31.7	34.5	28.7	37.5
Unpaid shares	0.0	21.4	9.8	42.9	31.9	0.0

Source: RLFS4, n = 229.

Table 6.17   Benefit entitlements for non-regular workers, by property form, all regions, mid 1994

Property form	State	Lease	Private	CJS	OJS	Social
Paid vacation	43.1	30.8	43.9	58.3	47.9	62.5
Additional vacation	15.3	23.1	14.6	16.7	20.2	50.0
Rest house	18.1	15.4	12.2	23.8	21.5	50.0
Sickness benefit	52.8	38.5	46.3	63.1	56.4	75.0
Paid health services	16.7	23.1	22.0	34.5	31.3	37.5
Subsidised rent	0.0	0.0	9.8	6.0	8.0	0.0
Subsidies for kindergarten	9.7	15.4	19.5	26.2	20.2	12.5
Bonuses	34.7	30.8	36.6	48.8	41.7	62.5
Profit sharing	15.3	7.7	26.8	35.7	30.7	37.5
Loans	29.2	7.7	36.6	47.0	38.7	50.0
Retirement assistance	19.4	0.0	17.1	27.4	29.4	12.5
Supplementary pension	0.0	0.0	2.4	2.4	3.1	12.5
Possibility for training	16.7	15.4	9.8	21.7	20.9	25.0
Subsidised food	5.6	15.4	7.3	13.1	12.3	25.0
Subsidy for canteen or benefit for meal	20.8	23.1	14.6	34.5	38.7	50.0
Subsidised consumer goods	1.4	7.7	4.9	9.5	9.9	12.5
Transport subsidies	12.5	15.4	12.2	14.3	16.6	0.0
Unpaid shares	0.0	0.0	0.0	13.1	9.9	0.0

Source: RLFS4, n = 229.

Table 6.18   Benefit entitlements for management, by corporate governance, all regions, mid 1994

Corporate governance	Emp.	Worker	Private	State
Paid vacation	98.9	100.0	100.0	100.0
Additional vacation	44.8	51.0	46.9	42.9
Rest house	46.6	47.3	37.5	39.0
Sickness benefit	89.8	94.5	96.9	89.6
Paid health services	50.0	53.4	59.4	41.6
Subsidised rent	15.9	19.2	14.1	11.7
Subsidies for kindergarten	36.4	51.4	48.4	41.6
Bonuses	77.3	72.4	65.6	70.1
Profit sharing	67.0	77.4	65.6	44.2
Loans	81.8	84.2	84.4	74.0
Retirement assistance	79.5	75.3	65.6	70.1
Supplementary pension	4.6	6.2	9.4	9.1
Possibility for training	47.7	59.6	40.6	44.2
Subsidised food	18.4	20.5	15.6	15.6
Subsidy for canteen or benefit for meal	45.5	64.4	43.8	39.0
Subsidised consumer goods	8.0	11.6	12.5	6.5
Transport subsidies	28.4	32.9	20.3	33.8
Unpaid shares	28.7	34.9	28.1	3.9

Source: RLFS4, n = 374.

Table 6.19 Benefit entitlements for regular workers, by corporate governance, all regions, mid 1994

Corporate governance	Emp.	Worker	Private	State
Paid vacation	97.7	100.0	100.0	100.0
Additional vacation	67.0	68.5	65.6	58.4
Rest house	45.5	47.9	37.5	37.7
Sickness benefit	90.9	95.2	96.9	89.6
Paid health services	50.0	53.4	60.9	41.6
Subsidised rent	17.0	20.5	14.1	11.7
Subsidies for kindergarten	36.4	51.4	50.0	42.9
Bonuses	75.0	74.0	68.8	70.1
Profit sharing	65.9	77.4	65.6	42.9
Loans	81.8	84.9	85.9	74.0
Retirement assistance	80.7	75.3	65.6	70.1
Supplementary pension	4.6	6.2	9.4	9.1
Possibility for training	46.6	59.6	46.9	46.8
Subsidised food	18.4	20.5	17.2	15.6
Subsidy for canteen or benefit for meal	46.6	67.1	46.9	39.0
Subsidised consumer goods	8.0	11.6	12.5	6.5
Transport subsidies	29.5	33.6	26.6	33.8
Unpaid shares	27.6	34.9	28.1	5.2

Source: RLFS4, n = 374.

Table 6.20 Benefit entitlements for non-regular workers, by corporate governance, all regions, mid 1994

Corporate governance	Emp.	Worker	Private	State
Paid vacation	48.9	50.7	47.6	42.7
Additional vacation	21.6	17.1	17.5	16.0
Rest house	21.6	22.6	14.3	18.7
Sickness benefit	59.1	54.8	54.0	53.3
Paid health services	30.7	30.1	31.7	17.3
Subsidised rent	6.8	8.2	6.3	0.0
Subsidies for kindergarten	18.2	23.3	22.2	10.7
Bonuses	43.2	43.2	39.7	36.0
Profit sharing	30.7	31.5	28.6	14.7
Loans	44.3	37.2	39.1	28.0
Retirement assistance	33.0	24.0	22.2	18.7
Supplementary pension	2.3	2.7	3.2	0.0
Possibility for training	18.2	21.4	15.9	17.3
Subsidised food	12.6	12.3	9.5	6.7
Subsidy for canteen or benefit for meal	29.5	39.0	25.4	21.3
Subsidised consumer goods	6.9	9.6	9.5	2.7
Transport subsidies	13.6	17.1	11.1	13.3
Unpaid shares	10.3	11.0	3.2	0.0

Source: RLFS4, n = 374.

concerns, but there was a need to ensure that social benefits were not needlessly removed altogether.

6.6   CONCLUSIONS

This chapter has tried to provide a broad picture of the evolving wage pattern in Russian industry, and it is appropriate to conclude by noting that although the RLFS made a great effort to solicit correct and thorough data on wages and earnings, one should be cautious about their accuracy. An abuse of statistics and a desire to conceal information from the authorities were features of the old system, and there are reasons to believe that official labour statistics suffer from many shortcomings, particularly in sensitive areas, including wages.

When asked to suggest the main cause of low labour efficiency, only 8 per cent of managements cited low wages, behind inadequate supplies of materials (23.4 per cent), poor equipment (18 per cent) and difficulty of selling their output (18 per cent).[24] Only 10.7 per cent gave low wages as the second main factor. This seems to symbolise the lack of perception of any link between wages, incentives and productivity, which should be a key issue in efforts to reform the wage system. Nevertheless wages are more flexible than is widely believed and are certainly not rigidly based on the wage tariff system. And whatever the perceived cause of low labour efficiency, the main means of trying to raise it was to raise wages, according to 44 per cent of the managers.

The picture that emerges from the RLFS is that by the mid 1990s wages had started to become responsive to market forces, wage differentials had widened, earnings differentials had widened even more, and wage flexibility had become potentially considerable. This combination of developments supports the view that, whatever the number of presidential decrees and other regulations issued, by 1993–4 the Russian labour market had become flexible and was operating to widen inequalities.

One implication of the emerging flexibility is that wage taxes and wage regulations will remain ineffectual, and are likely to have perverse effects, adding new forms of distortion. Another implication is that the most promising form of wage policy, in terms of efficiency and equity, would be one based on multilayered collective bargaining, as long as it is conducted by independent trade unions and employers and goes with a wholesale restructuring of the large enterprises that in 1993–4 still dominated the industrial landscape. In both respects – independent collective bargaining and enterprise restructuring – there is a long way to go.

APPENDIX 6.1 PERCENTAGE OF FIRMS PROVIDING SPECIFIED BENEFITS FOR EMPLOYEES AND WORKERS, 1993

Table A6.1 Types of benefit provided for management, by industry, all regions, mid 1993

Benefit	Metals	Engineering	Food proc.	Constr. materials	Textiles, garments	Chemicals	Wood & paper
Paid vacation	100.0	100.0	100.0	100.0	100.0	100.0	100.0
Additional vacation	100.0	52.2	53.5	60.0	33.9	58.3	59.4
Rest house	62.5	61.4	82.5	66.7	68.3	75.0	75.0
Sickness benefit	100.0	98.3	100.0	100.0	100.0	100.0	100.0
Paid health services	71.4	56.5	56.6	56.0	52.8	69.6	44.8
Subsidised rent	16.7	10.2	21.7	25.0	19.2	19.0	16.7
Subsidies for kindergarten	57.1	41.7	68.3	66.7	52.6	50.0	53.3
Bonuses	75.0	83.3	87.7	88.5	80.6	83.3	93.8
Profit sharing	87.5	58.9	81.4	66.7	77.0	77.3	67.7
Loans	100.0	90.0	92.3	84.6	93.5	92.0	100.0
Retirement assistance	100.0	73.5	81.7	79.2	87.5	76.0	90.3
Supplementary pension	40.0	8.0	14.6	26.3	6.7	19.0	9.7
Possibility for training	85.7	74.1	80.6	72.0	85.0	87.5	68.8
Subsidised food	83.3	27.6	60.7	65.2	23.9	31.8	40.6
Subsidy for canteen or benefit for meal	71.4	64.3	83.3	75.0	64.8	86.4	46.9
Subsidised consumer goods	50.0	21.6	33.3	38.1	26.1	30.0	12.9
Transport subsidies	66.7	42.6	38.0	45.0	43.4	23.8	31.3

Source: RLFS3, n = 338.

Table A6.2   Types of benefit provided for regular workers, by industry, all regions, mid 1993

Benefit	Metals	Engineering	Food proc.	Constr. materials	Textiles, garments	Chemicals	Wood & paper
Paid vacation	100.0	100.0	100.0	100.0	100.0	100.0	100.0
Additional vacation	100.0	75.4	70.7	80.0	58.6	83.3	75.0
Rest house	62.5	61.4	82.5	66.7	68.3	75.0	75.0
Sickness benefit	100.0	98.3	100.0	100.0	100.0	100.0	100.0
Paid health services	71.4	56.5	58.5	56.0	52.8	69.6	48.3
Subsidised rent	16.7	12.2	23.9	25.0	23.1	22.7	16.7
Subsidies for kindergarten	57.1	42.6	68.3	66.7	54.4	54.2	53.3
Bonuses	75.0	83.3	87.7	88.5	79.0	83.3	93.8
Profit sharing	87.5	58.9	81.4	66.7	77.0	72.7	67.7
Loans	100.0	90.0	92.3	84.6	93.5	92.0	100.0
Retirement assistance	85.7	74.4	81.7	79.2	87.5	80.0	90.3
Supplementary pension	66.7	8.0	14.6	26.3	6.7	19.0	6.5
Possibility for training	85.7	75.2	83.9	80.0	83.6	95.8	71.9
Subsidised food	83.3	27.6	62.3	65.2	24.4	31.8	40.6
Subsidy for canteen or benefit for meal	71.4	66.1	83.3	76.0	64.8	90.9	46.9
Subsidised consumer goods	50.0	21.6	33.3	38.1	26.1	30.0	12.9
Transport subsidies	66.7	43.0	40.0	47.4	45.3	23.8	28.1

Source: RLFS3, n = 338.

Table A6.3 Types of benefit provided for non-regular workers, by industry, all regions, mid 1993

Benefit	Metals	Engineering	Food proc.	Constr. materials	Textiles, garments	Chemicals	Wood & paper
Paid vacation	33.3	38.5	37.9	42.3	57.1	50.0	45.2
Additional vacation	20.0	15.1	7.5	20.0	9.4	4.8	9.7
Rest house	0.0	13.2	11.1	8.7	12.7	20.0	3.2
Sickness benefit	83.3	69.4	60.3	61.5	80.7	81.8	75.0
Paid health services	40.0	26.5	22.4	12.5	26.5	15.8	13.8
Subsidised rent	0.0	3.2	4.3	5.0	4.1	0.0	6.7
Subsidies for kindergarten	0.0	14.9	18.9	13.0	15.4	4.8	12.9
Bonuses	66.7	45.1	49.1	56.0	47.4	38.1	53.1
Profit sharing	66.7	21.9	19.6	26.1	21.8	10.5	20.0
Loans	66.7	26.1	26.3	19.2	32.1	27.3	19.4
Retirement assistance	20.0	13.9	11.8	8.7	21.6	13.6	10.0
Supplementary pension	16.7	1.0	0.0	5.3	2.3	0.0	0.0
Possibility for training	33.3	22.6	18.9	20.8	27.3	20.0	21.9
Subsidised food	80.0	18.6	43.6	43.5	16.3	25.0	31.3
Subsidy for canteen or benefit for meal	66.7	47.1	58.8	60.0	42.0	47.6	31.3
Subsidised consumer goods	40.0	14.3	20.8	19.0	22.7	27.8	12.9
Transport subsidies	60.0	21.2	28.3	20.0	18.4	5.6	15.6

Source: RLFS3, n = 338.

Table A6.4 Types of benefit provided for management, by employment size, all regions, mid 1993

Benefit	1–250	251–500	501–1000	1001+
Paid vacation	100.0	100.0	100.0	100.0
Additional vacation	44.9	56.3	56.1	54.4
Rest house	50.9	74.2	77.2	87.0
Sickness benefit	100.0	97.9	100.0	100.0
Paid health services	41.3	53.8	61.5	78.5
Subsidised rent	8.4	24.0	17.0	19.3
Subsidies for kindergarten	40.4	57.0	52.7	66.7
Bonuses	81.0	89.5	79.7	89.9
Profit sharing	65.5	70.7	78.6	70.1
Loans	86.3	93.7	98.3	94.2
Retirement assistance	73.0	87.9	82.7	80.9
Supplementary pension	11.6	11.9	10.9	12.9
Possibility for training	66.4	83.3	75.0	92.8
Subsidised food	31.2	46.8	47.9	38.7
Subsidy for canteen or benefit for meal	54.6	76.8	71.7	77.8
Subsidised consumer goods	15.5	32.9	27.7	32.8
Transport subsidies	32.3	54.4	37.3	35.5

Source: RLFS3, n = 338.

Table A6.5 Types of benefit provided for regular workers, by employment size, all regions, mid 1993

Benefit	1–250	251–500	501–1000	1001+
Paid vacation	100.0	100.0	100.0	100.0
Additional vacation	62.7	77.3	77.2	81.2
Rest house	50.9	74.2	77.2	87.0
Sickness benefit	100.0	97.9	100.0	100.0
Paid health services	43.3	53.8	61.5	78.5
Subsidised rent	9.5	24.0	19.1	25.9
Subsidies for kindergarten	40.4	59.3	52.7	68.2
Bonuses	81.0	89.5	78.0	89.9
Profit sharing	65.5	69.5	78.6	70.1
Loans	86.3	93.7	98.3	94.2
Retirement assistance	73.9	89.0	82.7	79.4
Supplementary pension	10.5	11.9	12.8	14.5
Possibility for training	69.3	84.6	80.4	92.8
Subsidised food	31.2	48.1	47.9	39.3
Subsidy for canteen or benefit for meal	55.6	78.0	71.7	79.7
Subsidised consumer goods	15.5	32.9	27.7	32.8
Transport subsidies	32.3	54.4	36.0	39.3

Source: RLFS3, n = 338.

Table A6.6   Types of benefit provided for non-regular workers, by employment size, all regions, mid 1993

Benefit	1–250	251–500	501–1000	1001+
Paid vacation	47.7	41.2	38.9	44.4
Additional vacation	7.1	8.6	15.1	21.0
Rest house	6.1	9.6	7.8	27.0
Sickness benefit	68.9	71.6	70.4	74.2
Paid health services	15.8	17.8	20.4	42.6
Subsidised rent	4.4	4.1	2.2	3.5
Subsidies for kindergarten	9.5	11.3	13.7	26.2
Bonuses	43.4	46.1	41.5	64.1
Profit sharing	22.3	20.3	26.0	20.6
Loans	29.0	23.3	21.2	33.8
Retirement assistance	19.0	13.6	6.3	14.5
Supplementary pension	2.2	1.5	2.2	0.0
Possibility for training	15.8	22.5	23.1	33.8
Subsidised food	22.8	28.0	33.3	33.3
Subsidy for canteen or benefit for meal	37.1	50.6	48.0	60.9
Subsidised consumer goods	13.2	19.7	17.8	25.4
Transport subsidies	18.9	27.0	10.4	24.1

Source: RLFS3, n = 338.

Table A6.7 Types of benefit provided for management, by property form, all regions, mid 1993

Benefit	State	Leasehold	Private	Closed joint st.	Open joint st.
Paid vacation	100.0	100.0	100.0	100.0	100.0
Additional vacation	52.3	34.6	50.0	55.6	54.5
Rest house	64.7	74.1	69.0	70.3	74.4
Sickness benefit	100.0	100.0	100.0	98.5	98.9
Paid health services	51.0	55.6	44.4	59.7	63.2
Subsidised rent	14.9	24.0	16.7	15.8	15.1
Subsidies for kindergarten	47.2	30.8	66.7	50.0	62.8
Bonuses	86.6	81.5	84.4	81.5	86.3
Profit sharing	53.2	74.1	90.0	88.7	69.7
Loans	86.6	96.3	87.5	97.0	95.8
Retirement assistance	79.6	74.1	77.8	82.8	82.2
Supplementary pension	9.6	24.0	12.5	9.4	12.2
Possibility for training	78.1	66.7	75.0	74.2	84.8
Subsidised food	26.7	40.7	34.6	49.2	48.8
Subsidy for canteen or benefit for meal	60.2	64.0	50.0	71.7	82.8
Subsidised consumer goods	20.0	20.0	32.0	26.3	32.9
Transport subsidies	38.0	30.8	37.0	43.3	43.6

Source: RLFS3, n = 338.

Table A6.8 Types of benefit provided for regular workers, by property form, mid 1993

Benefit	State	Leasehold	Private	Closed joint st.	Open joint st.
Paid vacation	100.0	100.0	100.0	100.0	100.0
Additional vacation	73.2	65.4	65.6	71.4	78.9
Rest house	64.7	74.1	69.0	70.3	74.4
Sickness benefit	100.0	100.0	100.0	98.5	98.9
Paid health services	52.1	55.6	44.4	59.7	64.4
Subsidised rent	17.9	24.0	20.8	17.5	16.4
Subsidies for kindergarten	49.1	34.6	66.7	50.0	62.8
Bonuses	85.7	81.5	84.4	81.5	86.3
Profit sharing	53.2	74.1	86.7	88.7	69.7
Loans	86.6	96.3	87.5	97.0	95.8
Retirement assitance	79.6	77.8	74.1	82.8	83.3
Supplementary pension	10.5	20.0	12.5	9.4	13.5
Possibility for training	78.3	70.4	78.1	75.8	89.2
Subsidised food	26.7	40.7	34.6	49.2	50.6
Subsidy for canteen or benefit for meal	61.5	72.0	50.0	71.7	82.8
Subsidised consumer goods	20.0	20.0	32.0	26.3	32.9
Transport subsidies	39.4	30.8	38.5	43.3	43.6

Source: RLFS3, n = 338.

Table A6.9 Types of benefit provided for non-regular workers, by property form, all regions, mid 1993

Benefit	State	Leasehold	Private	Closed joint st.	Open joint st.
Paid vacation	46.8	41.7	53.6	40.7	39.8
Additional vacation	12.0	4.2	10.7	12.3	14.1
Rest house	12.5	4.2	11.5	9.1	15.3
Sickness benefit	71.2	58.3	64.3	73.3	74.4
Paid health services	17.4	12.5	12.5	35.7	26.8
Subsidised rent	4.3	4.5	4.3	7.5	0.0
Subsidies for kindergarten	11.2	8.7	21.4	12.5	18.5
Bonuses	42.2	16.7	48.3	52.6	59.8
Profit sharing	14.9	12.5	29.6	30.4	24.4
Loans	19.4	12.5	34.5	38.6	30.8
Retirement assistance	14.7	8.3	16.7	16.4	14.1
Supplementary pension	3.3	0.0	0.0	2.0	0.0
Possibility for training	22.3	12.5	11.1	28.6	26.4
Subsidised food	18.6	20.8	16.7	36.4	38.8
Subsidy for canteen or benefit for meal	38.6	31.8	29.6	53.6	65.1
Subsidised consumer goods	14.1	9.1	29.2	18.5	23.0
Transport subsidies	17.2	8.7	24.0	22.2	26.7

Source: RLFS3, n = 338.

7 Corporate Governance and Trade Unions in Russian Industry: A Drift towards Collective Individualism?

The Soviet trade union . . . is not formed to fight anybody.[1]

7.1 INTRODUCTION

Management and trade unions have been in turmoil in Russian industry since the late 1980s, when their traditional role as 'transmission belts' for the Communist Party was disrupted. Since then, old-style managements and old-style trade union functionaries have been on the defensive, often drawn together inside enterprises in cosy relationships. However they have had to try to adapt to the rapid and diffuse property-form restructuring and the associated moves to new forms of industrial governance.

The mid 1990s are likely to be recalled as the critical moment in the evolution of labour relations in Russian industry. The old model was undoubtedly an obstacle to enterprise and employment restructuring, yet no new model was in place to produce an industrial relations climate conducive to dynamic efficiency or a situation in which workers and their representatives were strong enough to regulate and constrain management decision making in a profitable and equitable manner.

Old-style Soviet labour relations were an impediment to dynamic efficiency, in part because unions focused on a social stabilisation function, keeping workers quiet and providing a mechanism for social stratification, and in part because the diverse structures of governance inside enterprises created a bureaucratic analogue of Taylorism, with 'production committees' and 'brigades' complementing trade unions in administrative functions.[2] Since the notion of craft unionism was deemed incompatible with the notion of a single 'working class', during the Soviet era unions were structured as industrial unions, with a single union for any individual enterprise. They were thus part of the complex monopolistic apparatus. As a means of labour-market regulation, they operated as a mechanism to *legitimate* a production and distribution process and as means of *coordinating* the work process.

At the end of the 1980s all this changed. Within enterprises, the institutions of governance began to crumble, with production committees being discontinued on shopfloors and with the overall 'work collective' becoming more of a focal point than the brigade, which was typically the domain of the union leadership.[3] Unions were put under unprecedented and immense pressure that was particularly difficult to bear because most union leaders had been in office for many years, and because they were out of touch with their members as the ritualistic production conferences at which they were periodically elected and reelected lacked real employee participation.[4] Suddenly stuck with the need to become bargaining agents in an environment of labour-market risk and uncertainty, growing market-based inequalities, a withering of bureaucratic regulation and pervasive threats to the level of real wages, employment and social benefits, unions were put in a position of wanting to combine political relevance and influence with a role as bargainers with those authorities with whom they had collaborated as system regulators. It would have been truly remarkable if they had succeeded.

The first task for unions in the 1990s was to emerge as champions of workers' rights, and for that they had to become active and influential in factories and other enterprises. Here the representatives of old unions were caught in a honey trap. How could they escape from being part of management without losing the cosy benefits that went with that role? They had to establish a new legitimacy with their actual and potential constituents – ordinary workers. Yet legitimacy requires worker representatives to play proper roles. Early efforts to evolve in that direction had very limited success. One analysis claimed that plant-level union leaders were spending more time trying to rectify individual worker grievances and trying to supervise workplace safety.[5] Others reported that there were no substantive changes.[6] A survey of presidents of enterprise trade union committees in 1993 found that 95 per cent of them saw themselves as part of management.[7] This view was commonly reiterated to us in the course of fieldwork for the RLFS. The difficulty was compounded by their previous lack of activity with regard to the workers' aspirations, epitomised by the widespread lack of respect for union representatives by management. In the visits to factories from 1991–4 the most common reaction of the general directors of industrial enterprises upon mention of the union was laughter. In industrial relations, laughter is akin to contempt.

The union representatives were thus truly caught in the honey trap, for if they became more aggressive as bargainers, the management were in a position to take back the prerogative of distributing the firm's social benefits, which was the union's source of status and legitimacy among the workforce. There was also the implied or actual threat that the management would recognise another faction of the union, or another union where it existed, as the bargaining unit.

For the purpose of our analysis, it might be useful to establish a few points of principle. In general, to merit full support among workers, trade unions should combine four characteristics – they should be *representative* of workers, they should *promote good wages, benefits and working conditions*, they should be a force for *dynamic efficiency* and they should have a *'sword of justice'* effect through reducing various forms of discrimination and inequality within enterprises. Achieving a successful balance of these four objectives is the art of collective bargaining. If a trade union represents only 10 per cent of the workforce, has no effect on wages or benefit levels, has no effect on workplace or labour-market inequalities and is an obstacle to efficiency and profitability, then it will scarcely merit support, even if it does manage to create an atmosphere of social solidarity and community. Yet if unions are able to achieve those four aims, they will offer the prospect of being the most effective and desirable form of labour-market regulation, since an instrument for what might be called 'voice regulation' (bargaining) is surely, in principle, the democratically preferable option to statutory regulation. This is particularly true in circumstances in which the capacity of the central state to implement laws and regulations has been undermined, and in which new decrees are ignored with impunity in enterprises around the country.

This chapter draws on the RLFS to see what has been happening to labour relations in Russian industry. It considers whether there have been changes in the level and pattern of unionisation, what effects, if any, unions have had on wages and other aspects of labour relations, and what has been happening to the character of corporate governance in Russian factories.

Underlying the analysis is the hypothesis that in the foreseeable future it will be impractical to establish legitimacy for conventional forms of trade unionism, as developed in Western European or other market economies, and that new forms of 'collective individualism' may emerge in the context of property form and other forms of enterprise restructuring within Russian industry.

7.2 PROSPECTS OF DE-UNIONISATION

Traditionally, under the Soviet system the unionisation rate of the workforce was virtually 100 per cent at the formal level. Membership was almost obligatory, and costly if avoided, since the union played the role of organising all social aspects of an enterprise, even if wages were low and scarcely affected by collective bargaining. Thus membership was essential to ensure access to benefits such as sick pay and 'rest houses'. Although legislative changes since the end of the 1980s have been designed to create what the government called a 'level playing-field', barriers to change in unionisation have persisted, since an employee or worker has had to take the initiative to opt out from the automatic deduction of union dues from his or her monthly earnings.

Nevertheless changes have been occurring that represent much more than might at first appear. There are two basic indexes of representation – presence of a union in the factory and the proportion of the workforce that belongs to a union. If there is a formal shell in every plant, but without active members, then the former index is scarcely meaningful.

According to the first round of the RLFS in 1991, 99 per cent of all firms had a recognised trade union, and in the third round (mid 1993) 93.5 per cent of all establishments still had one. In all industries more than 90 per cent of the firms had unions in 1993. Thus at the formal level unions were firmly entrenched.

Between 1993 and 1994 there was a more pronounced erosion in the share of firms with unions, attributed by some managers and workers to the position of the trade union leadership in the political upheavals in Moscow in 1993, and probably related in part to the removal of trade unions from administration of the federal social security system at the end of 1993. By mid 1994 87.5 per cent of all industrial establishments had trade unions, with a low of 81.3 per cent in textiles and garments and a high of 100 per cent in metals (Figure 7.1). Smaller factories were less likely to have a union, and the decline in union representation occurred mainly among those establishments with fewer than 250 workers. One reason for the observed decline between 1993 and 1994 was the inclusion of Ivanovo, where fewer firms were unionised than in the other regions. This is strange, in that Ivanovo is famous for its radical union activity in the early years of the twentieth century, when it was a cradle for the first Soviets. However, although among the establishments that were in both RLFS3 and RLFS4 the decline was not observed, the slide in representation was most marked in St Petersburg.

In both 1993 and 1994, union presence was least likely in private establishments. The fact that one quarter of all private firms in 1994 did not have a union (compared with only 6.3 per cent in 1993) is surely a sign that trade unions were under a long-term threat, especially as, with the desired break-up of the big industrial enterprises, the number of smaller

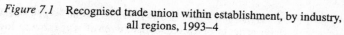

Figure 7.1 Recognised trade union within establishment, by industry, all regions, 1993–4

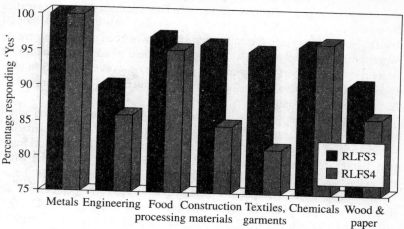

Source: RLFS3, RLFS4; n = 348 and 384, respectively.

establishments should grow in number relative to large concerns. Also conducive to declining union presence was the fact that firms that had cut employment were more likely to have had unions than those that had expanded or not changed their staffing level (Figure 7.2).

Yet it is the second index of representation that should receive the bulk of attention. *More significant than the growth in the number of firms without a trade union is the fact that in 1993–4 there was a substantial decline in the unionisation rate, that is, the percentage of the workforce in firms that were in trade unions.* Overall the unionisation rate was 85.4 per cent in mid 1993 for all firms covered in that round of the RLFS. By mid 1994 it had dropped to 73.8 per cent, expressed as an average for all firms covered in the fourth round.

If we consider only those factories that were in both RLFS3 and RLFS4, the average (unweighted) rate of unionisation fell by 8 per cent in 1993–4 – an extraordinarily rapid rate of decline.

Can we discern a pattern in the changing unionisation rate? First, one might expect some variation by sector, with the unionisation rate remaining highest in those sectors that remained relatively unscathed by economic shocks from 1991. This was the case. The sector that performed least badly in terms of sales and employment, namely food processing, retained the highest unionisation rate. Although there may be something

Figure 7.2   Recognised trade union within establishment, by percentage
employment change, all regions, 1993–4

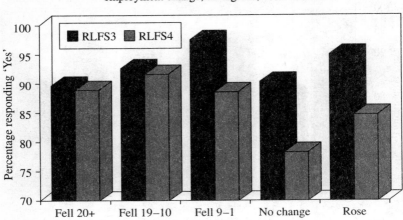

Source: RLFS3, RLFS4; n = 348 and 384, respectively.

specific to that sector, it is likely that it was the economic position of the
industry that helped maintain union membership, rather than the unionisation rate having a positive (or negative) effect on industrial performance.

In mid 1994 the unionisation rate ranged from 86.2 per cent in food
processing to 67.6 per cent in textiles and garments (Figure 7.3).[8] In those
firms with a union, on average 85.6 per cent of workers belonged to the
trade union in mid 1994, ranging from 92.2 per cent in food processing to
80.6 per cent in chemicals. In those establishments that were in the survey
in both 1993 and 1994, the unionisation rate declined most in chemicals
and textiles and garments, although it fell in all sectors (Figure 7.4).

Second, it could be expected that, as in most countries, larger establishments would have a higher unionisation rate. This was borne out by the
data from the RLFS, although it was predominantly among firms with
fewer than 250 workers that the unionisation rate was low (Figure 7.5).
More interesting perhaps is that the unionisation rate tended to be lower
in factories that had cut employment.

Third, because of the association between the state, management and
trade unions as the transmission belt of management, it could be expected
that the unionisation rate would be relatively high in the state sector, and
lowest in private enterprises. In fact the unionisation rate tended to be
highest in open joint-stock firms (Figure 7.6). Taking the merged file, the

Figure 7.3 Unionisation rate, by industry, all regions, 1993–4

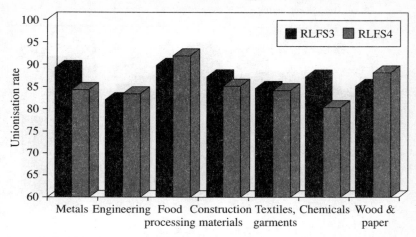

Source: RLFS3, RLFS4; n = 348 and 384, respectively.

Figure 7.4 Change in unionisation rate, by industry, all regions, 1993–4

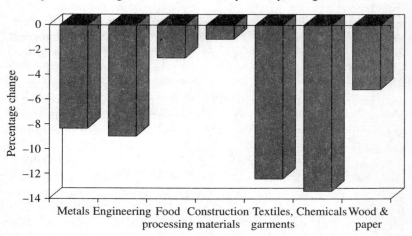

Note: In all tables and figures that include the merged data from the third and fourth rounds, Ivanovo plants are automatically excluded. The straightforward RLFS4 results include them.
Source: merged RLFS, n = 229.

Figure 7.5   Unionisation rate, by employment size, all regions, 1993–4

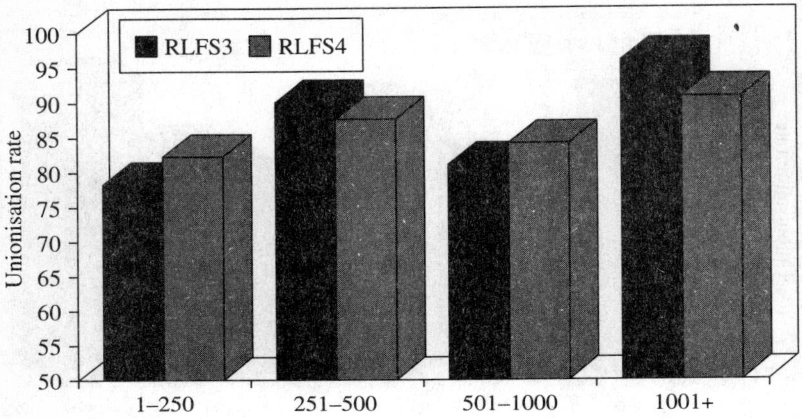

Source: RLFS3, RLFS4; n = 348 and 384, respectively.

unionisation rate was highest in those firms that had been and remained closed joint stock (85 per cent) and lowest in leaseholds that had been leaseholds before (58 per cent) and in those that had been and remained private (63 per cent). Those that had been and remained open joint stock also had a relatively low unionisation rate (70.6 per cent). This suggests that a decline in the unionisation rate could follow the move to open joint stock with a lag. It was in those that had only recently become open joint stock that the unionisation rate was well above average.

The decline in the unionisation rate was particularly large in establishments that had been private in mid 1993, although it is notable that state firms also had substantial declines (Figures 7.6 and 7.7). In terms of association of de-unionisation and change in property form, those that were open or closed joint stock in 1993 declined the least. Those that had been private for a relatively long time had the largest drop in the unionisation rate.

Fourth, one might anticipate some differences between local labour markets, perhaps linked to the organisational capacity of regional trade union federations, but more probably linked to the general level of the local economy and labour market.

Overall, by 1994 considerable regional variation had indeed emerged. The levels were lower in the depressed labour market of Ivanovo and in St Petersburg than elsewhere.

Fifth, it was anticipated that firms that were relatively labour intensive

Figure 7.6 Unionisation rate, by property form, all regions, 1993–4

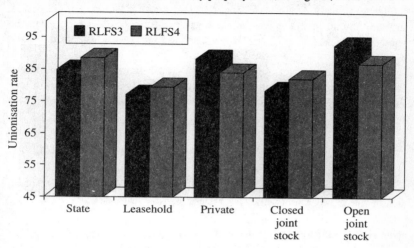

Source: RLFS3, RLFS4; n = 348 and 384, respectively.

Figure 7.7 Change in unionisation rate, by property form, all regions, 1993–4

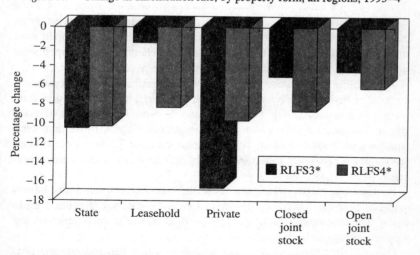

Note: The dark columns refer to changes in firms that had the designated property form in mid-1993; the shaded columns refer to those with the property form in mid 1994.
Source: merged RLFS, n = 229.

and had a high proportion of manual production workers would have a higher unionisation rate than firms that had relatively more employees. In fact, in tabulations there was only a weak positive correlation between the share of manual ('blue-collar') workers in the factory and the unionisation rate.

To try to identify the determinants of interfirm variation in the unionisation rate more systematically, an ordinary least-square regression was estimated, in which the percentage of workers belonging to a union was the dependent variable ($\%TU$), as follows:

$$\%TU = a + b_1\Sigma(\text{IND}) + b_2\Sigma(\text{PROP}) + b_3\text{EMP} + b_4\Sigma(\text{REG}) + b_5\%\text{BC} + b_6\%\text{FEM} + e$$

where the independent variables are defined as follows:

$\Sigma(\text{IND})$ = set of binary variables for industry of establishment, the missing sector being the energy sector.

$\Sigma(\text{PROP})$ = set of binary variables for property form of establishment, the missing form being state enterprises.

EMP   = size of establishment by number of workers and employees as of June 1994.

$\Sigma(\text{REG})$ = set of binary variables for *oblast* of establishment, the missing region being Moscow City.

%BC   = percentage of workforce consisting of manual production workers.

%FEM   = percentage of workforce consisting of women.

e = error term.

The functions were estimated by means of an ordinary least-square regression for both 1993 and 1994. The results are given in Table 7.1. A separate function, not reported, included a variable for whether or not the management was in the union.

The third and fourth columns reproduce the regression results for the subsample of firms that were in both rounds of the RLFS. It is not surprising that the fit of the equation is better for 1994, since with the restructuring and greater differentiation of firms there was more variation in the unionisation rate in the latter year. Note that a key variable in both 1993 and 1994 was whether or not the management was in the union. If so, the overall unionisation rate was much higher. But that certainly does not mean that the union was more effective or representative.

Table 7.1 Unionisation in Russian factories, 1993–4 (OLS regression coefficients)

Variable	Unionisation rate/RLFS3	Unionisation rate/RLFS4	Unionisation rate/RLFS3*	Unionisation rate/RLFS4*
(Constant)	81.7071	36.6723	75.2071	3.6189
Industry				
Metals	-3.1873	4.7454	-4.9315	4.4832
Engineering	-5.6361	-0.3578	-6.0247	4.0433
Food processing	3.4791	12.0945**	5.4207	14.4525*
Construction materials	-1.3035	-0.8750	-4.9833	6.9737
Chemicals	-0.5811	4.0094	1.6031	3.9201
Wood & paper	0.5404	8.9937	8.2194	17.7412*
Property form				
Leasehold	-6.8744	-8.7761	-12.1582	-2.5615
Private	1.4108	-9.4221	1.5197	-2.1119
Closed joint stock	-7.4682*	-1.8753	-8.5693	-1.5035
Open joint stock	3.8678	10.3398**	0.3310	6.1034

Table 7.1 Cont'd

Variable	Unionisation rate/RLFS3	Unionisation rate/RLFS4	Unionisation rate/RLFS3*	Unionsation rate/RLFS4*
Region				
Moscow Region	7.4007	9.5897	8.0071	13.1123*
St Petersburg	−4.8211	−12.4442***	−5.7827	−11.8402**
Nizhny Novgorod	0.1207	2.1569	3.3998	0.4294
Ivanovo	N/A	−13.8581**	N/A	N/A
Employment size	0.0028**	0.0027***	0.0029*	0.0036**
Manual workers' share	0.1007	0.4433**	0.2370	0.8808***
Women's share	−0.0708	−0.0415	−0.1623	−0.0767
R^2	0.0781	0.1743	0.1167	0.2000
F	1.6880	4.2098	1.6160	3.0739

* Statistically significant at the 10% level of probability.
** Statistically significant at the 5% level.
*** Statistically significant at the 1% level.
Source: RLFS3, RLFS4, merged RLFS; n = 348, 384, 229 and 229, respectively.

In 1994 the unionisation rate was significantly lower in Ivanovo and St Petersburg than in the other three regions, and was higher in larger firms, open joint-stock companies and food processing.[9]

Functions were also estimated for the *change* in the percentage of workers in unions between mid 1993 and mid 1994 for those factories that were in both RLFS3 and RLFS4. These functions were similar to those for the unionisation rate, with the addition of employment change over the year and the 1993 unionisation rate. Several variables were statistically significant. Thus if employment fell in a plant, it was relatively likely that the unionisation rate of the remaining workers also fell. The larger the number of women employees, the greater the fall in the unionisation rate. It also fell to a relatively large extent in basic metals, engineering and chemicals, and did so far more in St Petersburg than in the other regions. But whether one used property forms or governance types, there appeared to be no independent effect from restructuring.

One of the main features of changes in the unionisation rate in 1993–4 was the widespread withdrawal of managers and senior employees from the unions. The fall in the overall unionisation rate was much greater in those firms in which the managers were not in the union – 28.6 per cent compared with 12.2 per cent – which was unlikely to be simply because their absence from the union automatically reduced the unionisation rate. Some managers were also taking a more overtly anti-union stance.

In 1994 nearly 12 per cent of managers had left their union since 1993, and a further 4 per cent had opted out before mid 1993.[10] De-unionisation of management (a nice concept) was greatest in chemicals and textiles and garments, and most in St Petersburg, the region in which de-unionisation generally was also the greatest (falling by 10.6 per cent). These changes were indicative of the changing industrial relations climate, yet in a related survey of union leaders, managers and workers carried out in early 1995 nearly as many managers (62 per cent) as union leaders (67 per cent) felt that it was appropriate for managers to belong to the same union as workers, whereas only 51 per cent of workers stated that this should be the case.

In sum, both the level and the character of trade union membership were changing. Although the unionisation rate remained quite high, this does not imply that the high rate represented union strength and worker representation.[11] The clear trend was towards de-unionisation, which continued throughout 1994.[12] Whether de-unionisation will slow once it falls from the unrealistically high levels of the Soviet era or will accelerate as enterprise restructuring and unemployment continue to rise will depend very much on reforms in the unions themselves and on how the industrial enterprises evolve.

7.3   UNION AFFILIATION

Under the Soviet system all unions were part of one composite body, and there was a corresponding body to represent 'employers' and managers, which participated in the International Labour Organisation's tripartite activities. Since the end of the 1980s numerous independent trade unions have been founded and numerous organisations have emerged to claim to be representatives of employers.

At the same time the old official trade union confederation has undergone a series of changes, first with its reconstitution in 1991 and then following the abortive coup of 1993, when its former leadership came out in support of the parliament and subsequently had to resign. In early 1994 that union body, the Federation of Independent Trade Unions of Russia (FITUR) claimed to have 56 million members, which would have been about 60 per cent of the adult population.[13] Meanwhile, new 'free' trade unions have claimed that the FITUR's membership figures are exaggerated, and analysts close to those unions have referred to 'dead souls' in the FITUR membership.[14]

In the manufacturing industry in mid 1993, according to RLFS3, in nearly 94 per cent of the firms that had unions the main (and usually only) union was affiliated to the FITUR.[15] It was roughly the same in 1994, although it may have slipped slightly, since 12.9 per cent of managements did not know whether the union was affiliated or not and only 82.8 per cent reported that the union was affiliated to the FITUR.

Interestingly the unionisation rate declined by much more in those firms in which the union was not affiliated to the FITUR, and the average unionisation rate was higher in firms with an FITUR union than in those with a union that was not affiliated to it. In sum, the data do not suggest that the hegemony of the reconstituted old trade union body was under threat.

7.4   COLLECTIVE BARGAINING

The notion of collective bargaining in Soviet-era industrial enterprises was highly formalistic. In the late 1980s and early 1990s legislative and institutional changes created a more realistic basis for genuine bargaining. Yet it is difficult to determine whether the collective bargaining taking place between unions and management in the period covered by the first four rounds of the RLFS had remained formalistic or had been growing more substantive, reflecting genuine differences of interest and pressure between

Figure 7.8 Duration of collective agreements, by industry, all regions, mid 1994

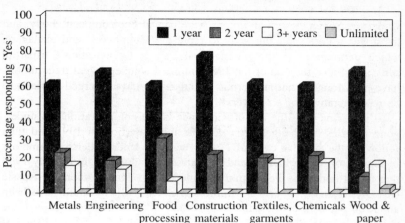

Source: RLFS4, n = 384.

managements and workers. The RLFS collected data on various aspects of such bargaining, which can be summarised quite briefly.

The *duration of collective agreements* on average became shorter in the early period of attempted 'shock therapy', probably in response to very high inflation and economic uncertainty. This trend seems to have been reversed in 1993–4. In 1993, according to RLFS3, just over three quarters of all agreements were for one year, and only 10.4 per cent were for three years or more. In 1994, according to RLFS4, fewer than two thirds of collective agreements were concluded for one year only, and 13 per cent were for three years or more.

There was little variation by industry (Figure 7.8), but state establishments were more likely to have one-year agreements than other property forms, which were tending to introduce two-year agreements. There was also a relatively high tendency for firms in Ivanovo to have one-year agreements, perhaps reflecting their parlous state and uncertainty in the local economy. There was no variation in duration by employment size or employment change. During discussions with some managers it emerged that most aspects of such agreements were agreed on a longer-term basis, whereas wages were subject to quarterly adjustments for inflation.

In 1994 most collective agreements were enterprise-level agreements, with a few at establishment level and a few at industry level. Among those firms visited in both 1993 and 1994 there seemed to have been a modest

Table 7.2   Collective agreements, by level of bargaining, all regions, 1993–4 (percentage of establishments with different forms of agreement)

	RLFS3	RLFS4	RLFS3*	RLFS4*
Industry	3.4	2.8	2.8	4.1
Regional	0.3	1.0	0.4	0.5
Enterprise	95.6	93.0	95.8	91.9
Production unit	0.6	3.2	1.0	3.6

* The data refer to the panel of 229 firms in both RLFS3 and RLFS4.
Source: RLFS3, RLFS4, merged RLFS; n = 323, 313, 210 and 196, respectively.

Table 7.3   Issues covered in collective agreements, 1991–4 (percentage of collective agreements that covered specific issues)

	RLFS1	RLFS2	RLFS3	RLFS4
Wage rates	91.3	97.8	91.2	93.8
Bonuses	93.7	94.5	89.6	83.0
Benefits	96.4	97.8	97.7	97.7
Working time	93.3	96.7	94.1	94.4
Dismissals	77.5	84.0	76.2	80.4
Job mobility	35.1	55.8	52.1	47.7
Promotion	17.2	36.5	29.9	29.4
Output norm	50.6	58.6	55.8	55.9
Release	N/A	N/A	48.5	51.1
Other	N/A	N/A	0.0	7.7

Source: RLFS1, RLFS3, RLFS4; n = 495, 181, 348 and 384, respectively.

shift to establishment-level (or production unit) agreements (Table 7.2). An implication is that the basis for a highly decentralised system of collective bargaining existed, and future industrial relations policy in the country will surely have to build on that reality.

In 1991, 1993 and 1994 most of the collective agreements covered a very broad range of labour issues, as shown in Table 7.3. The only items that seem to have been covered in an increasing number of agreements were promotion, job mobility and possibly 'dismissals', as well as all aspects of employment restructuring. The main issue that seems to have become more of a prerogative of management outside the collective agreement was the determination of bonuses.

Overall the differences were small and mostly not statistically signicant.

There was little to suggest a major change in the character of agreements, although it might turn out to have been a harbinger of a reorientation that collective agreements in non-state firms were more likely to cover issues of labour mobility and redundancy. There was also some evidence from the 1993 survey that, in the first three years of radical reform and stagflation, wage rates had become more central to collective agreements, in that fewer of the agreements negotiated in 1990 had covered wage issues.

7.5 STRIKES

Labour disputes in the form of strikes are usually regarded as symbolic of genuine collective bargaining, especially in a period of industrial upheaval and rising unemployment. Much has been written about the growth of strikes in Russia since the end of the 1980s, yet they were really prominent only in 1990–1, with the miners to the fore. In industry the long tradition of subordination of workers masked incipient worker protests concealing a bitter crisis in industrial relations.[16] This tendency to channel conflict into other forms of worker action seems to have persisted into the 1990s.

There were very few reported strikes in industrial establishments in any of the rounds of the RLFS. In 1991 only 2.4 per cent of the firms in the first round had experienced a strike during the previous two years, and 2.8 per cent of the firms reported that strikes were prohibited. In 1993 only 1.3 per cent had experienced a strike in the previous two years, all in engineering. In 1994 the corresponding figure was also 1.3 per cent, a few strikes having occurred in wood products, textiles and engineering. All strikes had been in factories experiencing declining employment.

The low incidence of strikes in a period of collapsing wages and contracting employment may be recalled in the future as a remarkable aspect of the evolving labour market, yet it is not surprising given the induced passivity of the workers and unions and the peculiarities of evolving labour relations.

The nature of the strikes is no less peculiar. It is generally accepted that the four main causes of strikes in Russian industry were abnormal by the standards of market economies. First, many were initiated by the managements themselves, with the intention of putting pressure on local authorities or the federal government to make concessions, provide subsidies, extend credit or give them commercial orders.[17] Second, some strikes were prompted by one management faction competing against another and mobilising the union on their behalf. A third cause was conflict resulting from one union faction trying to oust another. A fourth was demands on

Figure 7.9   Average wages, by unionisation rate, all regions, 1993–4 (average wages in establishments according to level of unionisation)

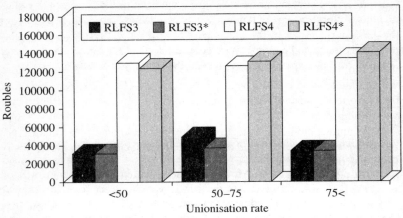

Source: *RLFS3, RLFS4, merged RLFS; n = 348, 229, 384 and 229 respectively.

management and others beyond them to actually *pay* wages, rather than wage levels *per se*. In sum, little can be read into strike data on whether there is genuine collective bargaining in industrial enterprises.

7.6   UNIONS' INFLUENCE ON WAGES

For workers in most countries the main rationale for trade unions is that they can bring about wage increases for those they represent. In the Soviet system that role was not developed as the unions were organs of the Communist Party. Since the reform of trade unions began in the late 1980s a greater interest in wage determination could have been expected. The trouble is that it is unclear whether unions have genuinely represented workers' interests in this respect in Russian industry.

The data from the RLFS allow a preliminary assessment of their effects. In both 1993 and 1994 there was no correlation between average wages and the unionisation rate (Figure 7.9). The wage functions estimated in the previous chapter showed not only that the unionisation rate variable was insignificant, but that the coefficient was the wrong sign, implying that if anything the higher the unionisation rate, the lower the wage. There is little reason to doubt that unions had no effect on wages at the establishment level.

The simple correlation between unionisation rate and earnings was slightly stronger than with wage rates. This may have reflected the fact that the standard wage tariff system was more influential in more union-ised firms – the tariff served to hold down wage rates because it was based on the statutory minimum wage and provided some sort of weak anchor on wages. Firms with high rates of unionisation were more likely to be using the wage tariff. Thus only a slight majority (51.9 per cent) of those with a unionisation of rate less than 50 per cent were still using it, whereas over two thirds of those with a higher than 75 per cent unionisation rate were doing so.

Were unions having an effect on the wage system and wage flexibility? As we have just seen, they did not seem to be associated with moves away from the old wage tariff system. However, more unionised firms were more likely to be operating a profit-sharing system, and, as found in Chapter 5, this was associated with greater (downward) wage flexibility.

Although no questions were asked about the subject in 1993, there was no apparent relationship between the unionisation rate and the percentage of wages in arrears in 1994. The percentage of wages not paid on time was actually highest in firms with a medium unionisation rate. This should be disquietening news for unions, since if they are to be an effective force for worker protection they should be successful in obtaining workers' wages.

In sum the unionisation rate at the time of the surveys was not correl-ated with higher wages and earnings, and unions had not succeeded in reducing the probability of workers finding themselves in wage arrears. Thus in one way and another one can conclude that unions had yet to exert much influence on wages.

7.7 UNIONS AND WAGE DIFFERENTIALS

Another traditional role of trade unions is to modify wage and earnings differentials – the so-called 'sword of justice' effect. In this respect, first impressions from the RLFS were more promising in terms of unions hav-ing an effect. We can consider three aspects of this type of impact, and will merely indicate the possible lines of future enquiry.

Occupational differentials

In most countries, unions have traditionally attempted to protect the wages of manual production workers to a greater extent than those of other oc-cupational groups, and as such have tended to reduce occupational wage

Figure 7.10   Wage ratio of managers compared with unskilled workers,
by unionisation rate, all regions, 1993–4

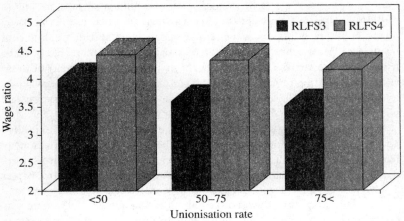

Source: RLFS3, RLFS4; n = 348 and 384, respectively.

differentials. Indeed various empirical studies in the United States, the
United Kingdom and elsewhere have found that unions have had a negative effect on profitability but a positive effect on productivity, implying
that they have had a redistributional effect on the incomes of stakeholders
in firms, improving those of workers to the detriment of those of shareholders.[18] In those countries where the unionisation rate has declined, it is
tempting to speculate that, with the effect of persistently high unemployment and the changing character of employment, it has been the declining ability of unions to arrest the growth of occupational and functional
inequality that has most eroded their appeal among workers.

   The evidence in Russian industry suggests that unions may have assisted
in moderating occupational earnings differentials, although one makes no
judgement about what differentials are desirable or undesirable in terms
of efficiency, labour mobility or relative demand. In both 1993 and 1994
the differentials between managements' and unskilled workers' wages and
earnings were lower in firms with high unionisation rates (Figure 7.10).
Thus in firms in which the unionisation rate was less than 50 per cent,
managerial employees' average wages were four times those of unqualified production workers, whereas in those in which the unionisation rate was
above 75 per cent the ratio was 3.6. This sort of relationship also emerged
for all other occupational groups compared with unqualified workers. Thus
unions *may* have helped reduce occupational wage inequality.

Figure 7.11 Women's wage as a percentage of men's (workers), by unionisation rate, all regions, 1992–4

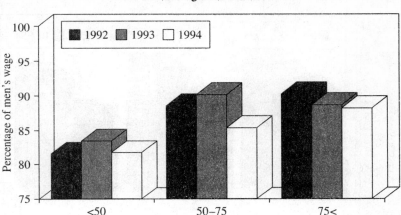

Source: RLFS3, RLFS4; n = 348 and 384, respectively.

Gender differentials

Less controversially (in that many economists believe that occupational differentials should have been increased), one would hope that gender-based wage differentials would be small and declining, and that unions would be an instrument for reducing those differentials. Although many critics of union behaviour in other countries have claimed that unions have acted to protect male 'insiders', the evidence that they have behaved in that way in terms of women's wages and earnings is mixed, if not positive. Even in countries where unions have been weakened by legislative and political factors, they have been associated with reduced gender-based wage differentials.[19]

Although the issue of women's employment is considered in Chapter 9, in Russian industry in both 1993 and 1994 there was no relationship between feminisation of the factory workforce and the rate of unionisation. Whether or not one can trace a causal relationship, women's wages relative to men's were greater in highly unionised plants. This applied to both workers and employees (Figures 7.11 and 7.12). Unions may thus have been associated with a lower level of wage discrimination against women, although the correlation may be spurious in that it may merely reflect the influence of other factors correlated with the unionisation rate.

Figure 7.12   Women's wage as a percentage of men's (employees), by unionisation rate, all regions, 1992–4

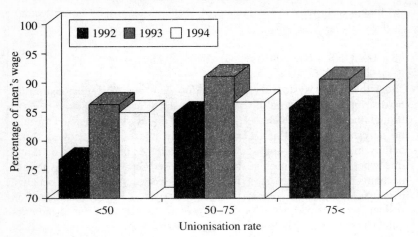

Source: RLFS3, RLFS4; n = 348 and 384, respectively.

Insider–outsider differentials

As discussed in Chapter 5, the RLFS identified a new phenomenon in Russian industry – the existence and growth of a substantial category of workers in factories paid well below the average wage in the firm. It will be recalled that questions were asked about the lowest wage actually paid to a group of workers and the percentage of workers being paid that amount. If unions were having any effect, then one would expect that where they were most strongly entrenched the size of the low-paid group would be small.

It seems that the minimum wages of workers and employees were relatively high in firms with very high unionisation rates, and the percentage of workers being paid the low wage was smaller in more unionised firms. These findings suggest that unions were limiting the growth of a very low-paid category of workers in firms where they were relatively strong.

Consequently the unions may have been more successful, whether inadvertently or not, in limiting wage and earnings differentiation in Russian factories. This could arise from the awkward and paradoxical tendency for unions to have been a force for institutional conservatism, or atavism, in the early 1990s. As shown in Chapter 6, property form, size and corporate governance restructuring were all tending to widen earnings differentials, as was the general growth of wage system flexibility. In the circumstances the 'sword of justice' effects may have been more fortuitous than a testimony to the pursuit of economic equity by union leaders.

7.8 UNIONS AND NON-WAGE BENEFITS

Under the Soviet system the trade unions were primarily responsible for the distribution and partial management of the allocation of social benefits through the extensive enterprise-based social policy. This persisted through the *perestroika* period and during the early phases of attempted shock therapy in 1992–3. As noted in Chapter 6, another paradox was that, at a time when the wage mechanism was supposed to act as a relative price mechanism, there was a shift from money wages to non-wage benefits, in part to compensate for high inflation, in part to convey privileges on 'insider' workers, in part to avoid the wages tax of the tax-based incomes policy, and in part because of barter exchanges encouraged by lack of funds and growing indebtedness among most industrial enterprises.

If provision of social benefits was the primary objective and rationale for trade unions, one would expect that unionised firms would have provided more benefits and preserved, if not extended, benefits to a greater extent than others.

The evidence from the RLFS supports those expectations. For 1994, Table 7.4 shows that factories with unions were more likely to be providing all sorts of benefits (except subsidised food) than factories where there was no union. The first column for each category of employee or worker gives the percentage of establishments in which the management reported that the specified benefit entitlement was provided, while the second column gives the figure for those factories in which there was no recognised union. Thus, for example, as can be seen for the case of rest houses, 48.2 per cent of unionised plants provided workers with access to them whereas only 18.8 per cent of non-union plants did so. Table 7.5 (and Table 7.6 for the merged file for 1993–4) shows that in most cases the more unionised the workforce the greater the probability of entitlement to a specified benefit for administrative employees (management), regular workers and non-regular workers. For example in 1994 rest houses were only provided in 19.2 per cent of firms with a lower than 50 per cent unionisation rate, whereas they were provided in over half of those with a higher than 75 per cent unionisation rate.

The direct causal role of trade unions in this differentiation must be doubted. The incidence of benefits and the extent of the unionisation rate

Table 7.4 Benefit entitlements, by category of worker, by unionisation, all regions, mid 1994

Recognised trade unions:	Administrative workers		Regular workers		Non-regular workers	
	Yes	No	Yes	No	Yes	No
Paid vacation	99.7	100.0	99.4	100.0	50.9	31.9
Additional vacation	49.4	37.5	67.6	54.2	20.1	8.5
Rest house	48.5	18.8	48.2	18.8	22.8	6.4
Sickness benefit	94.0	85.4	94.6	85.4	59.0	34.0
Paid health services	53.9	31.3	54.2	31.3	31.1	6.4
Subsidised rent	17.0	6.3	17.9	6.3	6.3	2.1
Subsidies for kindergarten	47.3	27.1	47.6	29.2	20.7	8.5
Bonuses	74.6	54.2	75.3	54.2	43.7	25.5
Profit sharing	68.2	52.1	67.9	50.0	29.3	17.0
Loans	83.6	68.8	83.9	70.8	39.9	21.3
Retirement assistance	77.7	41.7	78.0	41.7	26.3	10.6
Supplementary pension	7.8	2.1	7.8	2.1	2.7	0.0
Possibility for training	53.3	29.2	55.4	27.1	20.7	6.5
Subsidised food	17.6	25.0	17.9	25.0	12.0	4.3
Subsidy for canteen or benefit for meal	53.3	37.5	55.4	37.5	34.4	10.6
Subsidised consumer goods	10.1	8.3	10.1	8.3	8.7	0.0
Transport subsidies	31.0	25.0	32.7	25.0	15.9	4.3
Unpaid shares	26.3	18.8	26.3	18.8	7.5	4.3

Source: RLFS4, n = 384.

could merely reflect two aspects of a corporate paternalistic enterprise. Nevertheless there is some suggestion in the data that between 1993 and 1994 the probability of unionised firms providing benefits to a greater extent than non-unionised firms had increased. This is shown by a comparison of those firms that were included in both 1993 and 1994 (Table 7.6). Although there was erosion in the provision of benefits generally – as in the case of sickness benefit, rest houses, kindergartens, subsidised food and subsidised consumer goods – the difference between unionised and non-union firms in most cases had increased.

In 1993–4, according to RLFS4, among firms with trade unions 21.4 per cent added a new benefit during the previous year, compared with 22.9 per cent of those without trade unions. In contrast 28.6 per cent of unionised firms had cut a benefit, compared with 22.9 per cent of non-unionised firms. This could reflect the erosion of union strength or the simple fact that unionised firms had more benefits to cut!

Table 7.5 Benefit entitlements, by category of worker, by unionisation rate, all regions, mid 1994

Unionisation rate:	Administrative workers			Regular workers			Non-regular workers		
	<50	50–75	75<	<50	50–75	75<	<50	50–75	75<
Paid vacation	100.0	100.0	99.6	100.0	100.0	99.2	44.2	39.5	51.3
Additional vacation	43.6	53.5	48.3	59.0	68.2	67.6	14.3	16.3	20.3
Rest house	19.2	38.6	53.4	19.2	38.6	53.1	10.4	14.0	24.9
Sickness benefit	89.7	90.9	94.3	89.7	93.2	94.7	50.6	51.2	58.2
Paid health services	35.9	47.7	56.1	35.9	50.0	56.1	18.2	23.3	31.8
Subsidised rent	7.7	15.9	17.9	7.7	15.9	19.1	1.3	2.3	7.7
Subsidies for kindergarten	29.5	38.6	50.4	30.8	38.6	50.8	9.1	16.3	22.6
Bonuses	56.4	68.2	77.4	57.7	68.2	77.9	35.1	32.6	44.8
Profit sharing	57.7	54.5	70.6	56.4	54.5	70.2	23.4	25.6	29.5
Loans	74.4	81.8	84.0	75.6	81.8	84.4	35.1	32.6	39.2
Retirement assistance	53.8	75.0	78.6	53.8	75.0	79.0	15.6	20.9	27.6
Supplementary pension	3.8	9.1	7.7	3.8	9.1	7.7	1.3	7.0	1.9
Possibility for training	38.5	47.7	54.2	37.2	54.5	55.7	10.5	16.3	21.8
Subsidised food	19.2	11.4	19.5	19.2	13.6	19.5	6.5	14.0	11.9
Subsidy for canteen or benefit for meal	41.0	54.5	53.8	42.3	56.8	55.7	19.5	34.9	34.5
Subsidised consumer goods	9.0	2.3	11.5	9.0	2.3	11.5	3.9	4.7	9.2
Transport subsidies	24.4	31.8	31.7	24.4	31.8	34.0	7.8	14.0	16.5
Unpaid shares	19.2	22.7	27.6	19.2	22.7	27.6	5.2	4.7	8.1

Source: RLFS4, n = 384.

Table 7.6 Benefit entitlements, by category of worker, by unionisation, all regions, 1993–4

| | RLFS3* | | | | | | RLFS4* | | | | | |
| | Administrative workers | | Regular workers | | Non-regular workers | | Administrative workers | | Regular workers | | Non-regular workers | |
Recognised trade unions:	Yes	No	Yes	No	Yes	No	Yes	No	Yes	No	Yes	No
Paid vacation	100.0	100.0	100.0	100.0	38.1	42.1	99.5	100.0	99.5	100.0	54.4	42.9
Additional vacation	47.1	42.1	71.0	73.7	8.6	5.3	46.6	42.9	68.8	76.2	22.8	14.3
Rest house	67.6	36.8	67.6	36.8	10.5	5.3	47.1	23.8	47.1	23.8	23.8	9.5
Sickness benefit	100.0	100.0	100.0	100.0	68.6	52.6	93.3	90.5	94.2	90.5	63.1	47.6
Paid health services	49.0	47.4	50.0	47.4	21.0	5.3	56.7	33.3	56.7	33.3	34.0	4.8
Subsidised rent	11.4	15.8	13.8	15.8	1.9	5.3	16.8	0.0	18.3	0.0	6.8	0.0
Subsidies for kindergartens	51.4	36.8	52.9	36.8	13.3	5.3	43.3	23.8	43.8	28.6	22.8	9.5
Bonuses	82.4	78.9	82.4	73.7	41.0	31.6	77.8	57.1	79.3	57.1	51.5	38.1
Profit sharing	68.1	63.2	67.6	63.2	21.0	15.8	71.6	52.4	71.6	52.4	32.5	28.6
Loans	91.4	94.7	91.4	94.7	23.3	21.1	85.1	76.2	85.1	76.2	42.2	38.1
Retirement assistance	79.0	52.6	79.5	52.6	12.9	10.5	80.8	52.4	81.3	52.4	30.6	19.0
Supplementary pension	10.0	5.3	10.5	5.3	1.9	0.0	8.2	4.8	8.2	4.8	2.4	0.0
Possibility for training	75.7	73.7	77.6	73.7	21.9	21.1	53.4	33.3	56.3	38.1	22.3	9.5
Subsidised food	34.3	21.1	34.3	21.1	22.9	10.5	20.3	14.3	20.3	14.3	14.1	4.8
Subsidy for canteen or benefit for meal	62.4	57.9	64.3	57.9	41.4	31.6	55.8	47.6	57.7	47.6	36.9	23.8
Subsidised consumer goods	22.4	5.3	22.4	5.3	14.8	0.0	10.6	0.0	10.6	0.0	10.2	0.0
Transport subsidies	33.3	47.4	33.3	47.4	17.2	15.8	33.2	14.3	34.6	19.0	19.4	9.5

Note: Invanovo excluded from merged panel set.
Source: *merged RLFS, n = 229.

There has been a tendency for administrations in industrial enterprises to take over direct responsibility for welfare functions.[20] This could reflect a desire on the part of management to increase its paternalistic control, growing friction between unions and management, or a transition in which management was seeing the social sphere as one area where costs could be cut. In a survey of the role of trade unions, conducted in early 1995, two in five worker respondents reported that the management was the main guardian of social benefits, and 37.6 per cent of trade union leaders in the firms reported the same. The big difference was that whereas over a third of the trade union leaders thought the union was the main guarantor, only 13 per cent of the workers thought so. And 59 per cent of union leaders claimed that workers often went to them for assistance, whereas only 15 per cent of the workers reported doing so. According to the union representatives, the main reason workers went to see them was to buy coupons for rest homes, with the second most common reason being to obtain other social services.

The erosion of the paternalistic position of trade union representatives coincided with important changes in the position and actions of management. Firms in which the management was in the union were more likely to be providing fringe benefits to both managerial employees and workers, with the exception of profitsharing. Most intriguingly, in factories in which managements had moved out of the union, the provision of holiday accommodation was much less likely than in firms where the management was still in the trade union. Could it be that, by distancing themselves from the union, managements were enabling themselves to cut non-wage benefits? Dropping out of the union and abandoning certain types of benefit may have been two strong signs that the enterprise was in the process of transforming itself from a paternalistic social entity into a commercial firm. This aspect of the restructuring of corporate governance may have profound implications on social welfare and distribution.

7.9 UNIONS AND 'DYNAMIC EFFICIENCY'

For most economists, trade unions are perceived either as a negative source of rigidities, wage inflation and inequality between those in and those out of employment, or as beneficial for workers through their effect on wages and benefits and through reducing wage differentials. A third potential advantage is less often recognised and has rarely been given much attention – unions can be agents of dynamic efficiency through imposing direct and indirect pressure on firms and managements to improve productivity,

Figure 7.13   Labour costs as a percentage of production costs, by unionisation rate, all regions, 1992–3

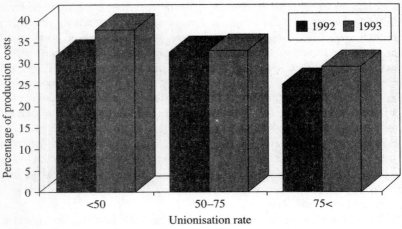

Source: RLFS4, n = 384.

skills and technological innovation.[21] As noted earlier, the negative effect on profitability has been offset by the positive effect on productivity, and the redistribution to workers away from profits has been greatest in monopolistic firms, which should be relevant in the emerging situation in Russian industry.

Given the passive if not discredited role of trade unions generally, one would anticipate that unions in Russian factories would have had neither positive nor negative effects on dynamic efficiency in the early 1990s. Yet it might be useful to consider a few stylised facts derived from the RLFS, for future comparison, should the character of trade unionism change.

For what it is worth, in mid 1994 managers in more unionised firms were more inclined to report that they were satisfied with labour efficiency. In terms of labour and wage costs, more unionised firms seemed to have lower costs (Figure 7.13), although one should be extremely wary about reaching any conclusions about this (and the differences between the means were not statistically significant). The result is presented merely to stimulate discussion on what should be a more important issue than seems to have been the case in Russian industry.

There is also a range of behavioural aspects of dynamic efficiency whereby unions could have some beneficial effect. For example unions might be expected to put pressure on managements to provide enterprise-

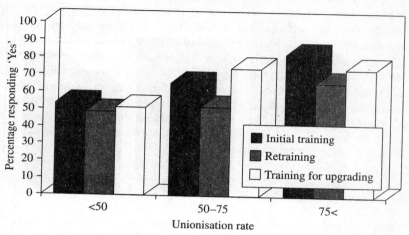

Figure 7.14 Initial training, retraining, training for upgrading, by unionisation rate, all regions, mid 1994

Source: RLFS3, RLFS4; n = 348 and 384, respectively.

based training, a relationship found in some industrialised and industrialising market economies.[22] In this regard, in both 1993 and 1994 there was a strong positive correlation between the unionisation rate and the provision of entry-level training, and a weaker positive relationship with retraining to improve job performance and retraining for upgrading (Figure 7.14). In 1993 and 1994 the more unionised firms may also have been more likely to be paying for their own training institutes. Perhaps unions were defending such institutes, and perhaps that was a reasonable action, despite scepticism about the value of the training provided in them.

We can extend the training link a little further. In deriving a composite human development index (HDE1 – see Chapter 11) we took into account all forms of training, as well as the type of training in each case and whether or not the firm was paying for a training institute or for workers to attend such an institute. It seemed that there was a fairly strong positive correlation between 'skill development' and unionisation rate.[23] We will expand on this concept in Chapter 11. The main point here is to suggest that further empirical work will have to consider whether Russian unions have had a positive effect on worker skills.

Another aspect of dynamic efficiency is the extent of technological innovation. One common claim internationally is that trade unions restrict such innovation, impeding managerial efforts to introduce change because of what they perceive as the potential threat to jobs. Although one should be wary of drawing conclusions from correlations in this respect, none of the three forms of technological change identified in the RLFS was negatively correlated with the unionisation rate.[24] In 1994 firms with a high unionisation rate had a higher probability of having broadened their range of products during the previous year and of having introduced new production technology. Although the probability of having made changes in work process organisation was lowest in firms with unionisation rates exceeding 90 per cent, those with medium and fairly high levels of union representation were more likely to have introduced changes than those with very low levels. In sum, there was little or no evidence that unions had been a force in lowering dynamic efficiency.

7.10   UNIONISATION RATE AND EMPLOYMENT

What, if anything, is the link between unionisation rate and employment change? In other countries, some studies have estimated that unions have had a negative effect on employment at the enterprise level, although some have concluded otherwise.[25] In Russian factories, for the same reasons that we should not expect unions to have influenced other aspects of the enterprise labour market, we should not expect any effect here, although for future monitoring and analysis a few summary statistics may be worth presenting.

There was no apparent link between labour surplus levels and the percentage of the workforce in unions (Table 7.7). It might be thought that if the unionisation rate were high, there would be worker pressure on the firm to retain more of those workers who were surplus to requirement. If so, one should expect the ratio of employment cuts to concealed unemployment (surplus labour) to be positively related to the unionisation rate. In fact there was no relationship at all.

There also seemed to be no relationship between the unionisation rate and the percentage of workers on administrative leave, or working short days or weeks, and there was no relationship with time lost through production stoppages or with the percentage of women on maternity leave.

Yet there was an inverse relationship between unionisation rate and employment change during the previous year. Those that had cut employment most sharply were least likely to have a unionised labour force. It is debatable whether one can interpret this as a sign that unions were protecting jobs (as some unionists like to claim), or that they were hindering employment restructuring, or that the relationship was merely coincidental.

Table 7.7 Indicators of labour surplus, by unionisation rate, all regions, mid 1994

Indicator	Unionisation Rate		
	<50	*50–75*	*75<*
Labour surplus 1	15.1	29.1	20.3
Labour surplus 2	19.6	27.2	21.2
Labour surplus 3	23.9	36.7	27.5
Percentage of workers on			
administrative leave	10.8	19.7	14.0
short-day work	1.8	3.1	1.6
short-week work	2.6	6.4	4.7
Percentage women on maternity leave	5.9	6.1	5.9
Percentage of time lost on production stoppages	8.8	7.5	7.2

Source: RLFS4, n = 384.

7.11 UNIONS AS PROTECTORS OF VULNERABLE-GROUP EMPLOYMENT

Finally, there is the issue of discriminatory employment protection. Throughout the world it is widely believed that unions are dominated by men and that they give priority to protecting the interests of prime-age male workers. If this also applies to Russian industry, one would expect an inverse correlation between unionisation rate and the share of employment taken by those usually classifiable as socially vulnerable.

At best the evidence is that unions have had little effect one way or the other. As far as women are concerned, there does not seem to be any relationship, although if anything there is a positive correlation between unionisation rate and women's share of employment (Figure 7.15). This issue is considered in more detail in Chapter 9.

The number of disabled was if anything higher in the more unionised firms. But there was a more pronounced relationship with respect to the age distribution of employment, reflecting perhaps that unions were protecting older workers, or perhaps that the unionisation rate was lower in firms with larger numbers of young workers precisely because young workers were not joining the unions. In any event there seemed to be a lower proportion of older workers in firms with low unionisation rates, although there was no difference if the unionisation rate was above 50 per cent. The proportion of older workers rose faster in firms with low unionisation rates, so one guesses that there was no relationship.

Figure 7.15   Percentage of female share of employment, by unionisation rate, all regions, mid 1994

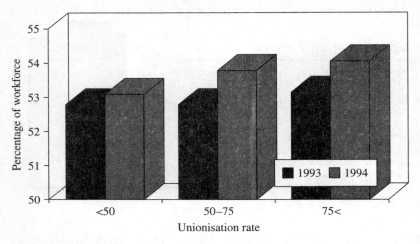

Source: RLFS4, n = 384.

There was a negative correlation between the unionisation rate and the percentage share of younger workers in the firm (Figure 7.16). Thus although the main point is that the unions did not appear to be acting on behalf of male 'insiders', as is commonly believed to occur in other countries, there was a possibility that unions might be acting as protectors of older workers' jobs.

7.12   MANAGEMENT AUTONOMY AND PARTICIPATION: AN ASIDE

So far attention has focused on the role of trade unions, or their weakness. Yet if labour relations are to become an arena for dynamic efficiency and enterprise restructuring, managements too must have proper roles. This means that managers must work in the interests of the long-term profitability and sustainability of their enterprise. Muddled, unclear aims lead to muddled, unclear performance, which leads to a lack of pressure to improve productivity.

This is a sensitive issue that looks likely to become one of the most contentious in the whole process of restructuring. As noted in Chapter 3, there are fascinating theoretical debates on managerial rationality during

Figure 7.16 Percentage of workers under age 25, by unionisation rate, all regions, 1993–4

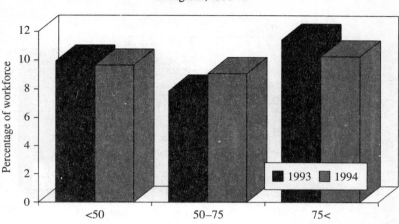

Source: RLFS3, RLFS4; n = 348 and 384, respectively.

economic transformation. Above all managers must have a sense of autonomy, be provided with adequate incentives and have a properly defined sense of accountability if they are to give high priority to the pursuit of efficiency, productivity and profitability. Incentives must be judiciously combined with knowledge that their performance is being monitored.

One index of managerial allegiance and the sense of having an independent role, as much symbolic as substantive, is membership of an association of employers and managers. The data on this from RLFS4, which was the first round to ask about this subject, may be rather embarrassing. The basic fact is that scarcely any managers were members of a representative organisation. The claims of the various bodies to be representative, which have been used to justify their membership of the national Trilateral Commission for the Regulation of Social and Labour Relations and their role in the ILO, should thus be treated with reservation.

In mid 1994 91.9 per cent of managers of industrial firms said they did not belong to an employer organisation. Only in joint-stock firms were more than 10 per cent of managers in an employer association (Figure 7.17), and only in large firms were more than 10 per cent in an association (Figure 7.18). In contrast only 4.5 per cent of managers of firms with fewer than 250 workers belonged to an employer organisation.

Only 4.4 per cent of managers were members of the Russian 'Union'

Figure 7.17   Managerial participation in employer organisation, by property form, all regions, mid 1994

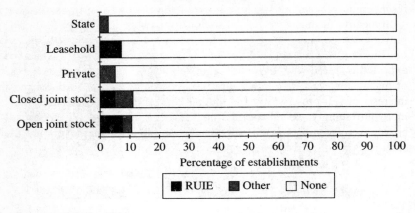

Source: RLFS4, n = 384.

Figure 7.18   Managerial participation in employer organisation, by employment size, all regions, mid 1994

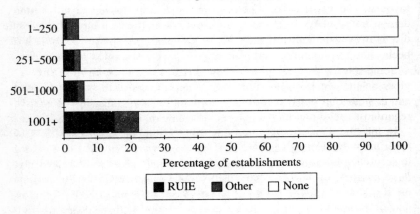

Source: RLFS4, n = 384.

of Industrialists and Entrepreneurs, the 'official' employers' body, often described by managers and known colloquially as 'Volsky's organisation', after its chairman. This small percentage effectively negates the representativeness of that body, since manufacturing enterprises were supposed to be its main membership base. Six other employer organisations had a few managers as members, but none of them had as much as 1 per cent.[26] It is perhaps time that the representativeness of bodies stating that they represent employers and managers is assessed objectively and dispassionately.

Ironically, no managers of non-union firms were members of an employer association, while *all managers that belonged to employer associations were also trade union members*. This corresponds to what would be expected by those who depict a 'corporate alliance' between certain types of management and traditional types of trade union, based on the shared interests of self-preservation and the habitual modes of existence.[27] Even more intriguingly, no managers who had been appointed by enterprise boards were members of an employer organisation. If employers are to emerge as a collective body, they have a long way to go.

7.13   CONCLUSIONS

For many decades workers, managers and the trade unions that were supposed to represent them in the 'work collective' colluded in a coalition of inefficiency and structured privileges that were based on a queuing system, time in the enterprise, party membership, personal contacts and favours. The experience of *perestroika* and then market reforms have demonstrated that it is easier for institutions to emerge than for them to die. However the edifice has begun to crumble and in some respects has been crumbling quite rapidly. What is likely to take its place?

Some observers, sympathetic to unions in general, have tried to put a gloss on the decline in the unionisation rate in Russia and other Central and Eastern European countries by claiming that apparent declines can be regarded as reunionisation on a voluntary basis.[28]

In the mid 1990s trade unions, whether affiliated to the FITUR or to other union bodies such as SOTSPROF, have been finding it very difficult to secure legitimacy, even though they have showed a capacity to mobilise large numbers of workers, pensioners and students for demonstrations, as on 27 October 1994 in a mass demonstration across the country against wage arrears. So-called independent trade unions have secured niches in only a few sectors, and have scarcely succeeded in wresting the initiative from the reconstructed old trade unions.[29]

One can predict that the unionisation rate will continue to fall, and it is likely that only a minority of workers will still belong to unions at the end of the twentieth century. The property restructuring of industrial enterprises may cause this decline to accelerate. One reason is that employers and managers are likely to continue to withdraw from, or not join, trade unions. Another is that more employers are likely to view unions as impeding their freedom to operate in an almost unregulated economy.

Another reason, and one with a less predictable outcome, is that workers and employees are more likely to have a triple role to play, quite unlike in the past. First, they will see themselves as *consumers*, and will experience a withering of the social provisions of the enterprises in which they work when these are transferred to local authorities or are provided by private firms and institutions, if at all. As such, workers will probably be less attracted to company-based trade unions, since the provision of social benefits and the apportioning of those benefits were the primary reason for trade union membership.

Second, they will see themselves as *workers* with interests more clearly opposed to those of their employers. This should strengthen the appeal of trade unions. Yet they are likely to see themselves as individual workers, with different interests from others, with more individualised salaries, positions and so on, and this is unlikely to contribute to a renewed sense of solidarity.

Third, they may see themselves as *owners*, since ownership of shares and enhanced voting rights over management appointments and reappointments are unlikely to disappear, even if they do evolve into a new form of corporate governance, with intermediary shareholding institutions emerging to acquire large blocks of shares.

In sum, the evolving 'class' position of workers will pose awkward challenges to trade unions. Yet the new set of functions may not promote pure individualism, for the imbalances of wealth, social status, ownership and corporate governance will reward those who coalesce into collective institutions, encouraging the emerging 'principals' to create new 'agents' to act on their behalf. It is most improbable that the old-style industrial, craft or plant-level trade unions will be able to serve the needs of the future.

In the restructuring of industrial enterprises, there is likely to be a continuing process of decentralisation of collective bargaining. International evidence shows that highly centralised, coordinated systems of social bargaining and highly decentralised systems work better in terms of their impact on inflation and employment than intermediate systems that have some elements of centralisation and some of decentralisation.[30] The trouble for Russian industry is that, although international evidence suggests that a centralised system based on democratic, representative bargaining seems most effective of all, it requires a history of legitimation, which only comes from a prolonged period of institutional trial and error. This cannot be imposed or institutionalised by laws, decrees or the sudden dictates of national trade union leaders, employer spokesmen or bureaucrats. The implication of this for Russian industry is profound. *Only a decentralised system is feasible*. If one starts from that premise, one can turn to the exciting question for the future: what type of decentralised system of bargaining and labour relations is desirable and feasible for enterprise restructuring and dynamic efficiency?

Before turning to that, it is important to recognise that a decentralised system can function inside a federal framework, in which a tripartite body exists to share and generate the information required to guide decentralised bargainers. This has been a secret of the success of some centralised systems, such as the Finnish negotiated incomes policy in the 1980s, before the strains of the break-up of the Comecon trading bloc led to a change of government to one ideologically opposed to incomes policy. Some parameters can be established at the national level, including agreements on social benefit levels, tax rates, inflation targets and so on. At the national level, securing agreements on the boundaries within which local bargainers can operate will be valuable.

Whether the Russian Trilateral Commission for the Regulation of Social and Labour Relations, set up at the end of 1991, can perform that function will depend in part on whether it is allowed to evolve as a quasi-independent body with a technically qualified secretariat not dominated by any particular interest group. Since 1995 there have been grounds for concern that the Trilateral Commission will not be able to foster a suitable macro-level structure that will allow decentralised collective bargaining to develop.[31]

What sort of decentralised bargaining offers the best hope for the future in the Russian labour market? There is powerful evidence that the old trade unions may have an intractable credibility problem inside industrial enterprises, which is surely associated with the declining unionisation rate, while new unions have been mostly a mystery, having had little impact. What interests will trade unions represent in the future? Will they represent workers as workers or will they represent workers and others as shareholders? They will not be able to represent both groups satisfactorily or consistently.

If the evolution of corporate governance restructuring continues along the route of joint-stock firms and worker minority shareholdings, substantive collective bargaining will have to be based on three interest groups in the enterprise of the future, and if these groups have sense they will go beyond that. One bargainer will have to represent the shareholders, most of whom may be workers; one will have to represent the workers, most of whom may be co-owners of the enterprise; and one will have to represent the management, whose responsibility it should be to sustain the commercial viability of the firm and maximise its long-term profitability. If the functions are muddled during bargaining, the outcome will be suboptimal and inefficient, and will probably lack the legitimation needed to secure a high 'effort bargain' from workers and managers.

The bargaining between different interest groups or agents concerns incentives as well as the distribution of benefits and gains from growth. In the twenty-first century, one wonders whether worker ownership of part of the capital rather than trade unions will be the main vehicle through which Russian workers will obtain an effective voice and negotiating status, because substantial unemployment and low levels of social protection from state transfers will continue to mean that workers *qua* workers will have a weak bargaining position. Strong unions could reduce managerial and other stakeholder opportunism and contribute to dynamically efficient corporate governance. But is such strength likely?

8 Restructuring Internal Labour Markets

8.1 INTRODUCTION

Firms shape labour markets by their practices and policies towards the allocation and development of labour resources. In turn, the labour markets within factories and other enterprises are shaped by regulations, technology, the social relations of production and various other external factors. What is beyond dispute is that, in order to understand labour markets and eventually restructure them, one cannot ignore the mechanisms of the internal labour process.

This chapter draws on information collected from the four rounds of the RLFS to see how the internal labour market in Russian factories has been evolving in the context of industrial restructuring. It attempts to treat the labour market as a process, and therefore it proceeds from worker recruitment and induction mechanisms to training and retraining, to occupational restructuring and the employment impact of technological innovation, to working-time developments and the growth of external labour-market flexibility.

The enterprise labour-market process is illustrated schematically in Figure 8.1, which shows the key decision-making elements, starting with recruitment and form of employment, through training and retraining to issues of labour turnover. There are other issues relating to the job structure and working-time practices that will be considered later. In an attempt to provide a picture of the internal labour market, this chapter presents evidence on the various elements as a means of identifying where practices could or should be modified in the interest of efficiency and flexibility.

8.2 RECRUITMENT AND INDUCTION

The initial point is the recruitment process, which is a mechanism by which labour markets are structured and a means by which both the *level* and the *incidence* of unemployment are determined. In the Soviet era, Russian enterprises traditionally recruited workers directly from schools and colleges, and since most factories were virtual monopolies within their

Figure 8.1   The enterprise labour market

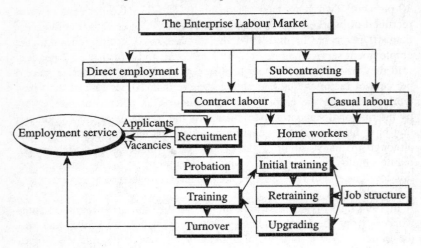

districts or *oblasts*, and were often huge entities, their main challenge was to secure a sufficient supply of labour in conditions of an artificial 'labour shortage'. They made little use of the official employment offices, which were mainly seen as handling social misfits, ex-convicts, alcoholics and others on the margin of society.

Since 1991 the new federal authorities have made a strong effort to develop an independent, credible, federal employment service, and by the end of 1994 there were over 2300 employment exchanges in the country. Under the 1991 Employment Act and subsequent legislation, firms are supposed to register all vacancies with the local employment exchange, inform workers being released of the need to register as a jobseeker with the local employment exchange, give the local exchange advance notice of 'mass releases' of ten workers or more, and make use of the employment service in their recruitment.

In 1991 information on recruitment practices was collected in RLFS1. Not surprisingly, this showed that the vast majority of firms did not make use of the employment service when recruiting workers or employees.[1] For production workers, two thirds of firms stated that their main recruiting method was advertisements, over 6 per cent relied mainly on direct applications, over 6 per cent relied on friends of existing workers and 4 per cent mainly recruited direct from educational institutions. Only just over 14 per cent relied mainly on the employment service.

In 1991, according to RLFS1, 45.1 per cent of those firms that had made recruitments said they had recruited no production workers through the employment service, and a further 44.9 per cent had recruited less than 10 per cent. Two years later, according to RLFS3, 60.6 per cent of firms recruited no workers through the service, and 31.2 per cent recruited less than 10 per cent. In mid 1994 the number not recruiting through the employment service had risen to 61.5 per cent, and a further 32.2 per cent said they had recruited 10 per cent or less through it. That left a mere 6 per cent of factories that had obtained more than 10 per cent of their new workers through the employment exchange. This placement rate is low by international standards, particularly by the standards of those countries that have also operated a quasi-monopolistic public employment service, although in many countries the proportion of placements made through public employment services is low and declining.[2] For the unemployed, this low placement rate must be a considerable deterrent to registering at the employment exchange.

In 1994 the only sector where more than half the firms recruited some workers from the local exchanges was construction materials; this was the same in 1991 and 1993. Significantly, in both 1993 and 1994 food-processing plants were least likely to have used the employment service. Even though they were in the only sector that had expanded its employment in net terms, those firms also typically had the highest wages, which would have made recruitment relatively easy.

Perhaps because they were recruiting very few workers and partly because they still had their established channels of recruitment, state establishments were actually less likely to use the employment service than others. In 1994 seven in ten state-owned industrial establishments did not use the state employment service at all to recruit workers. A further irony was that firms in Moscow City were the least inclined to use the employment service, and the proportion of workers recruited through the service declined over the four years (Figures 8.2–8.5).

Only in the first round of the RLFS were questions asked about the *reason* for non-use of the employment service. The main reason given by managements in 1991 was that the service sent only 'low quality' or unsuitable workers for the jobs on offer. Whether this was correct or not, their perception is the important point, and it is apparent from the declining use of the employment exchange that the reasons for not using the service increased in the 1990s rather than diminished. The second most common reason given in 1991 was that appropriate workers were not available from the service. The third most commonly mentioned reason was that the service was slow and ill organised.

Administration of the Federal Employment Service almost certainly improved after 1991, although the growing demands placed on the service by jobseekers may have prevented it from improving its efficiency,

Figure 8.2　Percentage of workers recruited from employment service,
by region, mid 1994

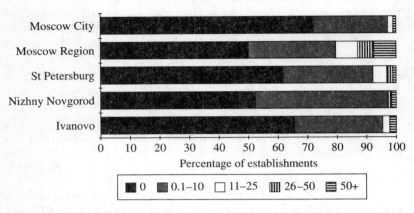

Source:　RLFS1, RLFS2, RLFS3, RLFS4; n = 503, 191, 348 and 384, respectively.

Figure 8.3　Percentage of workers recruited from employment service,
Moscow City, 1991–4

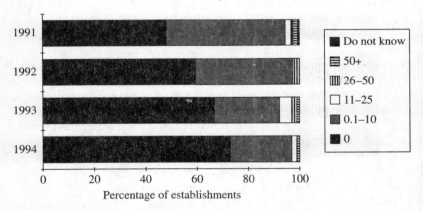

Source:　RLFS1, RLFS2, RLFS3, RLFS4; n = 503, 191, 348 and 384, respectively.

especially as the ratio of jobseekers to staff remained very high by international standards. The declining use of the service points to a failure of the formal labour-market mechanism to evolve as dis-employment accelerated and employment restructuring needs intensified. This lack of progress in institutional development was due ultimately to the low priority given to unemployment by policy makers.

Figure 8.4 Percentage of workers recruited from employment service, Moscow region, 1991–4

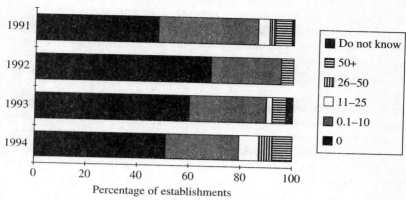

Source: RLFS1, RLFS2, RLFS3, RLFS4; n = 503, 191, 348 and 384, respectively.

Figure 8.5 Percentage of workers recruited from employment service, St Petersburg, 1991–4

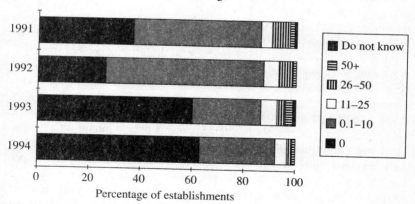

Source: RLFS1, RLFS2, RLFS3, RLFS4; n = 503, 191, 348 and 384, respectively.

The picture that emerges is that Russian firms had retained their institutional and personal recruitment channels, and that in the mid 1990s they were actually using the employment service *less* than at the outset of the federal employment service. The most reasonable explanation of this is that firms were recruiting fewer workers and had a much larger pool of unemployed from which to choose. But non-use of the employment service was also indicative of a basic reality of unemployment. If real unemployment was anything like the level suggested by the registered unemployment rate (a little over 1 per cent at the time of the fourth round of the RLFS), one would have expected that firms' use of the employment service would have been much greater. *If there were such a tight labour market, firms would have used every channel available.*

The picture is mirrored by the firms' registration of job vacancies. Although this was only asked about in RLFS4, it turned out that in 1994 more than one in every three firms did not inform the local employment service of job vacancies when they had them, even though under the 1991 Employment Act they were supposed to do so. Presumably most firms were unaware of this obligation, and this was confirmed by a few managers in conversations. In food processing, nearly one in two plants did not bother to inform the local employment exchange of job vacancies.

An indication that registration of vacancies nationally would have been even lower than recorded in the survey is that factories in Moscow City and Moscow Region, situated near the home base of the Federal Employment Service, were more inclined to register vacancies than firms in the other three regions. Nearly half the factories in Ivanovo did not bother to register vacancies with the local employment exchange. No doubt that was more typical of the country than Moscow. There was no significant difference between property forms, and although slightly more of the large firms did not inform their local exchanges, the differences between size categories were not large enough to be significant.

In 1994, of those that did so at all, only 35 per cent informed the employment service of their vacancy situation once a month, the remainder doing so at longer intervals. In textiles and garments and food processing, only about 22 per cent reported their vacancies once a month. Private and small firms were least likely to register them monthly. Firms in Ivanovo were not only much less likely to inform the local exchange of vacancies, but if they did so at all they were much less likely to do so once a month. As the reporting of vacancies seemed to reflect the initiative of the employment exchanges themselves, this was not surprising, since the understaffed and overworked exchange in Ivanovo had less time to visit or telephone enterprises to secure vacancy registrations.

The concept of job vacancies is notoriously complex, since it is not clear whether a declared vacancy is a stock or a flow. Some posts may be empty and the firm may be seeking to fill them at the prevailing wage rate as soon as possible; others may be empty but the firm may be prepared to fill them only if funds become available, if particular candidates become available or applicants emerge who are prepared to take jobs at much less than the prevailing wage. There are other difficulties with the concept, particularly in a bureaucratic environment in which the uncertainty is located in the demand for wage funds to pay for artificial posts.

Given the potential ambiguity of the notion of vacancies, it is still clear that the average vacancy rate in Russian factories declined steadily between 1991 and 1994. At the end of 1991, according to RLFS1, the overall vacancy rate was 6.0 per cent, being highest in construction materials (9.4 per cent) and lowest in food processing (2.7 per cent). Of the three regions covered, vacancies were highest in firms in Moscow City and in state firms. Two years later, in the four regions covered by RLFS3, the overall vacancy rate was 3.8 per cent, ranging from 5.8 per cent in Moscow City to a mere 1.1 per cent in Nizhny Novgorod. The vacancy rate was highest in state establishments (5.2 per cent) and lowest in private firms (2.6 per cent).

By mid 1994 the vacancy rate had fallen again, drastically, such that it ranged from 2.5 per cent in Moscow Region to 1.1 per cent in Nizhny Novgorod. Between different types of property forms it was highest in leaseholdings (2.6 per cent) and state establishments (1.7 per cent). These are extraordinarily low vacancy rates. The rate was highest in construction materials (3.9 per cent), probably reflecting seasonal factors, and lowest in food processing (0.34 per cent), which is notable because that was the sector that had been expanding employment. The vacancy rate was also inversely related to employment size of establishment.

It is indicative of the heterogeneity of the workforces and jobs that the vacancy rate was not highly correlated with the recent change in the firm's level of employment (Figure 8.6). Yet regardless of whether the employment change was positive or negative, the vacancy rate was still under 2 per cent.[3] In short, vacancies had virtually dried up. But the overall figure concealed yet another perverse phenomenon of Russian industry.

In terms of labour demand, in 1991 the vacancy rate for manual jobs was much higher than for employee categories, reflecting the character of Russian industry and the overwhelming use of manual labour. The vacancy rate was highest for qualified production workers (7.1 per cent), followed by unqualified production workers (6.6 per cent), whereas for employee groups it was about 3 per cent, depending on the level. Between 1991 and 1994 the vacancy rate declined for all categories, but the basic pattern remained (Figure 8.7). In 1994 the vacancy rate was 5.4 per cent for qualified production workers, 4.2 per cent for unqualified production workers and less than 1 per cent for employees. This reflected the outmoded technology that continued to prevail, and the emphasis on manual labour rather than on industry's longer-term needs.

Figure 8.6   Vacancy rate, by employment change during previous year, all regions, 1991–4 (average number of vacancies as percentage of employment at time of survey)

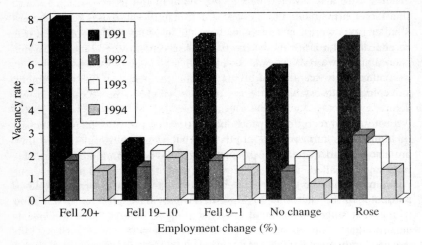

Note: The vacancy rate refers to end of the reference period for each round of the RLFS.
Source: RLFS1, RLFS2, RLFS3, RLFS4; n = 503, 191, 348 and 384, respectively.

Figure 8.7   Occupational vacancy rates, all regions, 1991–4

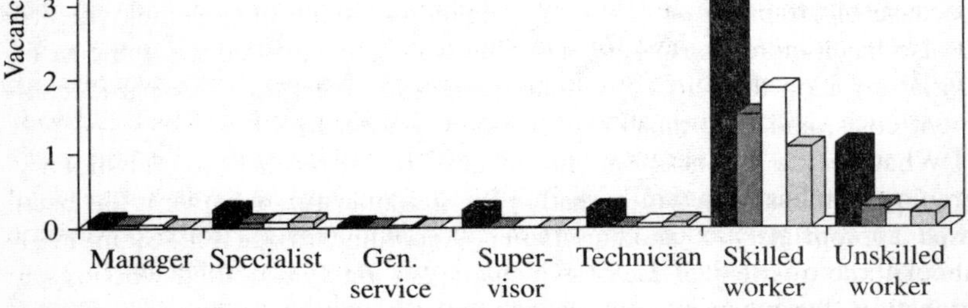

Source: RLFS1, RLFS2, RLFS3, RLFS4; n = 503, 191, 348 and 384, respectively.

As for the characteristics of workers sought by enterprises, the crucial issue of gender discrimination is covered in the next chapter. Other criteria were also covered in the first round of the RLFS, which showed that larger firms tended to recruit predominantly young workers, whereas smaller firms were less concerned with the age factor. The same was true of educational qualifications: larger firms screened by reference to formal schooling, but smaller firms were much less likely to do so. This sort of pattern may have implications for the incidence of unemployment, since large, old-established firms are least likely to be recruiting in the future.

Professional recruitment procedures are important for reducing the costs of high labour turnover that come from haphazard recruitment, and they are also an inadequately appreciated factor in determining labour productivity and so-called 'frictional unemployment'. However, although labour economists have given some attention to the recruitment process, and in particular to the use of screening criteria, they have given little attention to the next stage of the labour-market process, namely induction mechanisms, that is, the method of integrating newly recruited workers into the firm's labour force. This may seem a very minor issue in the context of employment restructuring in Russian industry, but as it is part of the process of developing an efficient and equitable labour market, it deserves a brief mention.

A well-known method of post-recruitment screening of worker suitability is *probationary employment*, whereby for some months workers may receive lower wages, less employment protection and fewer benefits. Experience in some labour markets has shown that this practice can be abused, and can be turned into a means of making workers insecure while undermining their pay and working conditions. In effect, it can be one method of creating a fragmented labour force. But its very existence weakens any claim that employment protection regulations deter firms from recruiting because of the costs of selecting inappropriate workers or because of the potential cost of subsequently having to cut employment.[4] It also has a more transparent economic value, since it reduces the cost of initial error on the part of the enterprise and potentially reduces recruitment costs, and may thus help to increase productivity.

Whatever its potential benefits or drawbacks, the use of probationary employment has been widespread in Russian industry. Whether it has been used appropriately is another matter. According to the RLFS, in 1991 about three quarters of factories usually put newly recruited workers on probation, the mean average duration of which was 2.3 months. It was most common in engineering and in larger factories. This issue was not investigated in subsequent rounds of the RLFS, since there was nothing to suggest that there was a major problem in this respect or the likelihood of any major change. The existence of an induction process of sorts did imply that there was no inherent obstacle to employment by virtue of high initial contract costs.

8.3   TRAINING AND RETRAINING: RESTRUCTURING SKILLS UNDER THREAT?

The next stage in the labour process story is one of the most complex, namely training and skill formation.[5] For some analysts, 'training' can become almost a fetish, both as the answer to labour-market restructuring challenges and as the cure for unemployment. It is neither of those. Yet it is a truism that enterprise-based training is potentially important for improving productivity and for economic and employment restructuring. Of the many forms of training, international evidence suggests that, typically, training received by workers within their enterprises yields a higher social and private (for worker and employer) return on the investment that training represents than does any other form of training. For instance studies have indicated that enterprise-based training yields more benefits than do vocational schools.[6] There is also strong circumstantial evidence that international differences in the extent of enterprise-based training explain part of the differences in average labour productivity within specific industrial sectors.[7] If industrial restructuring is to succeed in the foreseeable future, such training seems essential.

Superficially, it might appear that factories in Russia have performed well in this respect, although as noted in previous analyses, over the past few decades training in Russian enterprises may have been partly a 'social good'.[8] The suspicion is that, in the Soviet era, sending workers on training courses was a form of social perk to enable them to spend some time away from the drudgery of the factory shopfloor – a phenomenon not unknown in other parts of the world.

In quantitative terms there has long been a high level of industrial training in Russian industry. It is the qualitative aspect and the appropriateness of the type of training that gives greatest cause for alarm. Among the main concerns are (1) the practice of 'contract training', by which vocational schools are expected to train worker-students sent to them on contract from industrial enterprises, (2) excessive specialisation, with numerous trades being designated as separate subjects, (3) overemphasis on engineering,

Table 8.1 The training nexus

Type	Institution	Form of training
Initial:		
Pre-labour-market training, vocational education	State, local authority	Institutional
Labour market training	Employment service, local authority	Institutional
Recruitment training	Enterprise	Enterprise, institutional, on-the-job
Retraining:		
Retraining for task performance	Enterprise	Enterprise, institutional, on-the-job
Retraining for upgrading	Enterprise	Enterprise, institutional, on-the-job
Retraining for mobility	Enterprise, employment service	Enterprise, institutional, on-the-job

and (4) lack of adaptability, reflecting the persistence of outmoded product lines and technological inertia.

In any labour market there is a set of training mechanisms and structures, and it may be useful to characterise the training and skill-formation process as a sequential one of pre-labour-market, enterprise-based and labour-market (re-)training. This is illustrated in Table 8.1. The old craft model of manufacturing put emphasis on the third, fourth and fifth elements (rows). During the first six decades of the twentieth century, in most countries increasing emphasis was put on the first, through colleges, universities and other training institutions. Then, in the industrialised market economies of Europe in particular, the rise of mass unemployment in the 1970s and 1980s led to increased emphasis on the second and sixth elements, labour market training and retraining.

By the early years of the twenty-first century it is probable that the most competitive economies will be those that give balanced emphasis to all forms of skill formation. The Russian labour market in 1995 had a very long way to go to attain such a balance, and it is a salutary fact that in the 1980s and early 1990s there was a sharp decline in the extent of vocational education and pre-labour-market training.[9]

This section is not an attempt to discuss the full range of training and skill-formation issues. It has the more modest twofold objective of identifying the *incidence* of enterprise training and retraining and *trends* in the extent and types of such training. Although undoubtedly more detailed information would be required to make a detailed assessment of the changing 'training culture' in Russian factories, the survey data do go beyond what is usually collected in surveys. In the RLFS, three levels of training were investigated – initial training of newly recruited workers, retraining for job performance and transfers between jobs of similar levels or ranges of skill, and retraining for occupational upgrading. An attempt was made to distinguish between 'formal' and 'informal' types of training, where the first is defined as involving specific courses in recognised training institutions, including apprenticeships, while the second is defined as 'on-the-job' training that does not result in specific qualifications.

Initial training is the form that usually receives the bulk of attention, if not all of it. In the RLFS, managements were asked if they usually provided newly recruited production workers with training. At the end of 1991 the vast majority of the 501 factories covered by RLFS1 provided such training, with 91.8 per cent overall, ranging from 97.8 per cent in construction materials and 96.4 per cent in chemicals to a low of 86.7 per cent in engineering plants. However no less than 85 per cent of those factories providing training were doing so informally, with 7.9 per cent providing 'classroom training' on the factory site and 7 per cent sending workers to institutional training in classrooms off the premises. Most factories said that the duration of the training was short.

The picture was clouded by the claim made by over three quarters of factory managements that they were concerned about retaining those workers they did train. They attributed the loss of newly trained workers to low wages, first of all, and then to poor working conditions and lack of housing (which was particularly common in Moscow Region). In 1991, firms in food processing that were concerned about losing trainees were least likely to attribute their losses to low wages, which was consistent with the sector's new status as wage leader in manufacturing. However, although wages were most often cited, one possible explanation was 'status frustration', that is, newly trained workers and employees were finding themselves having to perform work beneath their qualifications or not requiring the technical skills they had acquired.[10]

In 1991–2 most firms said that newly trained workers were mainly leaving to go to 'cooperatives', the euphemism at the time for the emerging private sector. Wages were – or were widely believed to be – relatively high in those firms, and therefore it was not surprising that most managements responded by raising wages, although those providing institutional training were more inclined to offer extra benefits or attempt to hold on to workers through 'trainee contracts'. Raising wages was the principal response even in those firms that mainly attributed the loss of trained

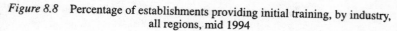

Figure 8.8 Percentage of establishments providing initial training, by industry, all regions, mid 1994

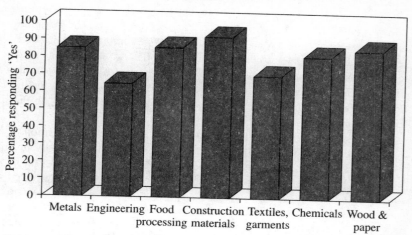

Source: RLFS4, n = 384.

workers to poor working conditions or lack of housing. In effect the labour market was beginning to work via compensatory wage payments.

Three years later, when firms were again asked what measures they were taking in response to the loss of newly trained workers, over two thirds said that they tried to raise wages. The only change of note since 1991 was that more firms were resorting to trainee contracts, particularly in textiles and garments and wood products.

The loss of trainees by factories should not be belittled simply because there is a large and growing labour surplus, or because most of the training is informal and thus expected to involve little cost. The probability of such losses could be a deterrent to more and better training, and it would have also involved the lost cost of sending workers to training schools.

After 1991 there was an erosion of enterprise entry-level training. In 1993, according to RLFS3 data, 82.5 per cent of firms were providing recruitment-level training, ranging from 100 per cent of construction materials firms to 72.5 per cent of engineering plants. In 1994 such training was provided to workers in 75.3 per cent of all firms, with the probability again being relatively low in engineering plants (Figure 8.8).

Underlying that erosion, were more structural concerns. A first source of concern was that private firms were less likely to provide training

Figure 8.9   Percentage of establishments providing initial training, by property form, all regions, mid 1994

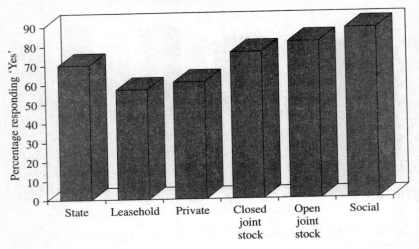

Source: RLFS4, n = 384.

(Figure 8.9), suggesting that in the context of property-form restructuring training mechanisms would need to be strengthened. A second concern was that the likelihood of such training was positively related to employment size (Figure 8.10), suggesting that size restructuring would also contribute to the erosion of training. A third concern was that the probability of training was much lower in firms in the depressed labour market of Ivanovo, and there must be a fear that cuts in training in response to worsening economic prospects could merely accentuate the disparities in regional labour markets. A fourth source of concern was that in most factories the training remained 'informal' or 'on-the-job'. Thus in 1993 84.7 per cent of firms that provided training were doing so informally. In 1994 the figure was 85.1 per cent, and only 9 per cent (8.9 per cent in 1993) were providing training in classes within the enterprise and 5.9 per cent (6.5 per cent in 1993) were providing it in classes outside the enterprise.

The one potentially positive correlation was that in terms of corporate governance forms, 'worker controlled' factories were 10 per cent more likely to be providing training than other non-state forms. Whether this was the result of worker pressure or merely reflected the type of firm involved is a moot point. Nevertheless there is reason to suppose that where workers have a greater say in the management of enterprises, training is more likely, an issue to which we will return in Chapter 11.

Figure 8.10 Percentage of establishments providing initial training, by employment size, all regions, 1991–4

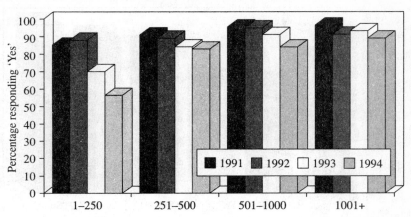

Source: RLFS1, RLFS2, RLFS3, RLFS4; n = 503, 191, 348 and 384, respectively.

Retraining for job performance was the second level of training for which information was gathered. In 1991 67.5 per cent of factories were providing such retraining, ranging from 82.2 per cent in textiles and garments to a low of 52.2 per cent in construction materials. The practice was relatively rare in small firms. In 1993 such retraining was provided in 61.4 per cent of firms, with a low of 51.3 per cent in engineering. In 1994 it was provided in 61.6 per cent of establishments, again with a relatively low number in engineering (55.5 per cent) and private firms (60 per cent). Such retraining was also relatively unlikely to be provided in Ivanovo. As with initial training, most retraining for job performance was informal – nearly 80 per cent in 1991 and 80.5 per cent in 1994. Thus, although the erosion was less than with recruitment-level training, the overall levels were lower and there were the same concerns associated with the probable impact of restructuring.

Retraining for upgrading was the third form of training considered. In 1991 this was provided in 89 per cent of firms, being more common in state enterprises and large factories, although in all sectors and property forms the type of retraining was predominantly informal. In 1993 the percentage of firms providing such retraining had shrunk to 81.7 per cent; in 1994 it was down to 70.1 per cent of establishments, with a relatively low incidence in textiles and garments (59.3 per cent), private firms (53.7 per cent) and firms in Ivanovo. As with other forms of training, in 1994

Figure 8.11   Percentage of establishments providing initial training, retraining for performance and retraining for upgrading, by corporate governance, all regions, mid 1994

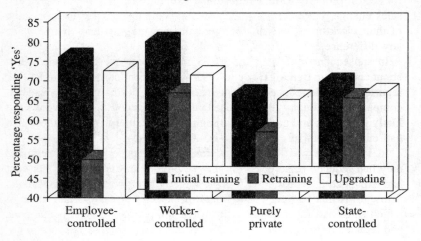

Source: RLFS4, n = 374.

most retraining for upgrading was informal (83.4 per cent), with only construction materials having a high propensity to provide formal training (41.2 per cent). The figures show that there had been a big drop in the percentage of factories providing retraining for upgrading compared with 1993.

It is worth noting that in terms of alternative forms of corporate governance, what were designated in Chapter 3 as worker-controlled and employee-controlled governance structures seemed to be more likely to be providing initial training and training for upgrading, although the situation was unclear for retraining for job performance (Figure 8.11).

Thus far we have considered whether factories did or did not provide training or retraining. Yet rather than give it up completely, it is more likely that firms changed the extent of such training. Accordingly, in the course of the four rounds of the RLFS more detailed information was gathered on the dynamics of training practices.

In 1991 managements on average estimated that about 17 per cent of workers had received some form of training or retraining during the previous year, ranging from 21 per cent in textiles and basic metals to 12 per cent in wood products, and from 11 per cent in firms with fewer than 250 workers to over 21 per cent in those with more than 1000 workers. In order to examine interfirm variation in the percentage of workers receiving training a regression was estimated. This showed that, controlling for sector, property form, occupational structure, employment change and sales change, larger firms were providing training to a larger proportion of their workforces, and that neither sales nor employment change made any difference.

In subsequent rounds of the RLFS more direct questions were asked about changes in training. In June 1992 40.8 per cent of the firms in RLFS2 reported they had reduced the amount of training during the previous year, compared with only 12.6 per cent that had expanded it. Cuts were most likely in textiles and garments, large firms, state enterprises and those that had cut employment.

In 1993 there was a further erosion. Nearly 36 per cent of firms said they had reduced training during the previous year, and only 6.8 per cent had expanded it. A reduction was particularly likely in large firms, private firms, firms that had cut employment or capacity utilisation and those in which sales had fallen. No less than half the textiles and garments firms had reduced training. Even among firms that had expanded sales, far more had cut training than had expanded it.

The erosion continued in 1994, when 42.8 per cent reported they had cut back on training and retraining during the previous year, compared with the 7.6 per cent that had increased it.[11] The decline was greatest in construction materials, chemicals and textiles and garments, and least in food processing. In terms of size, the most widespread reduction was in large firms – over 55 per cent of those with more than 1000 workers had cut training. And firms that had cut employment were more likely to have cut training as well (Figure 8.12). In turn, it is probable that this compounded restructuring difficulties, for it is in such factories that skill formation is most valuable as a means of promoting labour-market mobility.

Another issue examined from the second round of the RLFS onwards was *training institutes* owned by the enterprises. Having a training institute was the norm for large Soviet enterprises. According to RLFS2, where a question on this was included for the first time, 72.3 per cent of the 191 firms had operated a training institute in 1990. By mid 1992 only 56.3 per cent of those factories were doing so, implying that one in five of those that had operated a training institute had closed it. Nearly a third of those still operating one stated that they planned to reduce the funding allocated to it, in particular those firms that had cut employment.

RLFS4 also examined the financing of training. In 1991–3, according to managements, 4.2 per cent of firms had been financing their own training institute, 46.1 per cent had been transferring funds to a training institute

Figure 8.12   Percentage reducing and percentage increasing training, by percentage change in employment during previous year, all regions, mid 1994

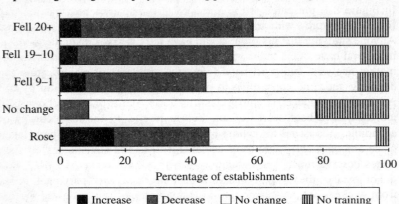

Source: RLFS4, n = 377.

to pay for trainees from their factory (particularly those in the chemicals sector), 13.5 per cent had paid for each trainee individually and 12.8 per cent had paid grants or stipends directly to trainees.

By mid 1994 over a quarter of those firms (27.6 per cent) that had paid for training in one of these ways had given up doing so, and over one in five (22.3 per cent) of those still providing such funding were planning to cut it. This represented a further erosion of enterprise-paid training, continuing the trend picked up in 1991–3. Yet paradoxically, nearly one in five firms considered that retaining skilled workers was likely to be their main employment problem over the next 12 months.

Another way of seeing the erosion of training and retraining is that in 1991 58.5 per cent of firms provided all three levels of training, while 2.8 per cent provided only recruitment-level training and a mere 1.8 per cent none at all. In 1994 43.5 per cent provided all forms, 7.8 per cent provided entry-level training only and 11 per cent provided none at all. At the same time there had been a shift from formal to informal, on-the-job training.

In sum, the actual process of enterprise restructuring was threatening to be a cause of the demise of enterprise training, and unless policies are introduced – perhaps training levies and grants, perhaps other fiscal incentives – lack of the most important form of labour-market training could jeopardise the restructuring process itself.

8.4 OCCUPATIONAL OR JOB RESTRUCTURING

In Figure 8.1, presented at the outset of this chapter, a box was inserted for 'job structure', with arrows going from it to the three forms of training. Anyone studying that diagram should have felt uneasy. Labour economists in general have failed to incorporate the issue of job structures into labour-market analysis, and most have found the problems of classification too daunting and time consuming to pursue the problems thrown up by it.[12] Attempts to produce statistical classification systems of occupational and job titles have been works of art. Yet in debates on the restructuring of economies, the issues thrown up by the protracted debates that have taken place among a select group of social scientists and statisticians on such issues deserve much more attention than they have received.

For instance the conventional view that 'structural unemployment' arises from workers not possessing the skills required by firms is flawed, in that the character of jobs and the distribution of types of job are *endogenous* to labour-markets and enterprises. They are not merely technologically determined. They reflect the influence of ideological factors, technology, labour-market conditions, wage structures and social factors. As such they can be altered by changing the pattern of incentives and much else. Indeed it can be argued quite cogently that in many spheres it would be easier and less costly to restructure jobs than to attempt to restructure people to fit the existing jobs.

Job restructuring is a critical aspect of employment restructuring. Here too one must be wary about the appropriateness of conventional concepts, and any evidence of change should be regarded as very exploratory. Classifying someone as belonging to a particular job or occupational title is often a matter of convenience or convention, rather than an objectively valid procedure, just as the dichotomy of 'skilled' and 'unskilled' is always questionable, since classifying skill depends partly on technical competence, partly on historically derived notions of social status and partly on notions of control.

These issues are particularly important in the context of Russian restructuring, since the job structures that emerged in the Soviet era were profoundly influenced by the Leninist admiration of Taylor's 'scientific management' – whereby technical division of labour was advanced as a means of controlling labour performance – and by the ideological commitment to a proletarian work ethic, in which manual labour was put on a pedestal – in many factories one could find images extolling the virtues and appeal of honest physical endeavour. The wage system and structure of differentials were adapted to fit the model of labour. It was one of the great ironies of the social system that the intended triumph of the 'working class' merely led to a systematic proletarianisation of the working population over seven decades of exhortation and incentive and monitoring structures.

A very exploratory attempt will be made here to see whether changes were taking place in the occupational or job structure of employment in Russian industry in the early 1990s, after the collapse of the Soviet system. It is hoped that the few insights gained will be sufficient to encourage much more detailed analytical work on what should be a crucial aspect of Russian labour-market restructuring

In the RLFS, current and retrospective information was collected on the different types of worker and employee, a dichotomy based on the custom of official *Goskomstat* statistics. The former category was divided into managerial and administrative, 'specialist' and general service employees; the latter was divided into supervisory (or shopfloor managerial), qualified manual (or 'skilled') and unqualified manual ('unskilled') workers, where the division of the last two groups depended on the amount of training and formal schooling normally required of the job, with a qualified job requiring at least three months of training.

Data on the number in each category were collected for the current period of the RLFS round and for the previous year. In this section we will do little more than present a description of the structure and of changes in the shares of total employment taken by the seven categories.[13]

Consistent with the prevailing idea that Russian industrial firms are overwhelmingly labour intensive, in 1991 skilled manual workers on average accounted for nearly 64 per cent of the firms' workforces. As unqualified workers accounted for a further 14.5 per cent, manual workers accounted for over three quarters of the total, an unusually high percentage by international standards. In the preceding two years there may have been a tiny shift towards managerial and administrative employees and supervisory workers, with a relative (and absolute) decline in qualified manual workers. In food processing and textiles and garments there was a clear shift away from unqualified towards qualified manual workers, while in other sectors the reverse was the case. The changes that occurred should be interpreted as the consequence of employment cuts, merely highlighting the fact that manual production workers were affected most by declining employment at the time. Thus those factories that had made employment cuts had also reduced their share of manual workers, whereas the few that had expanded employment had also expanded their share of manual workers. Another indicator of change was that non-state enterprises were most likely to have cut the share of manual workers, although in all property forms there was a net shift away from workers towards employees.

Figure 8.13 Occupational distribution of employment in Russian industry, all regions, 1991–4 (percentage of workforce in identified occupational categories)

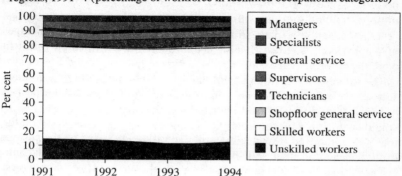

Source: RLFS1, RLFS2, RLFS3, RLFS4; n = 502, 191, 348 and 384, respectively.

At the end of 1991 managements were asked whether they planned to increase, decrease or leave unchanged the number in each of the seven occupational categories. Overall they were planning or expecting cuts in total employment. Yet it was clear that they anticipated a relative *growth* in skilled manual jobs, while expecting a net decline in all other categories. Thus in 1991 there was little evidence that there had been any shift away from manual labour in Russian industry, or that any was expected in the near future. Developments over the next three years bore out those expectations, as shown in Figure 8.13.

The basic fact is that employment in Russian industry declined across all categories but continued to consist predominantly of manual labour, perhaps with small changes between the share of unskilled and more skilled workers.[14] According to data from RLFS3, the share of the workforce consisting of workers in jobs classified as 'unskilled' fell in 1992–3, by 0.43 per cent on average. This concealed substantial sectoral variation. Whereas the share fell in wood and paper products, chemicals and food processing, it rose in engineering, textiles and metals. The decline occurred in all size categories, but by more so in small firms. There was no relationship between the change and the percentage change of total employment. Perhaps most surprising was the fact that, whereas the unskilled share declined by 0.78 per cent in state factories, it fell by only 0.14 per cent in private firms and by 0.15 per cent in closed joint-stock firms, while it actually rose in open joint-stock firms, by 0.55 per cent.

The RLFS4 data highlight two features of the occupational structure – the continuing predominance of manual workers, particularly those classified as 'skilled', and a slight shift from skilled to unskilled jobs. Thus over 84 per cent of the workforces in food processing and nearly 82 per cent of those in textiles and garments were manual workers. Although the percentage change was small, in all sectors the skilled manual worker share of employment declined. It also declined in firms with more than 500 workers, whereas it rose in firms below that size.

The impression one draws from the data is that, while there were some sectoral variations and perhaps some modest change, there was no systematic shift from manual to non-manual jobs, and none of the upgrading that would be desirable for restructuring and productivity improvement. Manual jobs still comprised over three quarters of all employment, and there was even evidence of a net shift from more skilled to less skilled jobs.

There was also little to suggest that managements were giving much attention to job restructuring. In all four rounds of the RLFS, senior managers were asked about expected or planned changes in the various categories of employment. In most cases the responses were no more than guesses, with little sign of strategic intention. If the pattern of responses showed anything, it was to indicate that the managers expected a net shift away from unskilled jobs towards skilled production jobs, coupled with a net cut in so-called 'specialist' employees (presumably reflecting the demise of planning departments and the effect of decentralisation of management to enterprise and establishment levels) and a general feeling of gloom about employment prospects.

The following summarises the noteworthy patterns of expectations with regard to job categories, as recorded in the fourth round of the RLFS.

Managerial and administrative: in mid 1994 21 per cent of firms expected to cut managerial and administrative employment during the coming year, while less than 1 per cent expected it to increase. Cuts were seen as most probable in the chemicals sector, in large plants and in private and open joint-stock companies. Expected cuts were also larger in firms that had cut employment during the preceding year.

Specialist employees: nearly 28 per cent expected to cut their employment levels, although 3.4 per cent expected them to rise. Expectations of cuts were greatest in metals, wood and paper products and textiles and garments (all over one third), in closed joint-stock firms, in larger and medium-sized firms, in St Petersburg, and in firms that had cut employment.

General service employees: just over 21 per cent expected to reduce the proportion of such employees, and 1.3 per cent to increase it. Expected cuts were greatest in metals, chemicals and textiles and garments, in closed and open joint-stock firms, and in large factories. Note that various clerical workers would have been included in this and the preceding categories.

Supervisory workers: just over 20 per cent expected to reduce the number of such workers, 2.4 per cent to increase them. Above-average expected cuts were in metals, chemicals, textiles, open and closed joint-stock firms, and medium-sized and large firms.

Technicians: employment of these workers was expected to decline in 21.7 per cent of firms and rise in 5 per cent of them. Above-average cuts were expected in metals, chemicals, closed and open joint-stock companies and large firms.

General service workers: 18.3 per cent expected to cut their employment, 1.1 per cent to increase it, the increases being well above average in metals, chemicals and textiles and garments, and in closed joint-stock firms.

Skilled workers: 22.5 per cent expected to reduce the employment share of skilled workers, but 20.1 per cent expected to increase their share. The expected decreases were relatively high in metals and textiles, whereas increases were relatively high in engineering and textiles. Decreases were also relatively high in private and low in state enterprises, and increases were easily highest in private firms.

Unskilled workers: 27 per cent expected a decline, 5.5 per cent an increase. Decreases were relatively likely in metals, textiles and chemicals, but in all sectors more than 20 per cent expected a decrease. Between property forms, decreases were most expected in closed and open joint-stock firms.

In sum, with the cuts in production and employment and the evidence of enterprise restructuring, one might have expected some restructuring of jobs. However there was apparently little systematic change in the occupational structure of employment in 1993–4. There was also no evidence that firms were planning to change their structure, except that more expected to cut unskilled workers and low-level employees to a greater extent than other groups (Figures 8.14 and 8.15).

A final point – or an item for further research – is that growth in the share of any occupational category was positively related to a change in the relative wage differential between that group and the wage of unskilled workers. This at least suggested that an occupational labour market was beginning to operate.

There was also some sign of *job flexibility*. In 1993 49.7 per cent of firms said they had made internal transfers to limit redundancies, and in 1994 62.3 per cent said they had done so, ranging from 84.6 per cent in metals to 54.4 per cent in textiles and garments. The practice tended to be less in state and leaseholding establishments, and was most widespread in joint-stock companies (Figure 8.16). This prompts the speculative

Figure 8.14   Expected employment change of skilled workers during next year, all regions, 1992–5 (percentage of establishments reporting expected change over next year)

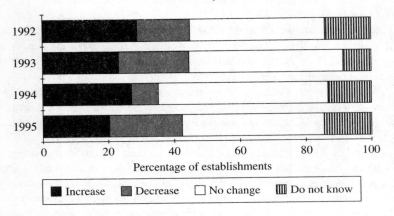

Note: The dates refer to the year after the time of the interview.
Source: RLFS1. RLFS2, RLFS3, RLFS4; n = 503, 191, 348 and 384, respectively.

Figure 8.15   Expected employment change of unskilled workers during next year, all regions, 1992–5 (percentage of establishments reporting expected change during next year)

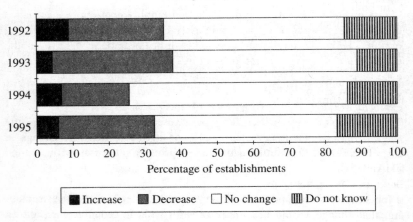

Note: The dates refer to the year after the time of the interview.
Source: RLFS1, RLFS2, RLFS3, RLFS4; n = 503, 191, 348 and 384, respectively.

Figure 8.16 Percentage of establishments making internal transfers of workers to limit redundancies, by property form, all regions, 1993–4

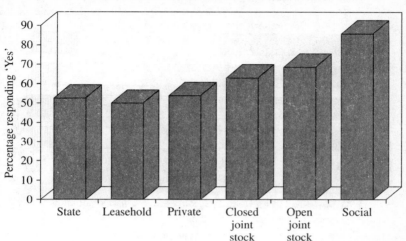

Source: RLFS4, n = 382.

hypothesis that worker pressure to retain redundant workers rather than release them was greater in such firms.

In both 1993 and 1994 the practice was far more likely in larger factories, as well as – predictably enough – in firms that had cut employment by a relatively large amount (Figure 8.17). Such necessary transfers may have been behind the fact that a large number of managements expressed concern about the longer-term threat to skills, since they had been obliged to transfer workers from posts where they used their skills to posts where they did not need them.

8.5   THE EMPLOYMENT IMPACT OF TECHNOLOGICAL CHANGE

If job structures are to change with enterprise and employment restructuring, that change should be connected with what is broadly classified as technological change. Throughout the 1980s Russian industrial enterprises were notorious for their lack of innovation, which was accompanied by stagnant and then declining productivity. As Chapter 3 suggested, this did begin to change in the 1990s, although much of the recorded change

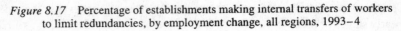

Figure 8.17   Percentage of establishments making internal transfers of workers to limit redundancies, by employment change, all regions, 1993–4

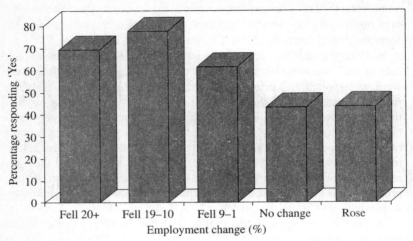

Source: RLFS4, n = 376.

was probably defensive or cost-cutting rather than an attempt to improve productivity.

The issue here is the employment restructuring implications of the changes. It will be recalled that in the survey technological change was divided into *product innovation*, *capital innovation* and *work process innovation*. In each case, if the management reported they had made a change they were asked about its perceived impact on employment, in terms of labour use or employment, and skill.

Determining the extent of product innovation was approached in 1991 by means of a question about whether the management had extended the product range during the previous year. Just over a third had done so. The probability of product extension was positively related to employment change – over 50 per cent of firms in which employment had risen had extended their product range, whereas less than a third of those that had cut employment had done so. But less than one in five firms that had extended their product range felt that the change had increased employment. More than two in five (47.8 per cent) felt that the change had increased the technical knowledge, or skill, required of production workers. If the implication of the change was that some product innovation was taking place, as some managers claimed, the perception that more technical skill was required was consistent with international evidence suggesting that the early stages of product innovation are associated with an increase in skilled employment.[15] However any impact would have been slight, since the figures imply that only about 15 per cent of firms were requiring more skill from their workforce purely as a result of product innovation.

In 1992 the question on product innovation was modified to include cuts as well as extensions in the range of products. Cuts in product range were widespread, and in itself that may have been advisable. However firms that had cut employment were five times as likely to have reduced the product range, while increasing the product range was positively associated with employment change. Of those that had increased the product range, 25.5 per cent reported that they believed the change had helped increase employment, and 51 per cent said that it had increased the *complexity* of the production process. Among those that had reduced their product range 55.8 per cent believed that the reduction had been labour-displacing.

In 1993 41 per cent of those firms that had increased their product range felt that this had increased employment, while 4.8 per cent thought it had led to a decrease because they had shifted to the production of less labour-intensive goods. This implied that on average product innovation had become more employment-generating than in the earlier stages of the restructuring. Of those that had reduced their product range, 65.4 per cent felt that the change had resulted in a lower labour demand. Of those that had increased their product range, 49.4 per cent felt that the expansion had increased the skill requirements of workers, the remainder said it had made no difference. The vast majority of those that had cut their product range said it had made no difference to skill requirements.

In 1994, as in previous rounds, firms that had increased their product range were far more likely to have increased employment than those that had made cuts in their range (Figure 8.18). And, as observed in Chapter 4, most of those that had cut products thought that doing so had resulted in less employment, whereas only a minority of those that had extended the number of products believed that it had resulted in more employment.

As for *capital innovation*, that is, changes in equipment, machinery and automation, in 1991 over two thirds of firms that had made an innovation reported that the main change had had no impact on employment.[16] In 21 per cent of cases the change was regarded as labour-displacing and in 12 per cent the main change was perceived as having boosted the demand for labour. Thus, overall, changes in machinery were perceived as labour-displacing. Over a third of the managements also felt that the changes had

Figure 8.18   Changes in product range, by percentage employment change, all regions, 1993–4 (percentage of firms reporting change in range of products)

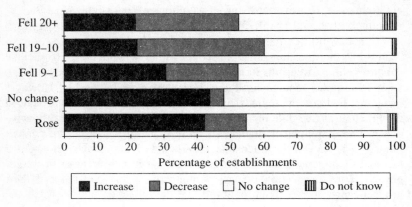

Source: RLFS4, n = 378.

increased the range of tasks of production workers – 35.4 per cent compared with the 17.1 per cent who believed they had reduced the range. A majority also believed that the changes had increased the level of technical knowledge required – 54.1 per cent, compared with the 14.4 per cent who believed it had reduced it.

In RLFS2 there was no correlation between capital innovation and employment change, although many managers reported that computerisation was helping them to increase employment. By 1994, in contrast, firms that had cut employment during the preceding year were less likely to have introduced new technology in the production process (Figure 8.19). In most sectors, as observed in Chapter 4, technological innovation was also thought to have had a positive effect on the level of employment.

The third dimension of technological change is *work process innovation*, that is, changes in the way work is organised. This covers a multitude of small and major changes, making any single measure somewhat unreliable. Nevertheless it may be useful to differentiate between those firms that had been static in this respect and those that believed otherwise.

In RLFS1 about 44 per cent had made work process changes, with change being most probable in engineering and 'cooperatives'. Work reorganisation was slightly more likely in firms that had cut employment, and more firms thought that the change had reduced employment (27.4 per cent) than increased it (10.7 per cent). The changes being made were also more likely to be perceived as increasing the knowledge required of

Figure 8.19 Percentage of firms introducing new technology during previous year, by percentage employment change, all regions, 1993–4

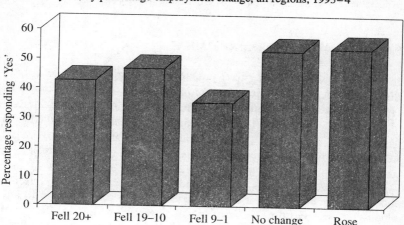

Source: RLFS4, n = 377.

production workers (36.8 per cent) than reducing it (4.5 per cent). The strong impression from the 1991 survey was that work reorganisation was fairly minor.

The tempo of work reorganisation seemed relatively stable, although this might have concealed a change in the type of reorganisation. In 1992 52.6 per cent of factory managements said they had conducted some form of work reorganisation during the previous year, and many believed this had reduced the need for labour (29.2 per cent) rather than increased it (9 per cent). In 1993 41.2 per cent of firms had made a change in work organisation, change being particularly common in textiles, and garments and basic metals.

In 1994 44.1 per cent of the firms claimed to have made a change in work organisation, ranging from 57.1 per cent in chemicals to 19.2 per cent in construction materials. In 1994 such changes may have been slightly more probable in private firms (53.7 per cent) than joint-stock firms, and were certainly more likely in large firms. The majority of those that had made a change claimed that the main modification had been a tightening of work organisation (52.4 per cent), followed by an increase in the range of tasks of production workers (17.1 per cent), an alteration in equipment and facilities to improve working practices (12.4 per cent) and an increase in work autonomy (6.5 per cent). Except in textiles and garments and chemicals, as observed in Chapter 4, the changes were generally thought to have enabled firms to reduce their labour requirements.

8.6   ASPECTS OF WORKING TIME

In Soviet industry, working-time practices were rigid, and there is little doubt that international developments in the sphere of what is known as 'functional flexibility' were not incorporated into employment in Russian industry in the early 1990s. Functional flexibility is concerned with improving the allocation of working time, refining the capacity to adjust to varying work requirements and responding to the needs of managers and workers.

Internationally there has been a trend towards more flexible working-time practices, an erosion of overtime premiums, increased shift working, the use of more part-time workers, job sharing, job rotation and the use of mechanisms to create multi-skilled workers. Resolving issues of functional flexibility will be important for the long-term restructuring of the Russian labour market. Moves to allow enterprises to set their own work schedules and working-time arrangements, and efforts to make them a subject of collective bargaining, were seen by some analysts as likely to lead to a reduction in the demand for labour.[17] Unless efficiency is improved by such methods, the long-term capacities of the factories to create employment will be undermined.

In the RLFS, information was collected on various aspects of working time. In 1991 the standard 40-hour week was the overwhelming norm for regular workers and employees, although on average the ubiquitous co-operatives were apparently working shorter weeks. At the time, manual workers were on average working about 45 minutes *overtime* per week, and employees none. There were centrally established restrictions on overtime, and some influential observers believed that their removal would lead to more overtime by some workers and the release of others into unemployment.[18]

There was considerable anecdotal evidence that in 1991 actual working time was often much less than the standard working week, although this issue was not examined in the first round. However there can be little doubt that the situation did not improve. Having refined the questions on working time in RLFS3, we found that in 1993 actual working time for employees and workers averaged 36.7 and 35.8 hours a week respectively. The big development was the reduction in working time introduced by managements in the face of a lack of demand. On average, besides other factors reducing working time, in mid 1993 workers and employees worked 1.1 fewer hours per week because of short-time working decided by the administration.[19] Overtime still existed in some factories, averaging about half an hour a week for workers, a little less than in 1991, and a few minutes for employees.

By mid 1994 the average working time had dropped considerably. Total hours were 31.8 per week for regular workers and 33.3 for employees, reflecting the greater incidence of short-time working among production workers. By then overtime had virtually disappeared, and non-working time due to short-time work decided by the administration was averaging 6.9 hours for workers and 5.8 for employees. As stressed in Chapter 4, this was a major feature of the surplus labour conditions that had come to dominate Russian industry. In a sense it continued the severe undervaluation of time that so characterised life in the Soviet era, with its queues and passivity. Anybody visiting a Russian factory in the mid 1990s would have been left in no doubt that most work was non-intensive and that the associated underutilisation of machines was severe.

Beyond the average working time and the extent of underemployment, working practices have been rather rigid. Perhaps the classic indicator of work flexibility in manufacturing is the extent of *shift working*. In some countries, most factories operate three shifts, and in certain sectors in some South-East Asian economies some even operate four per day.[20] In the European Union in the 1980s it was estimated that 29 per cent of industrial firms were operating two shifts per day, 23 per cent had three and 17 per cent had four.[21] Russian factories have a long way to go to reach anything like that stage.

At the end of 1991 38.3 per cent of factories operated only one shift and 44.7 per cent operated two per day, and some of those with only one shift had been operating two the previous year. The main reasons for cutting shifts were the shortage of raw materials at the time and the perception that there was a labour shortage. In the textiles and garments sector, over one quarter of those operating only one shift attributed this to the fact that they had mainly women workers, although this seems to have been an excuse since in many firms with a high proportion of women, two or three shifts were operated. In over three quarters of those factories with only one shift, the management estimated that they would have been able to sell the increased output, had they been able or willing to increase to two shifts.

Although shift working was low in 1991, in the ensuing three years the share of firms with two or three shifts per day declined quite sharply. In 1993 about half the firms were operating only one shift per day, or seven

Table 8.2 Main reason for single shift working, all regions, 1991–4 (percentage distribution for all establishments operating one shift)

	1991	1992	1993	1994
Raw material shortage	29.6	29.6	18.1	8.5
Labour shortage	29.1	9.2	11.3	6.3
Workers' opposition	4.2	6.1	3.4	5.4
Women workers	5.3	12.2	7.9	5.8
Low demand	—	15.3	20.9	33.1
Not required for production	—	12.2	—	4.5
Cut in production	—	—	9.0	24.7
Other	—	15.2	28.3	11.4

Source: RLFS1, RLFS2, RLFS3, RLFS4; n = 189, 98, 177 and 223, respectively.

or fewer shifts per week. At one extreme, two in five food-processing plants operated three shifts per day for five or more days a week. At the other extreme, less than 2 per cent of engineering plants operated three shifts a day and only one in four operated two shifts. In terms of work shifts per week, in May 1993 the mean average was 9.2; a year later it was down to 8.3. The mean fell in all sectors except food processing. It fell in all property forms of establishment.

According to RLFS4, shift working declined quite sharply in 1993–4. Thus 44.8 per cent of the factories were operating only one shift a day in 1993, 37.4 per cent two shifts and 17.9 per cent three shifts. For the same firms one year later, 56.6 per cent were operating only one shift, 28.5 per cent had two, and only 14.9 per cent had three. Engineering plants, with their links to military–industrial activities, experienced the greatest decline, and were also most likely to be operating only one shift (over 68 per cent were doing so), whereas food-processing plants were not only overwhelmingly likely to be operating two or three shifts, but by 1994 over 44 per cent were operating three shifts. One indicator that positive changes were taking place was that whereas 72.6 per cent of state firms were operating only one shift, 46.9 per cent of open joint-stock firms were doing so, a higher percentage than among private firms.

The reasons for operating only one shift per day changed during the four years, as shown in Table 8.2, which reports the responses of the general directors of the plants when asked to cite the main reason for having only one shift. At the outset of the economic shock the main factors were a shortage of raw materials, which reflected the supply shock associated with the break-up of the Soviet economic and political system, and the legacy of perceived labour shortage. Demand constraints were not mentioned. By mid 1992 labour shortage had ceased to be a major constraint, whereas lack of demand had become the second most common reason. A year later it had become the main factor, with low demand and cuts in production accounting for nearly 30 per cent of the total, and many of those classified as 'other reasons' were indirectly linked to lack of demand. By mid 1994 the absence of demand for the output was overwhelming the main factor, highlighting the tremendous slack in the economy.

Functional flexibility comes in many forms. Besides shift working and the need for more flexible working schedules, it may seem strange to consider perverse forms of work flexibility in factories. Time on the job and in the enterprise having so little value, the two main forms of perverse flexibility have been shirking and *absenteeism*, that is, unauthorised leave. Traditionally there have been many claims that Russian industry has been characterised by a high degree of absenteeism, and it has been claimed that this has contributed to the desire by managements to hire more workers than required. It was even suggested by one manager that both managements and workers built in absenteeism as part of the labour contract to compensate for low wages and poor working conditions. The trouble with this is that absenteeism is then largely institutionalised out of existence, because it is accepted as normal.

Bearing in mind this difficulty of interpretation, in RLFS1 several questions were asked about absenteeism, defined as unauthorised absence from work.[22] Consistent with our interpretation, which was based on discussions with personnel managers in factories, it turned out that the rate of absenteeism was remarkably low. It was relatively high in basic metals and in other male-dominated sectors – a significant point in view of the common excuse for discrimination against women that they have a relatively high rate of absenteeism. Managers believed that the main reasons for absenteeism were low work discipline and alcohol.

Another more positive aspect of work flexibility is the practice of *job rotation*. It has been claimed that transferring production workers between different sets of work tasks can improve productivity, as long as this is part of managerial policy rather than an expediency to fill gaps due to absences from work or labour turnover. It has been claimed that Japanese factories attain higher productivity and skill development by judicious use of job rotation, designed to prevent the lowering of efficiency due to excessive repetition of a narrow range of tasks.

In 1991 only, several questions on job rotation were included, and 56 per cent of firms claimed to practise it. Thus, if one accepts the responses at face value, this form of flexibility seemed quite widespread. Questions were not included in subsequent rounds of the survey, being supplemented by more detail on other matters. Yet the fact that internal transfers were widely resorted to, as mentioned earlier, suggests that in this respect there continued to be some flexibility, and that the capacity of managements to move workers around was not substantially constrained. This was borne out in a few large factories where managers informed us of how skilled workers in workshops that were being closed or cut back were moved to others, often at the expense of less favoured groups of worker.

Related to that practice, there was evidence of what might be called limited *reactive flexibility*. This is important, since to understand a work process one should have a reasonable idea of how firms react to a sudden shortage of work or a partial production stoppage.

For instance, when there were partial stoppages of production, in 1994 the most common responses by management were to cut the normal hours of the workforce (the main measure according to 28.6 per cent of the managements that had experienced partial stoppages in 1993–4) and to put workers on partially paid leave, which accounted for another 28.6 per cent of firms. A further 12.1 per cent said they put workers on unpaid leave, 6.6 per cent said they transferred workers to other work, 4.9 per cent said they cut wages and 4.4 per cent said they increased fully paid leave. Other firms said that their main response had been to encourage resignations or to offer some workers early retirement. Those in food processing were much more likely to cut hours, those in chemicals and building materials were relatively likely to resort to administrative leave. Closed and open joint-stock firms were much more likely than other firms to resort to partially paid administrative leave.

In 1993–4 the pattern of second main measures indicated that unpaid and partially paid leave were the most common secondary reactions by those that did not resort to this as their main measure. Cutting working time was the second measure in 14.4 per cent of firms, which implies that cutting working time was regarded as the appropriate or feasible response to partial stoppages of production among only a minority of managements.

To summarise the patterns identified in this section, Table 8.3 presents a stylised version of the typical pattern of working practices in Russian factories in the mid 1990s, compared with the international pattern. In some respects the suggested trends represent hypotheses. But the main message is that Russian industrial enterprises have a set of changes they need to make in order to become comparable to industrial firms operating in other parts of the world. These changes represent a major challenge in industrial restructuring.

Table 8.3 Schema of working-time practices in Russian factories compared with international trends, mid 1990s

Work form	Russian factories	International trend
Standard hours	Rigid, widespread	Flexible, declining
Overtime	Limited, declining	Limited, declining
Short-time work	External, rising	Limited, avoided
Shift work	Very limited, falling	External, rising
Absenteeism	Disguised	Variable
Production stoppages	High, growing	Low
Part-time work	Low, static	Rising
Multiple jobholding	Common, disguised	Rising
Job rotation	Some, uncertain	Growing

8.7 CHALLENGES OF EXTERNAL FLEXIBILITY

One international labour-market trend that will probably spread in the Russian labour market, particularly in a situation of high and rising unemployment, is a shift away from regular, full-time, protected employment towards more insecure and non-regular forms of work. This has usually been discussed under the rubric of 'external flexibility'.

One can produce an elegant taxonomy of work-status categories to show the potential diversity. For the RLFS we contented ourselves with four forms of non-regular work status – temporary or casual labour, contract labour, part-time works and labour subcontracting, the latter involving contracting out all or a specific part of the production process.[23] The following briefly summarises information from the RLFS on the extent and trend in each case. As with a number of issues covered in this chapter, more information was gathered in the first exploratory round of the RLFS.

The starting point was the view that at the beginning of the major reforms the Russian labour market had considerable rigidity in this respect, implying that enterprises could not make rapid employment adjustments because the workforces were essentially wedded to those enterprises.

Labour turnover is considered in the next section. It should be noted here, however, that the use of workers with insecure employment status gave firms an almost automatic capacity to alter employment levels fairly speedily. As far as *temporary or casual labour* is concerned, in 1991 about three quarters of factories stated that they had utilised such labour over the previous two years, mainly for manual work, and mainly because of the legacy of 'labour shortage'. Yet only in food processing was the share of total employment taken by casual labour more than 2 per cent, and in 1990–1 36 per cent of factories reported that they had reduced temporary employment, compared with the 9.6 per cent that had increased it. The most reasonable interpretation of this is that they were cutting the type of employment that was easiest to cut in the worsening recession.

There were cost factors that might have inclined more commercially minded employers to employ rather more temporary workers. Although more than nine in ten firms paid temporary workers the same rate as others doing similar work, they were seriously disadvantaged in entitlement to social benefits provided by the enterprise. Few firms provided temporary workers with holiday facilities, housing, severance pay (only 4.8 per cent of firms gave temporary workers this benefit), training, access to subsidised goods or even paid leave. In most firms they at least had a written short-term labour contract, although in a substantial number of firms they merely had an oral arrangement.

In 1992 86.9 per cent of firms said they had employed temporary or casual labour at some point during the previous two years, and in 1993 the figure was 81.7 per cent. There was little sectoral variation. Thus in 1993, although the figure was 90.6 per cent in wood products, it was over 75 per cent in all sectors. But more than two in five firms (43 per cent) that had used temporary workers were now employing fewer, while 11.8 per cent had engaged more, an increase being most likely in construction materials and a decrease most likely in textiles and garments.

Consistent with that net decline, in 1994 67.2 per cent said they had used temporary workers, ranging from 85 per cent in construction materials to 53 per cent in textiles and garments; this was down on 1993. Over a quarter of the firms (27.4 per cent) reported that they had reduced their use of temporary labour, compared with the 14 per cent that had increased it. Perhaps indicative of a behavioural change was the finding that private firms were more likely to have increased their use, whereas those firms that had become closed joint-stock enterprises were most likely to have cut back on temporary labour. It was too early to determine whether property restructuring and the changing corporate governance associated with it would lead to a shift towards additional temporary employment contracts – a phenomenon linked to privatisation in other economies – but it would be consistent with greater employee control if employment restructuring in closed joint-stock establishments were to lead to cuts in temporary worker employment, whereas in firms controlled by other stakeholders there might be a cutback in regular worker employment, so as to give management greater employment flexibility.

In 1994 that issue seemed to lie in the future. More relevant was the apparent growth in the extent of another form of external flexibility, namely *contract labour*. Few firms (about 15 per cent) employed such labour in 1991, although even then, as in other countries, the percentage was much higher in the construction materials sector. At that time the main reasons cited for using such workers were the perceived labour shortage, and in a few cases higher productivity and the greater sense of responsibility such workers were seen to possess. Contract workers were typically paid more than regular workers doing similar work, and it was the norm to provide such workers with a series of short-term contracts. In contrast with temporary or casual labour, contract labour seemed to be a growing phenomenon, with 31.5 per cent of managements reporting that their use of contract workers had increased.

In mid 1992 29.3 per cent of the firms in the second round of the RLFS reported that they had employed contract labour, nearly twice as many as in 1991. In mid 1993 the figure was up to 54.1 per cent, ranging from 40 per cent in chemicals to 73.1 per cent in construction materials and 67.7 per cent in textiles and garments. Although 43 per cent of those that had used such labour had reduced their use of it, 11.8 per cent had increased it, the increases being greatest in construction materials and the reductions being most common in textiles and garments. In 1994 55.2 per cent of firms reported that they had used contract labour, ranging from 65 per cent in construction materials to a low of 40 per cent in food processing. It was most common outside state enterprises. Over a third of all establishments reported that they had increased their use of contract labour, compared with the 13 per cent that said they had reduced it. There had been a net increase in all industrial sectors, the increase being most marked in non-state establishments. So while a growing proportion of firms were using contract labour, there had also been an increase in the use of such labour within firms that had already been employing it.

Another form of external labour flexibility that has been growing internationally is the *subcontracting of work* by industrial establishments to outside firms, primarily as a means of reducing fixed costs and providing enterprise flexibility. In Russian industry at the time of the study, although most production was still carried out in the large-scale, horizontally and vertically integrated enterprises that had been formed in the Soviet era, subcontracting was fairly common. In 1991 over two thirds of firms subcontracted some work, the practice being most common in engineering. Although much of the work involved maintenance, transport and repair, one third was primarily components production. About a third of firms said they had increased the amount subcontracted during the previous two years and nearly 14 per cent said they had reduced it. At the same time, nearly a third of firms were doing work on contract for other firms, and these on average had a much greater employment decline than other firms.

The pattern was similar in mid 1992. With the economic slump of 1992–3, however, subcontracting may have declined. In mid 1993 it had been reduced in 21 per cent of the firms included in RLFS3 and had been increased in 10.4 per cent, cuts being most common in the construction materials sector. In mid 1994, although over two thirds said they still subcontracted work, 38.6 per cent of the factories in RLFS4 reported that they had reduced the extent of subcontracting, compared with the 15.2 per cent that had increased it. By 1994 the most likely units to which firms subcontracted work were joint-stock enterprises (45.4 per cent), and even among state-owned establishments only 42 per cent subcontracted mainly to other state enterprises.[24]

In 1994, for the first time, we also asked if firms did work on contract for other firms. Nearly a third did so. Nothing should be read into the fact that this was about half the number that subcontracted work to other firms, since some of them subcontracted services, some were subcontracting to agricultural concerns and some to foreign firms. The most important point is that the data reveal an extensive practice of interestablishment networking. Over half the factories in the engineering sector worked on contract for other firms, suggesting that the degree of internal, vertical–horizontal integration of the production process was not as extensive as often presumed, even in post-Soviet Russia.

The amount of work contracted from other firms shrank from 1992–4, in that 35 per cent experienced a decline, compared with less than 23 per cent that expanded such work. However it was clear that this type of enterprise flexibility had become a feature of Russian industry, and establishments that had experienced rising sales in real terms had increased the amount of work provided to subcontractors as well as the work they did on contract for other establishments.

The final form of flexible labour combines elements of working-time flexibility and external flexibility, in that *part-time working* gives enterprises some working-time options and often can provide variation in the contractual status of workers. The most significant point about part-time employment in Russian industry is that it has been minimal, both in absolute terms and relative to what has been happening in other countries.

In 1991 about two thirds of factories reported they had employed some part-time workers in the previous two years, and the only industries in which only a minority of firms employed part-timers were construction materials (37.0 per cent) and food processing (48.1 per cent). The form of part-time work was slightly different from the more typical pattern in other countries, since it was usually taken by full-time workers wishing to go on a part-time basis for a short period, most commonly women with young children.[25] As in other countries, women predominated among part-timers, and in two thirds of the cases they were expected to return to full-time work. But what was most notable about part-time employment in 1991 was that while a majority of firms resorted to it, its extent was very limited and rarely accounted for more than 2 per cent of total employment. Moreover, more firms reported that they had cut part-time employment in the preceding two years than had increased it. Part-time employment had only grown in net terms in the few firms that had expanded total employment.

Although less detailed data were collected on this in subsequent rounds, they were sufficient to indicate that in the wake of the massive decline in output and employment, part-time employment also declined. In mid 1992 nearly 73 per cent of establishments reported the use of part-time employment during the previous two years. In 1993 only 56.5 per cent said they used part-time workers, with 76 per cent in chemicals and 75.8 per cent in textiles and garments. As in 1991, the only sectors where only a minority of firms reported having part-time workers were food processing (36.9 per cent) and construction materials (46.2 per cent). The low incidence in food processing is harder to explain, for a large number of its workers were women. It probably reflected the greater demand for labour in that sector. However the key points are that the number of firms using part-time workers had declined and that, among those that did employ part-timers, 7.4 per cent had increased the amount of part-time work while 21.3 per cent had reduced it. Reduction was particularly common in textiles and garments, in which sector two in five factories had reduced it, as had nearly a third of chemicals plants.

In 1994 47.8 per cent of the factories employed part-time workers, ranging from 61.5 per cent in textiles and garments to 20 per cent in construction materials, suggesting that the decline in the use of part-timers was continuing. Among the firms that did use them, their share of total employment was very low, and 24 per cent of the firms had reduced part-time employment while 22 per cent had increased it. A modest net increase was evident only in engineering plants.

Overall, part-time work had not become a feature of industrial employment, and this was despite the fact that in mid 1994 two in five firms that had employed part-timers said they paid them lower wages. The main reason given by about 70 per cent for not using part-timers, or not using them more, was that there was no labour shortage. A further 9.6 per cent

Figure 8.20   Percentage of establishments using non-regular employment, by form of employment, all regions, 1991–4

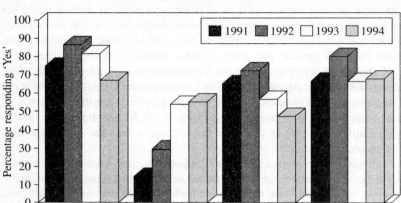

Source: RLFS1, RLFS2, RLFS3, RLFS4; n = 503, 191, 348 and 384, respectively.

did not wish to employ part-timers because they wanted 'a stable workforce'. So the mentality was still that this was a stop-gap, contingency form of employment, rather than one designed to give factory and worker an element of flexibility.

In sum, labour-market flexibility defined in terms of non-regular employment contracts had yet to become very substantial in Russian industry, although contract labour had become a widespread phenomenon (Figure 8.20).

The factors that are likely to lead to a more pronounced trend towards 'external flexibility' are the same as in other countries, where it has grown considerably in recent years. Persistently high unemployment will be a contributing factor, as will any weakening of unions, a shift towards what has been called external corporate governance, and a more conscious pursuit of profit maximisation. A shift towards higher wages and a reduction in the extent of wage flexibility would encourage managements to turn to non-regular forms of employment, because the costs of regular employment would become harder to bear in times of declining demand. Moreover, tighter labour regulations on employment protection, or more effective implementation of existing regulations, might also encourage a shift towards greater reliance on non-regular forms of employment. As most of these factors seem likely, with the exception of the last, one can predict that external labour flexibility will grow in the near future.

8.8 LABOUR TURNOVER AND RETRENCHMENT

As indicated in Chapter 2, Russian industry in the 1990s was not characterised by rigid employment, and in particular the rate of *labour turnover*
was quite high, as it had been for some years. However some changes in
both the level and the character of labour turnover did take place.

Labour turnover can be defined as the number of quits, dismissals, re-
tirements, redundancies and transfers to other establishments divided by
total employment over a specified period. In 1991 it was highest in chemicals and wood products, and was higher in factories that had been cutting employment than in others, which did not reflect the predominance of
redundancies in such firms. It was widely reported that the main component of turnover was resignations (71.9 per cent), although there is reason
to believe that many of these were 'induced resignations', with those
leaving being first eased into unpaid status, whether on leave or allowed
to continue to attend the work place, until they 'quit' in despair, conveniently saving the establishment the cost of severance pay. Those formally
made redundant accounted for only 5.4 per cent of total departures from
employment.

In 1991 questions were also asked about the establishment's retrenchment policy. Most managements responded that they were prepared to
make retrenchments, and most operated the standard practice of giving
two months' notice to workers made redundant. Some labour economists
argue that the type of employment security regulations in operation in
Russian industry have adverse employment effects. But only 15.4 per cent
of the managers reported that the notice period limited retrenchments; 1.4
per cent thought it might have restricted employment, 77.7 per cent said
it had no effect whatsoever, while 5.3 per cent were unsure whether it had
any effect.

As for the reasons for different forms of labour turnover, in 1991
over 60 per cent of managements attributed voluntary resignations to wages
being higher elsewhere, that being the case for over 70 per cent of the state
enterprises. The main reason cited by managers for employment termina-
tion was worker conduct, which was the main factor in three quarters of
establishments. Although lay-offs and production cuts were given as the
main reasons in only 5.6 per cent of the factories, this was sufficient to
indicate that even then enterprises could cut and were cutting employment
by making workers redundant, albeit in small numbers. Actually the highest release rate was for general-service workers and employees.

Even in 1991 the labour market seemed to be working in this direction.
The rate of labour turnover was inversely related to the average wage in

the firm, which is consistent with standard economic theory. Thus in 1993–4 labour turnover was 20.1 per cent in firms with wages averaging less than 100000 roubles, whereas it was 12.9 per cent in those with average wages of more than 200000 roubles. Although one should be wary about interpreting this correlation, multiple regression analysis suggests that the correlation is fairly robust, in that the statistical effect remains even when account is taken of the influence of other variables.

In 1992–3, according to RLFS3, labour turnover was 17.9 per cent, the highest rate being in textiles and garments and engineering. It was higher in state establishments (21.1 per cent) and in private firms (20.3 per cent) than in joint-stock companies, was inversely related to employment size, and was much higher in St Petersburg than elsewhere. If intra-enterprise transfers are excluded, the overall rate dropped to 16.8 per cent, but this did not change the picture of the incidence of turnover by type of firm.

According to the factory administrations, in 1992–3 most of the labour turnover still consisted of resignations or 'quits'. The aggregate retirement rate was 1.3 per cent and the aggregate quit rate was 10.5 per cent (with 12.5 per cent in state firms and 11.1 per cent in private firms, with lower rates in open and closed joint-stock firms). The aggregate dismissal rate was 1.0 per cent and the aggregate redundancy rate was 1.2 per cent (2.0 per cent in private firms, 1.6 per cent in state firms; and compared with other industries textiles had the highest rate at 2.5 per cent). The residual 'other' departure rate was a rather high 2.6 per cent, which was particularly high in private firms (4.5 per cent). In what was a period of employment decline the redundancy rate was remarkably low. The reason for this is surely that workers were being induced to quit, typically by being put on low pay, no pay or administrative leave until they drifted out of the firm's workforce. To call that 'voluntary' would be a misnomer, yet this is the image given and believed by those who merely reiterate official *Goskomstat* data showing a low redundancy rate.

In 1993–4 labour turnover declined in relation to the 1992–3 figure, and overall was 15.5 per cent, being highest in the newly included region of Ivanovo, as observed in Chapter 4. Excluding intra-enterprise transfers, it varied from a high of 24.0 per cent in construction materials to a low of 12.2 per cent in chemicals. Thus industrial variation had changed since 1993. More significantly, turnover had dropped in state firms, to 15.1 per cent, whereas it had stayed much the same in other property forms. The turnover rate had gone down most in the smaller firms, although the largest firms still had the lowest turnover. The fact that it was below 12 per cent in those with more than 1000 workers would lead some labour

Figure 8.21 Labour turnover, by percentage employment change during previous year, all regions, 1993–4 (average percentage leaving the establishment in previous five months, all reasons)

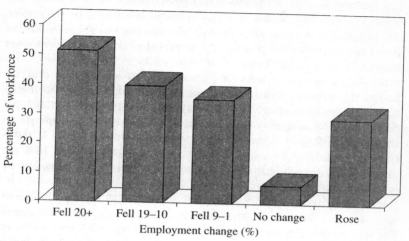

Source: RLFS4, n = 384.

economists to describe the firms in question as having a predominantly 'internal labour market regime'.[26] Once again, turnover rates were only moderately inversely related to employment change (Figure 8.21).

In 1994 redundancies comprised 8.5 per cent of all departures from employment, ranging from 5.5 per cent in food processing to 21.2 per cent in metals. The share of redundancies was relatively low in state and leaseholding establishments, and was much higher in large firms. It was more than twice as high in Ivanovo (13.3 per cent) as in Nizhny Novgorod (5.9 per cent). And not surprisingly, the more employment had been cut the greater the share of redundancies in total turnover.

Under the 1991 Employment Act, when releasing workers firms are meant to tell them to go to the employment service. In 1994 managements were asked whether they informed redundant workers that they should register with the employment service. Over 20 per cent admitted that they did not do so, and in Moscow City about one third. One may be confident that of those who claimed that they did, many would have done so only irregularly. The smaller firms were much less likely to tell them to do so, implying that with restructuring the tendency to ignore the Act would intensify. There was no incentive for firms to send workers to the employment service; indeed there was a strong disincentive, since in principle if released workers did not register they could lose their entitlement to the third month of severance pay.

Given that redundant workers would probably not know that they were obliged to register in order to be eligible for the third-month severance pay, this substantial non-compliance by firms of a basic procedural dictate should be a matter of concern for local and national policy makers, particularly in Moscow City, where one third did not inform workers. Establishments in food processing and wood and paper products seemed less likely to inform the workers, and ironically state and leasehold firms were less likely than others to do so. Despite that latter pattern, 29.5 per cent of small firms with fewer than 250 workers did not follow the correct procedure, compared with 10.3 per cent of large factories with more than 1000 workers.

We end this section by recalling the idea of internal labour markets. This has been a much debated issue since the seminal analysis of Doeringer and Piore,[27] preceded by work on the 'balkanisation' of labour markets by Kerr, and stemming from the insights of classical economists such as Mill and Cairnes. Although the approach has been subject to much sceptical criticism, here is not the place to review the arguments between neoclassical and institutional economists over the past 25 years. However it should be a consideration in the development of labour-market analysis in Russia to link up ideas of diverse forms of internal labour-market with the fragmentation tendencies that typically emerge within the labour force both inside enterprises and in the wider labour market.

The important point here is that within Russian factories one can identify a particular form of internal labour market, characterised by a limited number of 'ports of entry' to employment, reliance on on-the-job training and retraining for upgrading. Some resort to job rotation and the internal transfer of workers from positions where there are surpluses to positions where there are work opportunities. While there have been internal barriers to mobility between 'worker' status and 'employee' status, there have been mobility channels within each category. Although the internal labour market in Russian factories has no doubt been rigid, there is no reason to assume that this rigidity has produced a socially stratified labour force. Crucially for the concept of the internal labour market, wages have been attached to jobs rather than to workers, which is one reason for the traditionally low 'rate of return' to educational qualifications in the Russian labour market.

8.9   CONCLUSIONS

The really important variables in the internal labour market are *management* and *transaction costs*, those unappreciated ingredients sometimes subsumed under such terms as X-efficiency. It is a trivial point that managers in Russian factories are not necessarily concerned or even aware of the need for efficient use of resources. To do something about this, the first priority is recognition of the need for improvement. In the RLFS, questions were asked about managers' perceptions of labour efficiency. It is what might best be described as a sociological variable, in that it probably tells as much about the respondent population as about labour efficiency itself.

In mid 1994 it was disconcerting that about 20 per cent of managers expressed themselves satisfied with the level of labour efficiency in their enterprise. A further 12.8 per cent said they were more satisfied than dissatisfied, leaving 31.7 per cent somewhat dissatisfied and 35.6 per cent who were sure they were not satisfied.

The managers identified the main form of low labour efficiency as low work intensity (32.8 per cent), followed by idleness due to fluctuations in production (24 per cent) and the low quality of work (12.7 per cent). Other factors mentioned were labour turnover, short working time, idling on the job and absenteeism. The main cause of low efficiency, in their view, was the difficulty in selling the establishment's products, which was mentioned as the main cause in 43.5 per cent of the firms, followed by inadequate supplies of raw materials (16.5 per cent) and low wages (12.9 per cent). Again, these results probably tell us as much about the managers as about the sources of low labour efficiency.

Over 47 per cent of the managers said that the main measure they had taken to improve labour efficiency was to raise wages, and 13.8 per cent said they had done nothing. In terms of managerial initiative, 6 per cent said they had introduced an incentive programme, 4.7 per cent said they had made changes in the way work was organised, and less than 1 per cent had introduced training to improve efficiency. In factory after factory, one was left with the feeling that little in the way of innovative approaches had been tried. There were no evident differences between property forms, although among those that had acted in response to low labour efficiency, managers in state establishments were more likely to have resorted to wage increases. Firms that had cut employment were far more likely than others to have done nothing to improve efficiency. Whether this lack of effort was a cause of the need to make employment cuts must be a matter for speculation.

So too must be the observed differences between corporate governance structures. Of those that were worker-controlled, about 36 per cent expressed the view that labour efficiency was satisfactory or reasonably so, whereas only 28.6 per cent of purely private firms and 27.3 per cent of employee-controlled establishments expressed this view (with 36.4 per cent of state-controlled firms expressing satisfaction). According to *t*-tests, the difference between worker-controlled and the other two non-state forms is statistically significant. The interpretation of this must also be a matter for speculation, since worker-controlled firms might be more likely to believe that any given level of labour efficiency would be satisfactory, or workers could be making a greater effort in such establishments because they have a greater say. This is an issue that it is hoped to explore in more detail in RLFS5.

In conclusion, at the time the managements of industrial enterprises had yet to escape from their past. The typical Russian factory was continuing to rely mainly on full-time, manual labour employment topped up by a nebulous employee stratum. The work process exhibited the old-style pattern of employment that conveys a picture of rigidity. Although recognition and even use of various forms of flexible employment were widespread, in the wake of the economic upheavals of the early 1990s the typical reaction was to preserve the core workforce. The standard full-time work schedule continued to account for over 90 per cent of all jobs. Working-time flexibility had been impaired by the reduction in multiple shifts. The scope for internal flexibility was reduced by the considerable erosion of training and retraining. Perhaps one could depict the decline in training institutes and formal training as a 'clearing of the decks', needed to allow for new, more appropriate and flexible forms of training and skill forma-tion. If so, there was little to suggest that factors were present to stimulate the emergence of new and better systems.

Yet the signs of pressure for change were there. The sheer absence of effective regulatory mechanisms meant that there were no inherent bar-riers to external labour flexibility, and little to prevent the development of internal labour flexibility. As an example of the latter, firms clearly had the capacity to transfer workers both internally and between plants. Tech-nological innovation, although nothing by the standards of South-East Asia, for example, or even Western Europe, was also having a series of effects that were likely to induce a growing sense of dynamic efficiency. A picture was taking shape of a work process hesitantly becoming more flexible, with more rapid development depending on the emergence of proper incentives, institutional support and a managerial comprehension of opportunities.

9 The Impact of Restructuring on Women Workers

9.1 INTRODUCTION

One of the most fundamental labour-market policy challenges in an economy undergoing a major restructuring is avoiding labour-force fragmentation and segmentation. Identifiable groups can easily be marginalised in the labour market or pushed into a narrow range of low-paid, low-status and relatively insecure jobs, and once people are in such jobs or are marginalised there may be considerable difficulty in reversing the outcome. Commonly, particularly in the wake of high unemployment, it is women who have been marginalised in this way, along with ethnic minorities, migrants, older workers and workers with disabilities of one kind or another.

In the Soviet era, it seemed that, whatever the faults and shortcomings of the labour process, the position of women was *relatively* favourable by international standards. There was concern about their arduous situation and the 'double working day' that was forced on most women, in particular because almost all jobs were full-time. Yet undoubtedly women were fully integrated into the so-called 'sphere of material production', supported by their higher average education level and the fact that, because there were more women than men in the population and because of their high labour-force participation rate, they long outnumbered men in the labour force. What caused concern was that so-called protective measures may have actually contributed to the exploitation of women workers, since regulations designed to protect women – such as the prohibition of night work and types of work deemed inappropriate for women – induced them to perform such jobs in more adverse conditions than if they had been doing so in normal circumstances.[1]

After 1990, with the deepening economic depression and anticipated restructuring, some prominent economists and demographers in Russia advocated that the employment of women should be cut, justifying their proposal by citing fears arising from the fact that the birth rate had dropped sharply and that unemployment was rising. This perspective led to a Supreme Soviet Decree of April 1991 providing for longer maternity leave (up to three years, with 18 months of that period being partially paid).

Many observers that did not agree with that approach nevertheless forecast that women's position in the labour market would deteriorate, and typically added that it had already done so.[2] The first sign of deterioration came almost immediately, in that from the moment when unemployment was legitimised women comprised a remarkably high share of the registered unemployed. This was accompanied by a widespread fear that women were bearing the brunt of job losses and that they would lose a disproportionately large share of the better-paid, higher-status jobs. This was expected particularly to be the case within manufacturing industries. Cutbacks in childcare facilities in enterprises and the costs associated with maternity leave were expected to lead to greater employment cuts and higher unemployment for women.

What happened to women workers in the early period of restructuring? And what brought about the changes? As will be indicated in this chapter, using RLFS data, one can identify eight means by which women workers could be disadvantaged in the course of enterprise restructuring and reorientation towards more 'open' labour-market relations. Although one must be cautious about interpreting the findings from the RLFS, and in particular about attributing changes to discrimination rather than to structural changes or changes in patterns of labour supply, it should still be useful for those concerned with creating a socially equitable labour market to consider how aspects of the restructuring might accentuate or ameliorate the disadvantages faced by women or men.[3]

The most striking point to bear in mind is that, according to the four rounds of the RLFS and contrary to expectations, between 1991 and 1994 women were not marginalised in Russian industry, at least not in terms of their share of employment. According to RLFS1, in 1991 they comprised 51 per cent of the total workforce in Russian factories, expressed as an unweighted mean average. According to RLFS2, in mid 1992 they accounted for 52 per cent of the workforce. By mid 1993, according to RLFS3, they comprised over 53 per cent, although for the firms that were in both RLFS2 and RLFS3 there was no change of any significance. Women's share of industrial employment on average fell in Moscow Region and St Petersburg, and rose in Moscow City and Nizhny Novgorod. In mid 1994, according to RLFS4, they comprised over 52 per cent, and in firms that were in both RLFS3 and RLFS4, the share was unchanged at 52.6 per cent, although it had fallen in some sectors and risen in others.

Thus, overall one really cannot suggest that women have been marginalised. But was this the result of the pattern of restructuring offsetting

Figure 9.1   Forms of labour-market disadvantage for women

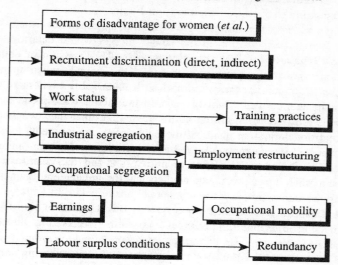

growing discrimination? Did it conceal a deterioration in certain respects? What were the factors explaining their apparently growing share of employment? And were there factors that would weaken their position in the longer term? We will consider these questions by examining the various sources of potential disadvantage.

If one considers the enterprise labour market as a process, then one can envisage that there may be several points at which women (or any other group) face some form of discrimination or some form of actual or potential disadvantage relative to other groups. The process is summarised in Figure 9.1. What should be borne in mind is that a disadvantage or discriminatory barrier at one stage, say recruitment, might either be accentuated by barriers or practices in other respects, or be offset by a compensatory practice. Cumulative disadvantage may be the most common outcome, although this is not necessarily the case.

The full range of determinants of women's disadvantage extend beyond the enterprise, encompassing the legal and fiscal systems, the education system, equality legislation, the system of wage regulation, the modes of labour regulation and so on. The enterprise labour market takes much of this as given, and reflects the outcome of these influences, although in the longer term it also helps shape developments in these spheres. All we can do here is try to tell that part of the story that can be captured in the short-run practices of managements within the factories. The internal labour market is displayed abstractly in Figure 9.1.

9.2 DISADVANTAGED BY DISCRIMINATORY RECRUITMENT?

Besides the more important cultural and educational barriers that have prevented women from gaining entry to the labour force in many countries, the most common source of labour-market disadvantage for women is direct discrimination in recruitment for wage employment.

In the RLFS we examined this by asking managers if they had a preference for men or women when recruiting, and this was asked separately for the main group of production workers and for employees. This attitudinal approach is not ideal, since many people are reluctant to admit to prejudices based on some stereotypical notion. But there is nothing illegal or improper in admitting to a preference, nor is it in the Russian character to be reticent about voicing personal preferences.

In 1991 about 29.5 per cent of managers said they had a preference for men when recruiting production workers (32.1 per cent in Moscow City, 25 per cent in Moscow Region and 29 per cent in St Petersburg, the three *oblasts* covered by the first round of the RLFS), compared with the 14.6 per cent who said they preferred women and the 55.9 per cent who said that men or women were equally acceptable. This suggests that there was much less recruitment discrimination in Russian industry than in similar sectors in other countries where comparable surveys have been carried out.[4] The industrial pattern was similar to that found in other countries, with a net preference for men in engineering, building materials and wood products, and a net preference for women in food processing, textiles and garments and chemicals.

On the recruitment of employees, 9.4 per cent of factories said they preferred to recruit men, 10.2 per cent women and the remaining 80.4 per cent had no preference one way or the other. So, besides revealing a lower incidence of gender discrimination when it came to employees, there was a slight overall preference for women. The industrial pattern corresponded to that found for production workers, in that those sectors and firms that had a preference for men as production workers tended to favour men as employees as well, and vice versa.

In mid 1992, among a smaller sample of firms, 24.6 per cent of managers said they preferred men as production workers, 13.1 per cent women and 62.3 per cent said they had no preference. On the recruitment of employees, more managements said they preferred women (8.7 per cent) than men

(6.3 per cent), although once again the main point is that the vast majority said they had no particular preference. If anything, the results suggested a slight decline in the incidence of gender discrimination, although this mainly reflected the changed composition of firms in the survey.

In mid 1993, for workers, 24.3 per cent of managements said they preferred to recruit men, 10.1 per cent women and 65.7 per cent were indifferent. For employees, 8.6 per cent said men, 7.4 per cent women and the remainder were indifferent, thus suggesting there was no discrimination either way in the case of employees and only limited discrimination in the case of workers.

In mid 1994 there was a suggestion that there had been an increase in gender discrimination in recruitment, insofar as 28.4 per cent said they preferred to recruit men as production workers, 12 per cent preferred women and 59.6 per cent had no preference.[5] In assessing that pattern, a point that emerged in the course of fieldwork during 1994 is that in our discussions with managements some stressed that their preference for men was because the share of women in their workforce had risen above what they regarded as 'normal' (*sic*).

On the recruitment of employees, in 1994 nearly four in five firms expressed no gender preference, and only 11.7 per cent reported a preference for men, compared with the 9.1 per cent that they preferred women.

As in previous rounds of the RLFS, in 1994 there was a strong preference for men production workers in engineering, basic metals, construction materials and wood and paper products, and a net preference for women in textiles and garments and food processing. The pattern was similar for employees, with only the chemicals sector having no net discrimination.

It is notable that in the one sector where average employment had grown, food processing, there was a net preference for women (Figures 9.2 and 9.3). In large firms there was a strong net preference for men, but encouragingly for women's employment there was less discriminatory preference for men in firms that had expanded employment during the previous year than in those that had cut employment.

The reasons given for a preference for men workers and employees were the conventional ones found in other countries and primarily related to a perception that men had better or more relevant skills. Among the most intriguing finding is that 11 per cent of those who expressed a preference for men as production workers cited labour regulations (Table 9.1). Among those who preferred women, the main reason given was their greater reliability, and many managers referred to women as less likely to drink or slack on the job.

Figure 9.2   Gender preference for production workers, by industry, all regions, mid 1994 (percentage of establishments indicating a preference for men or for women)

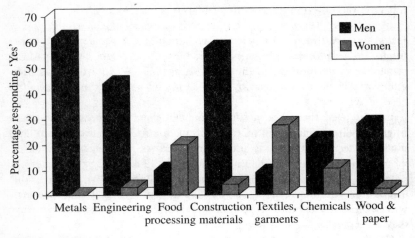

Source: RLFS4, n = 384.

Figure 9.3   Gender preference for employees, by industry, all regions, mid 1994 (percentage of establishments indicating a preference for men or for women)

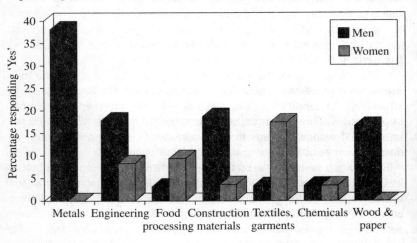

Source: RLFS4, n = 384.

Table 9.1 Reasons for gender preference, by gender, mid 1994

	Workers		Employees	
	Men	Women	Men	Women
Better skills	25.7	13.0	36.4	8.6
Higher productivity	11.9	8.7	9.1	5.7
Higher work quality	1.8	15.2	6.8	11.4
Lower absenteeism	2.8	2.2	9.1	0.0
Men need work more	3.7	0.0	6.8	0.0
Lower labour costs	0.0	4.3	0.0	5.7
Men unavailable	0.0	8.7	0.0	0.0
Higher mobility	0.9	0.0	2.3	2.9
Reliability	7.3	23.9	13.6	40.0
Discipline	0.9	6.5	2.3	22.9
Labour laws	11.0	0.0	4.5	0.0
Specific production process	8.3	8.7	0.0	2.9
Other	25.7	8.7	9.1	0.0

Source: RLFS4, n = 376.

In sum, one can conclude that while there was some preferential discrimination in recruitment, and while there were justifications along the lines that men were more skilled and women were more reliable, it does not seem that discrimination was substantial, and there is little to suggest that it had increased or that the process of restructuring was worsening it.

9.3   DISADVANTAGED BY TRAINING PRACTICES?

For women to retain an equal share of employment in the course of restructuring, it is crucial that they have access to training and retraining opportunities. This is a complex issue, since although there might be discrimination against women in the allocation of training, this might be counteracted by greater provision of training opportunities in factories in which women have a large share of employment.

The RLFS collected three types of information on this issue. In the first round no questions were included on the management's gender preferences in the allocation of training. In mid 1992, according to responses in RLFS2, 9.4 per cent of managements preferred men to be trained, compared with the 5.8 per cent who preferred women and the 83.8 per cent who claimed that they treated men and women equally. In mid 1993, according to RLFS3 data, there was still only a slight tendency for managements to express a preference for training men – 8.6 per cent stating this, compared with the 3.3 per cent that said they had a preference for training women workers. This meant that in seven in ten factories managements at least claimed that they were operating a non-discriminatory training policy.

In mid 1994, according to RLFS4, 10.2 per cent of firms preferred to train men, 3.4 per cent preferred women. As in the previous year, in the construction materials, basic metals, engineering and wood and paper products sectors there was a relatively strong preference for training men, whereas only in textiles and garments factories was there a net preference for women.[6]

A second indicator of potential gender disadvantage in training is the probability of being in a firm that provides training. In this respect, in 1991 women's share of employment tended to be higher in firms that provided training and retraining than in those that did not. Two thirds of firms in which women accounted for more than three quarters of the workforce provided entry-level training, retraining for skill improvement and retraining for upgrading, whereas only 43 per cent of firms in which women accounted for less than a quarter of the workforce were doing so.

In 1992 training was also more likely to be provided in firms in which women took a high share of total employment. Although there were proportionately more women in factories in which training was being cut back in 1992, in mid 1993 the opposite was observed. They had a higher share of employment in factories that had expanded training generally during the preceding 12 months (40.5 per cent) than in those where training had been cut (34.7 per cent). Women's share of employment was higher in firms that provided training, retraining for job performance and retraining for upgrading. Although this did not apply to retraining for upgrading, in 1994 women also tended to make up a larger share of the workforce in firms that provided training and retraining (Table 9.2).[7] Women also had a higher share of training in firms that had expanded training than in those that had cut it. Overall, their share of training was 2 per cent higher than in 1992–3.

The third indicator of gender disadvantage in this area is the actual share of trainees. Again the information gathered in the four rounds of the RLFS differed somewhat. What is clear is that, compared with their share of employment, women consistently made up a smaller share of those provided with training. In 1991, on average women reportedly comprised 43.6 per cent of all apprentices in all sectors, ranging from 83 per cent in textiles and garments to 5 per cent in construction materials. Given that women made up 51 per cent of the workforce, they were slightly underrepresented in that form of training. However apprenticeship was not very extensive (this was the reason for dropping the question on it in 1992, when other issues were given priority).

Table 9.2 Female share of employment, by provision of training, 1993–4 (per cent)

	Initial training		Retraining		Upgrading	
	Yes	No	Yes	No	Yes	No
1993	54.0	49.3	53.9	52.2	53.3	52.5
1994	55.9	48.4	57.1	49.1	54.1	56.4

Note: 'Initial training' refers to whether or not new workers were provided with training; 'retraining' refers to subsequent provision of retraining for work performance; 'upgrading' refers to retraining for promotion.
Source: RLFS3, RLFS4; n = 340 and 384, respectively.

Figure 9.4 Female share of all those trained during previous year, by industry, all regions, mid 1993

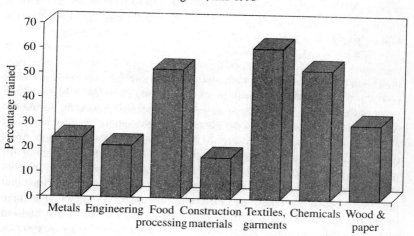

Source: RLFS3, n = 292.

More significantly, the RLFS2 data indicated that in 1992 women made up 42 per cent of all those who had received training during the previous year, and in large establishments with more than 1000 workers they made up nearly 57 per cent. A year later, women's share of training was a disappointing 36.3 per cent. The 1993 level ranged from 61 per cent in textiles and garments and 52.3 per cent in chemicals to 16.2 per cent in construction materials and 21.1 per cent in engineering (Figure 9.4). In mid 1994, on average firms reported that women comprised 38.7 per cent of all workers

Figure 9.5   Female share of all those trained during previous year, by industry, all regions, mid 1994

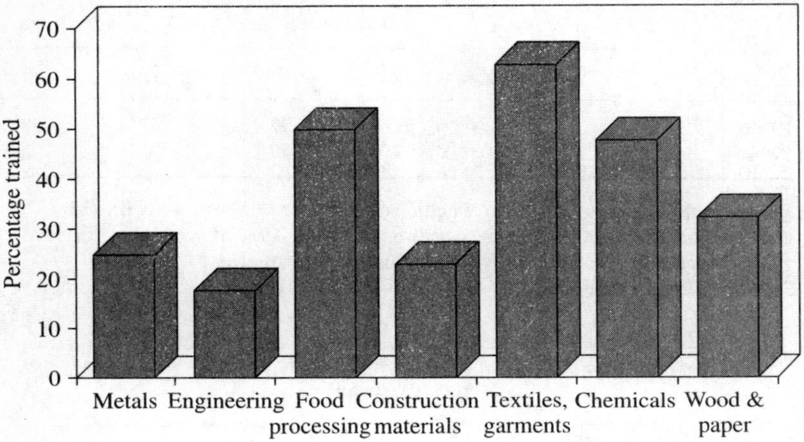

Source: RLFS4, n = 384.

that had received training during the previous year. As expected, women comprised a majority of trainees in textiles and garments and in food processing (Figure 9.5). But overall their share of training or retraining was considerably less than their share of employment.

In sum, the situation is that there has been overt discrimination in the provision of training and women make up too small a proportion of those provided with training. This should lead policy makers to monitor the situation and encourage managements to give equal treatment to women. However, because women are relatively concentrated in firms that have been providing training, and because the very notion of training in Russian factories has been subject to some abuse, it is unlikely to be a strong factor in any deterioration of women's labour-market situation.

9.4   DISADVANTAGED BY INDUSTRIAL SEGREGATION?

A third means by which women could be disadvantaged is by being increasingly concentrated in a few industrial sectors. This is part of a long-standing view that women are disadvantaged in labour markets through being 'crowded' into a narrower range of jobs than men, which drives down wages and their employment opportunities.[8]

Figure 9.6   Female share of employment, by industry, all regions, mid 1994

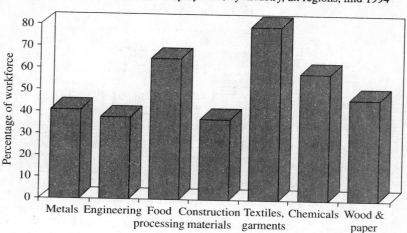

Source: RLFS4, n = 384.

In the factories covered by the first round of the RLFS, in late 1991 women's share of employment ranged from 77.6 per cent in textiles and garments and 61.8 per cent in food processing to 35.9 per cent in construction materials and 36.9 per cent in basic metals. The industrial pattern of male and female employment was very similar to that found in many other countries, although there was probably less concentration than in most.

However, in the ensuing three years there may have been a tendency for industrial segregation to grow, with the female share growing in the highly 'feminised' sector of textiles and garments, and declining most in wood products and basic metals. Thus in mid 1994 women's share of employment ranged from 80.1 per cent in textiles and garments and 64.2 per cent in food processing to 37.6 per cent in construction materials (Figure 9.6).

We saw earlier that gender-based recruitment preferences varied systematically by sector, as did training preferences and outcomes. This implies that the process of industrial segregation was firmly entrenched. It is also pertinent that when managements were asked whether they planned, or expected, either to cut or to expand women's share of employment in the coming year, a larger proportion of firms in sectors with a low proportion of women indicated that they expected to cut women's employment (Figure 9.7).

Thus, although industrial segregation was not very pronounced, there was some suggestion that it could be increasing. Experience in market-oriented

Figure 9.7   Expected change of female employment during next year, by industry, all regions, mid 1994

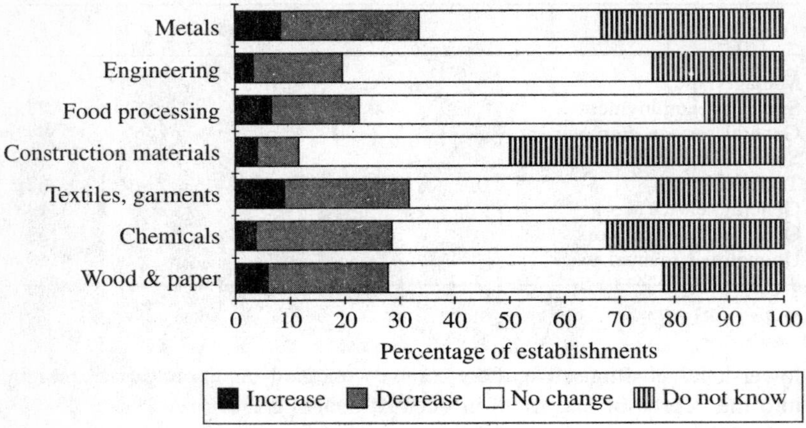

Source: RLFS4, n = 383.

economies suggests that unless a trend towards sectoral concentration is addressed, women will be 'crowded' into a narrow range of sectors, which would lead to a decline in their relative wages and benefits.

9.5   DISADVANTAGED BY OCCUPATIONAL SEGREGATION?

Perhaps the main means by which women have been disadvantaged in most labour markets is through being concentrated in a smaller number of occupational categories and being squeezed into lower-status, less well-paid jobs. This is a pervasive international phenomenon, and the degree of occupational segregation has not corresponded closely to overall levels of female labour-force participation or employment.[9] In Western European countries, gender-based occupational segregation seems to have declined in recent decades, although it has persisted, and some observers believe it may have increased in a few countries.[10]

Within Russian industry, we can present a rough picture of the extent of gender segregation of jobs, although the occupational categories for which information was collected were not as detailed as would be ideal for this purpose, since research in other countries suggests that within more aggregative occupational categories women tend to be concentrated in the

Table 9.3 Women's share of occupational category, all regions, 1992–3
(percentage of category consisting of women)

	1992	1993
Managerial	47.6	47.4
Specialist employment	78.3	79.0
General service employment	95.6	94.3
Supervisory work	49.5	50.1
Technical	71.4	68.3
General service work	94.2	93.6
Qualified manual work	47.4	47.1
Unqualified manual work	60.1	60.6

Source: RLFS3, n = 340.

lower-level positions. Nevertheless we can gain an approximate insight into the degree of and trend in occupational segregation.

In 1991 women's share of different occupational categories ranged from 94.9 per cent of general service employment (clerical jobs) to a low of 44.1 per cent of skilled manual work. The data do not suggest a very strong degree of occupational segregation by international standards.[11] Although the pattern varied enormously by industrial sector, there was a tendency for women's share to be relatively low in managerial and supervisory jobs and relatively high in jobs requiring less 'skill'.[12] And in industries where women made up a high share of one occupational category, they typically made up a relatively high share of other occupational categories. This suggests that industrial segregation was more important than occupational segregation *per se*.

If women lost higher-income, higher-status jobs more than others, then they would be disadvantaged by occupational restructuring. In 1991–2 there was some suggestion that this was happening, the second round of the RLFS showing a small decline in women's share of managerial and supervisory jobs. In 1992–3, according to an examination of their shifting share of the various occupational groups, there was little apparent trend except for a slight decline in the share of technicians, offset by a slightly expanded share of professional and technical employment and supervisory grades. Perhaps *within* the rather wide bands of occupational categories, women might have been disadvantaged, but there was little evidence of growing occupational segregation (Table 9.3).

In RLFS4 the results were encouraging for those concerned about the prospect of women being marginalised in the labour market. Bearing in mind the difference in the samples, the important point is to observe the

Table 9.4   Women's share of occupational category, all regions, 1993–4
(percentage of category consisting of women)

	1993	1994	1993*	1994*
Managerial	50.5	50.9	47.2	48.1
Specialist employment	74.6	76.3	79.0	79.6
General service employment	87.3	85.5	94.7	95.0
Supervisory work	41.8	38.8	48.4	46.5
Technical	63.7	64.6	68.4	66.4
Qualified manual work	51.5	52.4	47.0	46.5
Unqualified manual work	56.6	56.7	60.7	58.1

* These refer to the 229 establishments that were in both RLFS3 and RLFS4.
Source: RLFS3, RLFS4, merged RLFS; n = 348, 384 and 229, respectively.

changes within the same firms. In 1993–4 women's share in the higher-level occupational categories increased, and only for manual-worker supervisory posts did their share decline (Table 9.4). Note that even in the managerial–administrative posts, women accounted for a slight majority of employees. If one took only the establishments that were in the survey in both 1993 and 1994, the data suggest that the proportion of women increased in managerial and other employee groups and fell slightly among worker categories, leaving the overall level unchanged.

In sum, although one might find that the occupational categories are excessively broad, the data do not suggest growing occupational segregation or any deterioration in women's occupational pattern of employment.

9.6   DISADVANTAGED BY INDUSTRIAL RESTRUCTURING?

Women's share of employment could fall or rise because of the industrial pattern of employment decline. In fact sectors that were declining relatively rapidly showed very small losses in the share of women (metals, engineering and chemicals, as well as wood products), whereas their share increased in food processing, construction materials and textiles and garments production. As food processing was the only industry in which there was employment growth from 1991–4, the pattern of industrial restructuring could be beneficial for the female share of employment.

There was consequently no reason to believe that the industrial pattern of labour-shedding was leading to a greater labour-market disadvantage for women.

Figure 9.8   Female share of employment, by employment change,
all regions, 1992–4

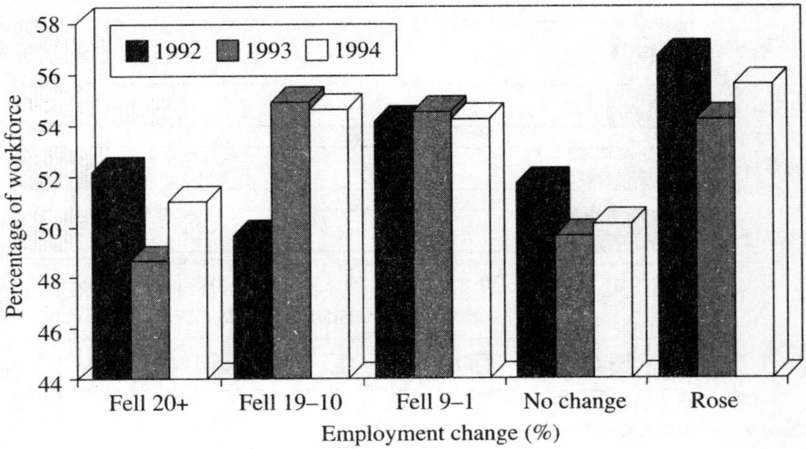

Source: RLFS3, RLFS4; n = 345 and 384, respectively.

9.7   DISADVANTAGED BY EMPLOYMENT RESTRUCTURING?

Another means by which women's labour-market position could be disadvantaged is through the pattern of employment restructuring. Two issues arise here. First, women could be adversely affected by the size restructuring of employment. The four rounds of the RLFS suggested there was little to be concerned about here, since although women tended to have the lowest share of employment on average in small firms with fewer than 250 workers, in all size categories their share exceeded 50 per cent.

Second, women could be disadvantaged by being concentrated in firms making relatively large employment cuts. Again the data suggest developments have actually been favourable for women. For example those firms that expanded employment in 1992–3 had a higher share of female employment than those that cut employment, both at the outset and at the end of the period (Figure 9.8).

While the overall employment decline of women was little different from that of men in 1992–3, female employment fell more in large firms, implying that the relatively sharp employment decline in such firms was particularly affecting women workers.

In 1992–3, according to RLFS3, the female share declined in firms that expanded total employment and fell slightly in firms that cut employment

Figure 9.9   Expected change in women's share of employment during next year, by employment size, all regions, mid 1993

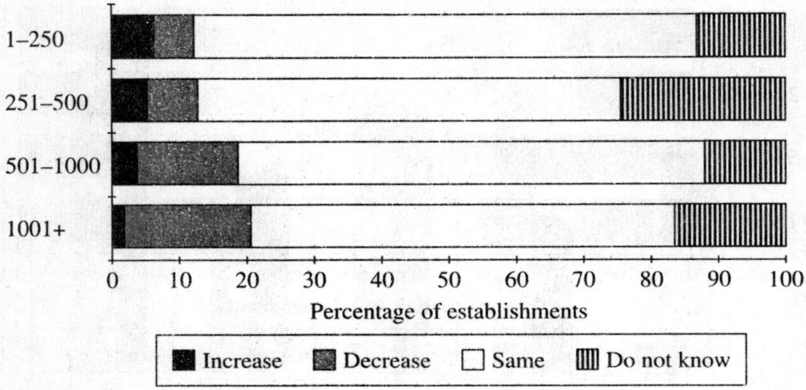

Source: RLFS3, n = 338.

by more than 20 per cent; women's share rose in the remainder. So, since large firms were likely to shed most jobs in the near future and because there would probably be large cuts in employment, which would involve redundancies rather than normal labour turnover (in which men seem to predominate), the future pattern of employment change may threaten women's employment share more than was the case from 1991–4.

Finally, and most worrying for those concerned to protect women's employment, in 1993 more firms expected women's share of total employment to decline (10.7 per cent) than to increase (4.4 per cent), although 68.3 per cent expected no change and 16.6 per cent were unsure. Expectations of a decline were much greater in large establishments (Figure 9.9), as well as in the 'heavy' industries of basic metals, engineering and chemicals. Similarly, in 1994 more firms expected women's share to decline (18.8 per cent) than to increase (5.5 per cent), although more firms were uncertain than had been the case a year earlier. Although the samples in 1993 and 1994 were somewhat different, again it was the large firms that most expected women's share to fall (Figure 9.10).

9.8   DISADVANTAGED BY PROPERTY RESTRUCTURING?

A question must arise as to the effect of property-form restructuring on the position of all groups that, for whatever reason, had been systematically

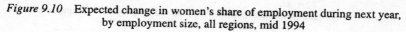

Figure 9.10 Expected change in women's share of employment during next year, by employment size, all regions, mid 1994

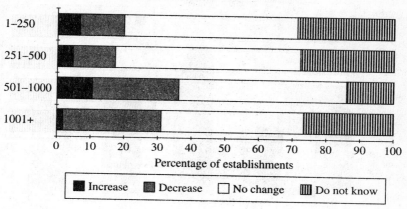

Source: RLFS4, n = 383.

integrated into employment in the Soviet era. The evidence is mixed as far as women are concerned. In 1991, according to RLFS1, the female share of employment was much lower in so-called 'cooperatives' – 34.7 per cent compared with 53.5 per cent of leaseholdings. But in mid 1992 the RLFS2 data suggested that women had a slightly higher share in non-state firms, whereas their share had fallen in state firms.

In 1993 and 1994, according to RLFS3 and RLFS4, it seems that although their share may have declined slightly in private and leaseholding firms, their share of employment was much higher in private firms, followed by closed joint-stock firms, than in state enterprises (Figure 9.11). Whether this is anything more than a coincidence is a matter for speculation.[13]

In sum, there is no evidence that property-form restructuring *per se* was eroding women's position in industrial employment, since women's actual share of employment was higher in non-state enterprises than in the state sector.

9.9   DISADVANTAGED BY LABOUR-SURPLUS CONDITIONS?

Women could be adversely affected by the incidence of labour surplus and labour shedding or by direct discrimination in dismissals.[14] The fact that their share of total employment has continued to be over 50 per cent

Figure 9.11   Female share of employment, by property form, all regions, 1992–4

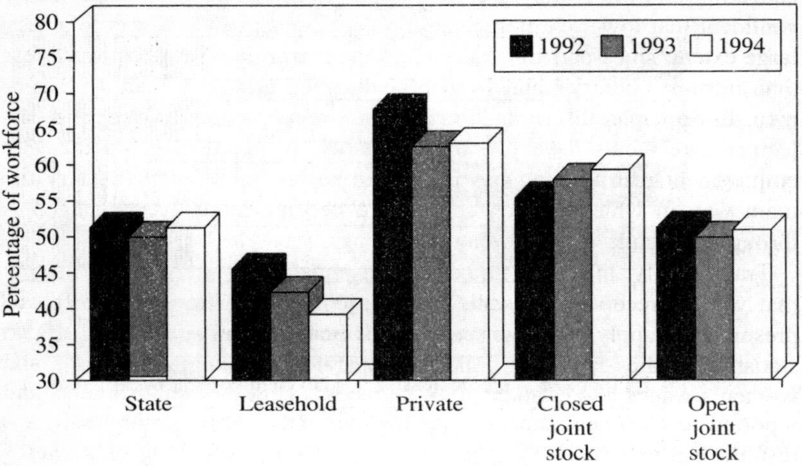

Source: RLFS3, RLFS4; n = 345 and 378.

suggests that there has been little direct discrimination in this respect. Although they could have been adversely affected by the pattern of restructuring, there is little evidence of that either.

Thus in 1993 women's share of employment was *lower* in firms that reported a labour surplus (as measured by the response to the question on whether the firm could produce the same with fewer workers), although on one measure they were slightly overrepresented in firms reporting that they had had too little work for their workforce during the previous few months.

Women were less likely than men to be in enterprises reporting that they foresaw a strong chance of bankruptcy in the near future. There is no link between the two, of course, yet it implies that if bankruptcies were to occur among those expecting or fearing bankruptcy, women would not be disproportionately affected by the resultant decline in employment.

9.10   DISADVANTAGED BY INCOME?

Finally, women's labour-market position could be disadvantaged by discrimination in terms of wages. Although one must be particularly cautious about interpreting correlations as resulting from discrimination or demand factors, since to some extent at least they might reflect differences in skill, education or work experience, in Russian industry one can be reasonably confident that lower earnings would reflect demand-side factors to a very large extent, since part-time and intermittent working has been much less than in most countries and women's education has been equal to that of men. In principle, discrimination against women is not allowed, and collective agreements have presumed equality. In practice, given the way employment restructuring has proceeded so far, in Russian industry the main way in which women could have become more disadvantaged is through a decline in their relative earnings.

Traditionally, in Russia equal pay for equal work was meant to imply that women received the same wages as men. Somehow this edict was presumed to apply, and this was the justification for the fact that official statistical bodies have not collected separate information on men's and women's wages and earnings. All the records kept by establishments and reported to *Goskomstat* have been for men and women combined. As a result it was extremely difficult to obtain reasonable estimates of women's relative wages and earnings, and accordingly we asked managers directly what women production workers earned and what women employees received, relative to their male counterparts. Because of the ideology of equal pay, one might presume that the resultant data were overestimates of women's relative pay. What might be more reliable are estimates of the patterns between firms of different types and estimates of the trends over the four rounds, which in this respect covered the five-year period 1990–4, since in each case we asked for the estimate for the current year and for the preceding year. We need to bear in mind that in the four rounds the size and composition of the sample of firms varied, and no doubt other changes occurred within firms, so it is advisable to focus on the changes within the two years covered in each round of the survey.

According to RLFS1, in 1990 women production workers on average received 88.6 per cent of the pay of their male counterparts in the same firms, ranging from a high of 94.7 per cent in textiles and garments to a low of under 83 per cent in basic metals. For employees, the estimate was 89.2 per cent, ranging from 95.4 per cent in chemicals to 84.2 per cent in basic metals. For 1991 the overall averages were little different, being 88.1 per cent for workers and 89.1 per cent for employees.

In mid 1992, according to RLFS2, women employees on average were earning 89.9 per cent of what their male colleagues were receiving, and women workers 87.6 per cent. Again, for the firms covered in this round there was little change from the previous year.

As of mid 1993, according to RLFS3, on average women employees were receiving 89.7 per cent of men's earnings, and women workers were receiving approximately 91.7 per cent of men's income. This could suggest that the situation of women workers had improved, but it seems rather to reflect the changing composition of firms in the survey. Compared with estimates for the previous year, the figures represented a deterioration of 4.7 per cent among employees and 2.5 per cent among workers. For employees and workers, women's relative position deteriorated most in construction materials and engineering, while it improved in textiles and garments; for workers, their position worsened most in Moscow City and scarcely changed in Nizhny Novgorod.

In 1993, according to RLFS4, women employees received 89.8 per cent of what their male counterparts were receiving, and women workers received 87.8 per cent of what male workers in the same firm were earning. The important point is the change within the same round of the survey; from the RLFS4 data it seemed that between 1993 and 1994 there might have been a further slight deterioration in women's relative earnings, since in mid 1994 the average figure was 87.5 per cent in the case of employees and 86.6 per cent among workers. Their relative wages deteriorated most in large firms, both for workers and for employees. Furthermore their relative wages had fallen in firms that had cut employment as much as in those that had increased it.

In the 229 factories that were in both the 1993 and the 1994 rounds, women workers' average earnings relative to those of male workers deteriorated from 91 per cent in 1992 to 85.3 per cent in 1994. For employees, remarkably the average was 86.4 per cent in 1992 and 86.4 per cent in 1994, although this reflected offsetting changes.

To see if we could identify the main determinants of changes in relative earnings more systematically, a basic function was estimated. It was hypothesised that there was an interindustry, interregional pattern of differences, and that the larger the share of women in total employment in the establishment, the smaller the differential between men's and women's earnings. It was also conjectured that property-form restructuring would lead to a widening of the gender differential, on the ground that managements of non-state firms would feel less bound by traditions of equal pay. However one could also argue that closed and open joint-stock firms – and 'cooperatives' in 1991–2 – would have relatively equal wages because of the stronger bargaining voice enjoyed by workers in such factories. Again, it was expected that there would be an inverse relationship between employment change and women's relative wage, on the ground that firms cutting employment would find it easier and more expedient to lower women's wages, perhaps as a cost-cutting device. Finally, the hypothesis that unions

Table 9.5 Log wages of women relative to men's, mid 1994
(OLS regression results)

Variable	Log. wage ratio workers	Log. wage ratio employees
(Constant)	1.9169	2.0550
Industry		
Metals	−0.0896**	−0.0304
Engineering	−0.0692***	−0.0444*
Food proc.	−0.0182	0.0043
Constr. mat.	−0.0252	0.0017
Chemicals	−0.0186	−0.0291
Wood & paper	−0.0214	−0.0196
Property form		
Leasehold	−0.0299	0.0108
Private	0.0195	0.0076
Closed joint stock	0.0002	−0.0170
Open joint stock	0.0071	0.0070
Social	0.0553	0.0529
Region		
Moscow Region	−0.0050	−0.0402*
St Petersburg	−0.0323*	−0.0213
Nizhny Novgorod	−0.0050	−0.0061
Ivanovo	0.0300	0.0391*
Employment size	0.000003	0.000003
% women's share, 1994	0.0007*	−0.0001
% unionisation	0.0085	−0.0439
% employment change	−0.0001	0.000004
R^2	0.1765	0.0872
F	3.3606	1.4980

* Statistically significant at the 10% level of probability.
** Statistically significant at the 5% level.
*** Statistically significant at the 1% level.
Source: RLFS4, n = 384.

have a 'sword-of-justice' effect, as suggested in Chapter 7, was tested by including the rate of unionisation as an independent variable.

For brevity, only the results for 1994 are presented in Table 9.5. Some of the results for previous years are worth noting however. For 1991, for instance, the results suggested that private firms had wider gender differentials for workers and for employees, that the larger the proportion of women in the plant the more equal the wages for both workers and employees, that firms in Moscow City were more egalitarian in this respect than elsewhere, and that to a small extent employment cutting was associated with a worsening of women's relative earnings among employees.

The results for 1994 suggest that there was a lack of adequate explanation for relative wages, since the percentage of variance explained by the equation was low. The only variables that were strongly statistically significant were sectoral variables – indicating that the gender differential was relatively large in engineering and metals – and regional variables, suggesting that in St Petersburg the gender differential was relatively large as well. The results also indicated that the higher the share of employment taken by women, the higher their wage relative to men.

These regression results are indicative, rather than strong. The main conclusion we can draw from these data is that over the five years there may have been a slight deterioration, but only a slight one, in the relative earnings of women workers in Russian industry. This view may be too sanguine, and relative wage developments should be monitored carefully by those concerned with protecting women's position in the labour market.

9.11 EXPLAINING INTERFIRM DIFFERENCES IN WOMEN'S EMPLOYMENT

Having considered the aspects of potential labour market disadvantage, and indirectly examined factors that could affect women's level and share of employment in industrial firms, we might appropriately conclude by presenting an exploratory function to explain interfirm variation in women's share of employment.

We may hypothesise that the female share of employment is explained, first of all, by industrial segregation and that there might be regional variations due to differential labour-market conditions. It might also be hypothesised, for reasons mentioned earlier, that women's share would vary according to the property form of the firm. It is also possible that their share would be cut in factories that have been cutting employment, if the 'marginalisation' thesis mentioned at the outset of the chapter were to be true. Another popular hypothesis is that the higher the share of manual production workers – or unskilled and semiskilled labour – the higher the share of women, and that the larger the size (mass production) the higher the share. Finally, it has been proposed by some observers that if the factory is operating multiple shifts women's share is higher; others feel that the necessity of night work in such circumstances would lead to a lower female share of employment.

Table 9.6 Female percentage share of employment, mid 1994
(OLS regression results)

Variable	Female share
(Constant)	70.6758
Industry	
Metals	−36.8406***
Engineering	−40.9935***
Food proc.	−14.0911***
Constr. mat.	−40.1695***
Chemicals	−20.6085***
Wood & paper	−32.3810***
Property form	
Leasehold	−7.8969*
Private	3.8365
Closed joint stock	2.0237
Open joint stock	−0.3917
Social	7.9139
Region	
Moscow Region	2.0474
St Petersburg	1.3983
Nizhny Novgorod	2.7993
Ivanovo	−3.9879
Employment size	0.0002
% manual workers, 1994	0.0318
Multiple shift	0.5409
Part-time workers	7.0220***
% employment change	−0.0104
R^2	0.6116
F	28.1073

* Statistically significant at the 10% level of probability.
** Statistically significant at the 5% level.
*** Statistically significant at the 1% level.
Source: RLFS4, n = 384.

The results for a function estimated for 1994 are given in Table 9.6. These show that sector of production was the most important determinant of variation in women's share of employment, as expected. Controlling for other factors, and compared to the reference category of textiles and garments, women's share of employment was much lower in construction materials, metals and engineering, was somewhat lower in chemicals and wood products and was a little lower in food-processing plants. The sectoral variables indicate the pervasive industrial segregation in the Russian industrial labour market, whereas there was no evidence that occupational structure was an important factor in explaining interfirm variation in female employment shares. What was encouraging, in a sense, was that neither the size of factory nor the change in employment made a significant difference to women's share of employment – further evidence against the view that employment cuts would lead to the marginalisation of women.

9.12 CONCLUSIONS

In sum, although women's relative earnings apparently suffered and although managerial plans and expectations about future employment were not encouraging, women's position in the industrial labour market scarcely weakened from 1991–4, contrary to most observers' expectations. Although the share of women on long-term maternity leave was high, it would certainly be an exaggeration to describe the situation as one of actual or imminent marginalisation. The slight strengthening of female employment during the 1990–4 period accords with the international picture, in which women's share of employment has been growing throughout the world and their unemployment relative to men has been declining.[15]

There is no reason for complacency, since discrimination against women could grow, particularly in the wake of persistently high unemployment, and particularly if industrial enterprises continue to abandon social facilities such as kindergartens, which may have facilitated women's employment. Yet one cannot avoid reflecting on the fact that in Russia in 1994 female life expectancy was *ten years longer than men's*. Acute stress in the labour market has been cited as one factor for the rising mortality of young and middle-aged men.[16] One of the many other reasons for differential mortality, and the corresponding differences in morbidity, might be that men have been more likely to be working in unhealthy and dangerous conditions. *Goskomstat* data indicate that in 1994 nearly 27 per cent of all male workers in industry were working in what were called abnormal or unacceptable working conditions, compared with 16 per cent of female workers (Table 9.7). Moreover the situation for men had deteriorated, as shown in Table 9.8.

Another factor that may have affected the relative position of men and women is the development of the education and vocational training system. In the 1980s and 1990s the number of men and women receiving education in universities and technical colleges declined quite sharply. But in the process women's share of those receiving such training remained consistently over 50 per cent, as Table 9.9 shows.

Table 9.7 Percentage of employed workers in abnormal (poor) working conditions, by gender, 1994

	Industry	Transport	Construction
Total poor conditions			
Men	26.7	13.6	9.5
Women	15.8	5.9	5.9
of which*			
Noise-related			
Men	11.5	5.7	2.1
Women	7.1	2.2	1.0
Vibration			
Men	2.8	2.8	1.2
Women	0.6	0.8	0.3
Atmospheric			
Men	16.9	5.1	6.4
Women	8.6	1.9	4.0
Radiation			
Men	0.7	0.2	0.2
Women	0.2	0.1	0.1
Hard physical			
Men	4.4	1.4	3.5
Women	1.1	0.6	2.8
Unsafe equipment			
Men	1.4	0.5	0.3
Women	0.7	0.2	0.1

* Some workers were subject to two or more forms of abnormal working conditions.
Source: Goskomstat of the Russian Federation, unpublished data.

No doubt there are factors other than those mentioned in this chapter that help to explain the high share of industrial employment taken by women. In the late 1990s the labour market should become much more flexible, and this could provide new working opportunities for women, including greater access to part-time work that could be combined with other forms of activity, including education.

This point recalls that there are so many ironies in the Russian labour market that one is constantly bumping into them. Thus, in the name of promoting full employment, the authorities and the ethos of the Soviet era ensured that as many people as possible had full-time employment for as long as possible, a peculiarly distorted vision of a triumph of the working class. Any deviation from the norm of full-time employment was regarded

Table 9.8   Percentage of employed workers in abnormal working conditions, Russian industry, 1991–4

	1991	1992	1993	1994
Total	17.8	21.4	21.4	21.6
Women	14.4	16.7	16.0	15.8

Source: *Goskomstat*, RF, unpublished data.

Table 9.9   Women's percentage share of students receiving training in universities and technical colleges, Russia, 1980–94

	1980–1	1985–6	1990–1	1991–2	1992–3	1993–4
University	53	56	51	50	50	52
Technical college	58	59	59	59	59	59

Source: *Goskomstat*, RF, unpublished data.

as an abnormality. Consequently, as shown in Chapter 8, part-time work was minimal. That was an important difference from what has been taking place in other countries, and there can be little doubt that many women, and some men, would welcome part-time employment on a continuing, regular basis. If unemployment continues to rise, barriers to part-time working should be dismantled. According to the labour-force survey of late 1993, 12.4 per cent of unemployed women wanted part-time employment, a further 12.2 per cent said they would not mind whether they obtained part-time or full-time employment, and only 57.5 per cent said they wanted only full-time employment. Thus the scope for part-time work for women may be considerable.

We come back to the fact that women comprised a majority of the registered unemployed, and it is that which led many commentators to assert that women were being marginalised. The main reason is simply that, once unemployed, women have had a much greater tendency to register as unemployed.[17] According to *Goskomstat's* national labour-force survey of 1993, women were 50 per cent more likely to do so. This is not the same as a greater tendency to become unemployed, although it may be that once unemployed, women face greater difficulties in reentering employment. The evidence presented in this chapter would not lead one to think that was the case either. Indeed, in the second round of the job-seekers' survey carried out in 18 districts in 1993–4, unemployed women were more likely to be offered a training place and, if anything, were more likely to leave the register and to have a shorter period of unemployment; and whereas 40 per cent of the women who left the register received jobs, only 37.4 per cent of the men who left it did so.

So far it seems that it is men who have suffered more from the labour-market developments of the early 1990s. However, as unemployment grows and as non-regular forms of labour relations spread, women's position could suffer. Perhaps significantly, in the women's survey carried out in 1994 in Ivanovo and Nizhny Novgorod, 58 per cent of the 852 economically active women questioned believed that women did not have the same chance of obtaining jobs as men, 48.5 per cent believed that women would not receive the same rate of pay as men (a further 21.6 per cent were unsure) and 21 per cent believed that women did not have the same chance of obtaining training opportunities.

For that reason among others, institutional voice mechanisms – in the form of non-governmental organisations to protect and enhance the position of women in Russian society – may be required to prevent the marginalisation that so many observers have predicted. The growth and promotion of such mechanisms has been a trend in Western Europe.[18] That will surely happen in Russian society too. It is to be hoped that women industrial workers will not be overlooked as special interest groups emerge to fill the institutional void of what is a market-regulated labour market.

10 Demographics of Restructuring: Older Workers, Youth and the Disabled

10.1 INTRODUCTION

The standard picture of employment restructuring in economies undergoing major economic restructuring has depicted 'vulnerable social groups' as being marginalised, and has typically presented them as being displaced by adult men from the majority group in the population. With employment cuts, those identifiable as belonging to some minority group are expected to be the most affected, and those who cannot obtain reentry into mainstream employment tend to drift out of the labour force altogether, or into long-term unemployment, or into the 'informal' or 'black' economy. In contrast those who are relatively employable transfer smoothly into the emerging private sector. This was the employment model underlying the shock therapy strategy for Central and Eastern Europe, and it has been the picture presented for Russia as much as for anywhere else.

An alternative hypothesis is the following. In contrast with the standard model, one may anticipate a *three-phase process of employment restructuring* and employment decline in emerging industrial labour markets such as those found in the Russian Federation. In the first phase employment cuts are small, and mainly involve cuts in empty posts and a reduction in vacancies. The changing incidence of employment in this situation depends on group-specific rates of labour turnover, and that in turn depends on relative probabilities of obtaining alternative jobs, on the relative need for income security, on the need for income and on the inertia and pecuniary advantages stemming from prolonged employment in a specific enterprise or organisation.

In this first phase, in contrast to the conventional model of employment decline, we would expect the share of employment taken by vulnerable groups to depend more on their capacity to hold on to their jobs, and to the extent that the employment decline involves a cut in the recruitment of young labour-force entrants, one would expect older workers' share of employment, for example, to stabilise or even rise.

In the second phase of employment restructuring, even replacement recruitment would decline, and rather than 'voluntary' labour turnover shaping the demographic pattern of employment, individual and group redundancies would begin to shape it much more. Given the usual tendency to displace relatively unskilled workers and administrative employees no longer required because of the demise or reduction of large planning and administrative departments, the impact on the employment share of various groups would depend on the preceding social division of labour. It is quite possible that vulnerable groups would be adversely affected in this second phase, yet this would depend in part on the age–gender distribution of jobs within the factory. Given the long stability of divisions of labour in the Soviet system – with particular groups being expected to do particular types of job, and little mobility between types of job – there would be rather little scope for 'bumping', whereby 'insider' groups of workers would push out 'outsider' groups if it so happened that the jobs adversely affected were those predominantly occupied by insiders.

The third phase of employment restructuring would be the most traumatic. Mass redundancies, plant closures, sell-offs and bankruptcies would predominate as employment cuts become much more substantial and 'lumpy', that is, involve large groups rather than a few individuals at a time. It could be expected that in this phase many older plants would be slimmed down or shut, and that older workers would be disproportionately affected. More generally, it could be predicted that in this phase most vulnerable social groups would face the strong prospect of socioeconomic and labour-market marginalisation. New property forms of firms might be more 'discriminatory' in the sense that they would be able to select workers from a more open labour market and apply more 'economic' and subjective criteria in recruiting and retaining workers, especially as they would almost certainly be under less regulatory pressure to abide by some socially determined rules and practices.

The following briefly examines the relevant data from the RLFS to determine whether the actual change in the demographic pattern of employment corresponds with this three-phase process of employment restructuring. It will begin with, and give greatest weight to, the changing employment of older workers, although in all cases it is hoped that the schematic picture presented will stimulate more detailed empirical investigation.

10.2 OLDER WORKERS IN RUSSIAN FACTORIES, 1991–4

Workers in their fifties, sixties and seventies have long comprised a substantial part of the workforce in Russian industry. The pension age has been very low by international standards – 60 for men and 55 for women, with scope for even earlier pensions in certain conditions. Yet, in part because of this, the amount of the pension has been very low too, so that most people have been obliged to try to combine their pension with continued wage employment well past the typical age of retirement in industrialised European countries. This has been encouraged by the fact that receipt of a pension has not prevented workers from remaining in wage employment, and vice versa.

In the Soviet era it was also the usual practice of enterprises to allow workers to remain in their posts into old age, even if they did nothing. In some respects it was to the advantage of managements to keep such workers on their payrolls, because this enabled them to demand larger wage funds and consumption funds from the relevant ministry.

This situation was expected to change with the onset of restructuring. Even in the *perestroika* period the cut in posts in the late 1980s resulted in the disappearance of some older people from the factory workforces. But with the onset of the attempted shock therapy, when the jobs haemorrhage was starting, the older workers' share of employment was expected to drop rapidly and permanently. Many expected there to be a substantial transfer of older workers from employment to full retirement, and anticipated this as a reasonable result of the tightening of budgetary constraints in enterprises and 'budgetary organisations' across the country. That expectation was also linked to the Pension Law of 1990, which came into effect in March 1991.

What was the situation of older workers in industry? The following presents the basic facts from the RLFS on the changing demographics of employment during the period of initial restructuring. The picture is essentially a statistical sketch, although it is clear enough to support the general explanation of demographic employment restructuring proposed at the end of the chapter.

To a foreign observer it might seem remarkable that in September 1991, 495 out of the 503 factories in RLFS1 employed pensioners, and pension-age workers accounted for nearly 14 per cent of total employment in the Russian factories covered in RLFS1. They represented 17.3 per cent of all workers in chemicals plants, and the larger the firm the higher the percentage of older workers. Yet the most revealing pattern that emerged from the first round of the survey was that the pension-age share of employment tended to be higher in those firms that had cut employment (Figure 10.1).

What seems to have occurred – and this was confirmed in a number of factories where the management spoke of this happening – was that in the wake of the worsening economic recession of 1991, older workers were

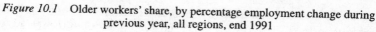

Figure 10.1   Older workers' share, by percentage employment change during previous year, all regions, end 1991

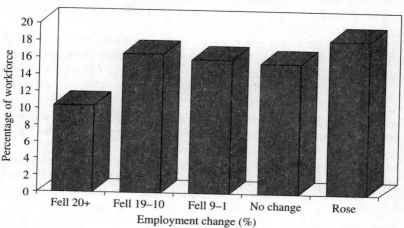

Source: RLFS1, n = 500.

staying in their jobs longer, while recruitment of young workers virtually stopped.

Even so, many more firms expected to reduce the number of older workers during the coming year (29 per cent) than expected an increase (6 per cent). The expectation of a decline was more likely in those sectors in which older workers comprised a relatively high share of employment, most notably basic metals.

Asked to give the main reason for the expected decline, more than two in five managements (43.8 per cent) said that it was because of the declining labour shortage in the firm and in the local labour market. But there was also a feeling that older workers were not mainstream or 'insider', workers, in that a substantial number of managers (15.7 per cent) gave as their main reason for expecting to reduce older worker employment that they wished to preserve the jobs of younger workers in the factory so as to sustain the morale of the work collective.

However there was no suggestion that older workers were simply in marginal jobs. In nearly three quarters of the factories the managements reported that the main jobs occupied by pensioner workers were in skilled production work, while 14.2 per cent said they were mainly doing unskilled manual jobs, 9.7 per cent technical work and 1.8 per cent clerical. In over three quarters of factories pensioners were employed mainly in regular employment, and only in a minority of firms were they hired for short-duration projects (26.9 per cent) and even fewer used them for stop-gap work. In the main, therefore, it seems that pensioners were regarded as part of the regular workforce.

What happened in the first phase of economic shock in the few months after the first round of the survey scarcely bore out the expectations expressed by managements at the end of 1991. In mid 1992 the share of pensioner workers in the sample of factories in RLFS2 was almost the same as in RLFS1 the previous year, again with over 16 per cent in chemicals. Thus, whatever the managements had expected, the pattern of employment cuts taking place at the time had evidently counteracted it. Again, their share had actually risen in factories in which employment had declined and had fallen in that small minority in which employment grew. In the subsample of factories that were in the survey in both 1991 and 1992, the pensioner share of employment rose during the 1990–2 period. Yet when asked about their expectations on pensioner employment, even more than in 1991 said they expected the share to decline in the coming year.

Once more, expectations were confounded. In mid 1993, according to RLFS3, pensioners represented 13 per cent of total employment. The figure in 1992 in RLFS2 was nearly 14 per cent, but one cannot draw any inferences from this since the sample differed. What was striking in RLFS2 was that within the same firms the share of older workers had *risen* in 1991–2. Within the firms in the third round of the survey there was also an estimated rise, albeit by a very small amount. As can be seen from Figure 10.2, the older workers' share of employment rose in large and small factories, and fell in medium-sized plants. We will return to this issue at the end of this section.

In RLFS3 a separate question referred to 'older workers', defined as all those over the age of 54, thus including men aged 55–59 as well as pensioners. As of mid 1993 the older workers' share was higher in heavy industry, with managements estimating that on average those aged over 54 represented nearly 20 per cent in basic metals, engineering and chemicals, compared with less that 15 per cent in other sectors. The share tended to be higher in firms that had cut employment the most and in Moscow City establishments.

Once again, in mid 1993 many more firms stated that they expected the pensioners' share of employment to decline (23.3 per cent) than to increase (4.2 per cent). A decline in their share was expected more among large enterprises and in the sectors where their share was relatively high in 1993, notably the heavy industries.

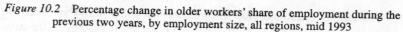

Figure 10.2 Percentage change in older workers' share of employment during the previous two years, by employment size, all regions, mid 1993

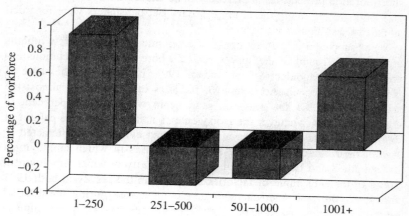

Source: RLFS3, n = 337.

In fact, according to RLFS4 the pensioners' share on average rose from 12.6 per cent in mid 1993 to 13.2 per cent in May 1994. As in the past, in mid 1994 the share was highest in metals. The overall figure was lower than in RLFS3 only because of two special factors. First, this was the first time the depressed economic region of Ivanovo was included in the survey, and as can be seen from Figure 10.3, the overall share of older workers in employment was much lower in Ivanovo. The main reasons for this are that employment cuts had been much greater there, the local labour market had a very high ratio of women to men, the population was unusual in that there were few male pensioners, and the region's labour market has traditionally relied relatively heavily on internal migrants. But what is striking is that only in Ivanovo had the pensioners' share of employment fallen, from its already much lower level.

Another reason is that for the first time a few 'social organisations' were included in the sample. Between 1993 and 1994 it seemed that many older workers had been pushed into earlier retirement in social organisations, whereas the older workers' share had risen in all other property forms.

Most significantly, once again the older workers' share of employment had risen in establishments in which total employment had fallen (Figure 10.4). This suggests that their share was rising mainly through non-recruitment of new workers to replace workers who were leaving the firm. Older workers were presumably holding on to their jobs, while

Figure 10.3   Older workers' share of employment, by region, 1991–4

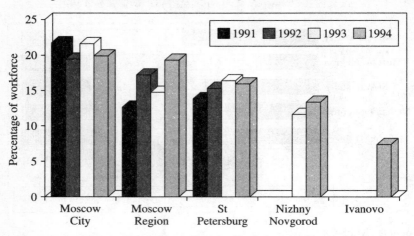

Source: RLFS1, RLFS2, RLFS3, RLFS4; n = 503, 191, 348 and 384, respectively.

Figure 10.4   Change in older workers' share of employment, by employment
change during previous year, all regions, 1993–4

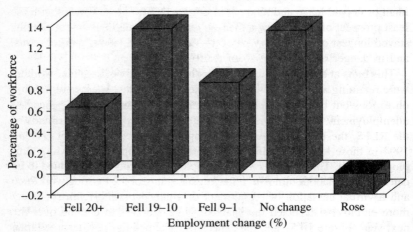

Source: RLFS4, n = 378.

Figure 10.5 Expected change in older workers' share of employment during the next year, by region, 1994

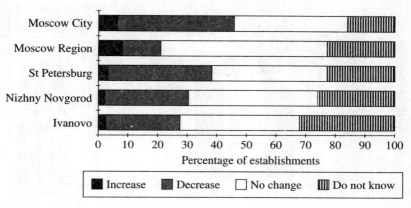

Source: RLFS4, n = 382.

the higher turnover at younger ages was tending to raise the older workers' share of the remaining jobs. This in turn reflected the peculiar way by which employment cuts were taking place, through concealed unemployment and the drift away from paid employment towards unpaid employment or unpaid leave and then out of employment. Those workers with the least prospect of obtaining another job or access to unemployment benefits stayed longest on the factory payroll – dead souls in labour-market terms, and in danger of becoming so in reality.

This hints at the twist in the peculiar story. It could be that older workers were retaining a high share of employment not because they were holding on to jobs but because much of their employment was merely concealed unemployment. For those firms that were in the first and fourth rounds of the RLFS, the pensioners' share of employment rose between 1991 and 1994 in those in which employment rose, and fell in those in which employment fell. This suggests that the employment structure continued to be determined by labour turnover, reflecting an ageing of the existing workforce and a virtual cessation of recruitment of young workers. Even so, many more employers expected the share of older workers to decline over the next year (Figure 10.5), and the expectation seemed more widespread than in earlier years.

One element began to be relevant from 1992 onwards, although it was at an early stage at that time. *Property-form restructuring* of firms could

Figure 10.6   Change in older workers' share of employment during 1993–4, by property form, all regions

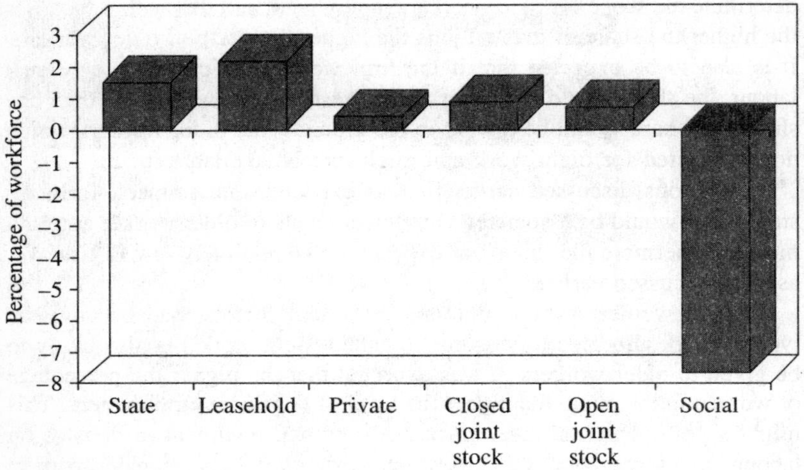

Source: RLFS4, n = 378.

be expected to make a big difference to pensioner employment, since one would anticipate that more profit-oriented firms would wish to reduce the number of those presumed to be of relatively low productivity. In 1990–2, according to data from the sample of firms in the first two rounds of the RLFS, in those firms that were private in 1991 the pensioners' share of employment declined, whereas it rose in both state and leaseholding establishments.

In 1992–3, according to RLFS3, both the pensioners' and the older workers' share of employment tended to be higher in state establishments than in closed or open joint-stock companies. While overall employment was falling, employment of older workers declined faster in privatised and private firms than in state enterprises. But in state and large factories, because worker recruitment had effectively been brought to a halt, once again the older workers' share of employment rose (Figure 10.6).

For all those establishments that were in the first, third and fourth rounds of the RLFS, that is, 126 factories in total, the share of older workers was 18.3 per cent in late 1991, 19.1 per cent in mid 1993 and 18.7 per cent in mid 1994. Thus the share was remarkably constant over the period.

To conclude this section, an attempt is made to explain the interfirm variation in the employment share taken by pensioner workers. It is hypo-thesised that technological and work schedules of different industries would determine the scope for older worker employment, and that within factories the higher the share of manual jobs the higher the share of older workers. It is also to be expected that if the firm were using part-time or casual labour, the share would be higher. In contrast, if there were more than one shift their share would be lower, on the grounds that older workers would not be wanted for night work and might not be available for it.

For reasons discussed earlier, it was expected that property-form re-structuring would be associated with lower levels of older worker employ-ment. Furthermore the share was expected to be relatively low in Ivanovo, as also discussed earlier.

Because women are concentrated in certain sectors, and because the type of work allocated to women (so-called 'light work') is also likely to be given to older workers, it was expected that the higher the percentage of women in the plant, the higher the level of pensioner employment. This might seem counterintuitive, since one common argument in debates on labour-force segregation is that there are substitutions between older workers and women. However Russian industry is peculiar in that respect. Al-though we collected such data only in RLFS1, women made up a larger share of pensioners (55.2 per cent) than they did of total employment. This must be an almost unique situation. The explanation is fairly simple. Women have an official pension age five years younger than men, and life expect-ancy is very much higher for women.

Finally, it was hypothesised that the higher the level of concealed un-employment in the factory, the higher the older workers' share, because of the dead-souls effect mentioned earlier.

Thus two functions were estimated by OLS regressions. The first sought to explain the variance in older workers employment drawing on the 1994 data, and the second sought to explain changes in the older workers' share between 1993 and 1994. The second excluded certain variables that seemed pertinent only to the shares. The first function was as follows:

$$\%PENS = a + b_1\Sigma(IND) + b_2\Sigma(PROP) + b_3\Sigma(REG) + b_4EMP + b_5CHEMP + b_6\%BC + b_7SHIFT + b_8PT + b_9CAS + b_{10}\%FEM + b_{11}\%LABSURP + e$$

where the dependent variable is the percentage of employment in the firm taken by pensioners in mid 1994, and where the dependent variables are as follows:

Σ(IND), ⎫ three sets of dummy variables for industrial sector, prop-
Σ(PROP) ⎬ = erty form of establishment and region of location, as
Σ(REG) ⎭ defined in preceding chapters.

EMP   = size of establishment in number of workers and employees as of June 1994.

CHEMP   = percentage change in employment in the firm during the
preceding year.

%BC   = percentage of total employment in the firm consisting of
manual production workers.

SHIFT   = 1 if the factory operated two or three shifts per working
day, 0 otherwise.

PT   = 1 if the factory employed part-time workers, 0 otherwise.

CAS   = 1 if the factory employed casual or temporary labour, 0
otherwise.

%FEM   = percentage of total employment taken by women.

%LABSURP = percentage of workforce identified as concealed unemployment, as defined in Chapter 4.

The function attempting to explain the changes in the pensioners' share merely focused on those variables that could have changed during the period. The results for both functions are presented in Table 10.1. The overall results were poor fits, explaining only about 10 per cent of the variance and suggesting that the pattern was fairly random. Attempts to explain the changing share of older workers had even worse outcomes.

Whatever the pattern of managerial expectations, one anticipates that once the second and third phases of employment decline predominate in Russian industry, when mass redundancies come to predominate over a combination of falling vacancies and high labour turnover, older workers will be hard hit.[1] It is a remarkable fact that in the mid 1990s they had retained as large a share of jobs as they had.

10.3 YOUTH

The position of young workers is not quite the reverse of that of pensioner and older workers. There has been anecdotal evidence that youths have been reluctant to enter factory employment in the 1990s.[2] An aversion to the lifestyle implied by such entities and the association with the previous regime were no doubt two factors. Another has been the lack of vacancies, and the resultant sense of an absence of a substantial peer group of young workers. A fourth factor may have been that young workers perceive few

Table 10.1 Old and young workers' share of employment, 1994
(OLS regression results)

Variable	Log. old workers' share	Log. young workers' share
(Constant)	1.3213	0.4731
Industry		
Metals	0.0733	−0.2024
Engineering	0.0360	−0.2061**
Food processing	−0.0642	−0.0561
Construction materials	−0.0326	−0.1845
Chemicals	0.1013	−0.1766*
Wood & paper	0.1155	−0.1996**
Property form		
Leasehold	−0.0111	−0.1247
Private	−0.0413	0.0915
Closed joint stock	0.0210	0.0976
Open joint stock	0.0385	0.0417
Social	0.1303	−0.2791*
Region		
Moscow Region	−0.0116	0.0649
St Petersburg	−0.0962**	0.1911***
Nizhny Novgorod	−0.1848***	0.0464
Ivanovo	−0.3407***	0.1097
Employment size	0.000001	0.00002**
% manual workers, 1994	−0.0018	0.0048*
% women, 1994	−0.00003	0.0008
Part-time workers	0.0541	0.0078
Several shifts	0.0517	−0.0748
Temporary workers	0.0142	0.0159
% employment change	−0.0002	−0.0001
Labour surplus	−0.0011***	−0.0009*
R^2	0.2314	0.1711
F	4.0848	2.8004

* Statistically significant at the 10% level of probability.
** Statistically significant at the 5% level.
*** Statistically significant at the 1% level.
Source: RLFS4, n = 384.

opportunities for job mobility once in such jobs, because of the stagnation of industrial employment.

In 1991, on average the factories surveyed estimated that 11.7 per cent of the workforce was under the age of 25, with 13 per cent in St Petersburg. Half the managements expected that the share of young workers in their

Figure 10.7   Young workers' share of employment, by region, 1991–4
(percentage of total employment taken by those aged 16–24)

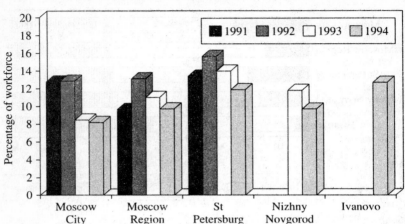

Source: RLFS1, RLFS2, RLFS3, RLFS4; n = 503, 191, 348 and 384, respectively.

factories would not change during the coming year, 15 per cent felt it would increase, 7 per cent felt it would decrease and nearly 28 per cent were uncertain. State enterprises were less likely to expect an increase in the young workers' share, and were slightly more likely to expect an increase. Two years later, in RLFS3, the results were rather similar – about 11 per cent expected an increase, 7.4 per cent a decrease, slightly over half thought there would be no change and the remainder were unsure. Rather worrying was the finding that over 13 per cent of managements in large factories expected the share to fall.

By mid 1994 young workers on average comprised exactly 10 per cent of the workforce in those factories included in RLFS4, and in all regions where two or more rounds of the RLFS had been carried out their share had declined (Figure 10.7). In mid 1994 their share of employment ranged from 14.3 per cent in textiles and garments to a mere 5.5 per cent in basic metals. They comprised 13.1 per cent in private firms compared with 9.3 per cent in state establishments; and they accounted for a statistically significant larger share in large establishments than in small ones. Consistent with the three-phase model of employment decline outlined earlier, youths made up 11.6 per cent of the workforce in establishments that had expanded employment during the previous year, compared with about 9.5 per cent in those that had cut employment. Only 6.6 per cent of the factory managements expected their share of employment to rise during

Figure 10.8 Expected change in young workers' share of employment during the next year, by region, 1994

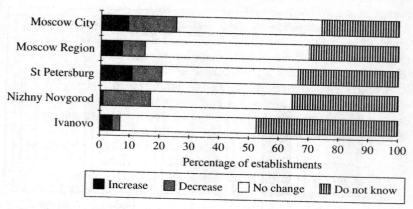

Source: RLFS4, n = 381.

the coming year, compared with the 12.1 per cent that expected it to fall (Figure 10.8).

Finally, considering only those establishments that were in more than one round of the RLFS, one can be reasonably sure that young workers' share fell during the four years of the four rounds of the RLFS. In those factories included in the first, third and fourth rounds, their share fell from 12.5 per cent in 1991 to 10.6 per cent in 1993 and 9.1 per cent in 1994.

The factories also employed some *students*, who would have been attempting to complement the very low stipends they were receiving. In 1991 the students' share was highest in Moscow City, followed by St Petersburg. But they were eased out of industrial jobs as employment contracted. The very small student share of total employment declined in 1992-3, from 1 per cent to 0.7 per cent, or by almost the same rate as that at which the older workers' share increased, which is not necessarily linked, although it is likely to reflect the fact that Russian industrial restructuring was still in the first or second phase of employment decline.

10.4 WORKERS WITH DISABILITIES

The statistics cannot adequately tell the story of what has been happening to the many workers with disabilities of one kind or another. The story is a sobering and disappointing one, and the telling of it is beyond the objectives of this analysis. Perhaps one part of it can be related by means of what happened in one particular factory that was included in all four rounds of the RLFS, and which the writer visited three times.

This old factory produced shoes and boots and was situated near the centre of one of the cities. Over the decade before the survey it had employed over 100 workers with various kinds of registered disability, ranging from physical handicaps to mental difficulties. In 1992 it employed 81 workers registered as disabled. The management had regarded the employment of such workers as part of its social responsibility in the district, where it was the largest employer. The trouble was that, as part of the paternalistic labour relations in such factories, these workers were concentrated in one workshop as a separate group. That workshop had the most obsolescent technology and the oldest machinery in the factory. The shoes produced in the workshop were the lowest quality and least profitable in the enterprise, and the noise and working conditions were unquestionably the worst. The management was under growing pressure to tighten the firm's 'budgetary constraint', and the firm was in mounting debt. Employment had to be cut, and had been reduced by a substantial amount. It was decided to close the workshop with the disabled workers, and as a direct result 81 workers with disabilities were released from employment. The general manager and the personnel manager were clearly unhappy about giving up their 'social employment', but reckoned they had had no choice.

That latter conclusion may be debatable, yet one was left with a feeling of ambivalence. The working conditions in the workshop were so bad that if one did not start work there with a disability, one could be fairly certain of obtaining one before long. The real tragedy was that the disabled were not so much integrated into the factory's workforce as segregated, and the segregation was transferred into the pattern of employment cuts. A year later none of the 81 disabled workers was employed in the factory, and it was extremely likely that they had been eased out of the labour force altogether.

This example was not an isolated one. More general analysis shows that between the late 1980s and the mid 1990s a majority of Russian workers with registered disabilities were displaced from employment.[3] From the RLFS, a little information is available on what happened in industry. In 1991, according to RLFS1, workers with disabilities accounted for about 2.5 per cent of total employment, ranging from 3.6 per cent in Moscow City to 1.2 per cent in St Petersburg, and ranging from nearly 4 per cent in textiles and garments and 3.7 per cent in engineering to 0.2 per cent in food processing. In 1993, according to RLFS3, such workers accounted for only 1.7 per cent of total employment, ranging from 4 per cent in textiles and garments and 2 per cent in engineering to an insignificant number in food processing.

In mid 1994, according to RLFS4, a first glance at the data suggests that the share was slightly higher than in 1993, but this was because a few sheltered enterprises were included for the first time as well as the region of Ivanovo, where the percentage of employed with disabilities was above average. Overall they accounted for 1.9 per cent of total employment, ranging from 3 per cent in engineering, 2.7 per cent in wood and paper products and 2.5 per cent in textiles and garments to less than 0.1 per cent in food processing. Thus the marginalisation of workers with disabilities had occurred in some sectors far more than in others.

10.5 MIGRANTS

Because of the sensitivity of the issues and the difficulty of obtaining meaningful or accurate information, little effort was made to collect data on the employment of foreigners or migrants from outside the *oblast*. Most managements confessed that they did not know where all their workers came from, and whether this was correct or not is a matter for speculation. Some had recruited from outside the *oblast*, usually in the Soviet era. In the case of Ivanovo, this was an area where workers traditionally had been attracted from many parts of the Soviet Union, while the opposite was true of Nizhny Novgorod, which had been a 'closed city' for fifty years.

For the record, in 1991 only a small minority employed any migrant or foreign workers, mainly in textiles and garments factories and chemicals, with internal migrants being found in relatively large numbers in food processing and construction materials. There was a net expectation that their employment shares would be cut. In 1993 only a few firms in the textiles and garments and chemicals sectors employed any foreign workers, according to RLFS3 data, and only a few chemicals and construction material plants stated that they employed 'refugees'.[4] As expected, no firms in Nizhny Novgorod had foreign workers or refugees, and none even had workers from outside the *oblast*. There had been a decline in the percentage shares of foreign and migrant workers in the two years. In net terms, there was an expectation that the employment shares of foreign workers, migrants and workers from outside the *oblast* would decline, although the numbers of firms reporting this was small, due to the small number employing such workers.

The main point that emerges from the information on migrant workers is that the regionalised, 'closed' character of the industrial labour market continued into the mid 1990s. If anything, rising unemployment has accentuated that phenomenon.

10.6   CONCLUSIONS

The main reason for the demographic pattern of employment change is that employment restructuring follows a three-phase process. In the first phase, employment decline comes about mainly from high labour turnover, coupled with the most intensive effort to retain jobs being made by groups with the lowest chance of obtaining alternative employment and with the most need for income. A rise in the employment share taken by pensioners in the context of Russian industry in 1991–2 was consistent with employment restructuring taking place in the first phase. Thereafter the story becomes more complicated.

In the second phase, which may roughly characterise the 1993–4 period, there are more redundancies as vacancies dry up and as enterprises take steps to cut the level of employment. The tendency is to reduce the employment of those perceived as marginal groups, which would include older workers, migrants, ethnic minorities and workers with disabilities.[5] In the Russian context, in this second phase one factor may have checked the expected decline in the older workers' share of employment: older workers put on unpaid administrative leave, partially paid administrative leave or minimal pay as part of the working impoverished would have been relatively inclined to maintain even the loosest of connections to their employment, simply because otherwise they would have had no access to unemployment benefit, whereas by staying on they had access to the social benefits of the factory.

11 Promoting the 'Human Development Enterprise': Enterprise Restructuring and Corporate Governance in Russian Industry

11.1 INTRODUCTION

> A just system must generate its own support.[1]

So far this book has been mainly about the employment and labour-market implications of industrial restructuring. This chapter is much more normative in character. For Russian industrial enterprises, the late 1990s represent a moment of crisis, bearing in mind the original Greek idea of crisis as both a threat and an opportunity.

In 1995 most factories were under threat of bankruptcy, as well as in danger of becoming more unpleasant places in which to work or through which to obtain the sort of social services they traditionally set out to provide. Industrial enterprises could be thoroughly rejected by young and old, associated as they were with a grimy, degraded past, with low wages, poor working conditions, Tayloristic working practices and heavy-handed bureaucratic controls. The old trade unions were losing members and had had their sense of legitimacy eroded, with little prospect of revival. The 'social enterprise', with its broad array of benefits and services, had frayed more than just at the edges, contributing to the socioeconomic fragmentation of society. The old training system, with all its faults, was withering, leaving a growing vacuum in skill formation. There had been massive 'downsizing' of factories, without the size restructuring needed to overcome the monopolisation of the economy. The result was very high concealed unemployment and a steady flow into open unemployment. Certainly there were ample grounds for Cassandras to feel comfortable.

Yet in the second half of the 1990s there is also an almost unique opportunity to alter the dynamics of enterprise culture and to create a new basis for *dynamic efficiency*. There has been a hardening of budgetary constraints, shown by the extensive employment cuts made in response to adverse economic performance and by the extensive fears of bankruptcy. There has been some technological awakening, as indicated in Chapter 3. Not only has there been extensive property-form restructuring, which could evolve in several distinct directions. Now that the umbilical chord between line ministries and management appointments has been broken, management accountability must grow. There is also the unresolved issue of relations between managers, workers, trade unions, shareholders and local authorities. This is the essence of corporate governance.

The old system has collapsed, but the era of experimentation has still to produce an ideal type likely to become the dominant model. One is inclined to predict that 'privatisation' is a misnomer for what has been happening and what will probably happen in the future.

This uncertainty in Russian industry is not unique as, fortunately or not, there is no suitable international model that could be imported. With all the emphasis on ideas embodied in such phrases as 'human development' and 'sustainable human development' (UNDP) and 'adjustment with a human face' (UNICEF) and other variants of the basic idea that development and structural adjustment must be guided by a normative perspective, it is remarkable that in the extensive international debate on structural adjustment and economic restructuring little attention has been devoted to the unit in which most people spend most of their lives, the *working establishment*.

This neglect has been mirrored in the dominant economic strategy supported around the world since the 1970s, namely supply-side economics. This has given *institutional* concerns minimal attention, and has been marked by a hostility towards collective entities of any sort. Put crudely, the supply-side economists' agenda has been oriented towards the liberalisation of all markets and the privatisation of economic and social policy, backed by a residual welfare state. At the level of the firm, the Chicago variant of neoclassical economics has been clear – business exists for one purpose only. As one of the fathers of the dominant approach of the past twenty years, the Nobel Prize winner Milton Friedman, put it, 'The *social responsibility* of business is to make a profit'.[2]

In Central and Eastern Europe the dominant mode of thinking about enterprises has been that under the Soviet system they operated with a 'soft budget constraint', in which profitability was not the main concern and in which there was an inherent excess demand for labour, because large workforces gave managements enhanced status and negotiating power with ministries and local clientele. Stemming from this view, which surely contains an essentially correct characterisation, the orthodox standpoint has been that only with privatisation would a hard budget constraint become operative, which in turn would lead to enterprise restructuring, including mass redundancies, bankruptcies and other responses to the need to increase profitability.

According to this line of reasoning, enterprise adjustment to the market would be assisted by the removal of regulations, most notably protective labour regulations, including minimum wages, employment protection rules, labour codes and even trade unions. This adheres to what is called the Chicago school of law and economics, in which the guiding ethical principle is 'Pareto optimality', leading to the view that regulations can be justified only if they promote economic growth and if some people gain while nobody loses. This restrictive view leads to support for wholesale 'deregulation', which as argued elsewhere is a misleading term.[3]

In the following, in contrast to the Chicago school, which has dominated so much of the economic policy in Russia and in other countries undergoing major economic restructuring, the basic ethical principle is closer to the Rawlsian 'difference principle'.[4] This states that, assuming an institutional framework provides *equality of opportunity* and *equal liberty*, distributive justice improves if a change in a practice or regulation improves the position of the 'worst-off' – or most vulnerable – groups. A second ethical principle guiding the following analysis and proposals is that they have powerful need to be protected from themselves.[5]

In less abstract terms, the main alternative to the orthodox perspective is one that looks to regulations, institutions and incentive structures to encourage and strengthen human development, while recognising that flexible markets are essential for economic growth. One can put this in several ways. However the fundamental starting point for constructive rethinking of social and economic strategy is the need to create conditions for thriving competition that is 'regulated' to ensure it is based on competition between strong partners who are simultaneously rivals and willing to cooperate. Paradoxically the competition must promote both social equity and dynamic efficiency, and as such it is important to recognise that it is a fallacy to depict a simple trade-off between 'equity' and 'efficiency'. *Dynamic efficiency* is derived from having rivals that are strong, and this is the ultimate justification for promoting cooperation and social consensus as the guiding principles for corporate governance.

This perspective is the basis of this chapter, which focuses on the normative issue of identifying the type of working environment that could be promoted in Russian industry to advance human development.

In the specific conditions of Russian industry in the late 1990s, the main question should be: 'What is a good enterprise for the twenty-first century?'

The notion of 'good' conjures up images of 'socially decent', and this may prompt a sceptical reaction from those who adhere to a neoliberal perspective. Accordingly one must state at the outset that the notion of a good enterprise cannot and should not be divorced from the pursuit of dynamic efficiency, and profitability, for without efficiency an enterprise will cease to be economically viable. Thus, in discussing what constitutes a good firm from a labour and employment point of view, it must be understood that ultimately it must be compatible with efficiency.[6]

Most people spend most of their adult lives working for enterprises and this experience shapes 'human development', in terms of both competence and status, as well as mental and physical health. A sweatshop does not contribute to the human development of those required to work in it, and an economy of sweatshops is unlikely to do much for human development generally. Nor can any contribution be made by the polluting, dangerous, noisy, hierarchically controlled factories that are the legacy of the Soviet era. On this most analysts would agree. Yet what *is* wanted is harder to determine – or agree upon -- than what is *not* wanted.

In the following an attempt is made to conceptualise and operationalise what is called a 'human development enterprise' (HDE), that is, a type of firm that in the specific circumstances of Russian industry in the mid 1990s could be regarded as having exemplary labour and employment practices and mechanisms to ensure development in terms of *skill, social equity, economic equity* and *democracy*. Although none is easy to define, all four are equally vital.[7]

Human development involves all those dimensions. Thus as individuals we need to develop and refine work skills, which we can achieve only in and through work. We need equitable treatment, in which discrimination based on non-changeable human characteristics is a denial of human rights and development. We need a fair distribution of the income generated by the efforts of workers, managers, employers and those working on their own account in some way. And we need to have voice in the work process, recognising that an absence of democracy in this most crucial of places for human development is a denial of meaningful democracy in general.

All these issues are relevant everywhere, and nowhere more so than in Russia, where enterprise restructuring is fundamental to the socioeconomic reform process. To give some substance to the ideas, provisional HDE indexes can be constructed by drawing on RLFS4.[8] For this purpose, RLFS4 was conducted at an inauspicious time. Nevertheless the data were opportune, in that enterprise restructuring was at an early stage of what had to be a tremendous upheaval, and in that there was a considerable range of options for the way in which the reform of corporate governance could go over the next few years.

11.2 CONSTRUCTING HDE INDEXES

In order to identify the type of enterprise that could be described as oriented towards human development, we need to identify proxy indicators that capture the essence of the practices, principles and outcomes that deserve to be promoted.[9] In most cases these will have to be measured by an indirect or proxy variable. Inevitably this means there will be a degree of subjectivity and a degree of pragmatism, in part due to the absence of data or the difficulty of obtaining measurable information on some issues.

A few methodological points should be borne in mind. We make a distinction between an *index* and an *indicator*. In developing what we may call an 'index' of an HDE with numerical values, we construct it from sets of 'indicators' of underlying phenomena. In putting indicators together as a composite index for any particular area of concern – such as the firm's orientation towards skill formation and training – there are difficulties of 'weighting' the different variables, or indicators.[10] There are various statistical techniques for dealing with this, including factor analysis and discriminant analysis. However in this sort of exercise there is a great virtue in transparency. The more complex the way in which an index has been constructed, the greater the suspicion that the data and reasoning have been 'massaged'. It is better to be able to interpret an index than to have to unravel it to try to make sense of it, even if we have to sacrifice a little in terms of 'scientific' accuracy. This is the main justification for the chosen technique in this analysis – using an ordinal scale for the indexes that are constructed. In subsequent refinements this could be modified.

A crucial point to make at the outset is that inclusion or exclusion of any particular indicator in an HDE index is a matter of preference, and does not affect the essence of the approach. Thus if the authorities choose to promote the HDE idea and do not believe that, say, economic democracy should be regarded as a desirable attribute, then the relevant indicators could be excluded. If, say, environmental concerns are deemed desirable, indicators capturing those concerns could be included.

In constructing HDE indexes we need sets of indicators that reflect four general considerations, as follows:

1. There should be indicators of *revealed preference*, or *ethical principles*, reflecting the firm's commitment to certain desirable practices and outcomes.
2. There should be indicators of *institutional mechanisms*, or *processes*, by which desirable outcomes could be translated into actual outcomes.[11]
3. There should be indicators of *outcomes*, which should reflect whether or not preferences and mechanisms are working.

Figure 11.1   Hierarchy of human development enterprise indexes

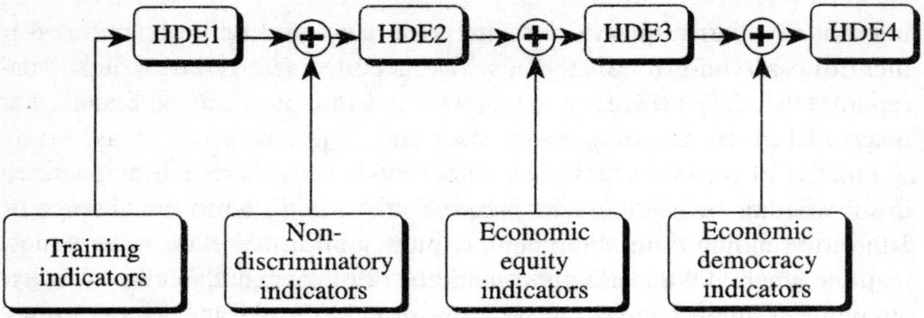

4. The indicators selected must be *sustainable*, since they must not be idealistic to the point where they would seriously jeopardise the enterprise's long-term viability and dynamism.

In this exploratory exercise a major objective is to construct an *hierarchy* of HDE indexes, to each of which is added a new set of indicators of one of our basic spheres of labour and employment practice – skill orientation, social equity, economic equity and democracy, in that order. We will proceed to construct four HDE indexes, as illustrated in Figure 11.1, starting with skill orientation, then moving on to integrate non-discriminatory practices, then economic equity and finally economic democracy.

11.3   HDE1: ENTERPRISE TRAINING

A good enterprise should provide opportunities for skill acquisition. In Russian industry, as we have seen, most training has been arranged by the large enterprises that have dominated the industrial landscape. What we can consider as the basic indicators of an orientation towards skill formation are the three layers of training, namely entry-level training for newly recruited workers, retraining to improve job performance or to transfer workers to other jobs with similar skills, and retraining to upgrade workers or promote them.[12]

In addition we need to take account of the type of training provided. If a firm gave only informal, on-the-job training, this would deserve less weight than if it involved 'classroom' and structured training, including apprenticeship. Accordingly, for each of the three levels of training a distinction is made between 'informal' and 'formal' training, the latter being presumed to have greater value, which is not always the case. Given the economic and institutional realities in Russian enterprises, the differences between formal and informal may be exaggerated. Yet concentrated training that involves a quantifiable cost should be preferable to 'on-the-job, pick-it-up-as-you-go' training. It will be recalled that although most firms reported that they provided training, few did so in a structured manner and many had given up doing so.

Finally, to construct the first index, HDE1, we included a factor measuring whether or not the establishment was paying for training directly, either by funding a training institute, or by paying the training fees to an institute where it was sending its workers, or by giving stipends to workers attending training courses. A substantial minority did at least one of the three, although it was a worrying trend that many others had ceased to do so and some others were planning to follow that course.

Thus the first index is constructed by a simple addition of the factors, as follows:

$$HDE1 = (TR + TRF) + (RETR + RETRF) + (UPTR + UPTRF) + TRINST$$

where the components are defined as follows:

TR = 1 if training was usually provided to newly recruited workers, 0 otherwise.

TRF = 1 if TR was apprenticeship or off-the-job in a classroom or an institute, 0 otherwise.

RETR = 1 if training was provided for established workers to improve their job performance or transfer between jobs of similar skill, 0 otherwise.

RETRF = 1 if that retraining was formal, in a class or an institute, 0 otherwise.

UPTR = 1 if training was provided to upgrade workers, 0 otherwise.

UPTRF = 1 if that retraining for upgrading was in a class or an institute, 0 otherwise.

TRINST = 1 if the firm paid for trainees at institutes, directly or indirectly, 0 otherwise.

Thus the basic HDE1 index, based on an ordinal scale, had values ranging from 0 to 7, with a zero value implying that the firm gave no training of any sort. In fact, for the whole sample of firms, the modal value was 3, the mean 3.0, with only 2 per cent having a value of 7 and with 4.6 per cent having a value of zero.

11.4   HDE2: INCORPORATING SOCIAL EQUITY

The second set of considerations is harder to conceptualise. For efficiency as well as the normally recognised equity reasons, a set of nondiscriminatory practices is essential: that is, an enterprise should be fair so as to reduce or avoid labour-market segregation based on personal characteristics such as gender, physical disability, age or ethnic origin. Earlier chapters have shown that the reverse has started to happen and has already become serious for disabled workers, and the situation could worsen for women in particular.

Measuring discrimination is notoriously difficult, yet the indicators in our survey instrument are probably reasonable first approximations, or sets of proxies. One could refine them, and in a different context from the countries of the former Soviet Union one would need to do so, to take account of ethnic factors in particular.

We measure socially equitable enterprises by reference to *revealed preference*, as stated by managements, and *revealed outcomes*. Neither stated preferences nor outcomes alone would be adequate; one might have preferences yet not put them into effect, or one might have no awareness of preferences yet discriminate on characteristics that had the perhaps inadvertent effect of excluding certain groups from various jobs.

Given the context and available data, the indicators of non-discrimination were mainly related to gender. In terms of hiring workers, if the management reported no preference for either men or women, this was regarded as a positive factor.

Note that in this regard it would be an inequity for men if we gave a positive value if the management said it preferred women, as was the case in some factories. However this reasoning could be stretched too far, because we are primarily concerned with redressing the typical case of discrimination against women.

Our second indicator of non-discrimination is a commitment to equal training opportunities for men and women. Preferences here are also likely to be revealed, especially as there is no law against discrimination in such matters. Thus, as shown in Chapter 9, there was some readiness on the part of managements to admit to a discriminatory preference for men, and in some cases for women.

Stated preferences are weak proxies, sometimes being rationalisations of what has happened, more often being norm-induced. To ignore revealed preferences altogether would be unjustifiable, yet in this respect it is particularly important to complement the preference factor with actual outcomes. Accordingly we incorporated an outcome variable of sex discrimination, one that may not be ideal but is a reasonable proxy for what we need. This second training factor is the percentage of higher-level 'employee' jobs taken by women. If this was greater than 40 per cent, then the firm was given a positive score in the index. In utilising this measure, one must admit to a degree of arbitrariness, because the outcome could be due to differences in the relative supply of men and women. However it does focus on the better types of job and is designed to identify relatively good performance in a key area of discrimination.

One could modify the selected share level to be sectorally specific, giving a positive score in the index if a firm had a relatively high percentage of women in training relative to the average for all firms in the sector. This could be justified because the ratios varied considerably by sector. But this is not as easily justifiable as it seems at first. It seems to allow for gender-based industrial segregation of employment.[13]

Besides the gender variables for employment equity, another indicator of discrimination is whether or not the firm was employing workers with registered disabilities. It will be recalled that, whatever the quota procedures, the disabled's share of employment had declined sharply, and we know from other sources that the share of the adult population with disabilities is high. So it is appropriate to use an indicator of whether or not the firm was employing any workers with disabilities. Coupled with the gender variables, this results in a proxy index of non-discrimination, as follows:

$$ND = Rs + Ts + FWC + D$$

where ND is the index of non-discrimination, and

Rs   = 1 if the management had no preference for either men or women when recruiting production workers, 0 otherwise.

Ts   = 1 if management stated it had no preference for either men or women when providing training for production workers.

FWC = 1 if the female share of employees (managerial, specialist or general service workers) was greater than 40 per cent, 0 otherwise.

D   = 1 if the firm employed workers with disabilities, 0 otherwise.

Adding ND to HDE1 gives us what might be called a 'socially equitable enterprise', which has a value of between 0 and 11. We now turn to the complex and more contentious issue of economic equity.

11.5   ECONOMIC EQUITY IN ENTERPRISES

The international literature on the notion of economic equity is vast, yet there is little on the issue of economic equity in terms of the microeconomics of the firm. What is an economically equitable firm? It is surely one in which the differences in earnings and benefits between members of it are minimised to the point where economic efficiency is not jeopardised. This might be called the 'principle of fair inequality' or 'efficient inequality'. It is rather utilitarian, and one should add a Rawlsian caveat – with priority being given to improvement of the 'worst-off' workers in the firm.[14]

There are also dynamic efficiency reasons to favour economic equity, whatever the bargaining position or market position of various groups in an enterprise. It is widely recognised that labour productivity depends in part on cooperation as well as on individual effort and performance. If there were wide differences between groups in the enterprise, there would be a tendency for the more disadvantaged, or those who felt they were inequitably treated, to withhold their 'tacit knowledge' and not commit themselves to the voluntary exchange of knowledge that contributes to dynamic efficiency.[15] There would also be a tendency towards implicit or explicit sabotage in factories.

To create a proxy economic equity index we consider three factors, giving greatest weight to the first, appropriately since this relates to treatment of the 'worst off' in the firm.

First, one of the less appealing phenomena to emerge in Russian industry in the mid 1990s is the growth of groups of workers in a firm who are paid much lower wages than anybody else, and typically there are some who receive very low wages indeed. An economically equitable firm should have few if any workers who are paid a small fraction of the average in the firm. So we can take the minimum wage received by the lowest-paid full-time workers as the initial yardstick. If more than 5 per cent of the workers received this wage, then the firm is given a low score on economic equity. But as this does not capture any distributional factor, we can complement it by giving a positive score to any firm in which the minimum payment was equal to or greater than 50 per cent of the average wage. These two indicators are only proxies for what we would like to measure, yet with the type of data one can collect in large-scale establishment surveys they are reasonable proxies.

A second consideration is whether the average wage itself is equitable relative to that paid in other firms. Here we do take as a proxy a sectorally relative measure, to reflect technological and market factors. The proxy used is whether the average wage in the firm is greater than the industry's average. If it is greater, then a positive score is given.

Finally, equity is improved if the enterprise provides benefits and entitlements that represent security against various personal contingencies and improve the stakeholders' standard of living. Since wages and incomes are only part of the remuneration system, we take as a proxy whether or not the firm provided ordinary workers with more than ten types of fringe benefit.[16] Thus the economic equity index is as follows:

$$EE = Min/Emp + M + AW/AWM + FB$$

where EE is economic equity index, and

Min/Emp = 1 if the percentage of the firm's total workforce receiving the minimum payment was below 5 per cent, 0 otherwise.

M = 1 if the minimum wage paid was greater than 50 per cent of the average paid in the firm, 0 otherwise.

AW/AWM = 1 if the average wage in the establishment was above the average wage for the industrial sector, 0 otherwise.

FB = 1 if the firm paid more than ten types of identified fringe benefit, 0 otherwise.

If we add EE to HDE2 we have what we can call the 'Socioeconomically equitable HDE'. This can take a value of between 0 and 15. Then we move into the politically most sensitive sphere of corporate governance.

11.6   THE ECONOMICALLY DEMOCRATIC HDE

To be governed by appetite alone is slavery, while obedience to a law one prescribes to oneself is freedom.[17]

There is something missing from Rousseau's famous aphorism. To be ruled by laws and regulations alone is not freedom either. What is crucial is that there should be voice regulation. In the workplace, as anywhere else, the direct stakeholders who bear the greatest risk and uncertainty should be able to regulate decisions affecting labour and employment practices. Put differently, what is human development without empowerment? This is perhaps the great quandary of corporate governance for the twenty-first century. Can the functions of management and productive decision making be made more democratic and accountable while promoting dynamic efficiency for the benefit of all representative stakeholders, which may include shareholders not working for the enterprise?[18]

Democracy must be more than casting a vote every few years. Democracy is also about institutional safeguards, and the most effective of these is the capacity of the vulnerable to exercise restraint and direction on those in decision-making positions, giving substance to the Rawlsian 'maximin' principle, which was alluded to earlier. Democracy is also about attempts to ensure cooperation in the interests of all representative groups. As some analysts have put it, successful cooperation requires 'the shadow of the future', that is, mechanisms to ensure that competitive interest groups will know that they will have to deal with each other and cooperate with each other in the future.

In the nature of an industrial enterprise, one side (management) has the scope for various forms of opportunism through control of information by, a limited circle of people and a capacity to take unilateral decisions (by fiat).[19] To limit opportunism on the part of the authorities there must be a process of reciprocal monitoring and a capacity to impose sanctions when abuses are detected.[20]

This is important in the area of enterprise restructuring in Russian industry, for unless there are mechanisms for voice regulation of the restructuring, the capacity of the vulnerable to influence the outcomes will be minimised. It is also unlikely that the process will succeed in achieving an atmosphere of dynamic efficiency if the workers are sullen and become 'excluded insiders' in factories.[21]

So to complete our idea of a human development enterprise we need to construct an 'economic democracy index'. This we can define in terms of six indicators.

First, we take it as axiomatic that the voice of the workers is strengthened – potentially at least – by a high degree of unionisation of the workforce. Quite simply, having a mechanism to represent workers and employees creates the basis for dynamic efficiency. Without a trade union, there would be no 'shadow of the future' to concentrate the minds of managers and workers on developing and maintaining decent and efficient employment and labour practices. This does not mean that we presume that unions will always behave appropriately. However a strong representative mechanism is a necessary condition for voice regulation. This, in the Russian case, is defined pragmatically as being the case if more than 50 per cent of the workers in a surveyed firm belonged to a trade union, because of the traditionally very high (artificially) level of unionisation. Ideally, it would be appropriate to identify the breadth of the union, since in principle an industrial union should be representative of a broader group of workers than a craft union, and a union that had members who were potential workers as well as those actually in employment would be more likely to ensure that the concerns of those in the labour market were also taken into account. The character of trade unions will have to change if such refinements are to make much sense in the Russian labour market.

Second, the democratic potential is greater if the main union is an independent one, which in the Russian context means, above all, that the administration or management should *not* be members of it.[22] Traditionally, in Soviet enterprises management belonged to the union and both managers and trade union representatives were subject to the commands of the Communist Party. Thus, symbolically and as an indicator of growing independence in bargaining, non-membership by management is an important indicator of independent voice in a country such as Russia. Elsewhere an alternative indicator of union independence would be more appropriate.

Third, to be meaningful there should be evidence of the existence of an operational mechanism for bargaining. For this, a collective agreement between the union and the employer is taken as a positive sign, even though it is recognised that in the mid 1990s a collective agreement would in most cases have been more formal than substantive.

Fourth, there is deemed to be a greater degree of democracy if workers own a large percentage of the shares of the company, which has been a feature of property-form restructuring of Russian industry. The critical level for a positive value is taken to be 30 per cent. Although this aspect of enterprise democracy has been controversial for many years, many empirical studies have suggested that minority employee ownership is conducive to efficiency, economic restructuring and equity.[23]

In Russian industry, given the lack of imbued work discipline and the legacy of the Soviet era in which the workers' effort bargain was low and erratic and the monitoring of it was ineffectual, if not wholly distorted, worker ownership and governance should have considerable *potential* benefits as a best-option means of overcoming the intrinsic incompleteness of labour contracts.[24]

Ownership of a flow of income should be distinguished from ownership of property rights. In terms of corporate governance, minority worker share ownership could be interpreted as turning workers into *outsider principals* – monitoring the performance of the agent (manager), and indirectly providing a mechanism for selecting, dismissing and replacing managers. The objection to the sole existence of *insider principals* is that a coalition between managers and workers as insiders could result in short-term concerns predominating over long-term strategy. However if share ownership is the mechanism, workers and managers effectively become outsider agents as well, having a direct interest in the long-term flow of income from their shares as well as their earnings from work.[25]

Fifth, at least in the Russian context, it is regarded as a positive element in enterprise democracy if the top management is elected by the workers, rather than being appointed by a ministry or by an enterprise board. This is likely to be the most controversial factor, for well-known reasons, although it is institutionalised in Germany in the system of codetermination. The essence of the pragmatic decision is that it recognises the positive value of direct accountability to actual stakeholders in the enterprise, limiting managerial opportunism and thus encouraging behaviour in favour of sustainable long-term profit maximisation, dynamic efficiency and human development practices.

As observed in Chapter 3, in the 1990s there has been diversification in the means by which Russian managements are appointed and reappointed. Achieving a balance in accountability of managements to workers and the firm is difficult, since commercial decisions might be jettisoned in favour of decisions that enjoy the short-term support of the workforce. Appointment by the workers could result in general managerial conservatism and a reluctance to restructure. This is an endemic problem in democracies.[26] Yet in the emerging Russian firms, workers are potentially becoming stakeholders, and this makes short-termism less likely, although the argument is a justification for sufficiently long periods to encourage managements to take decisions that combine concern both for today's workers and for the future of the firm.

Sixth, economic democracy is taken to be greater if there is a profit-sharing pay system in operation, implying a sharing of risks and rewards. This is a particularly sensitive issue, since many trade unionists have been against profit sharing on the ground that it introduces income insecurity for workers who are not involved in the decision making and who rely almost entirely on their wage income to maintain their standard of living. However if one is giving a positive value to the broadening of democratic decision making, it is appropriate to balance this by valuing mechanisms that share the risks and potential benefits. Moreover a firm with high income dispersion ('delevelling' in the jargon favoured by Russian labour economists) that is due to the working of incentive systems should be regarded differently from one in which high inequality reflects power relations and managerial fiat.

In sum, taking account of the various considerations, we can define an economic democracy index (ED), which can take a value of between 0 and 6, as follows:

$$ED = TU + IND + COLL + SH + MA + P$$

where

TU   = 1 if more than 50 per cent of the workforce is unionised, 0 otherwise.

IND   = 1 if the management is not in the trade union, 0 otherwise.

COLL = 1 if there is a collective agreement, 0 otherwise.

SH   = 1 if more than 30 per cent of the firm's shares are owned by workers and employees, 0 otherwise.

MA   = 1 if the top management is appointed by the workers, 0 otherwise.

P   = 1 if there is a profit-sharing element in the wage determination system, 0 otherwise.

By adding the ED index to the HDE3, as shown in Figure 11.1, we obtain the full 'human development enterprise index', which we designate as HDE4.[27] This has a maximum possible value of 22, and if the index is supposed to identify exemplary standards, there should be a tapering in the distribution of firms, with relatively fewer as the scores rise above the median value, and no excessive bunching of values. We now turn to an assessment of the HDE indexes in Russian industry.

11.7 IDENTIFYING THE HUMAN DEVELOPMENT ENTERPRISE IN RUSSIAN INDUSTRY

The attraction of the HDE index is that we can look at a firm to assess its performance in absolute terms or to assess its performance relative to others in the country, or even within a sector, region or size category. Thus, when discussing the values of the indexes and patterns, the following refers exclusively to Russian industry, and is primarily concerned with identifying those enterprises that have performed relatively well as an HDE in the context of Russian industry.

The first point to note is that, in terms of HDE4, 6.8 per cent of establishments had scores of more than 14, and these should be designated as the leading group in the Russian context, even though there were none with values above 17. At the other end, 35.6 per cent had values of below 11, and those should be regarded as unsatisfactory.

There are four further points to bear in mind. First, the way the HDE4 index is constructed gives a relatively heavy weight to skill formation (the

Table 11.1 Correlation matrix of human development enterprise indexes, all regions, mid 1994

	Econ. dem. index	Econ. equity index	Non-discr. index	HDE1	HDE2	HDE3	HDE4
Economic democracy index	1.00	-0.02	0.15	0.31	0.34	0.30	0.70
Economic equity index	-0.02	1.00	-0.01	0.07	0.05	0.40	0.29
Non-discriminatory index	0.15	-0.01	1.00	0.02	0.59	0.54	0.47
HDE1	0.31	0.07	0.02	1.00	0.82	0.78	0.73
HDE2	0.34	0.05	0.59	0.82	1.00	0.93	0.86
HDE3	0.30	0.40	0.54	0.78	0.93	1.00	0.89
HDE4	0.70	0.29	0.47	0.73	0.86	0.89	1.00

Source: RLFS4, n = 384.

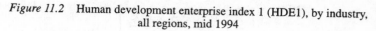

Figure 11.2   Human development enterprise index 1 (HDE1), by industry, all regions, mid 1994

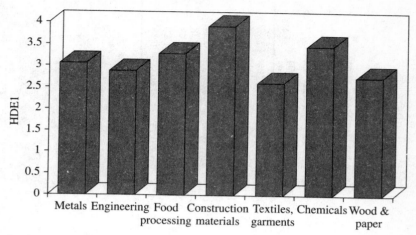

Source: RLFS4, n = 384.

base of human development in many models). Second, there was a low correlation between the four component indexes – non-discrimination, social equity, economic equity and economic democracy – implying they were measuring distinctive and different phenomena (Table 11.1). Third, the few social organisations are excluded from the analysis, since they were unique, special enterprises. Fourth, when considering interenterprise patterns it is worth noting that the averages for the various components may not translate into substantial differences overall, since in many cases firms that did well on some indicators did relatively poorly on others.

Turning to distributional patterns across the 384 firms in 1994, we start with HDE1. In terms of mean values, the average was highest in the construction materials and chemicals sectors, and lowest in textiles and garments (Figure 11.2). It was lower in private establishments than in other property forms, reflecting the low degree of training given in the private sector thus far (Figure 11.3). And it was highest in large firms (Figure 11.4). In terms of corporate governance, as defined in Chapter 3, it was highest in establishments designated as 'worker-controlled', followed by 'employee-controlled' (Figure 11.5). The patterns could be interpreted as suggesting that policy makers should concentrate most on improving training in small firms, in textiles and garments and in private firms. The message is that there is a need to couple property-form and size restructuring

Figure 11.3   Human development enterprise index 1 (HDE1), by property form, all regions, mid 1994

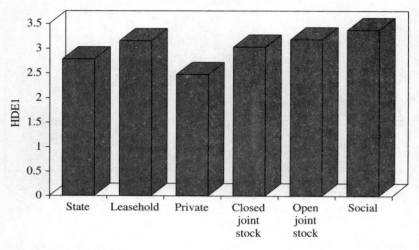

Source: RLFS4, n = 384.

Figure 11.4   Human development enterprise index 1 (HDE1), by employment size, all regions, mid 1994

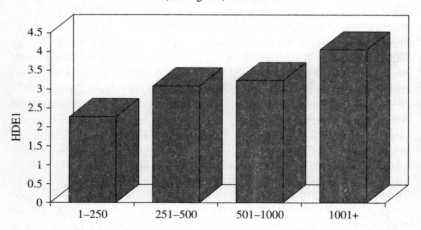

Source: RLFS4, n = 384.

Figure 11.5   Human development enterprise index 1 (HDE1), by corporate
governance, all regions, 1994

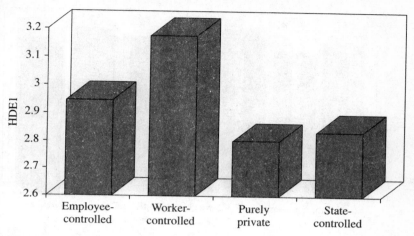

Source: RLFS4, n = 375.

and corporate governance reform with a policy of promoting enterprise
training and retraining.

Adding the non-discrimination index, in HDE2, made little difference to
the structural pattern (Figures 11.6–11.9). However adding the economic
equity index strengthens the relative performance of closed joint-stock
firms, as would be expected, and it is notable that worker-controlled
governance was associated with a statistically significant higher value
of economic equity, translated into a high value of HDE3. For HDE3,
in terms of mean values, open joint-stock firms appeared to perform better
on average than other property forms, whereas state firms did relatively
badly (Figures 11.10–11.12).

Finally, adding the economic democracy index gives the full index of
an ideal type of 'good enterprise' for the Russian context, HDE4. In terms
of economic democracy, larger firms tended to score higher than smaller
firms, and open and closed joint-stock enterprises tended to score much
better than other property forms (Figure 11.13). In terms of HDE4, the
average values were higher in closed and open joint-stock establishments
than in other property forms and appeared slightly higher in large firms
than in small firms (Figures 11.14–11.16). Worker and employee governance types performed best, as expected given their positive value to economic democracy (Figure 11.17).

Figure 11.6   Human development enterprise index 2 (HDE2), by industry, all regions, mid 1994

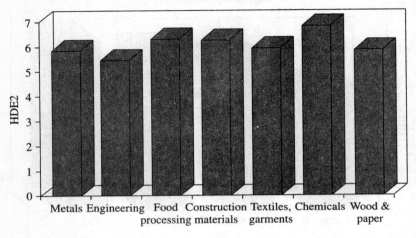

Source: RLFS4, n = 384.

Figure 11.7   Human development enterprise index 2 (HDE2), by property form, all regions, mid 1994

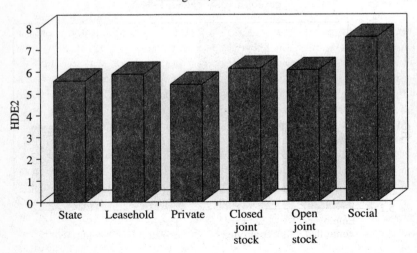

Source: RLFS4, n = 384.

Figure 11.8 Human development enterprise index 2 (HDE2), by employment size, all regions, mid 1994

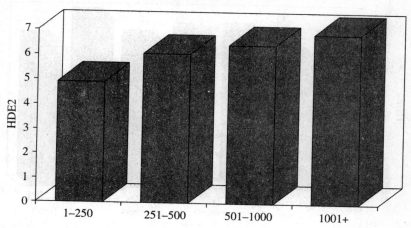

Source: RLFS4, n = 384.

Figure 11.9 Human development enterprise index 2 (HDE2), by corporate governance, all regions, 1994

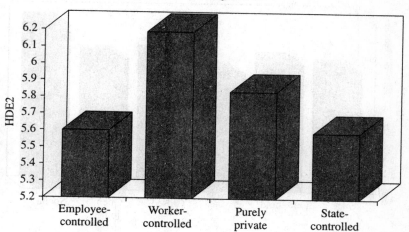

Source: RLFS4, n = 375.

Figure 11.10   Human development enterprise index 3 (HDE3), by industry, all regions, mid 1994

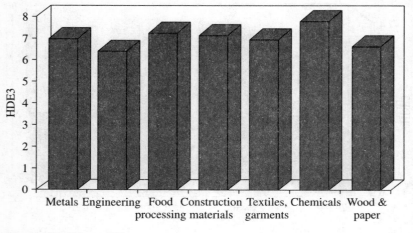

Source: RLFS4, n = 384.

Figure 11.11   Human development enterprise index 3 (HDE3), by property form, all regions, mid 1994

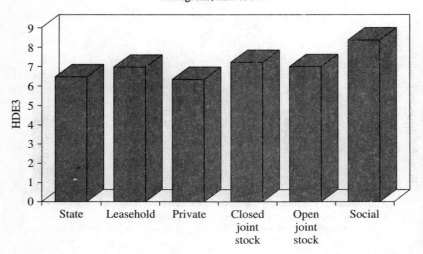

Source: RLFS4, n = 384.

Figure 11.12   Human development enterprise index 3 (HDE3), by corporate governance, all regions, 1994

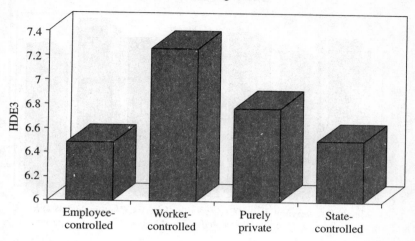

Source: RLFS4, n = 375.

Figure 11.13   Economic democracy index, by property form, all regions, mid 1994

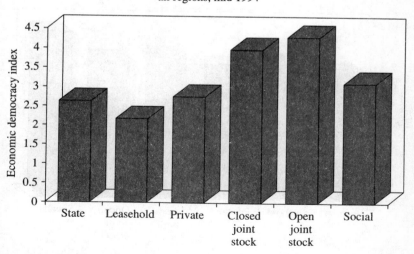

Source: RLFS4, n = 384.

Figure 11.14   Human development enterprise index 4 (HDE4), by industry, all regions, mid 1994

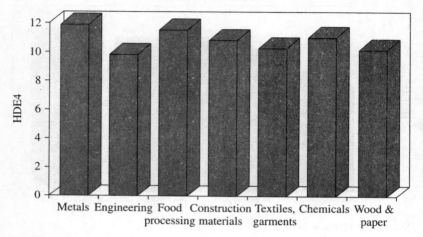

Source: RLFS4, n = 384.

Figure 11.15   Human development enterprise index 4 (HDE4), by property form, all regions, mid 1994

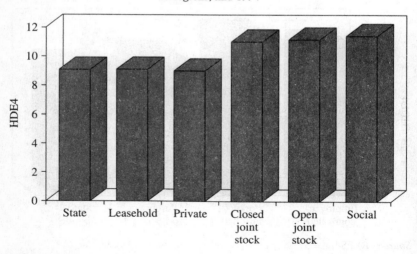

Source: RLFS4, n = 384.

Figure 11.16   Human development enterprise index 4 (HDE4), by employment size, all regions, mid 1994

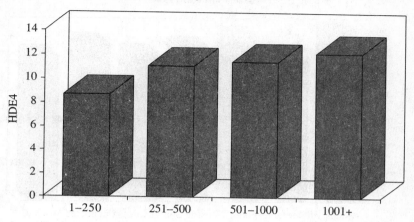

Source: RLFS4, n = 384.

Figure 11.17   Human development enterprise index (HDE4), by corporate governance, all regions, 1994

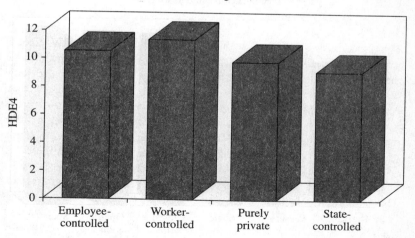

Source: RLFS4, n = 375.

In order to assess the structural determinants of the values of HDE1, HDE2, HDE3 and HDE4, a basic, ordinary least-square multiple regression function was estimated, as follows:

$$HDE = a + b_1\Sigma(IND) + b_2EMP + b_3\Sigma(PROP) \text{ (or } \Sigma CORP) + b_4EMPCH + b_5\Sigma(ELECT) + b_6CHSALES + b_7UNION + e$$

where

$\Sigma(IND)$	=	binaries (1,0) for industrial sector, the omitted category being food processing.
EMP	=	employment size of establishment.
$\Sigma(PROP)$	=	binaries for property form of establishment, the omitted category being state establishments.
$\Sigma(CORP)$	=	binaries for corporate governance form of establishment, the omitted category being state governance.
EMPCH	=	percentage employment change during the past year.
$\Sigma(ELECT)$	=	binaries for method of appointment of senior management, the omitted category being appointment by a ministry.
CHSALES	=	binary, 1 if sales rose in real terms during the past year, 0 otherwise.
UNION	=	percentage of workforce in a trade union.
e	=	error term.

The equation was estimated with and without the union variable, since it was included in the definition of HDE4, and with and without the variable measuring the means of appointing the top management, for the same reason. Whether included or not, the results in Table 11.2 suggest that, *controlling for the influence of other factors*, open joint-stock companies were more likely to score higher than other property forms, larger firms tended to have higher values of HDE4 and economic performance in terms of sales change was inversely related to the value of the HDE index.

Of course there is a possibility that the correlations between some of the explanatory variables and the HDE indexes mix cause and effect. The regression was little more than a check on the tabulations underlying the figures. In some respects, property form has defined the scope for the score on the HDE indexes, but in all cases there was considerable intragroup variation, and as the correlation matrix showed earlier, a firm scoring high on one component index or indicator did not necessarily score high on another. This is important, for if high scores are simply a reflection of size or one property form, the policy prescription would be

Table 11.2 Determinants of human development enterprise, Russian industry, 1994 (OLS regression results)

Variable	HDE1	HDE2	HDE3	HDE4
(Constant)	2.2716	5.2796	6.7062	9.9106
Industry				
Metals	0.3590	−0.3414	−0.2994	0.9882
Engineering	0.1728	−0.6937**	−0.8313***	−0.6895*
Food processing	0.4103	−0.1128	−0.0379	0.8554*
Construction materials	1.2574***	0.2105	−0.0097	0.0694
Chemicals	0.5994*	0.5237	0.3890	0.4384
Wood & paper	0.0831	−0.3894	−0.5879	−0.1468
Corporate governance				
Purely private	0.0338	0.0466	0.1027	0.5295
Worker-controlled	−0.1284	−0.3906	−0.4457	0.8363*
Employee-controlled	0.2205	0.2269	0.2755	1.6975***
Region				
Moscow Region	−0.3106	−0.4168	−0.3647	−0.1431
St Petersburg	−0.2646	0.2136	−0.0233	−0.4614
Nizhny Novgorod	0.1730	0.2361	0.1372	0.4060
Ivanovo	−0.4577	−0.6921*	−1.1814***	−1.9137***
Employment size	−0.0002***	0.0001**	0.0002***	0.0003***
% employment change	0.0008	0.0010	0.0015	0.0028
% sales change	0.0000	0.0000	0.0000	0.0000
Unionisation rate	0.0049**	0.0110***	0.0106***	—
R^2	0.1524	0.1480	0.1578	0.2107
F	3.6814	3.5565	3.8364	5.8215

* Statistically significant at the 10% level of probability.
** Statistically significant at the 5% level.
*** Statistically significant at the 1% level.
Source: RLFS4, n = 348.

restricted to a straightforward industrial strategy, leading to a simple recommendation to promote a particular enterprise size and property form. That is not the case. There were large firms with low HDE scores and small firms with high scores, and private firms with high and low scores. This implies that *if* one wished to promote the characteristics of an HDE (or variants of them), specific incentives to move in those directions would be advantageous.

Much more research is needed into the determinants of relatively good or bad enterprise performance in terms of 'human development', and this should be assisted by the data from the fifth round of the RLFS, which was being planned at the time this book was being finalised. The purpose here is merely to identify a way of approaching enterprise restructuring. It would surely be regrettable to talk about restructuring without having a reasonable set of criteria to guide that restructuring.

11.8   ECONOMIC PERFORMANCE AND THE HDE

Having identified a measurable set of indexes of the good HDE, we should address three potential criticisms. All three are likely to come from the orthodox, neoclassical economist. First, and most importantly, a critic is likely to claim that by being a good enterprise the firm would undermine its commercial viability. If it were shown that scoring high on the HDE were associated with low dynamic efficiency and poor responsiveness to market forces, the long-term viability of the enterprise would be jeopardised, and thus the rationale for promoting an HDE would be weakened.

In other words an orthodox neoclassical – or anti-institutional – economist might claim that the pursuit of the characteristics of an HDE would result in escalating costs, stronger internal rigidities, plunging economic performance and inadequate responsiveness to market forces, leading to higher costs, labour hoarding and so on. This is a legitimate concern.

What is the evidence? First, while correlations do not demonstrate causation, it appears that labour costs as a share of total production costs were lower in firms with high HDE values and also in firms that scored high on the economic democracy index, which would probably be the most contentious set of indicators in the construction of the HDE (Figures 11.18–11.21). These are encouraging results. What they suggest is that if a firm does well on its HDE index, and practises economic democracy, it has higher levels of labour productivity.[28] At the very least, this is *prima facie* evidence against the potential sceptics.

Second, since in Russia and other parts of the former Soviet Union it has been claimed that enterprises have not been responsive to market pressures, it might be claimed that high HDE values indicate resistance to change and strong protection of 'insiders'. High levels of 'labour hoarding' have been attributed to persistence of the soft budget constraint and a lack of concern about labour costs. In fact all forms of enterprise had cut employment by large amounts, and it is notable that firms with low values of any of the four indexes of HDE had cut employment by more than those with higher values (Figures 11.22–25). One might interpret these results as implying that firms with higher HDE values performed better in terms of employment. However this is neither necessary to support our concept, nor

Figure 11.18   Labour-cost share of production costs, by human development enterprise index 1 (HDE1), all regions, mid 1994

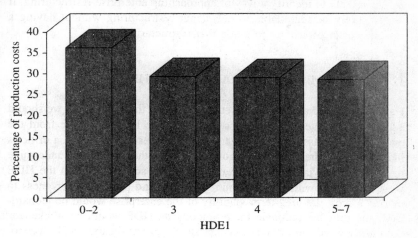

Source: RLFS4, n = 384.

Figure 11.19   Labour-cost share of production costs, by human development enterprise index 2 (HDE2), all regions, mid 1994

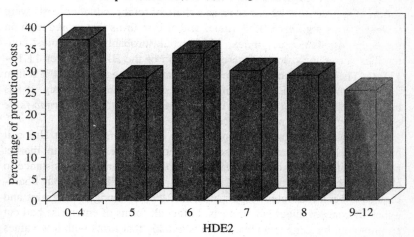

Source: RLFS4, n = 384.

Figure 11.20   Labour-cost share of production costs, by human development enterprise index 4 (HDE4), all regions, mid 1994

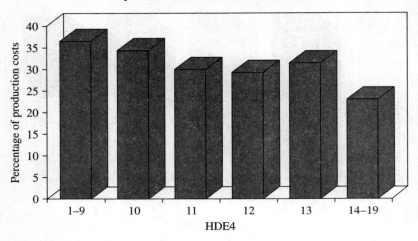

Source: RLFS4, n = 384.

Figure 11.21   Labour-cost share of production costs, by economic democracy index, all regions, mid 1994

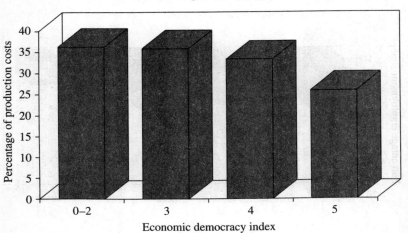

Source: RLFS4, n = 384.

Figure 11.22 Percentage employment change, by human development enterprise index 1 (HDE1), all regions, mid 1994

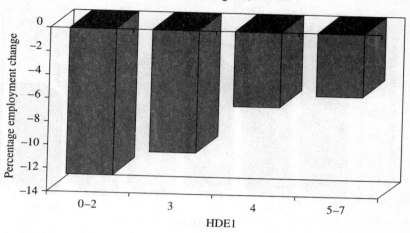

Source: RLFS4, n = 384.

Figure 11.23 Percentage employment change, by human development enterprise index 2 (HDE2), all regions, mid 1994

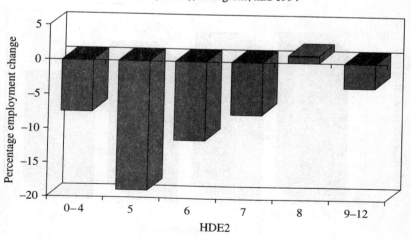

Source: RLFS4, n = 384.

Figure 11.24 Percentage employment change, by human development enterprise index 3 (HDE3), all regions, mid 1994

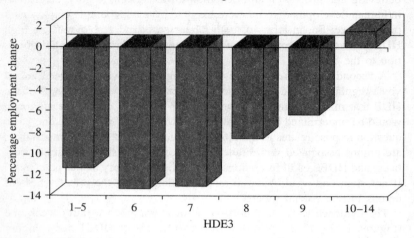

Source: RLFS4, n = 384.

Figure 11.25 Percentage employment change, by human development enterprise index 4 (HDE4), all regions, mid 1994

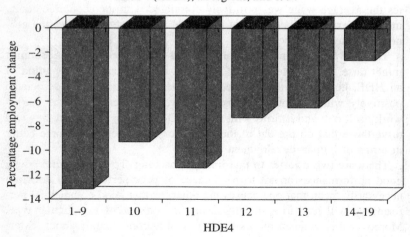

Source: RLFS4, n = 384.

necessarily correct. It merely means that there is a *prima facie* case for believing that firms with an orientation towards being a 'good enterprise' in human development terms were likely to have a favourable employment performance. So, in terms of both labour costs and employment, a high HDE is favourably correlated, which should weaken one potential objection to the concept.

A second criticism might be that strengthening what has been called voice regulation could jeopardise attainment of those basic aspects of the HDE that managements and owners value, so that a composite approach would be undermined by internal contradictions. In this respect, one basic question to pose relates to the effect of trade union presence. For instance, are unions associated with higher values of HDE1 (skill formation practices) and HDE2 (skill formation and non-discriminatory labour practices)? If not, then one would have to raise questions about the effectiveness of unions in two crucial spheres.

The evidence suggests a positive association, albeit a fairly weak one (Figures 11.26–11.27). Firms with higher scores of HDE1 had a higher average unionisation level, and this was also the case with HDE2.

Another question relating to voice regulation that is sure to arise concerns the association of HDE indexes with the wage level in the firm. If the HDE value were inversely correlated with wages, then the appeal for workers and their representatives would be weakened. In Russian factories the average wage was positively correlated with the economic equity index, as expected, but was not correlated with either HDE4 or the economic democracy index.

This leaves the third potential criticism that a neoclassical economist might raise. This is the standard argument against market intervention. If an HDE, however it is measured, is so desirable and if it is associated positively with economic performance, why intervene? Let the market work itself out, and if firms with a high HDE perform well, then they will drive those that do not out of the market or force them to become better in terms of human development policies.

There are two ripostes to that line of reasoning. To be *compatible with* good performance (or not to be a cause of poor performance) does not necessarily mean that one causes the other, or that good commercial performance will lead to a socially desirable outcome of a particular type. Moreover the criticism makes implicit assumptions, mainly about 'externalities', market failures, the dynamics of enterprise restructuring and the reversibility of change. In a period of major economic upheaval, firms taking a low-wage, anti-union, trainee-poaching approach and discriminating against women or those workers with disabilities may easily undercut the

Figure 11.26   Unionisation rate, by human development enterprise index 1
(HDE1), all regions, mid 1994

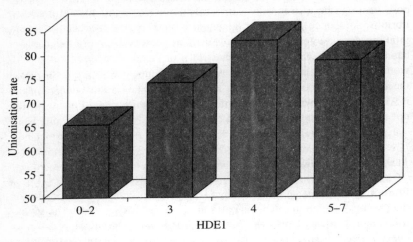

Source: RLFS4, n = 384.

Figure 11.27   Unionisation rate, by human development enterprise index 2
(HDE2), all regions, mid 1994

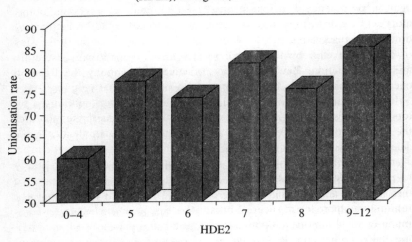

Source: RLFS4, n = 384.

firm that pays decent wages, legitimises a genuine trade union, provides training and so on. This is more than a matter of externalities, although the poor firm can be a 'free rider'. It is the nature of a fundamental disequilibrium. And once a highly fragmented labour market has been created, vital pressures to generate a virtuous path are removed. Once a mechanism has been eroded, it is harder to resurrect it or create something better that would be derived from it than it would be to create it in the first place. Once unionisation in Russian industry has declined, it is most unlikely that it will rise again, which does not mean that unions *per se* do not or could not play a positive role for workers or firms.

11.9 CONCLUSIONS

Promoting good enterprises is a key to the promotion of a good society for the twenty-first century. This is particularly so in Russia, where the industrial enterprise has been, for better or for worse, a crucible for almost every aspect of civil society. It is also apparent that enterprise restructuring is a key to effective structural or social adjustment. The idea of a human development enterprise, defined in terms of democratic, equitable labour practices, is suited to an era in which there is, and should be, an increasing emphasis on incentives to good practice rather than sanctions against bad practice. If labour standards are presented as something obligatory and rigid, then even those who support them would be inclined to do so with reservation. Some would pay only scant attention to the sins of others lest their own sins, real or imaginary, be exposed to scrutiny and condemnation. Rewarding good practices and shining the light on exemplary cases would be in keeping with mature social cultures.

It also corresponds to advanced management thinking, epitomised by top companies in the United States and elsewhere.[29] Enterprises that put the interests of their workers first appear to perform better than others.[30] There are also important externalities. Thus economically democratic firms – and this is the issue that is most ideologically controversial – are likely to promote democratic behaviour *outside* them.[31] One does not have to turn this into an ideological battleground. Rather one has to seek ways of refining the approach to secure a broadly based consensus and foster communities of human development, bearing in mind the 'network externalities' that come from large numbers of enterprises adopting systems of practices oriented towards human development.

In sum, the HDE is a useful heuristic device. Undoubtedly it could be refined, its components can be challenged and modified to take account of different points of view, and it can be adjusted to meet the specific conditions of different countries. It is an organising concept, which can be used to grade enterprises by explicit criteria – principles, mechanisms and outcomes – that can be justified as desirable or otherwise. This is its potential appeal.

As one famous political economist quipped, the point is not to interpret the world, it is to change it. The objective of identifying HDEs is to change enterprises into something closer to the ideal. Regrettably there is a long way to go in Russian industry. Now is the time to start.

12 Policy Reflections for the Russian Labour Market

12.1 THE IMPORTANCE OF THEORY

Most markets are not like the markets of the simple price theory found in economics textbooks, and this is certainly true of any labour market. They are always circumscribed and shaped by institutions and political structures that reflect the influence of generations of decision making. Prices, monetary variables and incentive structures also influence these changes, and altering relative prices will always affect behaviour. Yet it is hard to say what these effects will be without knowledge of the context in question, and the constraints in which workers, managers, bureaucrats and others are required to operate.

At the end of the 1980s it was a common occurrence in the former Soviet Union to meet economists and others, foreign and Russian, who would calmly assert that there was no labour market in the country. In the ensuing years it was common to hear from economists and others that it was essential to create a labour market.

Those views reflect a particular image of markets. In contrast, an underlying theme of this book is that analysis simply in neoclassical terms of relative prices, which determined the economic reform strategy, is not able to lead to the appropriate concerns or policy prescriptions. Of course one can gain insights from neoclassical price theory. Yet to understand labour markets one must look beyond that to incorporate institutional concerns, and what has become known as 'transactions costs theory', 'property rights theory' and the currently unpopular Marxian ideas of social relations of production and distribution.

Consider the idea of an employment contract. It is far more than a simple matter of a supply curve and a demand curve interacting at a given wage. When a person applies for a post, the employer acquires 'labour power' if the firm recruits, while the worker acquires a commitment to a flow of income. However this does not deal with the main point of the contract, which is an agreement for some 'effort bargain' on the part of the worker and some social responsibility on the part of the employer.

Thus if a worker applies for jobs under threat of impoverishment or starvation, he or she may take a job that pays an extremely low wage.

Such a wage could be described as the worker's 'reservation wage'. However, at that wage the effort bargain would be low and the worker would feel free to indulge in opportunism, pilfering, sabotage or simply idling. His or her dignity would be affronted, or at least it should be if such a person is to become efficient and acquire firm-specific skills. At that wage the worker would be looking for better options from the outset, either in the form of a second job at the same time or in the form of an alternative job. The worker may have in his or her mind an 'aspiration wage', that is, a wage that he or she thinks is fair and appropriate to accept a job. That will be above the reservation wage. However, even then, to accept employment and regard it as morally acceptable is not the same as exerting an optimal effort to be productive in the current period, let alone to invest in skill acquisition specific to the firm. Thus there must be an optimum 'efficiency wage'.

This complex notion of wages is not just relevant at the lower end of the wage-effort curve. If remuneration rewards are easy to acquire, the tendency to shift from work effort to opportunism becomes powerful. This is more than just a question of a backward-bending supply curve, since it relates to the type of activity and response behaviour. This had become a critical issue of the Russian labour market by the mid-1990s, with different opportunism encouraged at both ends of the earnings spectrum.

It is a truism that the effort bargain of workers in Soviet industry was low. The previous institutionalised labour contract was roughly as follows. The worker was guaranteed employment security, as long as basic performance criteria were fulfilled and certain disciplinary rules were followed, deference to the right people was shown and opportunistic behaviour was practised within tolerable norms. In return the worker was provided with a low wage, from which he or she was unable to save very much, which created the obligation to work into old age. Workers were paid their reservation wage, little more. As a means of retaining workers and ensuring the reproduction of the workforce, as well as moulding a social and political institution, the enterprise provided extensive social benefits to workers and their families. Implicitly, the worker thereby sacrificed entitlement to alternative benefits, which were denied to those outside enterprises.

As a result of this form of employment contract, the high ratio of benefits to wages ensured a lower labour turnover than would have transpired had the wage been the only labour-market variable. But of course the high ratio was a prescription for opportunistic behaviour and a low effort bargain.

The long-term cost of that system was terrible. However the price liberalisation and macroeconomic stabilisation policy of 1992 cut into this institutional labour market in the most disruptive way possible. It resulted, first of all, in a dramatically sharp fall in real wages. To pile on the agony, the attempted 'tax-based incomes policy', in the form of the excess wage tax, encouraged firms to shift from money wages to social benefits, and encouraged the strengthening of an opportunistic coalition between enterprise managements and workers to limit tax obligations. Lowering wages even further below the efficiency wage was scarcely a sensible way of tackling the fundamental labour-market challenge of the early 1990s – the need to overcome stagnant labour productivity. There was no need to try to preserve a stable (low turnover) labour force in obsolescent jobs. The primary task should have been to raise the effort bargain reached between workers and enterprises, and between managers, as employees, and their firms. The economic policy reforms – in the absence of an integrated policy to restructure the incentives system and labour-market mechanisms – was a prescription to generate a period of plunging productivity and pervasive opportunism.

It is not good enough to dismiss behavioural reactions as 'corruption', metaphorically throwing up one's hands as if to say that had it not been for corruption the policies would have worked. A system is an institutional structure of incentives and relationships that require systemic reform. To reiterate a point made earlier, a strategy that does not take behavioural and institutional reactions into account is unworthy of the name.

Allowing the minimum wage to fall to an extraordinarily low level and allowing the continuation of the direct link between the minimum wage and new labour-market social transfers, such as unemployment benefits, meant that there was no incentive for workers whose jobs were surplus to requirement to enter the labour market. It also meant that there was moral pressure on firms to retain such workers. The era of the social, paternalistic enterprise was prolonged by the macroeconomic policies of the time, contrary to the intentions of those formulating them. During the course of 1992, 1993 and 1994, numerous well-intentioned, decent men and women in charge of industrial enterprises informed us that they did not wish to turn 'our workers' out on to the streets when the threat of impoverishment was so strong.

The behavioural reactions to the macroeconomic policies did not stop the decline of industrial employment, although it surely slowed that decline. It distorted employment restructuring, encouraged the growth of concealed unemployment, as described in Chapter 4, and made it increasingly difficult for firms to value labour properly. It also accentuated the growth of labour-force fragmentation, since the institutional employment contract norm gave insiders in the more successful or protected enterprises access to a wide and increasing range of benefits, while a growing minority were cut out of that circuit. In the circumstances, the wage rate could not be an equilibrating mechanism.

Some institutional restructuring of the labour market had taken place by the mid 1990s. Yet, as we have seen, most of it was done in reaction to adversity, rather than as a means of formulating a constructive alternative to discredited aspects of the past model. The reform strategy singularly failed to stimulate an environment of dynamic efficiency.

In this concluding chapter, it might be useful to sketch the main types of labour market policy designed to promote employment and enterprise restructuring.

12.2   RECOGNISING LIVING SOULS

It took a long time to persuade some people that there was much more unemployment than the registration statistics suggested. Failing to recognise reality had ugly consequences. The most notable of these was the low priority given to social policy reform, and the miserably low benefits provided to those few unemployed who managed to obtain them. By 1995 it was essential to extend the labour-force survey approach to the collection of labour-market information. This had been started by *Goskomstat*, although insufficient attention had been paid to the results of the two national surveys carried out in 1992 and 1993. It was not sufficient to identify the numbers affected by open unemployment and the number discouraged from remaining in the labour market or from entering it. Those tasks were important. However it seemed as if international and national policy would focus adequately on the needs of the unemployed only if the plight of the unemployed and those at the margin of the labour market were adequately exposed.

In recognising the reality of unemployment more systematically, the importance of labour market policy will be reassessed. The federal employment service has made considerable progress since 1991, but it has been subject to troublesome pressures. The structure of financing of the Employment Fund created a recipe for a crisis if registered unemployment rose to much more than its level at the end of 1994. There was also a risk that budgetary politics would put powerful pressure on the employment service, to shift from what some labour economists call 'passive' labour-market policy to what is commonly called 'active' policy. If that occurred, officials might be induced to try to persuade, or coerce, the unemployed to take very low-paid 'public works' jobs, or to enter labour-market training schemes in much greater numbers. Particularly in the Russian labour market, that could reawaken well-known memories of things past.

As of early 1995, unemployment benefits (misleadingly called passive policy) were extremely low, and there was surely scope to raise them towards something like a survival income through the Employment Fund. An average unemployment benefit that represented about one-quarter of the income needed for survival was, perhaps inadvertently, a mechanism for holding down the level of unemployment. Perhaps fear of an increase in registered unemployment was a factor holding down the benefit level. One should not suggest that this was a conscious policy. However the fact remains that total expenditure on unemployment benefits comprised merely 14 per cent of total expenditure from the Employment Fund in 1994, and just over 13 per cent in 1993. Unemployment benefits represented merely 8.5 per cent of the total income of the Employment Fund in 1994. These figures imply there was considerable scope for raising unemployment benefits. The constraint was the structural problem associated with the regionalisation of labour-market policy. Thus if the unemployment benefits had been raised nationally, many *oblasts* and numerous districts would have been plunged into acute financial difficulties. In Ivanovo, to cite an example, unemployment benefits in 1994 comprised over 54 per cent of total Employment Fund expenditure, and the financial reserves were being rapidly depleted. Doubling the average unemployment benefit in such cities, which would still have left it at poverty level, could not have been achieved without a series of policy changes beyond the scope of the employment service.

Nationally, in 1994 3.8 per cent of the expenditure from the Employment Fund was used for labour market training, 0.5 per cent was used for so-called public works, 2.8 per cent for early retirement, 24.1 per cent for financial support of jobs (wage subsidies), 25.7 per cent for employment service needs and the remainder for payments to the federal budget, for building up employment service reserves and for miscellaneous expenditure.[1] A debate within the FES and among labour-market policy makers was whether the FES should become more of an 'unemployment benefits' agency or whether it should evolve into a labour-market restructuring agency, focusing more on job saving, labour-market training and employment promotion. Support was growing for an 'active' labour market policy. This would have had a number of pitfalls, including the simple one of cost. As of July 1994 the expenditure per participant in labour-market training was six times the cost of the average unemployment benefit, and the cost per participant in so-called public works jobs was over 1.7 times the average unemployment benefit. Still more provocatively, it might be appropriate to mention two salutary tales.

In an industrial town visited a number of times during the course of this work, although outside the *oblasts* covered by the enterprise survey, there was a large chemicals plant that in 1992 had employed nearly 4000 workers. The manager was a man with connections who exuded concern for his firm. Unfortunately he had presided over its slow demise, so that by 1994 the workforce was down to about 1000, with the administration having plans to release another 250 workers in late 1994. The firm had been obliged to abandon the production of insulin, because a larger enterprise in Moscow had gross excess capacity and had been given contracts that previously went to this firm. In desperation the manager had gone to the local employment service and proposed to convert part of the plant to the production of vodka. The employment service obliged, providing a large loan at a negative real rate of interest and without a firm commitment on the part of the enterprise to preserve jobs for any specific period, let alone a marketing plan to show that the conversion was commercially viable.[2] The loan made to that firm was more than the total amount paid to the district's registered unemployed in benefits that year.

This example raises all sorts of labour-market and production concerns, and it was by no means an isolated or freakish case. There are familiar 'deadweight' and 'substitution' effects in such measures intended to preserve or convert jobs. The cost of employment saving is actually much greater than is implied by simply dividing the number of workers kept in employment by the amount of direct transfers. There are also the implied costs of not allowing a labour market to function. When nearly a quarter of the country's Employment Fund expenditure was going on employment retention schemes, the best one can say is that the process was distorting the employment restructuring process.

The second example relates to the notion of 'public works'. As there is a long history of such schemes in various guises in Russia, there has probably been more scepticism about their use than about job-preserving subsidies. Yet hopes have been invested in their usefulness for responding to rising unemployment, and they have a certain appeal among some officials, although not inside the FES. In practice, public works seem to have been a vehicle for subsidising jobs. In one district, some of the unemployed had been put on a so-called public works scheme to shear sheep for a local agricultural enterprise. The firm thus acquired very cheap labourers who were paid little more than the minimum wage by the employment service, which meant that, first, they did not have to recruit other workers and, second, that there existed a body of dependent workers whose very presence put downward pressure on the wages of others.

As for labour-market training, tales abound about the reluctance of the unemployed to participate in schemes, and about some starting in them and then finding that the stipends were too low, the costs of attending too high and the prospect of jobs too low. Any shortcomings might be attributed to the fact that by the mid 1990s such schemes still had only a very short history. Again, substitution and deadweight effects should be considered before great hopes are placed in labour-market training. The fact (if it is a fact) that a high percentage of those who completed labour-market training schemes found jobs afterwards does not necessarily mean that the training scheme reduced unemployment or created skills where none would have existed otherwise. Labour-market training in some circumstances could be a deciding factor in inducing a local enterprise to abandon its own training programme.

Nobody should question the proposition that labour-market training could have a valuable role to play in the labour-market restructuring process. But to be viable in that respect, participation in training should be done on merit, as a matter of individual choice based on the perception of labour-market returns to the investment, rather than because of a directive to do so. Participation in training should be kept quite separate from the question of entitlement to unemployment benefits.

12.3   LINKING SEVERANCE PAY TO RESTRUCTURING

Since the introduction of unemployment benefits, enterprises making workers redundant have been obliged to pay severance pay, and, as described in earlier chapters, that payment has been seen as an alternative to unemployment benefits. From the point of view of labour-market adjustments, this is unfortunate. Receipt of severance pay should be kept distinct from receipt of unemployment benefits. However it would be sensible to go one stage further.

It would help encourage employment restructuring if enterprises releasing workers were allowed to pay a lower amount of severance pay if they found the workers alternative employment. This would be similar to what is done in Japan, where some firms negotiate with others to transfer redundant workers.

This could help reduce frictional unemployment and make employment restructuring less traumatic for managements and for the workers directly affected. But the scheme would not be costless. It could increase insider–outsider problems, in that it would tend to give workers about to be made unemployed an inherent advantage in obtaining employment over those who were already unemployed. To limit this would require a greatly improved employment service. In any case, receipt of severance pay should not be a barrier to receipt of unemployment benefits, and enterprises should not be enabled to avoid severance pay obligations by inducing resignations through the extended non-payment of contractual wages.

12.4   SEEKING EQUIVALENCE IN FLEXIBILITY

The Russian industrial labour market has been characterised by a much greater degree of wage-system flexibility than of employment flexibility, as Chapters 4 and 5 indicated. The balance has been unfortunate. For various reasons, including economic and social ones, perverse forms of wage-system flexibility should be reduced, which in itself would tend to increase employment flexibility. There is no need to reiterate the arguments made in earlier chapters. Suffice it to note that the arguments in favour of flexibility are primarily connected with dynamic efficiency. This means that collective bargaining should become much more substantive and be backed up by legally binding and enforceable contracts. *Excessive wage flexibility can be and has been a source of labour-market instability and can prevent effective employment flexibility and restructuring.*

12.5   REPLACING A TIP WITH A BIP

The excess wage tax, or tax-based incomes policy, has been an interesting example of a policy intended to alter relative prices, misguided because it took no account of the institutional and behavioural realities. In circumstances where real wages were so low that there was no incentive to allocate labour resources efficiently and where the high ratio of social benefits to wages at the enterprise level induced a low effort bargain, a tax designed to hold down money wages was distortionary and impeded the pursuit of higher productivity. It should be replaced by a benefits-based incomes policy designed to reduce the emphasis on non-wage forms of remuneration and encourage the communalisation of enterprise social benefits.

The pattern of benefits has contributed to the growth of socioeconomic inequality and is likely to accentuate the trend as firms in difficulty shed their 'social enterprise' functions. The danger is that many of those facilities will be run down or closed rather than maintained and developed as sources of employment and social welfare, if the process is left to mysterious market forces. What is needed is a policy to encourage the transfer of the facilities and benefits to the local authorities, leaving firms to concentrate on their commercial and labour-market functions.

12.6 FUNCTIONAL FLEXIBILITY AND SKILL FORMATION

One could interpret the decline of institutional and enterprise-based 'training' either as catastrophic or beneficial. Probably it was a mixture of the two. In the late 1990s there is an opportunity to restructure the work process to create pressures in the labour market to upgrade and diversify skills and upgrade and diversify forms of work. The rigid division of working life into the three phases of education/training, full-time work and retirement, inherited from industrial society, is ill-suited to the more flexible society and relations of production and distribution of the future. Institutional mechanisms, regulations and incentive systems will be required to encourage firms to restructure jobs, diversify working-time schedules and allow greater life-cycle flexibility in the allocation of time to work, skill acquisition and labour-force withdrawal (raising the prospect of lifetime sabbaticals for all).

Labour-market retraining schemes and institutions will have to be greatly strengthened in the late 1990s. But the most important need is a more flexible working environment to permit the spread of training leave and training-with-work employment contracts. The Russian labour market in 1995 was woefully behind its counterparts in Western Europe in its orientation to skill formation. However, as in so many respects, the lack of even residual credibility in the old system of training and job structuring meant that the scope for reform was considerable, because institutional inertia should have been rather weak.

The other important requirement is that training opportunities should be provided on the basis of positive incentives for skill formation and skill utilisation, rather than through direction coupled with sanctions if individuals do not participate in them, and penury if directives are refused. International experience shows that mandatory participation of unemployed jobseekers in labour-market training schemes is much less effective than if the participation is voluntary.

12.7 'WORKFARE' FIRMS

One proposal intended to assist in the restructuring of industrial enterprises and limit the growth of open unemployment is that of maintaining workers in jobs through the provision of public subsidies. In a sense, that is what happened through the resort to administrative leave. However some economists have suggested that large loss-making enterprises should be kept temporarily afloat as 'workfare firms'.[3]

The idea is that it would pay the government to do this as long as the value added produced by the workers equalled or exceeded the excess of their wages over the cost of unemployment benefits plus the administrative costs arising from such benefits. But this raises all sorts of problems. Administering a workfare firm policy on a substantial scale would create enormous administrative and monitoring costs. The provision of a new form of employment subsidy would create scope for renewed opportunism, and enormous deadweight and substitution effects.

Extending jobs that were not viable would merely postpone employment restructuring and hinder the real reintegration of those workers retained in dead jobs. Indeed the employment subsidy would discourage workers from moving precisely at a time when mobility is required. In the context of this sort of danger, it has been suggested that the management of those designated as workfare firms be transferred to an agency that is aware of budget constraints, such as the Ministry of Finance. This idea presumes what cannot be presumed – that the regulatory and monitoring capacity of any governmental authority stretches much beyond its own bureaucracy.

Ignoring the awkward problem of selecting enterprises to be maintained as workfare firms, the next problem is that of incentives. If the payments are available, will not workers and managers become passive recipients? Advocates of the approach respond to this by claiming that 'admission to workfare status' should be 'made singularly unattractive' and there should be 'harsh adjustment measures for both workers and managers, such as mandatory lay-offs, wage freezes and replacement of top management'.[4] Thus the essence of the scheme emerges. Once it is recognised as a recipe for opportunism it becomes a mechanism to be converted into a coercive, regulatory device, without any assurance that it will assist in the process of enterprise or labour-market restructuring.

12.8 COLLECTIVE INDIVIDUALISM AND HDEs

The ideal labour market of the twenty-first century, in the Russian Federation as elsewhere, will be one of 'collective individualism'. Essentially this involves a labour market in which individual flexibility and autonomy are combined with collective security. Complete individualism is neither desirable nor feasible in a modern society, especially one such as the Russian Federation with its historical roots in collective community, which long predated the Soviet era. In the 1990s it is scarcely a matter of controversy to assert that the collective agencies of that era have a credibility problem that is so huge it would be better to start with the assumption that their legitimacy cannot be recreated.

Will the Russian Federation emerge as a share-owning democracy? Will industrial, social and economic democracy accompany the growth of political democracy? When the revolutionary dust has settled, the inequalities and inequities of the 1990s will need to be redressed and the enterprises of employment will surely be a fulcrum of distribution and social democracy. In their shedding of one set of paternalistic functions, they will focus much more on the generation of profits, or economic surplus. It is at least possible that as enterprise restructuring takes more constructive shape in the years leading up to the next century, policy makers will want to tilt them towards being something close to what we have characterised as 'human development enterprises'. In doing so, it will be essential to ensure that their pursuit of profitability is not sacrificed to the social enterprise mentality. The productive system must be internationally competitive, and this means that adequate and legitimate incentives to the generation of economic surplus must be developed and maintained.

12.9 CORPORATE GOVERNANCE AND THE LABOUR MARKET

When visiting Russian factories between 1991 and 1994, and talking to dozens of managerial employees, union officials and ordinary workers, we found it impossible to escape from non-intellectual reactions, and a hundred images of decay and disillusion remain. Among those are the long array of faded photographs of workers who had given their lives to factory life, to be displayed for posterity in their medals as exemplary workers, often following fathers or mothers and in turn being followed by sons or daughters. Many would have made it into management, and for better or worse the future seemed unlikely to reproduce the sense of stability and continuity that such picture displays sadly conveyed.

Between 1991 and 1994 many faces in 'boardrooms' changed, as did management structures and attitudes. Distances and discontinuities seemed to be growing, and a whole host of actors were trying to find their appropriate behavioural mode. Even in 1994, most directors of enterprises were products of the *lumpenisation* of the Stalinist and Brezhnev era. This is not to say they were all bad or dishonest, any more than any other group of people in Russia or elsewhere. It is too easy to make categorical assertions about corruption, authoritarianism and incompetence – and some foreign observers and advisers were inclined to do just that. However nothing is what it seems in a revolution, and many of those who rose to the higher echelons of corporate authority were no doubt skilful, above all in the bureaucratic traits of adaptability and conformity.

The *nomenklatura* may have ruled Russia since the 1920s, but the bureaucratic conservatism that characterised the management of the 'social' industrial enterprises that were supposed to be the productive strength of the country was so pervasive by the end of the 1980s that a management revolution was a more urgent requirement than any other aspect of restructuring, including privatisation. Indeed privatisation without prior restructuring of enterprises was doomed to reproduce the bureaucratic managerial structures and make them much harder to remove in the near future. As one journalist noted when referring to the adaptive behaviour of those placed in positions of authority after 1991, without restructuring of enterprise governance there would be a process by which 'the dead seize the living'.[5]

In other countries, for efficiency one might not attach great hope to having the workers being involved in the appointment and monitoring of managers. However in the Russian factories of the 1990s it might be a promising development, if – and it *is* if – appointments and monitoring could become genuinely democratic within the factory gates. Why hold out much hope for that? Just consider whose living standards are most directly affected by poor management, low productivity and lack of profits.

A crucial question in the mid 1990s was whether or not the emerging forms of corporate governance were compatible with efficiency and with the development of high-value HDEs. By the end of 1994 it was still too early to reach strong conclusions, other than that the remainder of the twentieth century would be a period of uncertainty and flux.

The key ingredients are *incentives, monitoring* and *the relationship between the two.* Many analysts have distinguished between 'employeeism' and private capitalism.[6] In the Russian context, one should make a further distinction between what in this book has been called 'employee control' and 'worker control' (in the complex sense defined in Chapter 3), as well as 'purely private control'. The implications of this threefold distinction should become clearer with the data from the fifth round of the RLFS, both for enterprise performance and for the pattern of human development. As of mid 1994 the changes in governance were too recent to trace behavioural changes with any confidence.

Nevertheless one can speculate about the implications on the basis of economic theory and evidence from elsewhere. In the Russian context, the most important point is that worker share ownership and worker 'control' were potentially the best *available* means of monitoring managerial opportunism and thus tilting managerial behaviour in favour of practices oriented towards dynamic efficiency. This is partly because neither workers nor managers had an ingrained ascendancy (associated with class status), and partly because there were no better established monitoring mechanisms, either as single, dominant, external shareholders (as in the so-called German–Japanese model) or as potential major stakeholders threatening inefficient incumbent managements (the so-called Anglo-Saxon model).

Whatever the governance type – although particularly if employee- or worker-controlled – it is important that the establishment should not be too large, for the greater the size the more diffuse and thus ineffectual the monitoring of management. The governance problem is more intractable the larger the enterprise.

Which of the forms of governance identified in Chapter 3 will prove to be superior in economic and labour-market terms? Both employee-control and worker-control governance may produce greater dynamic efficiency than state or purely private governance structures, and thus be associated with rising labour productivity and HD skill formation. Given the enormous scope in Russian industry for improvements in productivity and dynamic efficiency, this factor deserves very considerable weight in arguments about the most desirable form of corporate governance for the latter part of the 1990s.

It is a common assumption in economics literature that employee control will always lead to employees paying themselves higher wages and preserving higher levels of employment.[7] There is no evidence that this was the case in Russian industry in the first few years of economic reform, as was seen in Chapters 4 and 6. In any case the view assumes myopia on the part of workers and employees and ignores the effects of participation in decision making. If the workers can control managerial opportunism (and of course under any form of governance they can do so only partially), they themselves may be more prepared to make short-term sacrifices in earnings in order to boost investment, pay off debts, avoid bankruptcy or improve dynamic efficiency. In contrast, managers who can forge alliances with commercial or political outsiders are likely to sell off or use up the assets of the firm to maximise their short-term incomes. This is especially likely if the managers are generally older than the workforce.

Similarly, if workers are able to monitor managers closely, because they are both strong stakeholders and workers inside the enterprise able to observe actual practices on a day-to-day basis, they may not wish to maximise the level of employment, whereas managers may wish to do so, because size of firm is a determinant of their earnings and status. Indeed it is often claimed by detractors of cooperatives that they restrict employment expansion because existing workers wish to keep average wages high and because of diminishing marginal productivity. In the Russian context, worker-control governance coupled with high labour turnover is likely to lead to managed employment reduction through the non-replacement of departing and retiring workers, not to employment maximisation.[8] So this form of governance may have neither the wages nor the employment consequences predicted by many economists drawing on their experience in other economic contexts or on economic models that do not take account of the peculiar institutional realities of Russian industry.

12.10   DYNAMIC EFFICIENCY

In the 1990s, the need to stimulate labour productivity and other forms of productivity in Russian industrial enterprises has been palpable. Productivity is not a technological variable, nor merely a matter of relative prices, or the availability of skills or markets. Productivity stems from all these and from institutional structures. To coin a phrase: getting governance right is as important as getting prices right.

By the mid 1990s there was a very long way to go to establish enterprises in which there were adequate internal mechanisms to promote dynamic efficiency, which arises most effectively from voice regulation and incentives to flexibility that do not spill over into pervasive insecurity. The latter promotes negative opportunism, whereas flexibility associated with adaptability of working-time arrangements, occupational restructuring, risk sharing and reward sharing promotes efficiency and profitability. The scheme for an HDE outlined hypothetically and normatively in the preceding chapter will not be the one that ultimately emerges in Russian enterprises. Yet some non-traditional patterning of the work process and enterprise governance involving bargaining roles for all stakeholders will be required to create and sustain a working environment that generates a balanced concern for production and distribution.

Perhaps trade unions in any of their traditional forms will be unable to secure the legitimacy to be effective. Perhaps workers and employees as owner–workers will have the collective strength to provide the presence needed to secure dynamic efficiency. The usual caveats about the limits of employee ownership – notably about sustainability in the face of competition from more conventional forms of capitalist firms – may not apply in circumstances in which a majority of firms have substantial minority or majority employee ownership. One should not rule out that possibility, especially if the structure of incentives in the wage system also evolve so as to be compatible with dynamic efficiency.

12.11 REDRESSING LABOUR MARKET FRAGMENTATION

Finally, all labour markets generate inequalities and insecurities. It is too easy to dismiss the distributional outcomes of restructuring as matters that will be rectified in the long run. There is a limit to which protective regulations can go, and in the Russian industrial labour market, with authorities that have not yet been legitimised, they are unlikely to go very far. They may even have the opposite effect to what is intended, as was noted with respect to night work. In the future, the best hope is that the individual rights of actual and potential workers should be strengthened and the institutional machinery created so that any individual, such as a disabled person, a member of an ethnic minority or a woman, can pursue claims against discrimination and disadvantage effectively and speedily. So far women and older workers have not been marginalised in Russian industrial enterprises, although the data show some emerging trends to accompany previous disadvantages. As unemployment rises, as bankruptcies spread and as labour market and employment restructuring gather pace, agencies to give voice to those threatened by labour-market marginalisation will have to become active, or the consequences could be severe. Such non-governmental organisations will in turn have to avoid the rent-seeking opportunism that has been so pervasive in the unregulated vacuum that has passed under the euphemistic title of 'transition'.

There is no reason for hopelessness in Russia. A crisis offers a moment of hope. In an environment where the past is discredited and where the institutional options are so numerous, an era of experimentation unfolds, and in doing so solutions can take shape in surprising ways. To warn is not to be pessimistic or negative, it is to hope.

Notes and References

1 The Russian Labour Market and 'Shock Therapy'

1. For an analysis of the evolution of 'scientific management' and its application in the USSR, see R. Linhart, *Lénine, les paysans, Taylor* (Paris, Editions du Seuil, 1976).
2. See, for reviews, see T. Kuznetsova, 'The growth of cooperatives in the Soviet Union', and M. Nuti, 'The role of new cooperatives in the Soviet economy', in G. Standing (ed.), *In Search of Flexibility: The New Soviet Labour Market* (Geneva: ILO, 1991), pp. 277–94, 295–318.
3. For a critique at the time, see G. Standing (ed.), *In Search of Flexibility*, op. cit. The full name of the Employment Act was *The Fundamentals of Employment Legislation of the USSR and the Union Republics, 1991*.
4. This was a common feature of the reform strategy throughout the central and eastern European region. R. Portes (ed.), *Economic Transformation in Central Europe: A Progress Report* (Luxembourg: European Commission and Centre for Economic Policy Research, University of London, May 1993). For a more general critique of the shock therapy approach, see United Nations Economic Commission for Europe, *Economic Survey of Europe in 1992–93* (Geneva: March 1993), pp. 6–10. For a critique that claims Eastern Europe should have adopted the strategy pursued in South-East Asian economies, see A. Amsden, J. Kochanowicz and L. Taylor, *The Market Meets its Match* (Cambridge, Mass.: MIT Press, 1995).
5. Critics have argued that the overemphasis on macroeconomic relative to microeconomic (structural) policy reflected the leading role of the IMF, with its macroeconomic conditionality, based on the view that macroeconomic stabilisation was a necessary condition for structural reform.
6. The classic analysis of Karl Polanyi showed how the creation of basic institutions is a necessary precondition for the establishment of a successful market economy. See K. Polanyi, *The Great Transformation: The Political and Economic Origins of Our Time* (Boston, Mass.: Beacon Press, 1957).
7. A. Tiraspolsky, 'Régions et transition en Russie', *Politique Étrangère*, no. 2, 1994.
8. In April 1992 the United States administration announced a US$24 billion aid package, but that failed to arrive. Food aid did come, but the main ingredient to materialise was short-term loans at market interest rates, which assisted exporters *to* Russia, not Russian producers. The World Bank announced that it was going to lend US$670 million, but that was not disbursed until a year later.
9. The failure to institutionalise enterprise restructuring in 1992–3 also contributed to very substantial capital flight, much of which took the form of (state) enterprise managements keeping export proceeds outside the country. European Commission, Directorate-General for Economic and Financial Affairs, *European Economy* (Brussels: European Union), Supplement A, nos 8/9, August–September 1994, p. 6.

372

10. The recorded output declines in the early 1990s are likely to be exaggerated, in part because the output levels were exaggerated in the Soviet era due to a tendency to show conformity with 'plan' targets and in part due to the underdeclaring of output to evade taxes. Nobody disputes that national income and production shrank very substantially.

11. European Bank for Reconstruction and Development, *Transition Report Update* (London: EBRD, 1995), p. 24.

12. No doubt, when some upturn or 'flattening out' of the decline eventually occurs, the economic advisers will be the first to claim that it is due to the policies that they advocated. They should not be taken seriously.

13. Ministries and Departments of the Russian Federation, *et al.*, *A Programme for Stepping Up Economic Reforms* (Moscow: Nachala Press, June 1992). Some estimated that in mid 1992 interenterprise debt was 20 per cent of GNP and that it was this that led the government to release credit and thus loosen monetary policy. Alexander Vorobyov, personal communication.

14. V. Koen and S. Phillips, *Price Liberalisation in Russia: The Early Record*, IMF Occasional Paper (Washington, DC: IMF, 1993).

15. *Financial Times*, 19 August 1994.

16. EBRD, *Transition Report Update*, op. cit., p. 25.

17. There is strong evidence of Kalecki price setting, in which mark-ups build in strong inflationary inertia. A.Y. Vorobyov, 'Russian economic growth: Lessons from the liberalisation experience, medium-term constraints and the role of the State', paper presented at Round Table on Forms of Organisation and Transformation in Central and Eastern European Economies, Paris, 26–7 January 1995.

18. One major debate about the macroeconomic reform policy concerns the nature of the inflation. The more it reflects structural factors, the less appropriate it is to treat it simply by tightening monetary policy.

19. The French Planning Commission estimated that in 1992 28 per cent of the population had less than the subsistence income; in 1993 the figure was 31.9 per cent. See Commissariat Général du Plan, *La Protection Sociale en Fédération de Russie* (Paris: Groupe de travail franco-russe, no. 3, April 1994).

20. Thus in January 1995 the proposal to raise the minimum wage from 20500 roubles per month to 54100 roubles was condemned on the grounds that this would have added 30 trillion roubles to government spending and thus would have 'wrecked the budget'. *The Economist*, 28 January 1995, pp. 29–30. The trouble arose because an instrument intended for one purpose was being used for another. Even at the higher level it would have been less than the equivalent of US$13 a month, which would have been insufficient to avoid starvation. The government proposed to raise it to 34440 roubles as of March 1995. The minimum wage, for better or for worse, is meant to be a variable for labour market protection, not a budgetary control mechanism.

21. M.-A. Crosnier, 'Russie: la protection sociale entre deux systèmes', *Le Courrier des Pays de l'Est*, no. 383 (October 1993).

22. M.-A. Crosnier, 'Ombres et lumières sur le niveau de vie en Russie', *Le Courrier des Pays de l'Est*, no. 383 (October 1993).

23. For reviews of evidence, see A. McAuley, 'Social welfare in transition:

What happened in Russia', mimeo (Colchester: University of Essex, January 1994); I. Savvatyeva, 'Inequality in Russia: The Gini coefficient is rising', *Izvestia*, 17 February 1994. Tchernina gave evidence that there was a 'washing away' of the medium stratum of incomes. N. Tchernina, 'Employment deprivation and poverty', paper presented to the International Institute for Labour Studies, Geneva, 23 April, 1993. See also V. Rukavishnikov, 'What is happening to income inequality in Russia?', Conference on Struggle against poverty, unemployment and social exclusion, Bologna, 1–4 December 1994. The growth of inequality was probably underestimated, since the official family budget survey excluded the top and bottom 10 per cent of the income earners, according to those who conducted the survey.

24. Among other analyses, see J. Sapir, 'Différences économique régionales, transition et politiques de stabilisation en Russie', *Revue d'Études Comparatives Est–Ouest*, 1st quarter, 1993.

25. For a savage, frightening official indictment of declining living standards, see 'Russia's White Book: The State Report on the Health of the Population of the Russian Federation in 1991' ('Belaia Kniga' Rossii'), *Chelovek*, no. 3, 1993, pp. 49–57; *Russian Social Science Review*, 1993, pp. 71–83.

26. The suicide rate rose from an already very high 26.5 per 100000 people in 1991 to 38 per 100000 in 1993, compared with about 12 in the United States. Deaths exceeded births by about 800000 in 1993. The birth rate was almost halved between 1987 and 1993. Life expectancy fell from over 65 for men and 74 for women to just over 58 for men and 68 for women, giving the largest gap between men and women in the world.

27. M. Boycko, A. Schleifer and R. Vishney, 'Privatising Russia', *Brookings Papers on Economic Activity*, no. 2, 1993 (Washington, DC).

28. 'The loveliness of bankruptcy', *The Economist*, 18 February 1995, p. 82.

29. V. Gimpel'son, 'Economic consciousness and reform of the employment sphere', *Sociological Research*, vol. 31, no. 5 (September–October 1992), pp. 16–32.

30. G. Yavlinsky and B. Serguey, 'The inefficiency of laissez-faire in Russia: Hysteresis effects and the need for policy-led transformation', *Journal of Comparative Economics*, vol. 19, no. 1 (August 1994).

31. See, for instance, M. Goldman, *The Lost Opportunity: Why Economic Reforms in Russia Have Not Worked* (New York: Norton, 1995).

32. In the well-known words of Nobel Prize winning economist, Herbert Simon, economic agents are '*intendedly* rational, but only *limitedly* so'. H.A. Simon, *Administrative Behaviour* (New York: Macmillan, 1947), p. xxiv.

33. G. Calvo and J. Frenkel, 'Credit markets, credibility and economic transformation', *Journal of Economic Perspectives*, vol. 5, no. 4 (1991), pp. 143–4.

34. J. Kornai, 'Transformation recession: The main causes', *Journal of Comparative Economics*, vol. 19, no. 1 (August 1994).

2 The Mystery of Unemployment

1. S. Commander, J. McHale and R. Yemtsov, 'Russia', in S. Commander and F. Coricelli (eds), *Unemployment, Restructuring and the Labour Market in*

Eastern Europe and Russia (Washington, DC: The World Bank, 1995), p. 171.

2. See, for instance, R. Layard and A. Richter, 'Labour market adjustment – The Russian way' (London: London School of Economics, Centre for Economic Performance, June 1994). They claimed that between 1991 and 1994 'employment has fallen by only 2 per cent' (p. 1).

3. Besides being repeated in World Bank reports and papers, this view has been expressed repeatedly by various foreign economists, such as Jeffrey Sachs, Richard Layard and Anders Aslund, all of whom have been 'advisers' in some capacity to Russian government agencies. See, for example, R. Layard, the *Financial Times*, 26 June 1992 and 8 February 1994; J. Sachs, quoted in the *Washington Post*, 27 September 1993; *The Economist*, 19 March 1994, p. 73. Incidentally, the number of economists calling themselves economic advisers to the Russian government has been enough to make the sharing of credit for the success of reforms a delicate matter.

4. They also stemmed from some misreading of the statistics. The Centre for Economic Reform, *Russian Economic Trends*, vol. 1, no. 2, p. 34 (London: Whurr Publishers, 1993), claimed that the Russian unemployment data that were cited related to those 'out of employment' seeking and available for employment. The data actually referred only to those registered at an employment exchange *and* counted as unemployed by the exchange.

5. G. Standing, *Developing a Labour Market Information System for the Russian Federal Employment Service* (Budapest: ILO Central and Eastern European Team, Policy Advisory Report, August 1993). One practice lowering the unemployment rate has been the tendency to measure it by dividing the number of jobseekers who attain unemployment status by the size of the working-age population, that is, including those outside the labour force, such as housewives, students and those in early retirement. This is not the normal procedure internationally, and automatically deflates the measured unemployment rate. Russian Federal Employment Service, 'The RF Employment Service – Strategy for the future', paper presented at the meeting of the FES Technical Assistance Coordinating Group, Moscow, 31 March 1993, p. 3.

6. For reviews and estimates in the 1980s, see P. Hanson, 'The Soviet labour shortage and Soviet economic policy', paper presented at the third World Congress for Soviet and East European Studies, Washington DC, 30 October–4 November 1985; S. Oxenstierna, *From Labour Shortage to Unemployment? The Soviet Labour Market in the 1980s* (Stockholm: Swedish Institute for Social Research, 1990), pp. 28–9. These and other studies highlighted the existence of substantial labour turnover in the Soviet era.

7. These were carried out by *Goskomstat*, advised by the ILO. They each covered about 200000 households.

8. These issues are discussed in detail in Standing, *Developing a Labour Market Information System*, op. cit. The most important factor inflating the employment *rate* was that if a pension-age person was employed he or she was counted as such, but the 'economically active' population only included pre-pension-age persons.

9. For an analysis of the first round of the survey of jobseekers, see G. Standing, 'Why is measured unemployment in Russia so low? The net with many

holes', *The Journal of European Social Policy*, vol. 4, no. 1 (February 1994), pp. 35–49.

10. This is one reason for it being incorrect to claim that the average duration of unemployment was short. A World Bank report supported this view on the basis of the registration data. If an unemployed person drops off the register without obtaining a job after a few months, that does not mean the duration of unemployment is short. D. Goodhart, 'Low mobility hits Russian jobless', the *Financial Times*, 6 October 1994. This cited a World Bank report. Incidentally, labour mobility was not low.

11. In this respect, it is unclear what was the effect of the regulation known as 'Ordinance 95', introduced in mid 1993 by the Ministry of Labour, by which firms were supposed to retain workers scheduled for redundancy for two months, during which time they were supposed to pay them the statutory minimum wage. If put into effect in the regions (which was questionable in the case of any regulations in the mid 1990s), it would have delayed some unemployment, but it would have meant that the workers affected would have lost out in current wage and subsequent unemployment benefits, since those were based on the earnings received in the last two months of employment.

12. As of 1993–4, unemployment benefit was only about 14 per cent of expenditure from the Employment Fund, which was set up to support the unemployed. This was about 7 per cent of the fund's income. So it was not a question of inability to pay higher benefits.

13. P. Smirnov, 'Disabled workers in the Russian Federation', paper prepared for the ILO's Central and Eastern European Team, Budapest, October 1993.

14. See, for instance, 'To save Russia from the revolution of the unemployed', *Rabochaya Tribuna*, 5 January 1995; L. Nemova, 'Labour market', *EKO* (Novosibirsk), no. 7, 1994, pp. 25–31.

15. For possibly the best estimate of long-term unemployment in the 1970s, see P.R. Gregory and I.L. Collier, 'Unemployment in the Soviet Union: Evidence from the Soviet Interview Project', *American Economic Review*, vol. 78, no. 4 (September 1988), pp. 613–32.

3 Restructuring in Russian Industry

1. Case studies are extremely useful, and in important respects they are superior to large-scale surveys. In particular, they are appropriate for identifying and clarifying hypotheses, particularly in a period of turbulence, in which old norms are dying and new norms have yet to take their place.

2. An establishment is a single entity usually on one work site, normally equivalent to a factory, whereas an enterprise may consist of two or more establishments under common control. The unit of the survey was the establishment. A distinction is sometimes made between an enterprise and a legal entity, the latter being the ownership unit. For a discussion of the definitions, see, for example, J.R. Baldwin and P.K. Gorecki, 'Measuring entry and exit in Canadian manufacturing: Methodology', Research Paper no. 23C (Ottawa: Analytical Studies Branch, Statistics Canada, 1990).

3. This stage was time-consuming yet essential. Particularly in 1991, notions of employment and unemployment, and more behavioural notions such as

absenteeism, were easily misunderstood by both the enumerators and the respondents. Consequently a great deal of time was taken to adjust the wording and instructions.

4. Although the writer went to many firms during the course of the RLFS, it was understood that the reactions would be different in the case of enumerators keeping rigidly to questionnaires. Survey designers everywhere have to take account of these realities and adjust their instruments accordingly, often ending up with proxy variables that a purist observer would dismiss as less than ideal.

5. Incidentally there seemed to be pleasure in some factories that there was interest in the information so dutifully recorded, and the response rate in general was remarkably good. Usually enterprise surveys are known to have low response rates, and many policy analyses are based on surveys that actually involve a very small number of respondents. This is usually because the survey is based on postal questionnaires. Not only would this be a waste of time in Russia, but in general one should recommend strongly against this capital-intensive technique. Its appeal to study-bound researchers is understandable.

6. The methodological complexities of firm panel data are part of an ongoing project on enterprise restructuring in the ILO's Employment Department. No claim is made that the statistical difficulties are overcome, such as the problem of dealing with the opening and and closure of firms and sampling over successive rounds. In the Russian case the former problem was a minor one, because in the period covered there were no closures and few new manufacturing establishments. The firms included in successive rounds were not selected on predetermined criteria. On the methodological issues of panel data, see J.B. Jensen and J.L. Monahan, 'Firm-level longitudinal linkages from establishment data: A preliminary appraisal', paper submitted to United Nations Statistical Commission and Economic Commission for Europe Conference of European Statisticians, 24th Session of the Working Party on Electronic Data Processing, Geneva, 21–4 February 1995; P. Lavallee, 'Business panel surveys: Following enterprises versus following establishments', mimeo (Ottawa: Statistics Canada, 1995).

7. It is hoped that the general 'story' told in the following pages will be complemented by a series of technical papers that go into specific issues in more detail and with more sophistication.

8. Note that in Figure 3.1 and in all subsequent figures, the reference to 'All Regions' refers to all regions covered in that particular round of the RLFS. The 'n' refers to the number of establishments for which there were data on the issues covered by the figure.

9. In 1994 a small number of special 'social organisations' were included in RLFS4, notably so-called sheltered enterprises for workers with disabilities of one kind or another. This category will be excluded from our comparisons of property-form performances, although they were included in the survey precisely because they did comprise a small but important type of enterprise in the Soviet system and because of the plight of the workers observed in several visits to factories employing disabled workers in an era of collapsing subsidies and the withdrawal of special orders for products from such firms.

10. This tendency has been attributed to *perestroika*, in that in weakening the Communist Party control and bureaucratic regulation, it allowed and encouraged the acceleration of regional decentralisation. J. Sapir, 'Transition, stabilisation and disintegration in Russia', paper presented to the Round Table on Forms of Organisation and Transformation in Central and Eastern European Economies, Paris, 26–7 January 1995, p. 9.

11. For a review of barter development, see L. Freinkman, 'Shaping a market environment and analysis of the enterprise interaction mechanism', *Studies on Soviet Economic Development*, vol. 3, no. 2 (1992), pp. 101–8.

12. *A priori*, one would expect that the growth of barter would have been under-recorded, simply because so much would have been informal.

13. In 1994 barter accounted for 20 per cent of sales of the two 'sheltered' enterprises included in the sample.

14. This perspective is usually attributed to the seminal work of Ronald Coarse in 1937, which has generated an increasingly fertile literature. See for example O.E. Williamson and S.G. Winter (eds), *The Nature of the Firm: Origins, Evolution and Development* (New York and Oxford: Oxford University Press, 1991); O.E. Williamson, *The Economic Institutions of Capitalism: Firms, Markets, Relational Contracting* (New York: The Free Press, 1985).

15. Z.L. Sadowski, 'Privatisation in Eastern Europe: Goals, problems and implications', *Oxford Review of Economic Policy*, vol. 7, no. 4 (Winter 1991), pp. 46–56.

16. P. Hare, 'The assessment: Microeconomics of transition in eastern Europe', *Oxford Review of Economic Policy*, vol. 7, no. 4 (Winter 1991), p. 7.

17. J.R. Blasi, 'The impact of privatisation on the enterprise and the impact of the enterprise on reform', proceedings of a Workshop on Conversion, Bonn International Centre for Conversion, Bonn, 10–13 August 1994, p. 25.

18. One ambiguity was the role of commercial banks, which by 1994 held less than 1 per cent of equity. Bank loans accounted for about 15 per cent of company finance and did not contribute significantly to enterprise restructuring. M. Sheppard, 'Constraints to private enterprises in the Former Soviet Union: Approaches and applications to Russia', in I. Lieberman and J. Nellis (eds), *Russia: Creating Private Enterprises and Efficient Markets* (Washington, DC: The World Bank, 1994).

19. This is one reason why size restructuring, in particular, should have started before privatisation, because the new agents could not respond to appropriate informational signals. S. van Wijnbergen, 'Enterprise reform in eastern Europe', *The Economics of Transition*, vol. 1, no. 1 (Jan. 1993), p. 22.

20. It is incorrect to presume that employee ownership leads to strong pressure to maintain employment. In conditions of high labour turnover where management bonuses and earnings are a positive function of employment size, a shift to strong worker share ownership could lead to managed downsizing, whereby departing workers are simply not replaced. Frydman and Rapaczynski presumed the opposite, and claimed that the Russian reforms in corporate governance were inadequate on the ground that they had not led to 'any significant unemployment'. R. Frydman and A. Rapaczynski, 'Insiders and the state: Overview of responses to agency problems in East

European privatisation', *The Economics of Transition*, vol. 1, no. 1 (Jan. 1993), p. 56.

21. G. Dow, 'The function of authority in transaction cost economics', *Journal of Economic Behaviour and Organisation*, vol. 8 (1987), pp. 13–38.

22. S. Peregudov, A. Zudin and I. Semenko, 'Social accord: The experience of the West and our problems', 'Sotsial'noe soglasie: Opyt zapada i nashi problemy', *Svobodnaia mysl*, no. 18 (1992), pp. 25–35.

23. J.R. Blasi, 'Corporate ownership and corporate governance in Russia: 1994 findings', paper presented at the Industrial Relations Research Association Meetings, Washington, DC, 8 January 1994.

24. Before 1994, when managers were appointed by an 'enterprise board' this usually meant that the general director had control, because the boards consisted largely of managers who reported directly to the general director. A presidential decree in early 1994 stipulated that henceforth no more than one third of directors could be employed in the enterprise and that each enterprise had to hold a new shareholders' meeting within 120 days of 1 January 1994 to choose a new board by cumulative voting, that is, ensuring that minority votes had some board representation.

25. Also included are the few cases where the management was appointed by a line ministry or a local authority but where at the time the establishment was a joint-stock company with majority employee ownership. Such cases arose from the timing of appointment and the timing of property-form change, and it is assumed that managers would become accountable to the current governance form.

26. These case studies included an analysis of the evolving restructuring of a giant oil refinery in northern Russia, in which by September 1994 the newly elected management had been made nervous by the prospect of shares being sold by the workers to outsiders.

27. This figure was reported by the State Committee on Privatisation. *Kommersant* (Moscow), no. 25 (July 1994), p. 56. The data seemed to relate to the spring of 1994 only. The minister of privatisation, Anatoly Chubais, stated that the country was not ready for an evaluation of the results of privatisation, and accordingly had not set up any monitoring mechanism. However it was estimated that the basic conflict was not between directors and work collectives but between directors and shareholders, and that non-shareholding general managers would soon lose power.

28. It has been estimated that expenditure on food rose from under one third of total personal expenditure in 1989 to over one half in 1993. ILO Central and Eastern European Team, *The Social Protection System in Russia*, a report prepared by a team coordinated by Marina Moskvina, Moscow and Budapest, September 1993.

29. By mid 1992 interenterprise indebtedness in Russia was officially said to be two trillion roubles, although one was surprised by the estimate. Ministries and Departments of the Russian Federation *et al.*, *A Programme for Stepping Up Economic Reforms* (Moscow: Nachula Press, June 1992), p. 10.

30. This followed a trend established in the 1980s, when the chemicals industry's capital depreciation was greater than for all industry. B. Lavrovskii, 'The paralysis of Soviet industry: Technological sources', *Problems of Economic Transition*, vol. 35, no. 1 (May 1992), p. 70.

31.   There were only eight social organisations in the sample. Given their special character, a separate analysis will focus on their specific and saddening plight. In most of this book they are excluded from the analysis, figures and tables unless otherwise stated.

32.   On this, see the work surrounding Williamson's seminal treatise on transaction cost analysis. Williamson, *The Economic Institutions of Capitalism*, op. cit.

4   Disappearing Jobs

1.   In Russian statistics a distinction has been drawn between 'workers', who are roughly equivalent to manual or 'blue-collar' workers in the statistics of industrialised market economies, and 'employees', who are roughly equivalent to the notion of 'white-collar' workers. Neither distinction is entirely adequate.

2.   J. Weeks, 'The size distribution of industrial enterprises', mimeo (London: University of London, 1992).

3.   Another peculiarly Soviet correlation was that the vacancy rate was higher in firms that had cut employment, an issue to which we will return in Chapter 8.

4.   See, for example, V. Gimpel'son, 'Economic consciousness and reform of the employment sphere', paper presented at a conference on New Directions in Worker–Management Relations, Hofstra University, Hempstead, New York, 12–15 March 1992, p. 4.

5.   This second measure of labour surplus raises a methodological problem, since an establishment taking prompt action to deal with surplus labour (that is, making workers redundant immediately the situation arose) would not have a labour surplus, as defined in the questionnaire, that is, too little work for a month or more. However, given the inertia in Russian industry this theoretical possibility probably did not arise in 1991–2, and at most would have led to a modest underestimate of the number of firms with surplus labour.

6.   The reasoning was that if a firm reacted quickly to surplus labour, using a longer reference period would have suggested that the firm did not have this problem.

7.   In addition, in 1993 a regulation introduced by the Ministry of Labour effectively subsidised workers on administrative leave, reducing the cost to enterprises and providing a minimum-wage income for some of those on such leave.

8.   In response to partial stoppages, managements reported that the main measure taken was to cut normal hours (28.6 per cent of all firms) and to resort to unpaid and partially paid leave (40.7 per cent).

9.   Report of the Federal Employment Service, Moscow, 12 September 1994 (internal document).

10.   One could estimate the share of maternity leave that constitutes hidden unemployment as being all that is above the mean value for all firms.

11.   Nevertheless, among the 14 factories thinking it would result in job cuts, the average expected decline was over 21 per cent.

12.   This three-phase model seemed applicable to all countries of Central and

Eastern Europe. G. Standing, 'Labour market developments in eastern and central Europe', ILO-CEET Policy Paper, no. 1 (Budapest: ILO Central and Eastern European Team, January 1993).

13. In this regard Russian labour market developments were by no means unique. In recessions in countries such as Italy, output decline can be three times the rate of employment decline. See, for instance, P. Auer, 'Sequences in rigidity and flexibility and their implications for the Italian labour market', in C. Buechtemann (ed.), *Employment Security and Labour Market Behaviour: Interdisciplinary Approaches and International Evidence* (Ithaca, NY: Cornell University Press, 1993), p. 420.

14. In estimating the function, property form was used as an alternative set of independent variables to corporate governance, being defined as leaseholding, closed joint stock, open joint stock, private and social, the omitted category being state ownership. Although the results are not shown, none of the property forms were statistically significant, and their inclusion made no substantive difference to the significance or otherwise of other variables. Also, tests with average wages as an independent variable made no difference to the general pattern of results, although in more complex modelling an attempt will be made to build a model incorporating the interrelationships between wages and employment change.

5 The Paradox of Wage Flexibility

1. J. Chapman, 'Recent and prospective trends in Soviet wage determination', in G. Standing (ed.), *In Search of Flexibility: The New Soviet Labour Market* (Geneva: ILO, 1991), pp. 177–202.

2. L. Gordon, 'Social policy on the remuneration of labour', *Soviet Sociology*, no. 2 (1988), pp. 59–88.

3. D. Lane and F. O'Dell, *Soviet Industrial Workers* (London: Martin Robertson, 1978), p. 85.

4. For an account of the evolution and attempted reform of the wage tariff system in the late 1980s, see V. Scherbakov, 'The labour market in the USSR: Problems and perspectives', in Standing, *In Search of Flexibility*, op. cit., pp. 19–44.

5. Labour productivity rose slightly in the 1980s, but declined sharply from 1990 onwards. International Monetary Fund, *Economic Review of the Russian Federation* (Washington, DC: IMF, 1992).

6. V.E. Gimpelson and V.S. Magun, 'Waiting for change: Workers' views on the situation at industrial enterprises', *Soviet Sociology*, no. 4 (1990), pp. 6–27.

7. A. Helgeson, 'Geographical mobility: Its implications for employment', in D. Lane (ed.), *Labour and Employment in the USSR* (Hassocks, UK: Wheatsheaf, 1986).

8. The impact of this policy has been analysed elsewhere. G. Standing, 'Wages and work motivation in the Soviet labour market: Why a BIP, not a TIP is required', *International Labour Review*, vol. 130, no. 2 (August, 1991), pp. 237–53.

9. This conclusion is based on measured changes in average wages for establishments included in both RLFS3 and RLFS4. The average rose by 367 per

cent in firms not using the wage tariff system and 315 per cent in those that did.

10.   There was considerable variation by occupational group.

11.   The decline was shown in each round and for the subsample of 229 factories that were in both RLFS3 and RLFS4, showing two successive years of decline.

12.   It is almost invidious to select references, because of the large number of reviews in recent years. However, for a review of studies, see M. Uvalic, *The Pepper Report* (Brussels: Commission of the European Communities, 1991).

13.   The role of the minimum wage in countries of Central and Eastern Europe was greater than elsewhere, so that the erosion in its value after 1991 had momentous effects. For a collection of national studies, see D. Vaughan-Whitehead and G. Standing (eds), *From Protection to Destitution: The Minimum Wage in Central and Eastern Europe* (London: European University Press, 1995).

14.   T. Chetvernina, *The Minimum Wage in Russia: Fact chasing Fantasy*, ILO-CEET Paper, no. 5 (Budapest: ILO Central and Eastern European Team, April 1994).

15.   The accumulated evidence is mixed, and it would be a foolhardy economist who stated with conviction that minimum wages have major effects on wages or employment in industrialised market economies. For robust statements in favour of minimum wages, see R.B. Freeman, 'Minimum wages – Again!', *International Journal of Manpower*, vol. 15, nos 2/3 (1994), pp. 8–25; Z. Shaheed, 'Minimum wages and low pay: An ILO perspective', ibid, pp. 49–61; D. Vaughan-Whitehead, 'Minimum wage in central and eastern Europe: Slippage of the anchor', in Vaughan-Whitehead and Standing, *From Protection to Destitution*, op. cit., chapter 2. For an agnostic view, see G. Standing, 'Minimum wage, workfare and citizen's income: Routes to distributive justice for the 21st century?', ibid.

16.   To reiterate once again how matters rarely correspond to simple theory in the Russian labour market, the majority of the remainder in both 1993 and 1994 believed the minimum wage had operated to *increase* wage differentials. This is because it acted as an anchor on the earnings of those near the bottom of the wage spectrum and its value was allowed to fall in real terms.

17.   In May 1994 the minister of labour considered putting a further high tax on wages that were twenty times the minimum wage. This proposal was not pursued.

18.   The arguments of these paragraphs were first presented in Standing, 'Wages and work motivation', op. cit., and some details are omitted here to avoid repetition.

19.   Those that reported they had paid wages with a delay, or had obtained a loan to pay the wages, may also have paid less than the full amount.

20.   In early 1994, 35000 enterprises in Russia owed their workers wage arrears, according to Mikhail Schmakov, President of the Federation of Independent Trade Unions of Russia, in a speech to the Conference on Tripartism and Incomes Policy, Moscow, 24 May 1994. This raises questions about International Labour Convention no. 95, which forbids this practice and which has been ratified by the Russian government.

21.   In one factory visited several times, one visit was on a Friday afternoon, when the general manager informed us that he had the unenviable experience that morning of finding out that the funds he had received to pay wages on the Monday came to less than one billion roubles when the factory wage bill was about six billion. He called a meeting of senior management and the union representatives and it had been agreed that senior employees would forgo wages altogether and that they were going to give most to those low-income workers most in need. This admirable response could scarcely be replicated.

22.   The average minimum payment for May 1993 in the same establishments covered in RLFS4 was 17615 roubles, the lowest being in engineering.

23.   In mid 1994 the statutory minimum wage was 14620 roubles, which was equivalent to about US$8 per month. As indicated in Chapter 1, that was less than 20 per cent of the income required for minimal subsistence.

6   Restructuring and 'De-Levelling' Wages

1.   The average wage was calculated by multiplying the average wage of each occupational category by the number in that category, adding up the totals and dividing the answer by the total workforce. Earnings included bonuses, profit shares, dividends and other non-wage payments.

2.   By coincidence, *Goskomstat* also reported that in May 1994 the average wage in industry for the whole country was 171000 roubles.

3.   Between 1993 and 1994 the standard deviation of the logarithm of average wages increased in all sectors except chemicals, and the inequality within sectors was greater for average earnings than for average wages.

4.   G. Standing, 'Industrial wages, payment systems and benefits', paper presented to the Conference on Employment Restructuring in Russian Industry, Moscow and St Petersburg, 21–8 October 1992.

5.   This is contrary to a claim made in a World Bank paper that there has been 'surprising stability in relative wages' in Russian industry. S. Commander, J. McHale and R. Yemtsov, 'Russia', paper prepared for the Conference on Unemployment, Restructuring and the Labour Market in Eastern Europe and Russia, Washington, DC, 7–8 October 1993.

6.   See also A. Stavnitsky, 'Wages policy and social partnership', paper prepared for ILO-CEET, May 1994, mimeo. A version was presented at a conference on Wages Policy and Tripartism, in the Ministry of Labour, Moscow, 24–5 May 1994, organised by the Ministry and ILO-CEET. Regions with the highest average wage were those richest in raw materials, notably Siberia, the northern region and the far east.

7.   Although Moscow and St Petersburg are the two great cities of the Russian Federation, wages in the *oblasts* in which they are situated (north western and central) have not been high-wage regions, although after 1991 their position improved relative to the national average.

8.   On these issues, see M. Nuti, 'Mass privatisation: Costs and benefits of instant capitalism', mimeo (London: London Business School, 1994).

9.   For a contrary view, see S. Commander and R. Yemtsov, 'Privatisation in Russia: Does it matter?', mimeo (Washington, DC: World Bank, 1994).

10.   This latter point is not as obvious as it might appear. According to 'solidaristic

wage theory', as epitomised by the Rehn–Meidner Swedish model, if relative wages do *not* adjust to productivity, profitability and sales, pressures to achieve economic restructuring will be intensified, whereas if wages merely fall in low-performance enterprises or sectors, pressures for restructuring will be weak. To subscribe either to this view or to the conventional wage adjustment model, one must emphasise the *ceteris paribus* condition.

11. Regional differentials highlight the need to reduce constraints on inter-regional labour mobility, meaning a full abolition of the *propiska* (residence permit) system, which was abolished formally by presidential decree in 1993, although as of 1994 it had not been put into effect in many *oblasts*. It also means creating a real housing market. Had other *oblasts* been included in the RLFS, the regional differentials would have been much greater.

12. In 1994, we launched a comparative study of wage payment systems in Central and Eastern Europe, examining the links between privatisation, 'employee-ownership' and such mechanisms as profit sharing, which may turn out to deserve another name in the Russian context.

13. This has been demonstrated in numerous empirical studies in other countries. For the United States, for example, see R.B. Freeman and J. Medoff, *What Do Unions Do?* (New York: Basic Books, 1984).

14. It may also reflect earnings differentiation coming through non-wage forms. The supposition must be that underdeclaring wages and salaries was greater in privatised enterprises. In any case, the results highlight the point that one should be wary about accepting simple correlations revealed in tables or figures.

15. T. Chetvernina, 'Labour incentives in alternative forms of production', in G. Standing (ed.), *In Search of Flexibility: The New Soviet Labour Market* (Geneva: ILO, 1991), pp. 203–20.

16. I. Gomber and L. Sushkina, 'Osnovnye napravleniia differentisiatsii zarabotnoi platy rabotnikov promshennosti', *Ekonomicheskie nauki*, no. 1 (1982), pp. 60–7, republished as 'Basic directions of wage differentiation in industry', *Problems of Economics*, vol. xxv, no. 11 (March 1987), pp. 36–50.

17. For the earlier results, see Standing, 'Industrial wages', op. cit.

18. The results for wage differentials were similar if occupational earnings were compared, that is, including bonuses and benefits. Including non-wage forms of remuneration did make some changes in the statistical significance of a few variables in the regressions for occupational earnings, but the results were similar.

19. In the mid 1990s it was claimed that many managers have concealed the amount they are paid by calling their salaries a 'commercial secret'. Stavnitsky, 'Wages policy', op. cit.

20. For an excellent and detailed description of the benefit system in Soviet-era enterprises, see M. Taylor, 'Non-wage labour costs in the USSR and the role of the trade unions', in G. Standing (ed.), *In Search of Flexibility; The New Soviet Labour Market* (Geneva: ILO, 1991), pp. 237–58.

21. Entitlements are not necessarily the same as provisions. For example an enterprise may provide loans to workers but only under certain restrictive conditions.

22. Even so the 'social consumption' elements were about one quarter of total labour costs on average, and that ignores the overheads of social facilities,

buildings and so on. Note that only in private firms did the social-cost share of production costs go down in 1992–3.

23. One World Bank report suggested that private firms were providing the same range of benefits as others. Commander, McHale and Yemtsov, 'Russia', op. cit., p. 170. This conclusion was based on a very small sample. It also claimed that subsidised food in enterprises was targeted at higher-level employees. That was not clear, since the subsidy was the same for all workers and thus represented a greater share of the earnings of lower-income earners.

24. 'Low wages' were much more likely to be cited in state enterprises and small establishments; 'poor equipment' was the reason most cited in small establishments, while 'inadequate supplies' was the most common in large firms. Incidentally, the main forms of labour inefficiency were 'low work intensity', 'periodic work stoppages' and 'high labour turnover'.

7 Corporate Governance and Trade Unions in Russian Industry

1. S. and B. Webb, *Soviet Communism: A New Civilisation*, vol. 1 (London: Gollancz, 1937), p. 137.
2. See, for example, B. Grancelli, *Soviet Management and Labour Relations* (Boston, Mass, and London: Allen and Unwin, 1988).
3. V. Gerchikov, 'Business democracy: Work collective councils and trade unions', in G. Szell (ed.), *Labour Relations in Transition in Eastern Europe* (Berlin: de Gruyter, 1992).
4. D. Slider, 'The brigade system in Soviet industry', *Soviet Studies*, vol. 39, no. 3 (1987), pp. 388–405. Various studies have reported the lack of turn-over of union leaders and brigade leaders in the Soviet era. See, for example, B. Ruble, *Soviet Trade Unions* (Cambridge: Cambridge University Press, 1981), Chapter 3; D. Van Atta, 'A critical examination of brigades in the USSR', *Economic and Industrial Democracy*, vol. 10 (1989), pp. 329–40.
5. A. Pravda and B. Ruble, *Trade Unions in Communist States* (London: Allen and Unwin, 1986).
6. Slider, 'The brigade system', op. cit.
7. S. Clarke and P. Fairbrother, 'Post-Communism and the emergence of industrial relations in the workplace', in R. Hyman and A. Ferner (eds), *New Frontiers in European Industrial Relations* (Oxford: Blackwell, 1994), pp. 387–8.
8. The term 'unionisation' is used to indicate that the establishment has a trade union. 'Unionisation rate' refers to the percentage of workers in trade unions.
9. Inserting a variable for the change in property form in 1993–4 from 'state to non-state' made no difference to the result, although the coefficient for the change variable was negative. The weakness of the relationship almost certainly reflected the recency of many of the changes.
10. Surprisingly, the biggest drop in managerial unionisation was in closed joint-stock companies. In a few firms the management actually joined un-ions in 1993–4, but these were outliers.
11. In an opinion poll of workers in 1992, 5 per cent regarded protection of their rights by unions as good whereas 73 per cent thought it poor or very

poor. Cited in D. McShane, 'Trade unionism in Eastern Europe and the CIS', in Hyman and Ferner, *New Frontiers*, op. cit., p. 350.

12. A survey of union leaders, managers and workers in early 1995 found that unionisation had declined extraordinarily rapidly in St Petersburg, a result that had been reported to us by the president of the region's union confederation, Evgeny Macarov, in conversations in late 1994. The survey results also showed that overall about 9 per cent of union members were intending to leave their union, and that a further 23 per cent were uncertain about whether they should remain or leave. For a report of the survey, see T. Chetvernina *et al.*, *Trade unions in the transition period* (Moscow: Centre for Labour Market Study, 1995).

13. The membership figure was kindly provided by the International Department of FITUR. The figure is less impressive when it is realised that it includes many economically inactive pensioners and students. FITUR's most impressive display of membership strength came on 27 October 1994, when an estimated eight million people participated in a day of demonstration against wage arrears. As a result the government agreed to negotiate on how to pay back the massive sums involved.

14. L. Gordon, 'Russia on the road to new industrial relations: From unipartite commands to tripartite partnership via bipartite conflicts and bargaining', *Problems of Economic Transition* (Armonk), vol. 35, no. 6 (Oct. 1992), pp. 6–38.

15. According to the first round of the RLFS, in 1991 about 90 per cent of the unions were affiliated to the official body, the General Federation of Trade Unions. If anything, therefore, the extent of affiliation to the main trade union body had increased by 1994.

16. Vera Kabalina and Alla Nazimova, 'Labour conflict today: Features and dynamics', in B. Silverman, R. Vogt and M. Yanowitch (eds), *Labour and Democracy in the Transition to a Market System: A US-Post-Soviet Dialogue* (New York and London: M.E. Sharpe, 1992), pp. 3–12.

17. Olga Kirichenko and Pavel Koudyukin, 'Social partnership in Russia: The first steps', *Economic and Industrial Democracy*, vol. 14, no. 4, Supplement (November 1993), p. 49.

18. See, for instance, K.B. Clark, 'Unionisation and firm performance: The impact on profits, growth and productivity', *American Economic Review*, vol. 74 (Dec. 1984), pp. 893–919.

19. G. Standing, 'Do unions impede or accelerate structural adjustment? Company versus industrial unions in a NIC', *Cambridge Journal of Economics*, 1992, pp. 327–54.

20. Vadim Borisov, Simon Clarke and Peter Fairbrother, 'Does trade unionism have a future in Russia?', *Industrial Relations Journal*, vol. 25, no. 1 (1994), p. 19.

21. See, for instance, R.B. Freeman and J. Medoff, *What Do Unions Do?* (New York: Basic Books, 1984); Clark, 'Unionisation and firm performance', op. cit. The positive effect of unions on productivity in American firms was first supported empirically in the 1970s. C. Brown and J. Medoff, 'Trade unions in the production process', *Journal of Political Economy*, vol. 86 (June 1978), pp. 355–78.

22. Standing, 'Do unions impede or accelerate structural adjustment?', op. cit.

23. For a description of the construction of human development enterprise indexes, see Chapter 11. Essentially, this involves the creation of an index combining indicators of training, retraining and other aspects of training practices in the firm.

24. In other countries, evidence suggests that unions have been *positively* associated with technological change. For instance this was shown in the British Workplace Industrial Relations Survey. W.W. Daniel, *Workplace Industrial Relations and Technical Change* (Shaftesbury: Blackmore Press, 1987), p. 24.

25. Of the former, see, for instance, D. Metcalf, 'Trade unions and economic performance: The British evidence', discussion paper no. 320 (London: London School of Economics, Centre for Labour Economics, 1988), and Daniel, *Workplace Industrial Relations*, op. cit., p. 226; for a sceptical view, see S. Wadhwani, 'The effect of unions on productivity growth, investment and employment: A report on some recent work', discussion paper no. 356 (London: London School of Economics, Centre for Labour Economics, 1989).

26. The organisation with the most managers was the Association of Moscow Entrepreneurs; others included the Union of Leaseholders and Entrepreneurs and the Union of Commercial Producers.

27. Olga Kirichenko and Pavel Koudyukin, 'Social partnership in Russia: The first steps', *Economic and Industrial Democracy*, vol. 14 (1993), pp. 43–54, especially page 48.

28. D. Blanchflower and R.C. Freeman, 'The legacy of Communist labour relations', Centre for Economic Policy Research discussion paper no. 180 (London: CEPR, November 1993).

29. For one study of a specific sector, see V. Borisov, P. Fairbrother and S. Clarke, 'Is there room for independent trade unionism in Russia? Trade unionism in the Russian aviation industry', *British Journal of Industrial Relations*, no. 3 (Sept. 1994), pp. 359–78.

30. One difficulty with intermediate solutions is that imperfect competition means that companies and unions in those companies can raise wages and pass on the cost in the form of higher prices.

31. Kirichenko and Koudyukin, 'Social partnership in Russia', op. cit.

8 Restructuring Internal Labour Markets

1. The question was put in a conditional way: 'If you were to recruit, what would be the main method of recruitment?' This avoided the likelihood of a large number of non-responses due to the fact that they had not recruited anybody in the recent past.

2. Even in the countries with a high placement rate, such as Sweden, Denmark and the United Kingdom, only about a quarter of employment placements are made through the public employment service, and in other industrialised countries the figure is less than 20 per cent. U. Walwei, *Developments in the organisation of job placement* (Geneva: International Social Security Association, 1995).

3. It is a common mistake to equate employment decline with an absence of vacancies. In certain circumstances, vacancies could increase in a period of

declining employment. The interesting idea that firms can be divided into two categories – a 'firing regime' and a 'hiring regime' – is hard to maintain. B. Lockwood and A. Manning, 'The importance of linked adjustment costs: Some evidence from UK manufacturing', in J. van Ours, G. Pfann and G. Ridder (eds), *Labour Demand and Equilibrium Wage Formation* (Amsterdam: North Holland 1993). Studies have shown that in market economies hiring usually continues when enterprises are making employment cuts. In one study of enterprises in the Netherlands, it was found that 40 per cent of hiring was done by firms that were not growing. D.S. Hamermesh, W. Hassink and J. van Ours, 'Job turnover and labour turnover: A taxonomy of employment dynamics', Series Research Memorandum, Vrije Universiteit, Amsterdam, November 1994.

4. For an analysis of the international trend towards employment of workers in various forms of non-standard work statuses, including long-term probationary status, see G. Standing, 'Labour regulation in an era of fragmented flexibility', in C. Buechtemann (ed.), *Employment Security and Labour Market Behaviour: Interdisciplinary Approaches and International Evidence* (Ithaca, NY: Cornell University Press, 1993), pp. 425–41.

5. Skill formation embraces more than training. The conventional terminology is a source of confusion. We typically refer to 'skilled' and 'unskilled' jobs and workers, when what we really mean is workers filling jobs for which some degree of skill is supposed to be required. The incumbents themselves are likely to have much more skill than is required for the job they have to perform. The issue is further complicated because the notion of 'skill' is at best hazy, often being the result of social convention or referring to positions of control and authority rather than technical competence.

6. H. Tan, B. Chapman, C. Petersen and A. Booth, *Youth Training in the US, Great Britain and Australia* (Santa Monica, CA: RAND Corporation, R-4022-ED, 1991).

7. See, for instance, J. Krafcik, *Training and the Automobile Industry: International Comparisons* (Washington, DC: OTA Report, 1990).

8. G. Standing, 'Training and retraining in Russian industry', paper presented to the Conference on Employment Restructuring in Russian Industry, Moscow and St Petersburg, 21–9 October 1992.

9. The absolute number of university students in Russia declined from 1627000 in 1980–1 to about 1310000 in 1993–4, a decline of about 20 per cent. The main area of decline was in industrial skills, notably engineering. The number undergoing technical college training also fell sharply.

10. At the time, several analysts estimated that over a third of all 'specialists' (graduates of institutes of technical or higher education) were being obliged to do simple manual work, and that millions of workers were in jobs that did not require the level or type of education they possessed. M. Bermant and M. Feonova, 'Training and retraining: The link with employment', in Standing, *In Search of Flexibility: The New Soviet Labour Market* (Geneva: ILO, 1991), pp. 319–38.

11. This understates the erosion, since nearly 11 per cent of firms had not carried out any training in 1993: the figure was over 20 per cent in Ivanovo.

12. In the following, the terms 'occupation' and 'occupational structure' are used because these are the accepted ones, yet in many respects it would be

more appropriate to refer to 'job' and 'job structure'. An occupation conveys the impression of a career, with progressive acquisition of technical skill, status and control, whereas a job is a humbler word to convey a post with limited potential. Usually a person defines himself or herself by reference to an occupation.

13. Analysis of occupational changes and restructuring should be presented in technical papers in due course.

14. In contrast, based on a much smaller sample of firms a World Bank study concluded that 'net job losses have been concentrated among clerical and other staff'. S. Commander, J. McHale and R. Yemtsov, 'Russia', in S. Commander and F. Coricelli (eds), *Unemployment Restructuring and the Labour Market in Eastern Europe and Russia* (Washington, DC: The World Bank, 1995), p. 159.

15. P.M. Flynn, *Facilitating Technological Change: The Human Resource Challenge* (New York: Ballinger, 1988).

16. Although the questions were partly subjective, in that one man's change might be classified as another's absence of change, the questions on capital and work process innovation included one that requested a description of the main change, so as to ensure that the change was relevant and substantial.

17. A. Shokhin and V. Kosmarskii, 'The labour market in the USSR in the transition period', *Problems of Economic Transition*, vol. 35, no. 1 (May 1992), p. 12.

18. Ibid., p. 11. Alexander Shokhin became the first minister of labour of the Russian Federation in late 1991, and Vladimir Kosmarskii became a deputy minister of labour.

19. In visits to factories, it was already common to find shopfloors virtually ide. This became increasingly common in 1993 and 1994.

20. This was found in the Malaysian Enterprise Labour Flexibility Survey. G. Standing, *Labour Flexibility and Structural Adjustment in Malaysian Manufacturing* (Geneva: ILO; Kuala Lumpur: Prime Minister's Department, 1991).

21. C. Hoffmann, 'Institutional barriers to job creation: Views and expectations of firms and workers in the European Community', in Buechtemann, *Employment Security*, op. cit., p. 447.

22. The concept and measurement of absenteeism are notoriously complex. Absenteeism should be distinguished from other forms of absence from work, but this is often difficult. For a review of the conceptual issues, see ILO, 'Statistics on absence from work', *Fourteenth International Conference of Labour Statisticians' Report* (Geneva: ILO, 1987), Chapter 3.

23. In 1991 questions were also asked about two other forms of flexible labour. First, for the sake of establishing a benchmark for future researchers, questions were asked about the use of 'homeworkers' (outworkers). This was very rare, except in textiles and garments. Second, we asked about the declining phenomenon of non-production work by production workers. This was a traditional form of work in the Soviet era, typically to help in community work or farming. According to managerial estimates, in the last three months of 1991 such work accounted for about 1.7 per cent of the labour input of production workers, although it was more common in Moscow Region than in the two cities. The decline of such work coincided with its

commercialisation. For instance, when Moscow Region's collective and state-farm managers requested the assistance of Moscow City dwellers for assistance with the harvest, they were surprised and offended to be asked for payment. B. Rakitskii, 'Specific historical peculiarities of the formation of a labour market in the USSR', *Problems of Economic Transition*, vol. 35, no. 1 (May 1992), p. 28.

24. For the first time, in 1994 a small number reported that the main subcontract was with a foreign firm.

25. Anecdotally, there were also cases where workers in full-time jobs took part-time jobs in the same factory. This was one opportunistic way of avoiding or limiting the excess wage tax.

26. See, for instance, A.J. Alexander, 'Income, experience and internal labour markets', *Quarterly Journal of Economics*, vol. 89 (1974), pp. 63–85.

27. P.B. Doeringer and M.J. Piore, *Internal Labour Markets and Manpower Analysis* (Lexington, Mass: D.C. Heath, 1971).

9 The Impact of Restructuring Women Workers

1. Natal'ia Rimashevskaia, 'Changes in social policy and labour legislation: The gender aspect', *Sociological Research*, vol. 31, no. 5 (September–October, 1992), p. 76.

2. See, for instance, UNICEF, *Women and Gender in Countries in Transition* (New York: UNICEF, Oct. 1994), pp. 91–9.

3. For a preliminary assessment of trends, based mainly on RLFS1 data for 1991, see G. Standing, 'Implications for Women of Restructuring Russian Industry', *World Development*, vol. 22, no. 2 (Feb. 1994), pp. 271–83.

4. See, for instance, G. Standing, 'Cumulative disadvantage? Women industrial workers in south-east Asia', paper presented at WIDER Conference on Patriarchy and Women's Status, Helsinki, 5–6 July 1992.

5. In the panel of 229 firms that were in both RLFS3 and RLFS4, in mid 1993 26.2 per cent said they preferred to recruit men, 10.5 per cent preferred women; in mid 1994 the figure was 29.3 per cent for men, 10.5 per cent for women.

6. Surprisingly there was a strong net preference only in Ivanovo, the so-called 'women's city'.

7. Although the results in Tables 9.2 and 9.3 are for the full samples in RLFS3 and RLFS4, the results for the panel of 229 firms that were in both rounds were similar.

8. This view seems to have been first articulated by Edgeworth, although its roots go back further still. F.Y. Edgeworth, 'Equal pay to men and women', *Economic Journal*, vol. 32 (December 1922), pp. 431–57.

9. This issue has attracted an enormous amount of research in recent years. Although derived from Edgeworth, the crowding hypothesis is often attributed to Bergmann. B.R. Bergmann, 'Occupational segregation, wages and profits when employers discriminate by race and sex', *Eastern Economic Journal*, no. 1 (April–July 1974), pp. 103–10. The ILO has recently conducted a comprehensive international comparative analysis of patterns and trends in occupational segregation. See R. Anker, *Gender-based Occupational Segregation Across the World* (Geneva: ILO, 1995). There are sev-

eral indexes of 'occupational crowding', although no consensus on which is superior. The 'Duncan index' has been the most popular. O. Duncan and B. Duncan, 'A methodological analysis of segregation indices', *American Sociological Review*, vol. 20 (1955), pp. 210–17. The Duncan index has been widely used, but also widely criticised. See, for example, Z. Tzannatos, 'Employment segregation: Can we measure it and what does the measure mean?', *British Journal of Industrial Relations*, vol. 28 (1990), pp. 105–11.

10. D. Berbezat, *Occupational segmentation by sex in the world*, Inter-Departmental Project on Women, Working Paper No. 13 (Geneva: ILO, 1993); J. Rubery and C. Fagan, *Occupational Segregation in the European Community* (Luxembourg: Office for Official Publications of the European Communities, Social Europe Supplement 3/93, 1993).

11. A common, albeit arbitrary rule in empirical studies has been to designate an occupational category as 'male dominated' or 'female dominated' if more than 70 per cent of those in the category are male or female respectively. For a review of studies, see M. Gunderson, *Comparable Worth and Gender Discrimination: An International Perspective* (Geneva: ILO, 1994). Gender segregation tends to be more pronounced if disaggregated by a two-digit classification of occupation rather than one-digit.

12. Various studies have claimed that women's opportunities to move into management were restricted in the Soviet era. A. Posadskaia and N. Zakharova, *To be a Manager in the USSR: Changes for Women* (Geneva: ILO, 1990); A. Posadskaia, 'Men's and women's potential social mobility and changes in working conditions', *Sociological Research*, vol. 31, no. 5 (Sept.–Oct. 1992), pp. 80–93.

13. One of the difficulties here is that many firms changed property form during the year.

14. The latter has often been claimed. See, for instance, Vadim Borisov, Simon Clarke and Peter Fairbrother, 'Does trade unionism have a future in Russia?', *Industrial Relations Journal*, vol. 25, no. 1 (1994), p. 19. 1994, p. 20.

15. G. Standing, 'Global feminisation through flexible labour', *World Development*, vol. 17, no. 1 (1989), pp. 1077–95; idem, 'Global feminisation revisited' (Geneva: ILO, Labour Market Paper 6, 1995).

16. Attitudes were strong on this issue. When asked why men were dying earlier than women, one knowledgeable woman in Ivanovo commented, quite seriously and memorably, 'Drink is the second reason. The first reason is that because women are more emotional, they cry, break cups and so on, whereas men keep problems to themselves. Men think too much'. The stress of adjustment may have been greater, although one should hesitate about any interpretation of the worrying statistics. The same woman, echoing others, explained the persistently high share of employment being taken by women and their declining share of unemployment by saying, 'Women in Russia are prepared to take any job. But for men, it is a big psychological problem, so that they cannot take a job below their past status'.

17. See, for instance, N.N. Popov, V.V. Sazonov and O.A. Reznikova, 'The credo of Russia's unemployed: "Believe not, fear not, ask not" ', *Segodnya*, 25 September 1993. This sociological survey also speculated that women were made redundant more than men, but gave no evidence. This does not

seem to have been the case. One factor that may have induced more women to register is that its seems to have been harder for men to obtain entitlement to, or receipt of, unemployment benefits.

18. A. de Jong and B. Bock, 'Positive action within the European Union', in A. van Doorne-Huiskes, J. van Hoof and E.J. Roelfs (eds), *Women in the European Labour Market* (London: Paul Chapman, 1995).

10 Demographics of Restructuring

1. This has happened in other Eastern European countries, such as Bulgaria. See G. Standing, G. Sziraczki and J. Windell, 'The changing position of vulnerable groups: A comparison of Bulgaria and Hungary', paper presented at the Conference on Labour Market Reforms in Bulgarian Industry, Sofia, 18–20 May 1993.

2. Besides anecdotal evidence, opinion-poll-type surveys have highlighted this aversion. See for example the work on the so-called 'social barometer' by Richard Rose of the University of Strathclyde, United Kingdom.

3. For a review of the evidence, see P. Smirnov, 'Disabled workers in the Russian Federation', paper prepared for the ILO's Central and Eastern European Team, Moscow and Budapest, October 1993.

4. In the first round (1991) one massive factory making trucks and various consumer durables employed hundreds of Vietnamese workers. Most were doing basic assembly-line work and in the ensuing period most suffered from being displaced from work and being unable to consider looking for alternative work. The employment of Vietnamese stemmed from a 1981 agreement, to last for ten years, by which many thousands of Vietnamese entered Russian factories as contract labour. According to discussions with the head of the migration department of *Goskomtrud* in 1991, there were about 150000 foreign workers in the USSR at that time.

5. Of course there may be institutional safeguards that protect some groups from the full effect of this tendency. In some countries this has given older workers some protection in times of economic downturn. For an assessment of the effects of labour-market conditions on older workers in the United States, see A.M. Sum and N.W. Fogg, 'Labour market and poverty problems of older workers and their families', in P.B. Doeringer (ed.), *Bridges to Retirement: Older Workers in a Changing Labour Market* (Ithaca, NY: ILR Press, 1990), pp. 64–91.

11 Promoting the 'Human Development Enterprise'

1. John Rawls, *A Theory of Justice* (Oxford: Oxford University Press, 1973), p. 261.

2. M. Friedman, 'The social responsibility of business is to increase its profit', *New York Times Magazine*, 13 Sept. 1970, pp. 32–3, emphasis added. See also, idem, *Capitalism and Freedom* (Chicago: University of Chicago Press, 1962).

3. G. Standing, 'Labour regulations in an era of flexibility', in C. Buecheteman (ed.), *Employment Security and Labour Market Behaviour: Interdisciplin-*

ary Approaches and International Evidence (Ithaca, NY: Cornell University Press, 1993).

4. Rawls, *A Theory of Justice*, op. cit., p. 75. It also relates to the less discussed ethical principle of fraternity.

5. It has been stated aptly that power is the facility not to have to learn. In effect, restricting an individual's power induces pressure on that person to learn, and to keep learning, the ultimate source of dynamic efficiency.

6. The notion of 'efficiency' is more complex than most who use the term in a rhetorical sense seem to believe. In this analysis we use the term to imply dynamic efficiency, whereby there are mechanisms to induce flexibility and cooperation that contribute to future efficiency as well as a high (long-term profit-maximising) level of utilisation of existing resources.

7. One is inclined to add a fifth desirable attribute: *work security*, or occupational health and safety. This is a prerequisite for the others, and is certainly a means to those objectives. Although not considered further in this chapter, it could be incorporated fairly easily. The issue is covered in RLFS5, the results of which it is hoped will be available in 1996.

8. We refer to a good *enterprise*, yet what most people would have in mind is what in statistics is an *establishment* or firm. In this era of multinational enterprises and conglomerates consisting of dozens or hundreds of firms, it would be more correct to refer to the 'good establishment', 'establishment restructuring', and so on.

9. Earlier variants of the approach developed in this chapter were developed in order to compare industrial enterprises in South-East Asian economies. See, for example, G. Standing, 'Towards a human resource-oriented enterprise: A South-East Asian example', *International Labour Review*, vol. 131, no. 3 (1992/3), pp. 281–96.

10. In constructing any complex index, conceptual and measurement difficulties abound. For the proposed HDE index, the most important concern *scaling* (justification of any particular weighting of indicators), *aggregation* (summarising multidimensional information in any single index) and *patterning* (determining that additivity is more or less appropriate than, say, a multiplicative approach).

11. In what follows, little explicit attention will be paid to an important set of concerns linked to mechanisms. A good enterprise should have mechanisms that minimise internal transaction costs, that is, costs required to ensure internal cooperation. It should also have mechanisms that reduce tendencies towards bureaucracy, that is, an hierarchical control system that exists because of high degrees of performance ambiguity and goal incongruency (or even goal indifference). On these issues, see, for instance, William Ouchi, 'Markets, bureaucracies and clans', *Administrative Science Quarterly*, vol. 25 (1980), pp. 129–41.

12. Possibly the second and third forms of training deserve greater weight than the first, yet it is usually only the first that is considered. The weighting of levels of training is a tricky issue. In an interesting commentary on the ideas proposed in this chapter, Professor Stephen Smith of George Washington University suggested, with respect to training in particular, 'Under the diminishing marginal utility principle, a social welfare function might weight HDE characteristics for those at the "bottom" of the firm more than

for those at the top'. S. Smith, 'The firm, human development and market failure', paper prepared for an ILO Meeting on Enterprise Restructuring and Labour Markets, Turin, 31 May–2 June 1995, p. 10.

13. For instance it would be inappropriate to give a positive score to a firm in the energy sector in which merely 12 per cent of its higher-level 'employees' were women just because the industry's average was 10 per cent.

14. Rawls, *A Theory of Justice*, op. cit. This point relates to what Rawls called the 'difference principle'.

15. For related points, see Geoffrey Hodgson, *Economics and Institutions: A Manifesto for a Modern Institutional Economics* (Oxford: Polity Press, 1988), p. 259. Others have shown that narrow pay differentials within firms are associated with group cohesion and trust of management, as well as with productivity gains. See, for example, D. Levine, 'Public policy implications of worker participation', *Economic and Industrial Democracy*, vol. 13 (1992), pp. 183–206. It has also been argued that narrow pay differentials induce worker commitment to management goals. See D.M. Cowherd and D. Levine, 'Product quality and pay equity between lower-level employees and top management: An investigation of distributive justice theory', *Administrative Science Quarterly*, vol. 37, no. 2 (1992), pp. 302–20.

16. In a different environment this threshold might be lower. Yet in Russia, and in other countries in Central and Eastern Europe, where it was the norm to provide an extraordinary array of benefits coupled with a low money wage, the wage measure of income is misleading.

17. Jean-Jacques Rousseau, *The Social Contract*, book 1, ch. viii.

18. The popular aphorism that we have reached 'the end of history' with the collapse of 'state socialism' is unacceptable. Now the challenge is to consider how to reverse atavistic thinking. Instead of the socialisation of property and essentially private management, is there an acceptable sphere in which one could envisage the privatisation of ownership through genuinely democratic, widespread and accountable share ownership and so on, coupled with socially accountable management?

19. Smith delineates five types of managerial opportunism, all of which could be moderated if workers had a monitoring role inside the enterprise. See S. Smith, 'On the economic rationale for codetermination law', *Journal of Economic Behaviour and Organisation*, vol. 16 (1991), pp. 261–81.

20. G. Dow, 'The function of authority in transaction cost economics', *Journal of Economic Behaviour and Organisation*, vol. 12 (1987), p. 22. Dow elsewhere makes the valid point that unilateral control by management may distort the choice of production technique away from the provision of firm-specific training. Idem, 'Why capital hires labour: A bargaining perspective', *American Economic Review*, vol. 83, no. 1, pp. 118–34.

21. One rarely appreciated reason for encouraging the establishment of effective 'voice mechanisms' in enterprises is to limit the growth of a 'survivor syndrome'. In factories subject to steady employment cuts, the remaining workers are likely to suffer from a sense of anger and insecurity that could reduce labour productivity. If workers are involved in the bargaining process, the 'shadow of the past' can be controlled, to some extent at least.

22. In South-East Asia, the relevant difference is whether the union is an industrial union or a company union. It turns out that this makes a substantial

difference to such outcomes as wage levels, wage differentials and training. G. Standing, 'Do unions impede or accelerate structural adjustment? Industrial versus company unions in an industrialising labour market', *Cambridge Journal of Economics*, vol. 16 (1992), pp. 327–54.

23. See, *inter alia*, H.A. Henzler, 'The new era of Eurocapitalism', *Harvard Business Review*, July–August 1992, pp. 57–63; D.I. Levine and L. D'Andrea Tyson, 'Participation, productivity and the firm's environment', in A. Blinder (ed.), *Paying for Productivity* (Washington, DC: Brookings Institution, 1990); Z. Acs and F. FitzRoy, 'A constitution for privatising large Eastern enterprises', *Economics of Transition*, vol. 2, no. 1 (1994), pp. 83–94. The argument against worker shareholding is often presented most forcefully by trade unionists. One claim is that it would weaken the workers' resolve to push for improved training.

24. The theoretical point was brought out in a famous article some years ago. A. Alchian and H. Demetz, 'Production, information costs and economic organisation', *American Economic Review*, vol. 62, no. 5 (December 1972), pp. 777–95. It is notable that worker ownership in the United States is greatest in such 'services' as legal practices, where monitoring of work is extremely difficult. It is ironic, however, that in what is often regarded as the bastion of capitalism, the states have *required* all law firms to be *worker owned*. This is not normally highlighted by those who regard worker ownership as incompatible with a capitalist economy.

25. One recognises that the argument could not stop there. In Central and Eastern Europe there have been efforts to promote institutional blockholders – large financial intermediaries holding large blocks of shares – that could control insider managements. See, for instance, E.S. Phelps, R. Frydman, A. Rapazynski and A. Shleifer, *Needed mechanisms of corporate governance and finance in eastern Europe* (London: European Bank for Reconstruction and Development, Working Paper no. 1, March 1993). An important consideration is that whatever blockholder is created, it should be active in corporate governance, and in this respect workers having a block of shares as a group (through the union?) could be beneficial. The risk to be avoided is that of workers being in substantial control, for then the management function would be distorted. One should be wary about the claim that worker share ownership would lead to short-term investments and profit maximisation, on the ground that they would be interested solely in the income flow during their work tenure. This cannot be valid. If the workforce owns shares, younger cohorts of workers would always be looking to a long-term future. On the contrary it is managements that are more likely to take a short-term perspective, since their tenure is likely to be short and on average they are likely to be closer to retirement age than the average worker. The conventional argument against workers becoming principals and for managers to turn from agents to principals could be reversed.

26. In established democratic societies, anybody over the age of 30 knows of past elections when incumbent politicians have indulged in tax cutting and avoiding budget cuts in the period beforehand.

27. It would also be appropriate to add some index of safety and health, or work security. Although no data were collected on this issue, they could easily be incorporated into future refinements of the approach.

28. For a review of theoretical arguments and evidence from other countries to suggest that economic democracy *per se* has positive effects on labour productivity, see H. Hansmann, 'When does worker ownership work? ESOPs, law firms, codetermination and economic democracy', *The Yale Law Journal*, vol. 99, no. 8 (June 1990), pp. 1751–816.

29. See, for instance, R. Waterman, *The Frontiers of Excellence: Learning from Companies that Put People First* (London: Nicholas Brealey Publishing, 1994). In the United States this was published under the title *What America Does Right* (New York: Norton, 1994). Waterman, with Tom Peters, was the management guru who first promoted the concept of *self-managed teams*, and recognised a basic principle of good management: 'Today's leaders understand that you have to give up control to get results'.

30. J. Pfeffer, *Competitive Advantage Through People* (Cambridge, Mass: Harvard Business School Press, 1994). The danger of corporate paternalism is not really recognised in the analyses of Pfeffer or Waterman. This is where our model is potentially more robust, by emphasising voice regulation.

31. There is empirical evidence that skills learned in participation inside firms improve participation in the wider community. See S. Smith, 'Political behaviour as an economic externality: Econometric evidence on the spillover of participation in US firms to participation in community affairs', *Advances in the Economic Analysis of Participatory and Labour-managed Firms*, no. 1 (1985), pp. 123–36.

12 Policy Reflections for the Russian Labour Market

1. Gratitude is expressed to the federal employment service for this information.

2. It would be mean to refer to the quality of the vodka.

3. S. van Wijnbergen, 'Enterprise reform in eastern Europe', *Economics of Transition*, vol. 1, no. 1 (January 1993), pp. 29–31.

4. Ibid., p. 30. It is also stipulated that all creditors not prepared to invest further in the firms should relinquish their claims.

5   O. Shkaratan, 'The old and the new masters of Russia: From power relations to proprietary relations', *Sociological Research*, vol. 31, no. 5 (September–October 1992), p. 67.

6. H. Miyazaki, 'Employeeism, corporate governance and the J-firm', *Journal of Comparative Economics*, vol. 17, no. 2 (June 1993); D.M. Nuti, 'Employeeism: Corporate governance and employee share ownership in transitional economies', mimeo (London: London Business School, April 1995). Nuti makes the good point that employee control is not the same as employee self-management, as in traditional cooperatives.

7. O. Blanchard, R. Dornbusch, P. Krugman, R. Layard and L. Summers, *Reforms in Eastern Europe* (Cambridge, Mass: MIT Press, 1991).

8. For a contrary view, see T.N. Ash and P.G. Hare, 'Privatisation in the Russian Federation: Changing enterprise behaviour in the transition period', *Cambridge Journal of Economics*, vol. 18 (1994), pp. 619–34. This article treated workers and managerial employees as one group.

Index

Index